P9-ECR-065

Europe's
Inner Demons

Europe's
Inner Demons

An Enquiry Inspired
by the
Great Witch-Hunt

NORMAN COHN

A MERIDIAN BOOK

NEW AMERICAN LIBRARY

TIMES MIRROR

BF
1584
.E9
C63

36,774

Copyright © 1975 by Norman Cohn

All rights reserved. For information address Basic Books, Inc.,
Publishers. 10 East 53rd Street, New York, New York 10022.

This is an authorized reprint of a hardcover edition published by
Basic Books, Inc., Publishers.

MERIDIAN TRADEMARK REG. U.S. PAT. OFF. AND FOREIGN COUNTRIES
REGISTERED TRADEMARK—MARCA REGISTRADA
HECHO EN WESTFORD, MASS., U.S.A.

Signet, Signet Classics, Mentor, Plume, Meridian and NAL Books are
published by The New American Library, Inc.,
1633 Broadway, New York, New York 10019

First Meridian Printing, October, 1977

3 4 5 6 7 8 9 10

PRINTED IN THE UNITED STATES OF AMERICA

Car c'est à la vérité une violente et traistresse maistresse d'escole, que la coustume. Elle establit en nous, peu à peu, à la desrobée, le pied de son autorité: mais par ce doux et humble commencement, l'ayant rassis et planté avec l'ayde du temps, elle nous descouvre tantost un furieux et tyrannique visage, contre lequel nous n'avons plus la liberté de hausser seulement les yeux.

Michel de Montaigne, *Essais*, Livre premier, chapitre xxii

For truly, Custome is a violent and deceiving schoole-mistris. She by little and little, and as it were by stealth, establisheth the foot of her authoritie in us; by which mild and gentle beginning, if once by the aid of time, it have settled and planted the same in us, it will soone discover a furious and tyrannical countenance unto us, against which we have no more the libertie to lift so much as our eies.

John Florio's translation, 1603

CAMROSE LUTHERAN COLLEGE
LIBRARY

CAMROSE LUTHERAN COLLEGE
LIBRARY

CONTENTS

ILLUSTRATIONS

between pages 256 and 257

1. "Waldensians" adoring the Devil in the form of a he-goat. From a manuscript of a French translation of a Latin tract or sermon by Johannis Tinctoris, *Contra sectam Valdensium*. Copyright Bibliothèque royale Albert Ier, Brussels (MS 11209, folio 3 recto). Date about 1460.

2. The witches' sabbat as imagined at the height of the great witch-hunt. From Pierre de Lancre's *Tableau de l'inconstance des mauvais anges*, second edition, Paris, 1613.

3. Goya: Capricho No. 71, with the caption: "Si amanece, nos vamos" ("When day dawns, we have to go").

4. Goya: Painting of witches, often known as El aquelarre (The witches' sabbat), in the Museo de la Fundación Lázaro Galdiano, Madrid.

5. Goya, Painting of witches, often known as El hechizo (The bewitching), in the Museo de la Fundación Lázaro Galdiano, Madrid.

6. Goya: Capricho No. 45, with the caption: "Mucho hay que chupar" ("There's plenty to nibble at").

7. Goya: Saturn devouring one of his sons, in the Prado, Madrid.

8. Rubens: Saturn devouring one of his sons, in the Prado, Madrid. Reproduced from the Mansell Collection, London.

PREFACE TO THE MERIDIAN EDITION

This book began as an enquiry into the origins of the great European witch-hunt. It ended as something wider. It argues that the stereotype of the witch, as it existed in many parts of Europe in the fifteenth, sixteenth and seventeenth centuries, is made up of elements of diverse origin, and that some of these derived from a specific fantasy which can be traced back to Antiquity. The essence of the fantasy was that there existed, somewhere in the midst of the great society, another society, small and clandestine, which not only threatened the existence of the great society but was also addicted to practices which were felt to be wholly abominable, in the literal sense of anti-human.

The fantasy is preserved in a literary tradition, which can be traced through many centuries in the polemical tracts of theologians and the tales of monastic chroniclers. The story of its transmission in the literate strata is a curious one, and it is told here for the first time. Nevertheless, that is not the book's main theme. The fantasy changed, became more complex, down the centuries. It played an important part in some major persecutions; and the way in which it did so also varied. Sometimes it was used merely to legitimate persecutions that would have occurred anyway; sometimes it served to widen persecutions that would otherwise have remained far more limited; in the case of the great witch-hunt it generated a massive persecution which would have been inconceivable without it. In pursuing its history one is led far beyond the confines of the history of ideas and deep into the sociology and social psychology of persecution.

The fantasy is first met with in the second century, when pagan Greeks and Romans attached it to the small Christian communities in the Empire. These unfortunate people found themselves accused of holding meetings at which babies or small children were ritually slaughtered, and feasts at which the remains of these victims were ritually devoured; also of holding erotic orgies at which every form of intercourse, including incest between parents and children, was freely practised; also of worshipping a strange divinity in the form of an animal.

In medieval Christendom various dissenting groups, or heretical sects, were accused of similar practices—and in addition of sacrilegious acts, such as spitting and trampling on the crucifix, and adoring Satan in corporeal form in some more or less obscene fashion. It came as a surprise to me to find that the dissidents who were so accused were not, as has commonly been supposed, primarily the exotic and non-Christian Cathars but, on the contrary, devoutly Christian groups such as the Waldensians and the Fraticelli. In all cases it proved possible, by a re-examination of the evidence, to clear these groups of charges which to some extent have hung over them for five or six centuries. Very similar accusations were used by the French king Philip the Fair to effect the destruction of the Order of the Knights Templars; and in this case too I argue that they were baseless.

The latter part of the book is devoted to showing how this age-old tradition contributed to the European witch-hunt. That great persecution reached its height only in the sixteenth and seventeenth centuries, and no attempt is made here to write its history; after seven years' labour, I felt entitled to stop at the threshold of that enormous task. The book scarcely ventures beyond the middle of the fifteenth century, but that was sufficient for my purpose. As I see it, for witch-hunting to reach massive dimensions, two conditions were necessary: the authorities in a given area had to believe in the reality of the witches' sabbat, and they had to have at their disposal a judicial procedure which permitted the use of torture. Both conditions existed in certain parts of Europe by the middle of the fifteenth century.

How the notion of the witches' sabbat came into being, indeed how the whole stereotype of the witch developed, is studied in detail. The results run counter to the three most widely accepted theories.

From the 1820's down to the present day, numerous writers, ranging in stature from the great historian Jules Michelet to the pseudo-historian Margaret Murray, have encouraged the belief that there really was a secret society of witches, or else a pagan cult which was so interpreted by the Church. This belief is responsible for the proliferation of "covens" and similar groups at the present time. But when scrutinized, the historical evidence simply dissolves: there are no grounds whatsoever for thinking that witch-hunting was directed against a real society or a real cult. Anyone who doubts this has only to read Chapter 6.

According to another theory, the witches' sabbat was a fantasy born of men's hatred and fear of women, and the great witch-hunt was a particularly bloody episode in the sex-war—aggravated, it is sometimes added, by celibate monks, friars and priests. In many recent works on relations between the sexes, and in much recent feminist propaganda, this theory is treated as a matter of established fact. It is nevertheless based on a confusion. The kind of witch who was thought of as necessarily a woman was the practitioner of *maleficium*, i.e. a person who was believed to harm her neighbours by occult means. That certain women could do this was an age-old belief, particularly amongst the peasantry. But precisely when the sabbat moved into the centre of the picture and the great witch-hunt began, witches ceased to be imagined as being invariably female: they could just as well be rich burghers, town-councillors, students, schoolboys, small children of either sex. The change is apparent in the earliest true witch-trials— those described at the beginning of Chapter 12.

The third theory was originally developed by nineteenth-century scholars, such as the American George Lincoln Burr, and the German Joseph Hansen, but has been revived and popularized in several recent works. According to this theory, the stereotype of the witch as a servant of the Devil was concocted in the thirteenth and fourteenth centuries, partly by Thomas Aquinas, partly by Pope John XXII, and partly by Nicolas Eymeric in his guide for inquisitors. Moreover already at that time trials are supposed to have been held in which the accused were tortured by inquisitors until they confessed to attending the sabbat. This theory cannot stand up to a careful study of the relevant texts. Chapter 7 demonstrates that the trials in question never took place at all: the only evidence for them turns out to consist of fabrications and forgeries concocted centuries later. In Chapter 9 I show that Aquinas, John XXII and Eymeric were concerned not with witchcraft, let alone with witches' sabbats, but solely with ceremonial magic, i.e. with the conjuring up of demons by magicians.

What, then, did create the stereotype of the witches' sabbat, and so launch the great witch-hunt? The process, which is described in some detail in the last four chapters of the book, can be summarized as follows.

In the late Middle Ages ceremonial magic became something of a vogue in the upper strata of society, and from the mid-thirteenth century onwards successive popes denounced it as a form of heresy. The fourteenth century witnessed the first heresy trials centring on charges of invoking demons. Some of these were also political trials, involving great personages in church and state: the earliest instances are the posthumous trials of Pope Boniface VIII and the trials of Guichard, bishop of Troyes, both arranged to serve the purposes of

Philip the Fair, king of France. But the first major step towards the great witch-hunt was taken when the charge of having direct dealings with a demon was brought not simply against an individual but against a group. This happened in the trial of Lady Alice Kyteler and her associates, held at Kilkenny in Ireland in 1324–5; and it happened again at Boltigen in Switzerland, some time between 1397 and 1406. In both cases a group was accused of conjuring up a demon and of performing *maleficium* with his help.

In neither case was the Inquisition involved. In Ireland the initiator and judge was a bishop, in Switzerland a secular magistrate. But they used the judicial procedure known as "inquisitorial", which was older than the Inquisition, and which normally involved the use of torture. The role of the Inquisition in initiating the great witch-hunt has been much exaggerated; but the replacement of the traditional, "accusatorial" procedure by the "inquisitorial" was decisive. The "inquisitorial" procedure was employed as much by bishops and lay magistrates as by inquisitors; and the effects of the torture are shown in the accounts of trials in Chapters 10 and 12.

In the fifteenth century the final step was taken. So long as the participants were supposed to proceed to their meetings on foot, those meetings could not be imagined as either very frequent or very large. Witches had to be able to fly, invisibly, to distant destinations. As it happened, in many parts of medieval Europe, as in many parts of present-day Africa, the peasantry had a tradition of trance or dream experiences which could be made—again, with the aid of torture—to fill this gap. This was achieved in the context of the pursuit of the scattered remnants of the Waldensians. At the same time everything that was believed about ritual magic was reinterpreted in terms of the traditional stereotype of the systematically anti-human, Devil-worshipping sect of heretics. The demon changed from slave to master, the secret meeting of magicians became the witches' sabbat, and the supposed participants were tortured not simply into confessing that they themselves had attended the sabbat but into naming others whom they were supposed to have seen there. So the great witch-hunt was born.

The essence of the offence known as *crimen magiae*, for which tens of thousands were burned alive on the Continent, was attendance at the sabbat. On the other hand, Mr Keith Thomas and Dr Alan Macfarlane have recently shown that in England supposed witches were commonly tried and executed for *maleficium* alone; and they have tried to explain the sudden increase in the number of witch-trials in the sixteenth and seventeenth centuries in terms of an increase of interpersonal tensions at village level. In Chapter 8 I argue that fear of *maleficium* was traditional amongst peasantry, but was prevented by the law of talion from expressing itself in legal action until the close of the Middle Ages. Chapter 12 throws further light upon this matter. There I show that at the height of the great witch-hunt there existed different notions of what witches were, and two different ways of pursuing supposed witches. The peasant depositions given in that chapter reveal an intense concern with *maleficium*; and they were directed against single individuals—almost always elderly women— or at most against single families. The mass witch-hunts, on the other hand, reflect the demonological obsessions of the authorities, ecclesiastical and lay. It was only where the authorities believed in the reality of the sabbat, and could use torture to substantiate their belief, that mass witch-hunts took place; circumstances which did not obtain in England. But there is a complication. The two different notions could be combined, and often were; so that many witch-trials represented a collusion, no doubt unconscious, between peasants and judges. Serious work on the dynamics of the great witch-hunt is only now beginning, but the interlocking of the divergent preoccupations and aims of peasants and judges would seem to offer a particularly fruitful field of enquiry.

Beneath all this one senses the presence of a deeper level of experience. The driving force behind the whole process studied in this book, up to its culmination in the great witch-hunt, seems to have been an ever-growing sense of the power of the Devil and his subordinates. This development, which provides the theme of Chapter 4, obtrudes itself again towards the close of the book. Where witch-hunting reached its greatest intensity, the witch was seen as an incarnation of apostasy, a living proof of the power wielded by the Devil in his battle against the Christian God. But can we go further, and argue from that that the witch was a scapegoat for an unconscious urge to apostasize? Was religious faith, at the close of the Middle Ages and in the early modern period, beginning to be felt by the laity as something of a burden? The postscript to the book offers this hypothesis—while admitting that, for the present, it cannot be regarded as more than a hypothesis.

A reader who happens to be familiar with an earlier work of mine, *The Pursuit of the Millennium*, may notice a certain relationship between it and the present work. Both books are conceived on the same scale, both cover roughly the same historical period, and both deal with the underside of Europe's history. The two books are in fact complementary to one another. Whereas the chiliastic fantasies portrayed in *The Pursuit of the Millennium* flourished amongst the marginal elements in society—free-lance intellectuals and semi-intellectuals, landless, rootless peasants, the poorest, most desperate elements in the urban population—the fantasies studied here were at home in what would now be called the Establishment. Monks, bishops and popes, kings and great nobles, orthodox theologians, inquisitors and magistrates—these were the bearers of this particular tradition. And the mass response they found did not necessarily come from the lowest strata, either.

The Pursuit of the Millennium and *Europe's Inner Demons* are related also in a deeper sense. Fundamentally, both are concerned with the same phenomenon—the urge to purify the world through the annihilation of some category of human beings imagined as agents of corruption and incarnations of evil. The social contexts are different, but the urge is unmistakably the same. What is more, it is with us still; and in the minds of some readers this book, like its predecessor, will prompt reflections not only about the distant past but about certain aspects of twentieth-century history too.

ACKNOWLEDGEMENTS

This book was originally written as a contribution to a series entitled "Studies in the dynamics of persecution and extermination", produced by the Columbus Centre in the University of Sussex. The research which went into it was generously financed by the Columbus Trust. Particulars of the Columbus Trust and the Columbus Centre are given in the British and American hardback editions.

During the years spent on this book various scholars helped me in various ways. Señor J. Caro Baroja, of Madrid, Dr Christina Larner, of the University of Glasgow, and Professor Jeffrey Russell, of the University of California at Riverside, generously put at my disposal either unpublished material or proofs in advance of publication. Miss Rosemary Handley, of Queen Mary College, University of London, assisted with the deciphering of the extraordinarily obscure shorthand notes of John of Capestrano's sermon at Nuremberg in 1451. Dr Michael Clanchy, of Glasgow, checked my comments on the accusatory procedure and the law of talion. I was able to discuss the postscript "Psycho-historical speculations" with Professor Meyer Fortes, Dr Robert Gosling and Sir Richard Southern, who commented on the argument from the points of view of social anthropology, psycho-analysis and medieval history respectively; though none of them can be held responsible for the postscript in its final form. I derived much intellectual stimulus from discussions with my colleagues in the Columbus Centre, and also from attending the annual conference of the Association of Social Anthropologists in 1968, which was devoted to the theme of witchcraft.

As so often in the past, I am greatly indebted to the staff of what is now the British Library, but which I still think of as the Reading Room and the North Library of the British Museum; and to the staffs of the Warburg Institute, the Bodleian, the Cambridge University Library and the Bibliothèque Nationale. But on this occasion I must also express my special thanks to the Librarian of the University of Glasgow, Mr R. Ogilvie McKenna, and his staff. Moreover, one particular riddle—the true nature of the witch of Orta (see the third section of

Chapter 7)—could not have been unravelled without the collaboration of the libraries of the Middle Temple, of three Cambridge colleges—Trinity, Magdalene and Trinity Hall—and (yet again) Glasgow. For this assistance too I am most grateful.

I am indebted to the boards of the British Library, the Bibliothèque royale Albert Ier, the Museo Lázaro Galdiano and the Prado for permission to reproduce pictorial material in their keeping. Particulars are given in the list of illustrations.

I am also indebted to the following publishers for permission to quote from the works listed: Basil Blackwell, Oxford, and the New York University Press, *Martyrdom and persecution in the early Church*, by W. H. C. Frend; the Cornell University Press, *Witchcraft in the middle ages*, by Jeffrey B. Russell: the Oxford University Press and the International African Institute, *Witchcraft and sorcery in Rhodesia*, by J. R. Crawford; Routledge & Kegan Paul, *The history of witchcraft and demonology*, by Montague Summers; the Stanford University Press, *Witch hunting in southwestern Germany, 1562–1684*, by H. C. Erik Midelfort; the Toronto University Press, *A razor for a goat*, by Elliot Rose; Weidenfeld & Nicolson, London, and Scribner, New York, *Religion and the decline of magic*, by Keith Thomas.

N. C.

University of Sussex

Europe's
Inner Demons

1

PRELUDE IN ANTIQUITY

–I–

In the second century after Christ the Christian communities in the Roman Empire—still small and scattered groups—were the object of strange suspicions and accusations. One of the first of the Latin apologists for Christianity, Minucius Felix, who probably wrote towards the close of the century, has recorded them in detail. He makes a pagan describe the practices of Christians as follows:

> I am told that, moved by some foolish urge, they consecrate and worship the head of a donkey, that most abject of all animals. This is a cult worthy of the customs from which it sprang! Others say that they reverence the genitals of the presiding priest himself, and adore them as though they were their father's. . . . As for the initiation of new members, the details are as disgusting as they are well known. A child, covered in dough to deceive the unwary, is set before the would-be novice. The novice stabs the child to death with invisible blows; indeed he himself, deceived by the coating dough, thinks his stabs harmless. Then—it's horrible!—they hungrily drink the child's blood, and compete with one another as they divide his limbs. Through this victim they are bound together; and the fact that they all share the knowledge of the crime pledges them all to silence. Such holy rites are more disgraceful than sacrilege. It is well known, too, what happens at their feasts. . . . On the feast-day they foregather with all their children, sisters, mothers, people of either sex and all ages. When the company is all aglow from feasting, and impure lust has been set afire by drunkenness, pieces of meat are thrown to a dog fastened to a lamp. The dog springs forward, beyond the length of its chain. The light, which would have been a betraying witness, is overturned and goes out. Now, in the dark, so favourable to shameless behaviour, they twine the bonds of unnameable passion, as chance decides. And so all alike are incestuous, if not always in deed at least by complicity; for everything that is performed by one of them corresponds to the wishes of them all. . . . Precisely the secrecy of this evil religion proves that all these things, or practically all, are true.[1]

If the passage in Minucius Felix stood alone one might suspect the author of rhetorical exaggeration; but other sources bear him out in almost every detail. The first really great writer of the Latin church, Tertullian, was familiar with these same accusations, and in the year 197 he set out to refute them. He describes how, in his own town of Carthage, a criminal who normally earned his living dodging wild beasts in the arena had recently been hired to display a picture of the donkey-god. It showed a creature with ass's ears and a hoofed foot, but standing erect, dressed in a toga and carrying a book; and it bore the inscription "The god of the Christians, ass-begotten".[2] Tertullian's answer is ridicule: "We laughed at the name and at the shape." Mockery is also his response to the tales of incestuous orgies, infanticide and cannibalism. If these tales were true, he comments, a would-be Christian would be confronted with some curious demands: "You will need a child of tender years, who does not know what death means, and who will smile under the knife. You will need some bread to soak up the blood; also some candlesticks and lamps, and some dogs, and some scraps of meat to make them jump and upset the lamps. Above all, be sure to bring your mother and sister. But what if the mother and sister will not comply, or if the convert has none? . . . I suppose you cannot become a regular Christian if you have neither mother nor sister?"[3]

Minucius Felix and Tertullian provide the fullest evidence for the suspicions under which the Christians laboured, but by their time the suspicions were already traditional. The most damaging can be detected already in the comments of the younger Pliny in 112 or 113. Installed as Governor of Bithynia in Asia Minor, Pliny had the task of examining some former Christians he found there; and he wrote to the emperor asking how they were to be treated. These people, he reported, admitted that they used to attend meetings where they took nourishment together; but they insisted that, whatever others might say, the nourishment was an innocent one.[4] There is little doubt what lies behind this cryptic phrase: Pliny had been trying to establish whether Christians did or did not practise collective cannibalism.

By 152 the Christian apologist Tatian, writing for the benefit of the pagan Greeks, thought it necessary to state explicitly, "There is no cannibalism amongst us."[5] In the same decade Justin Martyr also refers repeatedly to these slanders. In his *Apology* he asks how a glutton who enjoys eating human flesh could possibly bring himself to welcome death, as Christians did; for would it not deprive him of his pleasure?[6] And in his *Dialogue with the Jew Trypho* he asks whether, like the Gentiles, the Jews believe that Christians eat human beings.[7] Justin recognizes, too, that this particular accusation does not stand alone: when Christians are accused of cannibalism they are also commonly accused of promiscuous and incestuous orgies.

It remained for Athenagoras, around 168, to find the appropriate technical terms for these imaginary offences: alongside "Oedipean mating", "the Thyestean feast".[8] The name is highly significant: the children of Thyestes were killed by his brother Atreus and served up to him at a banquet. If the cannibalistic feasts in which Christians were believed to indulge could be called "Thyestean", that means that the supposed victims were not adults but children. And that is confirmed both by Minucius Felix and by Tertullian.[9]

Tertullian might make fun of such beliefs, but they were really no laughing matter. They were very widespread, both in the geographical and in the social sense. Christian apologists referred to them as flourishing in all the main areas where Christians were to be found—north Africa, Asia Minor, Rome itself; and not only amongst the unlettered populace, either. In the 160s M. Cornelius Fronto made a speech accusing the Christians of infanticide, cannibalism and incest—and Fronto was not only a famous orator and an influential senator but the tutor and adviser of the emperor Marcus Aurelius. In fact, these rumours constituted a mortal threat to the Christian community. It is quite possible that Fronto influenced Marcus Aurelius in his persecution of the Christians, which was severe. And in the frightful persecution which struck the Christians at Lyons towards the end of his reign these same accusations certainly played an important part.[10]

This persecution, which took place in 177, is exceptionally well documented; for one of the survivors sent a full account to the churches of Asia and Phrygia, and this has been preserved in the *Ecclesiastical History* of Eusebius.[11] The Christian community at Lyons was at that time still quite small. It consisted largely of Greek-speaking immigrants from Asia Minor whose spiritual home, to which they turned in their hour of need, was still in Asia Minor; but it also included some Romano-Gallic converts. These Christians belonged to various social strata—some were highly respected physicians and advocates, rich enough to own slaves, while others were themselves slaves—but together they formed a close-knit minority clearly marked off from the pagan population around them.

The immediate motive for the persecution may well have been simple self-interest on the part of the leading citizens of Lyons. Normally, the expenses of the gladiatorial games in the provinces of the

Empire fell largely on the rich landowners. A few months before, a measure had been introduced by Marcus Aurelius and the senate which enabled these local notables to purchase condemned criminals for use as ritual sacrifices at the games. Condemned criminals could be purchased at a very much lower cost than the hire of a gladiator. It has been pointed out that the public torture and execution of Christians could well commend itself to the leading citizens of Lyons and to the Gallic priests, as an even more expedient operation—one which would not only provide ritual sacrifices at minimal expense, but at the same time eliminate an alien and potentially troublesome group. [12]

However that may be, the authorities and the populace collaborated in the persecution. Officially banned from public places and in effect outlawed, the unfortunate Christians were hounded by the mob, beaten and stoned in the streets; after which they were arrested and thrown into prison. At this point pagan slaves belonging to the prisoners were arrested and tortured to obtain incriminating statements; and in the end some asserted that their masters killed and ate children and indulged in promiscuous and incestuous orgies. They would never have voiced such accusations without prompting—which suggests that the persecutors had from the start planned to saddle the Christian community with these crimes. Certainly once these charges were uttered, they set the tone for the rest of the proceedings. As Professor Frend has remarked, "for many of the pagans these revelations confirmed their worst suspicions. Popular rage knew no bounds, and the few moderate-minded individuals who had previously tried to protect their Christian friends felt themselves deceived and let matters take their course. . . . Few seem to have had any doubt that the Christians were in fact cannibals. Hence, the final punishment, the refusal of burial. . . ." [13] For, contrary to normal Roman practice even in cases of treason, the bodies of the executed were not buried but were burnt, and the ashes scattered in the Rhône.

The Christians were horribly tortured first, both in prison and in the amphitheatre. But nothing could induce them either to deny the faith they held or to admit to crimes they had never committed. As one of them, called Attalus, was being roasted alive in an iron chair, he still cried to the crowd: "What you are doing is indeed to eat men, but we do not eat men, nor do we do anything else wicked." [14] And the woman Biblis also cried out under torture: "How would such people eat children . . . ?" [15]

−2−

Some of the specific accusations which were brought against Christians had previously been brought against other communities or groups.

In the great city of Alexandria, Greek and Jewish communities lived side by side in a state of perpetual tension; and some time in the first century B.C. the Alexandrian Greeks started a rumour that the god of the Jews had the form of a donkey.[16] The idea may have been inspired by the fact that the name Yahweh somewhat resembled the Egyptian word for "donkey"; in any case it became a stock theme of anti-Jewish satire. In the first century A.D. the Greek writer Apion embroidered on it.[17] According to him a Greek called Zabidos contrived to enter the Temple in disguise and to steal the donkey's head that was worshipped there; and he added that some two centuries earlier, when the Seleucid monarch Antiochus Epiphanes broke into and plundered the Temple, he too removed a donkey's head of great value, which had been the central object of Jewish worship.

In the ancient world it was of course not uncommon for a god to be symbolized by a sculptured animal—even apart from the Egyptian gods, there was Graeco-Roman Pan. But few animals were as poorly regarded as the donkey, "that most abject of all animals", as Minucius Felix calls it; and a cult centred on a donkey-god could only be ridiculous and shameful. That is why Apion told his stories; for Apion was an Alexandrian Greek and the leading anti-Jewish publicist of his day. And for generations after Apion's time similar tales concerning the Jews continued to circulate in Alexandria. As late as the fourth century Epiphanius knew of a book possessed by Alexandrian Gnostics which treated the theme in a particularly colourful way. It told how Zachariah saw in the Temple a being which was both man and donkey. When he described what he had seen to the Jews, they killed him.* Those Gnostics maintained that because of this incident it had been decreed that the high priest should wear bells, so that when he entered the Temple to do priestly service, the being who was worshipped there would be warned in time to hide himself and the secret of his donkey-shape would be preserved.[18]

The fantasy of the donkey-cult was easily extended from the Jews to the Christians, not only because the Christian religion was long regarded as a mere offshoot of Judaism but because the Christian god presented much the same problem to pagan imagination as did the

* The reference is presumably to Zachariah, son of Baruch, who was murdered in the Temple, along with the high priest Ananias, by the Zealots in A.D. 67.

Jewish god. It was never easy for pagan Greeks and Romans to conceive of a god who was omnipotent and omnipresent and yet invisible. But whereas, so far as we know, Jews were accused of worshipping a donkey-god only in and around Alexandria, when the same charge was brought against the Christians it spread far and wide through the Empire. It was as familiar in the Rome of Minucius Felix as in Tertullian's Carthage.

Christians were not the first to be accused of ritual murder and cannibalism, either; indeed, the true significance of the charge becomes apparent only when one realizes what other groups were similarly accused. The Roman historian Sallust, writing in the first century B.C., has this to report of the Catiline conspiracy which occurred in his lifetime: "Many say that, when Catiline bound his associates by oath to his criminal deed, he mixed the blood of a man with wine and passed it around in a bowl; when all had uttered the curse and had drunk from the bowl, as is the custom in holy rites, he revealed his plan." [19] This was mere fiction; otherwise Catiline's great enemy Cicero would certainly not have omitted it from his Catiline orations. But the story flourished and expanded, until some three centuries after the event another historian, Dio Cassius, could write that Catiline and his associates had killed a boy, sworn an oath over his entrails and then eaten them together in a sacrificial meal. [20] Bearing in mind that this story is demonstrably false, we are justified in distrusting the same Dio Cassius when he says that the Egyptians who waged the Bucolic war against Rome in the second century A.D. began by slaughtering a Roman centurian, swearing an oath over his entrails and then devouring them. [21]

If such tales could be woven around well-documented historical events, it is no wonder that they could be woven into the half-legendary material inherited from a more obscure past. This happened when the Greek biographer Plutarch, writing in the second century A.D., came to tell of a conspiracy against the infant Roman Republic, six centuries earlier. After the last king of Rome, Tarquinius, had been expelled, his supporters plotted a restoration. "They decided," says Plutarch, "that all should swear a powerful and fearful oath, and while doing so they should shed the blood of a murdered man (instead of pouring a libation of wine) and should touch his entrails." [22] A less celebrated Greek writer of the second century, Polyaenus, has a more gruesome tale to tell about an obscure tyrant, Apollodorus of Cassandreia, who lived some four centuries before his time. When Apollodorus was plotting to seize power he sacrificed a boy, had a meal prepared from his entrails and set before his fellow-countrymen. "When they had eaten, and also drunk the victim's blood, which was dissolved in dark wine, he showed them the corpse and so, through this shared pollution, ensured their loyalty." [23]

What was the reality behind these stories? It is true that cults involving the killing and devouring of children or adolescents are not wholly unknown to history or to anthropology. There are grounds for thinking that the cult of Dionysos as originally practised in Thrace may have involved the devouring of an infant as representative of the god. It is certain that in our own century, in Sierra Leone, the secret society of "human leopards" killed and ate young people. None of this, however, has any bearing on our stories. If children ever were devoured as part of the Dionysian cult, it will have been done in a state of frenzy—just as animals were torn to pieces and eaten raw. As for the human leopards of Sierra Leone, their cannibalism seems to have been a form of magic, performed for the purpose of increasing their own virility and prosperity.* Our stories point in quite a different direction. In each case the murder and the cannibalistic feast form part of a ritual by which a group of conspirators affirms its solidarity; and in each case the group's aim is to overthrow an existing ruler or regime and to seize power. There is no evidence that such murders and feasts really took place—on the contrary, save in the dubious case of the Egyptian Bucolics all the stories either concern the remote past, or else can actually be disproved. But even if it could be shown that groups of conspirators really did sometimes indulge in such practices, that would not affect our argument. Ritual murder and cannibalistic feasts belonged to one particular, traditional stereotype: the stereotype of the conspiratorial organization or secret society engaged in a ruthless drive for political power.

Apion tried to fit this stereotype on to the Jews. As with his story of the donkey-god, he harked back to the exploit of Antiochus Epiphanes. He tells how when the Greek king penetrated into the Temple he found there an imprisoned Greek, who revealed the terrible secret of the Jews. Once a year the Jews would take a captive into the woods, where they would kill him as a sacrifice to their god. Then they would

---

* The main evidence for cannibalistic infanticide in the cult of Dionysos consists of a red-figured vase at the British Museum. It shows that by the fourth century B.C. the Athenian worshippers of Dionysos regarded the idea with horror. Even in the Thracian religion itself, by that time the sacrificial victim had long been an animal. Cf. W. C. K. Guthrie, *Orpheus and Greek religion*, London, 1935, pp. 130–32; E. O. James, *Sacrifice and sacrament*, London, 1962, pp. 97, 243. On the human leopards of Sierra Leone see K. J. Beatty, *Human Leopards: an account of the trials of Human Leopards before the Special Commission Court*, London, 1915.

taste of their victim's entrails and swear eternal enmity against the Greeks. The captive Greek was himself about to be sacrificed when Antiochus arrived and liberated him.[24] But this story of Apion's failed to convince: in the ancient world Jews were not believed to practise ritual murder or cannibalism. Though the pagan Romans might regard Judaism as a bizarre religion, they also knew that it was a *religio licita*—an officially recognized religion which deserved at any rate that respect which Romans paid to all ancient institutions. Above all, it was impossible to regard Jews, who were a very visible and active element in all the provinces of the Empire, as a secret society.

It was quite another matter with the obscure, unauthorized sect known as Christians. As we have seen, Christians were very widely believed to practise both ritual murder and cannibalism; which means that they were very widely regarded as a body of ruthless, power-hungry conspirators.

As it happened, there was one feature of Christian ritual which could easily be interpreted as cannibalistic: the Eucharist. The earliest known account of the Eucharist, which is that of St Paul in I Corinthians, shows that originally the faithful assembled periodically in a church and ate together, sharing their provisions. The high points of the meal consisted in the breaking and eating of a single loaf and the sharing of a cup of wine. Behind the ceremony lay the tradition which Paul claimed to have received from Jesus: ". . . the Lord Jesus the same night in which he was betrayed took bread. And when he had given thanks, he broke it, and said, Take, eat: this is my body, which is broken for you: this do in remembrance of me. After the same manner also he took the cup, when he had supped, saying, This cup is the new testament in my blood: this do ye, as oft as ye drink it, in remembrance of me." [25] Although several Fathers during the first three or four centuries tried to spiritualize the Eucharist, so that Christ's flesh and blood could be taken to mean simply the Word, this was not the view taken by most Christians. For many the Eucharist already possessed the meaning which it now possesses for all Roman Catholics. Few of the early Christians would have demurred at the authoritative definition which the Council of Trent was to give in the sixteenth century and which remains binding today: "If any one . . . shall deny that wonderful and singular conversion of the whole substance of the bread into (Christ's) body and of the wine into his blood . . . let him be anathema." [26]

Once more Tertullian offers valuable glimpses into the mentalities of Christians and pagans alike. He notes that many priests were careful that no crumb of the bread or drop of the wine should fall to the

ground, lest the body of Christ should thereby be exposed to harass-
ment.[27] Such crude interpretations of the Eucharist were bound to
reinforce the rumours of cannibalism; and Tertullian recognizes that
they did so. In warning against mixed marriages he asks, "What (pagan
husband) will without suspicion let (his Christian wife) go to the
Lord's supper, which people speak so badly of?" And if the wife takes
the Eucharist in her own home, "will the husband not want to know
what you are enjoying, secretly, above all other food? And when he
learns that it is bread, will he not think that it is the kind of bread which
is the subject of rumour?" [28] Indeed, to many pagans the Eucharist
must have seemed not merely cannibalism but, quite specifically, a
"Thyestean feast". Christian missionaries must often have used the
version of Jesus' words given in the Gospel of John: "Except ye eat of
the flesh of the Son of man, and drink his blood, ye have no life in
you." [29] In Greek, the mysterious phrase "Son of man" could easily be
understood as "child". It is significant that in Minucius Felix the child-
victim is coated in dough, i.e. is disguised as bread.

But what of the accusation of promiscuous and incestuous orgies?
The usual explanation is that the pagans confused the main body of
Christians with certain Gnostics who really did indulge in such practices. Yet when one examines the evidence in detail, it tends to dis-
integrate. The earliest source, Justin Martyr, merely says that he does
not know whether various Gnostic sects indulged in the nocturnal
orgies of which Christians were accused.[30] Irenaeus, writing after the
persecution at Lyons had already taken place, merely says of one particular Gnostic sect—the Carpocratians—that, being indifferent to good
and evil, they were promiscuous, and thereby brought discredit upon
the Christians, with whom they were confused.[31]* Clement of
Alexandria, writing around 200, is the first to attribute to these Carpocratians erotic orgies such as had long been attributed to the Christians; [32] while Eusebius, writing more than two centuries later, does
little more than repeat these earlier sources. But whatever this obscure
Gnostic sect may or may not have believed or practised, it can hardly
account for the constant and widespread accusations against the main
body of Christians.†

---

* A passage in I Corinthians 5 has sometimes been taken as showing that
already in the days of St Paul a gnostic sect at Corinth was practising "libertinism";
cf. W. Schmithals, Die Gnosis in Korinth, Göttingen, 1954. But the references to
fornication do not even suggest mass orgies.

† Apart from Carpocratians, the Borborians or Phibionites of Alexandria have
sometimes been blamed for the accusations brought against the Christians; see S.

It would seem that here too we are dealing with a real Christian custom, misinterpreted under the influence of a traditional stereotype. The custom was the *Agape*, or love-feast.[33] In the first two centuries of Christianity it was customary for a private person to invite baptized Christians to his house for a communal meal. The meal was an affirmation of Christian fellowship: the poor were invited, charity was dispensed. It was also a religious rite; and at least down to the middle of the second century it commonly included a celebration of the Eucharist. The imaginary orgy described by Minucius Felix is like a caricature of a real *Agape*, which has been summarized as follows: "Towards evening the ceremony begins. On the arrival of the bishop, the deacon brings the lamp and lights it. . . . The common meal follows, at the conclusion of which every one rises from his seat. The youthful participants of both sexes recite prayers and psalms as a preparation for the climax of the ceremony"—which is the Eucharist.[34]

It is true that the *Agape* sometimes became an occasion for excessive feasting and drinking, inspired by joyous expectation of the Second Coming of Christ. But in imagining and portraying it as an unbridled erotic orgy the pagan Romans were fitting it into a pre-existent stereotype—in this case the stereotype of the Bacchanalia. The "affair of the Bacchanalia" occurred in 186 B.C. and is described in details in Livy's history.[35] Originally, we are told, the Bacchanalia were celebrated by a small association of women, in broad daylight. But imported from Greece to Etruria and thence to Rome, the cult grew and changed until it involved large-scale nocturnal orgies. According to Livy,

> there were initiatory rites. . . . To the religious element in them were added the delights of wine and feasts, that the minds of a larger number might be attracted. When wine had inflamed their minds, and night and the mingling of males with females, youth with age, had destroyed every sentiment of modesty, all varieties of corruption first began to be practised, since each one had at hand the pleasure answering to that to which his nature was more inclined. . . . If any of them were disinclined to endure abuse or reluctant to commit crime, they were sacrificed as victims. To consider nothing wrong . . . was the highest form of religious devotion among them.[36]

Benko, "The libertine Gnostic sect of the Phibionites according to Epiphanius", in *Vigiliae Christianae*, vol. 21, No. 1, Amsterdam, 1967, pp. 103–19, and Dolger, *op cit.*, p. 220. The arguments do not convince me. The displeasing practices attributed to these people are very different from those attibuted to the Christians. Moreover, whatever Epiphanius may have observed in 330–340, it can throw no light on the state of affairs in the second century.

But the Bacchanalia were not condemned simply as erotic and some-times murderous orgies. The consul who had the task of enlightening the people about the danger is reported by Livy as follows:

> Not yet have they revealed all the crimes to which they have conspired. . . . Daily the evil grows and creeps abroad. It is already too great to be purely a private matter: its objective is the control of the state. Unless you are on guard betimes, citizens, as we hold this meeting in the day-time, summoned by a consul, in accordance with law, so there can be one held at night. Now, as single individuals, they stand in fear of you, gathered here all together in this assembly: presently, when you have scattered to your homes and farms, they will have come together and they will take measures for their own safety and at the same time for your destruction: then you, as isolated individuals, will have to fear them as a united body. . . . Nothing is more deceptive in appearance than a false religion. [37]

In other words, those who attended the Bacchanalia were regarded as conspirators aiming to seize political power; and the senate took stern measures. Decrees for the repression of the Bacchanalia were dispatched throughout the Italian provinces, and vast numbers of adherents of the cult—men and women, noble and plebeian—were executed or imprisoned. There has been much debate as to whether the Bacchanalia really needed suppressing, or whether the persecution was simply an exercise in government by terror. For our purposes the question is irrelevant. What the story shows beyond doubt is that by Livy's time—that is to say, on the eve of the Christian era—erotic orgies of a more or less perverted kind belonged to the stereotype of a revolutionary conspiracy against the state. Directed against the Christians, the accusation of holding such orgies points in precisely the same direction as the accusation of cannibalism. By assimilating the Christian *Agape* to the Bacchanalia the pagan Romans were, once again, labelling Christians as ruthless conspirators, dedicated to overthrowing the state and seizing power for themselves.

Yet this is not the whole story. If one compares the accusations against the Christians, as described by Minucius Felix, with the stereotypes concerning conspiratorial groups, the former are much the more outrageous; they represent, as it were, fantastically exaggerated variations on the traditional material. The conspiratorial groups around Catiline, Tarquinius and Apollodorus were said to have eaten flesh and drunk the blood of a man or a boy on one occasion only, to inaugurate the conspiracy; but Christians were said to devour babies as a matter of routine, every time a new member was initiated. And whereas the Bacchanalia were said to include homosexual practices, the erotic orgies of the Christians were said to be absolutely promiscuous and to include even incest between brothers and sisters, parents and their children. Moreover, it seems that only Christians were accused of worshipping the genitals of their religious leader. Such fantasies have a deeper meaning.

In almost every society sexual intercourse between close relatives— father and daughter, mother and son, brother and sister—is absolutely forbidden and is regarded as "against human nature". The same may be said of the worship of a man's genitals; that too is generally felt to be "against human nature". Similarly, babies and small children, as help-less beings who are nevertheless the bearers of new life and the guaran-tors of the future, are expected to be protected and nurtured. To kill them and use them for one's own nourishment is felt to be as "un-natural" an act as anyone could perform. To this one may add that, in societies which are not cannibalistic, cannibalism in any form is felt to be "against human nature". In most societies, therefore, to say that a group practises incest, worships genitals, kills and eats children, amounts to saying that it is an incarnation of the anti-human. Such a group is absolutely outside humanity; and its relationship to mankind as a whole can only be one of implacable enmity. And that is in fact how the Christians were seen in the Graeco-Roman world in the second century.[38] That the Christian god was supposed to be worshipped in the form of a donkey points in the same direction.

The explanation lies in the absolute incompatibility of primitive Christianity with the religion of the Roman state. Roman religion had always been less a matter of personal devotion than a national cult. Ever since the days of the Republic the gods of Rome had been regarded as, collectively, its guardians—indeed, they were religious embodiments of the supernatural power and holiness which were felt to be indwelling in the Roman community. It was the duty of all Roman citizens to pay them due respect and reverence, in rites which were rigidly prescribed by traditions of immemorial antiquity. If this was done, the gods in turn would carry out their task of protecting the Roman people; but any slackness in observance would bring disaster upon the whole community. Innovations could be made, and were made over the centuries, without affecting this basic attitude. Thus when, from the second century B.C. onwards, vast numbers of foreigners streamed into Rome, every effort was made to harmonize their deities with the indigenous gods. The resulting syncretism was still a national cult.

Under the Empire, the Roman gods were intimately associated with the imperial mission. They came to be seen as guardians of the peace and order that the Empire brought, guarantors that the Empire would never pass away. And in addition, the emperor himself was deified. The worship of the emperor began in a veiled form already under Augustus, and was carried on quite openly under his successors. Deriving partly from the Hellenistic concept of divine kingship, partly from the Roman habit of identifying high office-holders with the protecting gods, and partly from political calculation, it bound together the western and eastern halves of the Empire. More and more, from around A.D. 70 onwards, a conscious policy of Romanization brought the native religions in the various provinces into association with the imperial cult. Throughout the Empire the emperor's birthday was a religious festival, on which libation was offered. The emperor and the traditional gods together upheld the Empire, and reverence for them created and sustained a unified Graeco-Roman world.

It was a world from which, by the very nature of their religion, Christians excluded themselves. Their god too was a ruler of the universe and demanded total allegiance; conflict between his claims and those of the world-empire and its religion was inevitable. Not that the early Christians were political revolutionaries—but they were millenarians. As they saw it the existing world was thoroughly evil, the realm of the Devil; it was about to go under in a sea of fire; and it would be replaced by a perfected world, in which all power and glory would belong to the returning Christ and his Saints. As for the Roman Empire, it was the representative for the time being of the Devil; and in opposing it the Christians were carrying on not a political but an eschatological struggle. With its pantheon of gods and its deification of the emperor, Rome was the embodiment of "idolatry", it was the Second Babylon, the realm of Antichrist.

This attitude was fully developed already in the sub-apostolic age, when the Roman authorities themselves were scarcely aware of the very existence of Christians. It was intensified from A.D. 70 onwards, as a protest against the Roman policy of associating the native religions in the provinces with the imperial cult; for though this policy was not consciously anti-Christian, it was interpreted by Christians as a further manifestation of idolatry. And the same attitude of rejection persisted into the second half of the second century. This was a time when the peoples of the Empire were enjoying unexampled prosperity and were

united in genuine loyalty to Rome and to the emperor. In this environ-
ment the Christian communities were singled out as small, inward-
looking communities which took not the slightest interest in civic
affairs and ignored civic obligations. Interested only in the speedy end
of the world, they took no part in the daily life in the city and refused
to make even token gestures of loyalty to the emperor, or of reverence
to the gods of Rome.

In all their ways, Christians negated the values and beliefs by which
the pagan Graeco-Roman world lived. It is not surprising that to pagan
eyes they looked like a body of conspirators intent on destroying
society. "A new and maleficent superstition", "an immoderate and
perverse superstition"—the phrases of Suetonius and Pliny show clearly
enough the mixture of contempt and anxiety with which Christians
were regarded. The very presence of such people was felt to be an
offence to the gods, such as might well induce them to withdraw their
protection; in which case a whole civilization would be engulfed in
earthquake, revolution or military defeat. It was precisely because he
was such a conscientious emperor, and so genuinely concerned for the
public good, that Marcus Aurelius permitted agitators and informers to
go into action against the Christians, and encouraged trials and executions. In the late second century, according to Tertullian, it was taken
for granted that "the Christians are the cause of every public catastrophe, every disaster that hits the populace. If the Tiber floods or the
Nile fails to, if there is a drought or an earthquake, a famine or a
plague, the cries go up at once: 'Throw the Christians to the lions!' " [39]
It was in the same period that Christians came to be suspected of
incestuous orgies, of killing and eating children, of worshipping a
donkey-god or a priest's genitals. In these fantasies and accusations the
Graeco-Roman world expressed its feeling that these people were
indeed outside humanity and hostile to it.

It was only in the second century that Christians were accused of
such things by non-Christians,* and it is easy to see why. Before that,

* If one excludes a curious revival in the mid-nineteenth century, which
involved no less a personage than Karl Marx. In 1847 Marx read and was impressed
by the newly published work by Georg Friedrich Daumer, *Die Geheimnisse des
christlichen Altertums* (The secrets of Christian Antiquity). In a speech delivered to
a meeting of German-speaking workers in London in November of that year
Marx summarized its argument as follows: "Daumer demonstrates that the
Christians really did slaughter human beings and eat and drink human flesh at
Communion. This explains why the Romans, who tolerated all religious sects,
persecuted Christians, and why the Christians later destroyed all pagan literature
that was directed against Christianity. . . . This history, as it is portrayed in

Christians were too few and obscure to attract attention, or to be at all clearly distinguishable from the main body of Jews. By the third century, they were becoming too numerous, and above all too widely dispersed through the population, for such tales to retain much plausibility. Countless aristocratic families had some Christian members, mostly women—and how could these people really be suspected of indulging in incestuous orgies and ritual cannibalism? Moreover the attitude of the Christians themselves was changing. They were no longer so obsessed by fantasies of the imminent end of this world and the coming of the Millennium. The hierarchy was becoming more developed, the clergy were acquiring wealth, the bishops were becoming important public figures and leaders. By about 230 Christianity had established itself as one of the principal religions of the Empire, and the Church was beginning to look upon the Empire less as a realm of demons than as a potentially Christian institution. Such persecutions as came after that date were imposed by imperial decree and no longer invoked these horrific fantasies.

To sum up: The explanation of the defamation of the early Christians is a complex one. When the Christians were a small minority, their attitudes, beliefs and behaviour were a denial of the values by which Graeco-Roman society lived and to which it owed its cohesion. Because of this, certain real Christian practices, notably the Eucharist and the *Agape*, were misinterpreted in the light of traditional stereotypes, so that a dissident religious minority came to look like a revolutionary political conspiracy. More than that—these practices were misinterpreted to such a point that they seemed absolutely anti-human, and those who indulged in them were put outside the bounds of humanity. And this mechanism could sometimes be used to legitimate persecutions, to which other motives, such as avarice and sadism, also contributed.

It is a pattern which was to be repeated many times in later centuries, when the persecutors would be orthodox Christians and the persecuted would be other dissident groups.

Daumer's work, is the final blow to Christianity, and we may ask what it means to us. It gives us the certainty that the old society is ending, and that the structure of deceit and prejudices is collapsing." The meeting was much impressed, and it was decided to purchase Daumer's book. Later Marx became more doubtful about the theory, while in 1858 Daumer himself formally renounced it and became a fervent Catholic. But the episode remains a curious one: Marx on Christian ritual murder appears in the same volume of the official German edition of the collected works as the *Communist Manifesto*. Cf. W. Schulze, "Der Vorwurf des Ritualmordes gegen die Christen im Altertum und in der Neuzeit", in *Zeitschrift für Kirchengeschichte*, vol. 65, Gotha, 1953-4, pp. 304-306.

2

THE DEMONIZATION OF MEDIEVAL
HERETICS (1)

– I –

From the beginning of the third century onwards Christians gradually ceased to be regarded, and to regard themselves, as a militant outgroup; the process of integration into, and accommodation with, Graeco-Roman society had begun. But not all Christians adapted themselves to the changing circumstances. In the East, both compromise with the world and institutionalism within the Church were challenged by the religious revival known as Montanism (after its founder, Montanus). Based on the remote depths of Phrygia, in Asia Minor, Montanism embodied above all a revolt against the increasingly easy-going Christianity of the Greek towns. With its consuming thirst for martyrdom and its urgent prophecies of the End and the Millennium, the sect first made itself heard towards the close of the second century. But it survived for several centuries after that; and by the time Christianity had become the official religion of the Empire, this relic of earlier times had come to be viewed with grave suspicion.

Between the middle of the fourth and the middle of the fifth centuries, several representative Christians hinted that these intransigent backwoodsmen practised a sort of cannibalism. Philastrius, bishop of Brescia, has this to tell of them: "People say that at the Easter festival they mix the blood of a child in their offering and send pieces of this offering to their erring and pernicious supporters everywhere." [1] Epiphanius also has the Montanists in mind when he says that certain sectarians "stick a little child all over with brass needles and so procure blood for the offering". [2] Even the great Augustine reports of these Phrygians: "People say that they have most lamentable sacraments. It is said that they take the blood of a one-year-old child, drawing it off through tiny cuts all over his body, and at the same time produce their Eucharist, by mixing this blood with meal and making bread out of it. If the boy dies, they treat him as a martyr; but if he lives, they treat him as a great priest." [3] The Montanists themselves of course reacted just as the second-century Christians had done—they rejected these tales as malignant slanders.[4] They knew they were innocent—indeed, this was even admitted by some leaders of the Church.[5]

St Augustine also hinted at strange customs amongst the Manichees. By his time the Manichaean religion, spreading outwards from its Persian homeland, was penetrating deep into the Graeco-Roman world. As it advanced westwards it came more and more under the influence of Christianity. In North Africa in particular it took on the appearance of a more "rational" version of Christianity, unencumbered by the Old Testament; and so became a serious rival to Catholicism amongst the educated. Augustine himself was a member of the Manichaean church for nine years, before his conversion to Catholicism. But he was only an *auditor*, or secular Manichee; and the tale he tells concerns the *electi*, who were religious virtuosi.

According to Augustine, in his Manichaean days a woman once complained to him that at a religious meeting where she was sitting alone with other women, "some of the elect came in; one of them put out the lamp, whereupon another, whom she could not recognize, made to embrace her, and would have forced her into sin if she had not screamed and so escaped. This happened on the night when the feast of the vigils is kept." [6] Augustine, while admitting that the offender was never traced, comments that such practices must have been very common. One may reasonably ask why, in that case, he himself never witnessed anything of the kind during all the years of his membership. In reality the Manichaean *electi* or *perfecti* were famed, even amongst their enemies, for their absolute chastity and rigorous asceticism; and there is no reason to think that this implausible story is anything but a watered-down version of those orgiastic fantasies which the pagan Romans had once woven around the Christian *Agape*.

Centuries later these tales of erotic debauches, infanticide and cannibalism were revived and applied to various religious outgroups in medieval Christendom. In the process they were integrated more and more firmly into the corpus of Christian demonology. In the eyes of pagan Greeks and Romans, people who indulged in promiscuous orgies and devoured children were enemies of society and of mankind. In the eyes of medieval Christians they were, in addition, enemies of God and servants of Satan; their fearsome deeds were inspired by Satan and his demons, and served their interests. As the centuries passed the powers of darkness loomed larger and larger in these tales, until they came to occupy the very centre of the stage. Erotic debauches, infanticide and cannibalism gradually took on a new meaning, as so many manifestations of a religious cult of Satan, so many expressions of Devil-worship.

Finally the whole nocturnal orgy was imagined as taking place under the direct supervision of a demon, who presided in material form.

These transformations can be observed quite clearly if one traces, in chronological order, the accusations brought against certain dissident sects in eastern and western Christendom. We may start with the sect of Paulicians, which in the eighth century was flourishing in south-eastern Armenia, outside the frontiers of the Empire and outside the control of the Armenian church. In 719 the head of that church, St John IV of Ojun (Yovhannes Ojneçi), known as the Philosopher, summoned a great synod which condemned these people as "sons of Satan"; and he himself produced a tract which shows quite clearly what was meant by that.[7] The Paulicians, he complains, come together under cover of darkness, and at these hidden meetings they commit incest with their own mothers. If a child is born, they throw it from one to another until it dies; and he in whose hands it dies is promoted to the leadership of the sect. The blood of these infants is mixed with flour to make the Eucharist; and so these people surpass the gluttony of pigs who devour their own brood. In this way John of Ojun brought the two originally independent fantasies of the erotic orgy and the "Thyestean feast" into logical relationships with one another; thereby providing a model for later generations. But that was not all—he also described how the Paulicians worshipped the Devil, bowing low and foaming at the mouth. This idea too was to be absorbed into the traditional stereotype.

In a later example from the East the role of Satan and his demons is more explicit. Around 1050 Michael Constantine Psellos, who was both a famous philosopher and a leading Byzantine statesman, wrote a Greek dialogue *On the operation of the demons*; and he included in it a couple of paragraphs about the sect of Bogomiles.* Psellos lived and wrote in Constantinople, and the Bogomiles were located in distant Thrace; so it is through the mouth of a visiting Thracian that Psellos

---

* He calls them "Messalians"; just as John of Ojun also refers to "Messalianism" in connection with the Paulicians. It is now established, however, that neither of the sects in question had anything to do with the sect of Messalians, or Euchites, which flourished in Mesopotamia, Syria, Armenia, Sinai and Egypt up to the seventh century. By the time of John of Ojun, and still more by the time of Psellos, "Messalian" was a mere term of abuse. See H.-Ch. Puech and A. Vaillant, *Le traité contre les Bogomiles de Cosmas le Prêtre* (Travaux publiés par l'Institut d'Etudes Slaves, No. 21), Paris, 1945, pp. 327 *seq*; and cf. Conybeare, *op. cit.*, Introduction, p. lvii. On the real nature and beliefs of the Paulicians and Bogomiles, see below.

offers his report. This is the "mystical sacrifice" which the Thracian claims to have witnessed, in person, at Easter time:

> In the evening, when the candles are lit, at the time when we celebrate the redemptive Passion of Our Lord, they bring together, in a house appointed for the purpose, young girls whom they have initiated into their rites. Then they extinguish the candles, so that the light shall not be witness to their abominable deeds, and throw themselves lasciviously on the girls; each one on whomever first falls into his hands, no matter whether she be his sister, his daughter or his mother. For they think that they are doing something that greatly pleases the demons by transgressing God's laws, which forbid marriage between blood relatives. When this rite has been completed, each goes home; and after waiting nine months, until the time has come for the unnatural children of such unnatural seed to be born, they come together again at the same place. Then, on the third day after the birth, they tear the miserable babies from their mothers' arms. They cut their tender flesh all over with sharp knives and catch the stream of blood in basins. They throw the babies, still breathing and gasping, on to the fire, to be burned to ashes. After which, they mix the ashes with the blood in the basins and so make an abominable drink, with which they secretly pollute their food and drink; like those who mix poison with hippocras or other sweet drinks. Finally they partake together of these foodstuffs; and not they alone but others also, who know nothing of their hidden proceedings.[8]

The Thracian is clear about the purpose behind these rites. The souls of those who take part in them are purged of every trace of divine influence and become the homes of demons. This applies equally to those who participate unknowingly: by eating child's flesh they too fall into the clutches of demons. And elsewhere in his tract Psellos puts the whole matter in an eschatological perspective. It is because the End is near that these fearful deeds are being done. The coming of Antichrist is at hand, and it must be ushered in by monstrous doctrines and unlawful practices. The deeds of Saturn and Thyestes and Tantalus, when they devoured their offspring; of Oedipus, when he mated with his mother; of Cinyras, when he mated with his daughters—all these abominations are being repeated now, as signs that the Last Days have come. In other words, they are manifestations of the final, desperate effort of the demonic hosts in their struggle against God.

Up to the eleventh century western Christendom had been far less troubled than eastern Christendom by movements of religious dissent. But by the time Psellos wrote his attack on the Bogomiles, the West too was becoming uneasily aware of the presence of heretics in its midst. The authorities, ecclesiastical and secular alike, reacted sharply to this unfamiliar situation: heretics were not only burned, they were defamed as well. The first execution took place at Orleans in 1022. And in connection with this same incident tales of incest and cannibalism were bandied about for the first time in western Europe; for the first time, that is, since the great execution of Christians by pagans, at Lyons, more than eight centuries before.

This heretical group consisted mostly of canons of the collegiate church of Orleans—learned and pious men, one of whom had even been the queen's confessor. It also included some aristocratic laymen, and some nuns and other women. The tone was one of deep piety—the leaders not only preached but also lived an outstandingly holy and simple life, and that is what attracted the followers. And these people were not afraid to confess their beliefs; for they were convinced that the Holy Spirit would protect them, and in the end they went to the stake laughing. The evidence they gave, when interrogated in the presence of the king and queen and the bishops, can therefore be taken as absolutely reliable. It shows them to have rejected much that was accepted Christian doctrine: they did not believe that Christ was born of a virgin, or that he suffered for men, or that he rose from the dead. They were not persuaded of the supernatural efficacy of baptism, or of the Eucharist, or of praying to the saints. At the same time they were mystics. They believed that each of them had received the Holy Spirit, which now dwelt in their hearts and guided them in all their ways.

Their doctrine, then, was not very different from, or more sinister than, the doctrine which the Society of Friends was to profess many centuries later. But these sectarians also talked of a certain "heavenly food", and this proved enough to set imaginations working. A contemporary chronicler, Adhémar de Chabannes, describes how these people had been deceived by an unlettered layman, who gave them the ashes of dead children to eat, and so bound them to his sect. Once they were initiated, the Devil would appear to them, sometimes as a Negro and sometimes as an angel of light. Each day he would supply them with heaps of money; in return, they would be required to deny Christ in their hearts, even while pretending publicly to be true followers of Christ. And the Devil would also instruct them to abandon themselves in secret to every kind of vice.[9]

A couple of generations later, around 1090, a monk of Chartres called Paul gave a more elaborate account of the matter. "They came together on certain nights at an appointed hour," he writes, "each carrying a light. And they recited the names of the demons as in a litany; until suddenly they saw the Devil descend among them in the guise of some animal or other. As soon as this vision seemed to appear, the lights were at once extinguished. . . ." After which the monk faithfully follows his precursors, and notably Adhémar de Chabannes and Psellos. And after covering the usual promiscuous and incestuous orgy, the burning of the babies, the concocting of the enslaving, diabolic potion, he concludes, "Let this be enough to warn Christians to be on their guard against this evil work. . . ." [10]

A hundred years later it had become a commonplace that the Devil, or a subordinate demon, presided over the nocturnal orgies of heretics in the form of an animal, usually a cat. And this belonged not to the folklore of the illiterate majority, but, on the contrary, to the world-view of the intellectual elite; learned clerics who stood at the very centre of affairs were thoroughly convinced of it. The Englishman Walter Map, for instance, was not only an important ecclesiastic but, at various times, a judge and an officer of the court of Henry II. He was also a wit, whom the count of Champagne was happy to entertain at his court, when Map was travelling to Rome to attend an ecumenical council. Yet this highly educated, urbane and experienced man was capable of describing the meetings of heretics in terms so fantastic that one would think he was joking, if it were not obvious from the context that he is perfectly serious. In his book *De nugis curialium* (*Courtiers' Trifles*) he reports what certain French heretics, who had abandoned their heresy and returned to the Catholic fold, were supposed to have said about their former practices. At night the sectarians would fore-gather in a house—Map calls it a "synagogue"—with all gates and doors and windows firmly shut. After a period of silent waiting, a black cat of monstrous size would suddenly come down into their midst by a rope. Thereupon the lights were extinguished, and the heretics, murmuring their hymns between closed teeth (presumably, so as not to attract the attention of outsiders), clustered around their master the cat. In the darkness they had to feel for the demonic animal; and as each found it, he would kiss it on whatever part of the anatomy seemed appropriate to his craving for self-abasement: feet, genitals, under the tail (just as the early Christians were said to worship the genitals of the presiding priest!). It was only after this performance, and stimulated by it, that the heretics would embark on the usual promis-cuous orgy. [11]

By the time Map wrote this account, around 1180, such ideas had entered into the thinking even of professional philosophers and theologians. The Frenchman Alain de Lille, whose reputation for learning was such that he was nicknamed *Doctor universalis*, shared them. When he came to write his tract *Against the heretics of his times*, between 1179 and 1202, he had to explain why one of the major heretical sects was called Cathars. He gives the correct answer: the name comes from the Greek *Katharoi*, "the pure ones"; but he still feels obliged to offer an alternative etymology—from the Low Latin *cattus*, "cat", because it is in this form that Lucifer appears to them and receives their obscene kisses.[12] The eminent scholastic Guillaume d'Auvergne, bishop of Paris, was equally credulous. "Lucifer," he writes, "is permitted (by God) to appear to his worshippers and adorers in the form of a black cat or a toad and to demand kisses from them; whether as a cat, abominably, under the tail; or as a toad, horribly, on the mouth." [13]

The atmosphere was changing. Fantasies which in the early Middle Ages had been quite unknown in western Europe were turning into commonplaces. As so often, by dint of repetition fictions were coming to be accepted as fact. Certainly by the time Guillaume d'Auvergne penned his comment, some time between 1231 and 1236, he could be sure of support in the highest possible quarters; for, as we shall see, in 1233 a particularly elaborate version of the fantasy was incorporated in a papal bull.

-2-

The (not very numerous) executions of heretics during the eleventh and twelfth centuries were almost all the work of the secular authorities or of the mob; the clergy, while keenly interested in the elimination of heresy, generally relied on persuasion and were reluctant to sanction the use of force. But even then there were exceptions. In 1025 Gerard, bishop of Cambrai, was making a visitation of his diocese. At Arras a group of heretics was denounced to him; he had these people tortured and, as they showed themselves fittingly penitent, reconciled them with the Church. In 1035 Heribert, archbishop of Milan, had some heretics denounced to him at Monteforte; having interrogated them and found them impenitent, he had them burned. As Gerard II, bishop of Cambrai, was passing through a small town on a visitation in 1077, a heretic called Rhamird was denounced; after interrogation Rhamird too was burned.

These were early examples of the type of legal procedure which lawyers and legal historians call "inquisitorial", and which stood in marked contrast to the accusatory type of procedure which was the norm throughout the Middle Ages. Whereas under the accusatory procedure the initiative in bringing a charge lay with a private individual,* under the inquisitorial procedure it lay with the authorities. The authorities were responsible for collecting, from the public, information which might lead to the discovery of crimes and the identification of criminals. This meant that they depended on denunciations. Once armed with sufficient denunciations, the judge himself proceeded to an investigation, or "inquisition", of the suspect.

The first beginnings of this type of procedure can be traced back to Roman law as it existed under the Empire. In Roman law, as in Germanic law, the norm was the accusatory procedure—but, there were exceptions. Notably in cases of *crimen laesae majestatis* the authorities were required to initiate an investigation, and private individuals were required to come forward with denunciations. Something of this attitude passed into the canon law of the medieval church. From a very early date the religious dissenter tended to be regarded as an offender against the divine majesty; and it is significant that all the earliest examples of the inquisitorial procedure occurred in the context of the struggle against religious dissent.

As religious dissent spread, from the second half of the twelfth century onwards, legislation was introduced for the purpose of combating it. At the synod of Verona in 1184 Pope Lucius III and Emperor Frederick I decreed the excommunication of heretics; moreover those heretics who refused to recant, or who after recanting had relapsed, were to be relaxed to the civil power for punishment. In response to the decrees of the fourth Lateran Council in 1215, various rulers decreed the death penalty for obdurate heresy. And in 1231 Pope Gregory IX and Emperor Frederick II, acting in concert, established a coherent legislation against heretics in the Empire. For the first time the various penalties for heresy—up to and including death—were clearly formulated.

Meanwhile the inquisitorial procedure was becoming institutionalized. Early in the thirteenth century that great administrator Pope Innocent III established it as the normal way of proceeding against clerics. A cleric could not, of course, be tried except by an ecclesiastical tribunal; nor could he, under canon law, be accused by a cleric of lower status than himself. In practice this meant that bishops, abbots and the like had been almost wholly exempt from legal sanctions. The inquisitorial procedure enabled the ecclesiastical authorities, when appropriate, to initiate proceedings against even the most exalted clerics. This was

* The accusatory procedure is more fully described at pp. 160-63, below.

doubtless a commendable reform; but it took on a new significance when the Inquisition came into being.

The Inquisition took its name from the inquisitorial procedure and not, as is sometimes assumed, *vice versa*: it carried out "inquisitions", or official enquiries, and held "inquisitorial" trials, along lines which had been worked out much earlier. But, as an institution, it also adapted the inquisitorial procedure to its own special purpose, which was the eradication of heresy. As used by the Inquisition, the procedure was extremely unfair to the accused. He was seldom allowed a lawyer, and when he was, the lawyer was less concerned to defend him than to urge him to confess. The proceedings—which under the old accusatory procedure had taken place in public—were now shrouded in secrecy. And while a confession was required from the accused (known as "the witness") before he could be convicted, torture could be used to extract it. The accused could also be imprisoned for an indefinite period on bread and water before interrogation and between interrogations. A prisoner who held out and continued to insist on his innocence could be imprisoned for life. A prisoner who confessed would be called upon to confirm his confession three days later; when he would have to state explicitly that he had spoken of his own free will, and not as a result of torture or from fear of torture. If he performed satisfactorily, he would be formally reconciled to the Church and would have to undergo some punishment or perform some penance, light or heavy. If, on the other hand, he withdrew his confession for any reason—for instance, on the grounds that it had been extracted by torture—he counted as a relapsed heretic and (since the Church was not permitted to kill) was handed over to the secular arm to be burnt alive. The procedure perfected and systematized by the Inquisition was indeed an instrument with terrible potentialities.

The papal Inquisition became fully organized only in the second half of the thirteenth century; but already in 1231, following the agreement between Gregory IX and Frederick II, the archbishop of Mainz appointed a certain Conrad of Marburg as inquisitor for his vast see. It was a fateful step, for the man turned out to be a blind fanatic. Moreover, there was as yet no established routine to restrain his fanaticism. The procedure later developed by the Inquisition, unfair as it was, was less arbitrary than the procedure concocted by this pioneering amateur.[14]

It seems likely that Conrad of Marburg was of aristocratic descent, and had once belonged to the monastic order of the Premonstratensians; but latterly he was simply a secular priest. He had had a university education, probably at Paris, and was celebrated for his learning;

but he was even more famous for his formidable personality and austere way of life. Thin with fasting, of sombre and threatening mien, he was both respected and feared. He was utterly incorruptible; though he spent long years at the court of the count of Thuringia, and exercised great influence, he refused all benefices and remained a simple priest. He was also terrifyingly severe. As confessor to the countess—now St Elizabeth of Thuringia—he treated his penitent with a harshness which was extraordinary even by the standards of the time. He would, for instance, trick the twenty-one-year-old widow into some trivial and unwitting disobedience, and then have her and her maids flogged so severely that the scars were visible weeks later.

Popes were accustomed to trust Conrad with the defence of the faith. In 1215 and again in 1227, when plans were being laid for yet another assault on Islam, Conrad was appointed to preach the crusade. As he rode from place to place—always on a donkey, in imitation of Jesus—he was followed by crowds of clerics and layfolk, men and women; at the approach to towns the inhabitants would come in procession to meet him, with banners and candles and incense. His success as a preacher of the crusade made him famous.

Conrad also had plenty of experience in defending the faith against inner enemies. By insisting that bishops were obliged, on pain of dismissal, to pursue and punish heretics in their dioceses, the Lateran Council of 1215 encouraged informers. Those consumed with an urge to exterminate all heretics rushed in with denunciations. Amongst these people Conrad distinguished himself, and his zeal did not pass unnoticed. In 1227 the Pope gave him the task of preparing dossiers on the basis of which formal denunciations could be lodged with the bishops. In 1229 Conrad preached against heretics at Strasbourg, and so effectively that two persons were burned. His appointment in 1231 as Germany's first official inquisitor was an appropriate culmination for such a career.

A couple of unofficial and, it would seem, self-appointed inquisitors were already at work. One was a lay brother in the Dominican Order called Conrad Torso, the other a one-eyed, one-armed rogue called Johannes; both were said to be former heretics. They must somehow have acquired the prestige which in those days was always enjoyed by holy men; for they had the support of the populace, which enabled them to intimidate the magistrates into burning whomever they designated. The friars, Dominicans and Franciscans alike, also took orders from them and assisted with the burnings.

Conrad Torso and Johannes began by discovering a few genuine heretics—people who not only admitted their beliefs but impenitently persisted in them; these were duly tried, condemned and handed over to the secular arm for execution. But soon the two men showed themselves less discriminating. They claimed to be able to detect a heretic by his or her appearance; and as they proceeded from town to town and village to village they denounced people on these purely intuitive grounds. Those burned now included perfectly orthodox Catholics, who from the midst of the flames still called on Jesus, Mary and the saints. "We would gladly burn a hundred," said the amateur inquisitors, "if just one among them were guilty." (15)

At first they found their victims amongst the poor; but that did not satisfy them, and they soon hit on a device which put the rich also at their mercy. The German king, Henry VII, had just issued a decree governing the disposal of the property of anyone condemned for heresy: part of the property was to go to the person's overlords, but part was to pass to his or her heirs. The inquisitors proposed a new arrangement: when a wealthy person was burned on their indication, the whole of the property should be confiscated and divided amongst the various overlords, including the king; the heirs were to receive nothing at all. It seems that for a while the proposal achieved its object; the inquisitors did receive support from the highest strata in society.

The shady characters Conrad Torso and Johannes attached themselves to the genuine fanatic Conrad of Marburg, and the resulting combination proved astonishingly powerful. Vast areas were subject to its arbitrary and despotic will. These judges feared no man, and their judgements struck indiscriminately at peasants and burghers, clerics and knights. Whoever they chose to accuse was given no time to think or to prepare a defence but was judged at once. If he was condemned he was not allowed even to see his confessor but was executed as soon as possible, often on the very day of his arrest. And there was only one way to escape condemnation and execution: the accused must confess to heresy. But then proof of repentance was required: the accused had to have his scalp shaved, as an outward sign of shame; more importantly, he had to name fellow heretics and specify the "heretics' school" where he had been instructed. If he was unable to provide satisfactory information on his own, Conrad of Marburg and his companions were ready to help. They would offer the names of leading nobles—whereupon the accused would commonly hasten to agree: "Those people are as guilty as I, we were in the same school together." Some did this in order to save their dependants from expropriation and poverty, but most did it simply from fear of being burned alive. Terror reached such a pitch that brother would denounce brother, a wife her husband, a lord his peasant and a peasant his lord.

Conrad also relied greatly on denunciations supplied by former heretics who had since returned to the Church. Whatever such people told him he accepted blindly, without troubling to check it; and this casual approach led to endless abuses. Real heretics were able to exploit his credulity to their own advantage. They arranged for some of their number to fake conversion, so that they could then denounce good Catholics as heretics—partly to avenge their brethren who had perished in the flames, partly to direct attention away from their brethren who were still alive. And the persecutory apparatus could also be exploited for purposes of private vengeance. A young woman called Adelheid voluntarily presented herself as a repentant heretic for the sole purpose of denouncing her relatives, who were trying to deprive her of an inheritance. Conrad obligingly had them all burned.[16]

Conrad's activity as inquisitor lasted about a year and a half and covered places as far apart as Erfurt, Marburg and the Rhine towns of Mainz, Bingen and Worms. It is impossible to say even approximately how many burnings it involved, but all contemporary sources agree that they were very numerous. Certainly the atmosphere of uncertainty and anxiety, the wave of false denunciations and false confessions, produced widespread disquiet in the population.

The higher clergy themselves were shocked. Conrad's own superior, Archbishop Siegfried III of Mainz, joined with the archbishops of Cologne and Trier in asking the fanatical priest to restrain himself. A synod held at Mainz on 25 June 1233 tried to introduce a more orderly procedure which would encourage the instruction and conversion of heretics rather than their physical destruction.[17] Amongst the more prominent ecclesiastics only one supported the inquisitor—the bishop of Hildesheim, who was himself a fanatic. The rest all counselled moderation; but such counsel merely increased Conrad's fury and drove him to further excesses. In the end he began to accuse people who were both of high birth and of notable piety; and this proved his undoing.

Count Henry of Sayn was a great lord who owned much land both along the Rhine and in Hesse. He was also a devout Catholic, who had not only endowed monasteries and churches but had even gone on a crusade. Yet Conrad summoned him to appear on a charge of heresy; for he had witnesses who claimed to have seen the count—presumably at some nocturnal orgy—riding on a crab. The archbishop of Mainz prudently arranged for the case to be heard at an assembly of the states of the Empire, to be held at Mainz immediately after the synod. The

count and the inquisitor both appeared with their witnesses; and whereas the count's witnesses unhesitatingly affirmed his orthodoxy and piety,
Conrad's all recanted, some admitting that they had denounced the
count only to save their lives, others that they had done so out of
personal malice. The clergy present were unanimously convinced of
the count's innocence, and said so. It was a crushing defeat for
Conrad.

Embittered and enraged, Conrad began to preach publicly against
certain other noble personages whom he charged with heresy; and
then set off to ride back from Mainz to his native Marburg. Blinded by
his anger and overconfident in the sanctity of his office, he refused the
escort which the king and the archbishop offered him. On 30 July 1233
he was murdered on the open road, either by vassals of Count Sayn or
by the nobles whom he was still attacking.

In all the regions where Conrad had been active the news of the
assassination was greeted with joy. His end was regarded as a judgement
of God, and he was assigned his place amongst the damned in hell. For
his accomplices, too, things went badly: Conrad Torso was stabbed to
death, and Johannes was hanged, while the false witnesses against
Count Sayn were imprisoned by the archbishop of Mainz. Thereafter,
although the laws against heresy remained in force, there were no more
major persecutions. As one chronicler remarks, it was the end of a
persecution the like of which had never been seen since the persecution
of the early Christians; now the times became milder and more
peaceable again.[18]

But not everyone rejoiced. In a circular letter to the German clergy
Pope Gregory expressed his anger and dismay.[19] Conrad of Marburg,
he proclaimed, had been a servant of light, a champion of the Christian
faith, the bridegroom of the Church which would have rejoiced in his
struggles and his victories. The news of his murder had struck the
Church like a thunderbolt. His murderers were men of blood and sons
of darkness; it was impossible to devise any earthly punishment that
would match their crime. It was nevertheless the pope's duty to demonstrate that he did not wield the sword of Peter for nothing, and to
ensure that the criminals should at least not boast of their crime. He
accordingly decreed that the clergy should excommunicate the murderers and their accomplices, should forbid people to have any dealings
with them, and should place under interdict any town, village or castle
that might give them shelter, until such time as the guilty ones should
come to Rome and beg him for absolution. And Gregory had other
proposals to make as well. In letters to the archbishop of Mainz and the

bishop of Hildesheim he tried to relaunch the campaign against heretics in Germany, even proposing that those who took part in such a campaign should be granted the same indulgences as those who went on a crusade to the Holy Land.

During the following year the gulf that separated the pope from the German clergy and people yawned ever wider. At an assembly of the states of the Empire, held at Frankfurt in February 1234, many who had been accused and shorn by Conrad appeared in procession, carrying crosses, and complaining bitterly of their treatment. A storm of indignation shook the assembly; one prince-bishop was even heard to say, "Master Conrad deserves to be disinterred and burned as a heretic." [20] Count Henry of Sayn appeared, and was formally cleared of heresy. Another of Conrad's victims, Count Henry of Solms, declared with tears that he had confessed to heresy only to avoid being burned; and he too was cleared. Finally six of those involved in Conrad's murder came forward, and they were treated leniently. Except for Conrad's old ally, the bishop of Hildesheim, hardly anyone showed any interest in a renewed hunt for heretics; and in April the archbishop of Mainz, on behalf of the German clergy, wrote to the pope pointing out what gross illegalities had accompanied Conrad's activities. [21] On the other hand, none of this impressed Pope Gregory, who continued to fulminate against Conrad's murderers—and also against the German clergy for protecting them.

Clearly the pope in Rome had a very different idea of Conrad and his role from those who had seen the man at work; and one must ask why. It was not (as has sometimes been suggested) that Conrad's appointment was a papal imposition which infringed the traditional jurisdiction of the bishops; Conrad was appointed by his own superior, the archbishop of Mainz. [22] The explanation of the discrepancy lies elsewhere. Conrad was a fanatic whose persecutory activities were inspired not simply by a detestation of heresy but by demonological fantasies about heretics. The German bishops in general did not share those fantasies; but the pope did—and it was almost certainly Conrad who had implanted them in his mind.

In 1233 Gregory IX had in fact issued a bull, known as *Vox in Rama*, which contains all the defamatory tales we have been examining, and more.* This papal pronouncement describes what happens when a

---

* It was long accepted, and is often repeated in present-day works as though it were established fact, that this bull was directed against the Stedinger, a peasant people who lived in the extreme north of Germany. Yet the text of the bull shows that it was directed against the heretical sects with which Conrad of Marburg was

novice is received into a heretical sect. Usually there first appears a toad, which the novice has to kiss either on the behind or on the mouth; though sometimes the creature may be a goose or a duck, and it may also be as big as a stove. Next a man appears, with coal-black eyes and a strangely pale complexion, and so thin that he seems mere skin and bone. The novice kisses him too, finding him cold as ice to the touch; and as he does so, his heart is emptied of all remembrance of the Catholic faith. Then the company sits down to a feast. At all such gatherings a certain statue is present: and from it a black cat descends, to receive the obscene homage already described by Walter Map.

After songs have been sung the master asks one follower, "What does this teach?" and receives the answer, "The highest peace," while another adds, "And that we must needs obey." There follows the usual promiscuous, incestuous, often homosexual orgy; after which a man comes out from a dark corner, radiant like the sun in his upper half, but black like a cat from the waist down. The light streaming from him illumines the whole place. The master presents this man with a piece of the novice's garment, saying, "I give you what was given me." The shining man answers, "You have served me well, you will serve me better still. What you have given me I leave in your care." And then he vanishes.

This report is followed by what purports to be a summary of the heretics' doctrine. God, in their view, acted contrary to all justice when he cast Lucifer down to hell. Lucifer is the real creator of heaven; and one day he will cast God out and resume his rightful and glorious place. Then the heretics, as they hope, will attain eternal blessedness through him and with him. From this they conclude that they should avoid doing anything that is pleasing to God and should do whatever is hateful to him. This doctrinal summary confirms what one would in any case have assumed—that the toad, the cat, the pale ice-cold man and the man half radiant and half black are so many guises of Lucifer or Satan.

Vox in Rama is concerned specifically with heretics in Germany. It is addressed to the archbishop of Mainz, as primate of Germany, but also, by name, to Conrad of Marburg and his ally the bishop of Hildesheim. It is in fact based on a report which those correspondents had previously sent to the pope, concerning heretics along the Rhine. That earlier report is lost, but there can be little doubt that it was mainly, if not wholly, Conrad's work. When, after Conrad's death, the archbishop of

concerning himself, in the Rhine valley and in Thuringia. Conrad never got near the Stedinger.

Mainz wrote his letter of protest to the pope, he complained that the inquisitor had forced his victims to confess to kissing the toad, the cat, the pale man and other monsters.[23]

Conrad of Marburg was a man driven by intense inner needs. It was his own personality that enabled and impelled this solitary priest, unsupported by any monastic order, to terrify German society from top to bottom. Far more of the impetus to persecution came from him than from the real situation: although there certainly were heretics in the land, they were far less numerous and powerful than he imagined. Even while he was active, reports of heresy were confined to the areas he visited; the rest of the land was uninterested. And once he was dead, there was a great silence: the chronicles have practically nothing more to report about heretics and before long even the pope forgot about them. Clearly the Satanic menace had no real existence but was the creation of a single obsessed mind.

The episode was nevertheless of crucial importance. For the first time the traditional demonological fantasies had figured not simply as a by-product of persecution but as a stimulus to it. For the first time, too, the pope himself had lent his authority to those fantasies: *Vox in Rama* transformed mere tales into established truths. These were important precedents. In the next two centuries other persecutions were to be stimulated in the same way, also with support and approval from the highest quarters. And each new persecution in turn lent fresh credibility and authority to the fantasies that had stimulated and legitimated it, until those fantasies came to be accepted as self-evidently true—first by many of the educated, and in the long run by the bulk of society.

3

THE DEMONIZATION OF MEDIEVAL HERETICS (2)

– I –

When the archbishop of Mainz wrote to Pope Gregory IX about Conrad of Marburg, he referred to the sect which the deceased inquisitor had tried to track down as "the poor of Lyons".[1] But "the poor of Lyons" was simply another name for the Waldensians or Vaudois.

The true history and nature of the Waldensian heresy have long been established.[2] In 1173 a rich merchant of Lyons called Valdès or Valdo was moved by a passionate craving for salvation. The words of Jesus, in the parable of the rich young man, seemed to point the way: "If thou wouldst be perfect, go, sell that thou hast, and give to the poor. . . ."[3] Valdès disposed of all his possessions and became a beggar. A group formed around him, intent on following the way of absolute poverty, after the example of the apostles. And soon these men began to preach.

So far the story exactly parallels the beginning of the Franciscan venture which was to come a generation later. But whereas St Francis and his companions succeeded, with some difficulty, in obtaining papal approbation for their way of life, and with it permission to preach, Valdès and his followers failed: when they appeared at the Lateran Council in Rome in 1179, the pope, though impressed by their piety, imposed restrictions on their preaching. Faced with the alternatives of giving up preaching or of disobeying the pope, "the poor of Lyons" chose the latter course, with the inevitable consequence that in 1181 they were excommunicated; and in 1184 were formally condemned as heretics.

Persecuted, expelled from one diocese after another, sometimes burned at the stake, the Waldensians (as they were now called) nevertheless multiplied. The original French movement spread north to Liège, east to Metz, but above all south, to Provence, Languedoc, Catalonia, Aragon. And meanwhile new branches appeared in Italy, where the stronghold was Milan; along the Rhine, at Strasbourg, Trier and Mainz; in Bavaria and Austria.

The Waldensians were of two kinds, roughly corresponding to the clergy and the laity in the Church of Rome. Only the first of these were "the poor"; the layfolk were simply "friends". Relatively few in number, "the poor" formed a religious elite; each member, after a noviciate of several years, pledged himself to observe strictly the law of Christ: to renounce the world, to model his way of life upon the apostles, to own nothing beyond what he needed to live from day to day, to be always chaste. Moreover "the poor" continued to specialize in preaching and to lead the hard life of itinerant preachers.

Unlike those other heretics, the Cathars, the Waldensians were practically untouched by non-Christian influences. They managed to get the Vulgate translated into their various vernaculars; and these (often rather inaccurate) renderings of the Bible supplied the framework of their faith. Though they were not learned people—being mostly peasants and artisans—they devoted themselves to an intensive study of the Scriptures; even the totally illiterate were often able to recite the four Gospels and the Book of Job by heart. All the peculiarities of their doctrine arose simply from a one-sided interpretation of the New Testament. For instance, they refused in any circumstances to take an oath; and they had an intense horror of any sort of lying, however trivial. They were opposed to capital punishment and also, it would seem, to military service. Passages to justify all these attitudes could easily be found in the New Testament.

Voluntary poverty remained the supreme value, and supplied the yardstick by which the Waldensians measured both themselves and their enemies, the Catholic clergy. As they saw it, in so far as the clergy failed to practise voluntary poverty, they could not really baptize, confirm, consecrate the Eucharist, ordain priests, hear confession or grant absolution. The power validly to administer these sacraments was reserved for the only true devotees of voluntary poverty, the Waldensians. Indeed, the "poor of Lyons" and their followers constituted the only true church; while the Church of Rome, because of its failure to impose absolute poverty on its clergy, was an abomination.

Such was the sect which, according to Conrad of Marburg and Pope Gregory IX, practised nameless orgies and worshipped the Devil. In the thirteenth century the discrepancy between the accusations and the reality was obvious to many even amongst the guardians of orthodoxy. The archbishop of Mainz, when he wrote to the pope after Conrad's assassination, was clearly unimpressed; and so was the celebrated preacher David of Augsburg when, around 1265, he wrote his *Treatise on the heresy of the poor of Lyons*. In this systematic account of the sect and its doctrines, the charge of Devil-worship is flatly rejected, and the orgies are reduced to mere transgressions by individual Waldensian preachers who, having given up their wives for the sake of their vocation, found perpetual chastity too much for them.[4] Nevertheless the old defamatory stereotype survived in the German-speaking lands, and early in the fourteenth century it woke to new life.

From 1311 to 1315 Duke Frederick of Austria joined with the archbishop of Salzburg and the bishop of Passau in a drive to clear the Austrian lands of heretics who, again, were clearly Waldensians.[5] As usual, those who would not recant were burned; and these seem to have been the great majority. A contemporary chronicler notes that "all showed an incredible stubbornness, even to death; they went joyfully to execution". The same chronicler summarizes the sect's doctrine—and amongst tenets which the Waldensians really hold he intersperses some which come straight from the bull *Vox in Rama*. These people, he says, believe that Lucifer and his demons were unjustly expelled from heaven, and in the end will find eternal blessedness; whereas Michael and his angels will be eternally damned. Meanwhile God neither punishes, nor even knows of, anything done under the earth; so the heretics hold their meetings in subterranean caverns, where they indulge in incestuous orgies—father with daughter, brother with sister, son with mother.[6] Conveniently, this view of the doctrine and behaviour of the Waldensians was confirmed by the confession which Dominican inquisitors extracted from one Ulrich Wollar, of Krems.[7]

Popes took these fantasies seriously and used their unique authority to disseminate them. Like Gregory IX before him, John XXII incorporated them into a bull; and in both cases the pope took this step under the influence of a single cleric in a distant country. Just as Pope Gregory in Rome took on trust the reports which Conrad of Marburg sent from Germany, so Pope John, resident at Avignon, accepted without question the tales concocted by a canon of Prague cathedral. The canon, Henry of Schönberg, was not even a genuine fanatic like Conrad but simply an intriguer, intent on ruining his bishop. Inspired by this man, the pope in 1318 fulminated a bull accusing the bishop of protecting heretics. Here, too, the heresy described is unmistakably Waldensian—but here, too, real Waldensian doctrine is blended with fantasies of Lucifer-worship and of nocturnal orgies in caverns.[8]

Already in *Vox in Rama*, in 1233, the Devil is shown as presiding in corporeal form over the nocturnal assemblies of the Waldensians; and the same fantasy is found a century later. Under the year 1338 the Franciscan John of Winterthur, in Switzerland, tells of heretics who were being tortured to death or burned at the stake, in Austria and the neighbouring countries. These too must have been Waldensians; and the rituals ascribed to them are strange indeed. When they have assembled in a subterranean hide-out, the proceedings open with a sermon in which the head of the sect expounds its doctrine. Next four youths appear, bearing burning torches; and then there enters a king, clad in precious robes, with a sparkling crown and strangely shining sceptre, and surrounded by a brilliant retinue of knights.

The king announces that he is the king of heaven—which means that he is Lucifer. He confirms the doctrine that has just been expounded and commands, in virtue of his authority, that it be observed and obeyed for ever. At once a grasshopper comes and settles on the mouth of each individual in turn; whereupon all are overwhelmed with such a joyous ecstasy that they lose all self-control. The moment has come for the customary orgy: the lights are extinguished and each has intercourse with his or her neighbour; often a man with a man, a woman with a woman. The chronicler ends with the comment that these sectarians are the special sons of Satan, for they imitate his words and works before other men.[9]

That is what people believed about the Waldensians in the southern-most parts of the German-speaking world—but in the far north the picture was apparently just the same. Around 1336 rumours reached the bishop of Brandenburg that the town of Angermünde was infected with heresy. Inquisitors were sent to investigate, and not in vain. They found a number of people who were suspected of "the heresy of the Luciferans"; and fourteen men and women, having refused to recant, were burned.[10] Details of the charges are lacking, but a story which reached John of Winterthur at least suggests what was meant by "the heresy of the Luciferans".

According to the Swiss chronicler—who bases himself on "a faithful report"—a schoolmaster in Brandenburg invited a Franciscan friend of his to come and see the Holy Trinity. Having obtained permission of his brethren, and armed himself with a consecrated wafer, the Francis-can accompanied the schoolmaster to what turned out to be an assembly of heretics. It was presided over by three strikingly handsome men, clad in shining robes, whom the schoolmaster identified as the Father, the Son and the Holy Spirit. Unimpressed, the Franciscan produced the Eucharist and held it aloft, crying: "Then who is this?" John of Winter-thur finishes his story: "The spirits which, in the guise of the Trinity, had so long fooled people and made them mad, vanished at the sight of the Eucharist; leaving behind a most evil stink. The Franciscan returned thankfully to his brethren, and reported on God's power and its wondrous effects. But the heretics who had let themselves be mocked and deceived by the spirits were sent to the stake and burned. When they were warned to cast off the filth of superstitions and devilish deceit, to reflect, and to profess the true faith, as they ought to do, they persevered in their heretical perversity, being too much ensnared and seduced. They preferred to perish in the fire, in the midst of their sins, to being saved by confession of the true faith. Indeed, they said that they saw in the flames golden chariots which would at once carry them over to the joys of heaven." [11] In 1384 a further group of "Luciferans" was discovered in Brandenburg, and on this occasion we know what they were accused of. Like the Austrian heretics, and like Conrad of Marburg's victims, they were supposed to believe that Lucifer had been wrongfully expelled from heaven, and would in due course return there and take over from God. Meanwhile they worshipped Lucifer as their god, and also held promiscuous orgies in underground cellars. The rest of the doctrine ascribed to these people is purely Waldensian, and everything suggests that they too were Waldensians. [12] ★

There is no reason to think that Waldensians were very numerous in the German lands at any time. Nor, after their earliest days, were they socially influential: by the fourteenth century they consisted almost entirely of artisans, modest tradesmen and peasants. Certainly when pitted against the massive structure and vast resources of the Catholic Church the sect was much too small, scattered and obscure to constitute any real threat. Yet in certain quarters it was felt not simply as a threat but as a destructive force of overwhelming, superhuman power. Again we may turn to the Franciscan John of Winterthur to discover not indeed how things were, but how they were imagined to be. In his view, only the most strenuous efforts of Catholic preachers—including of course Franciscan preachers—prevented the Church from being altogether overwhelmed and obliterated: "These people would over-throw the faith of Peter, if the teachers did not each day fortify it with the word of truth. So Peter's little boat, which sails on the billows of the sea of this world, is battered by the blows of the tempest; but it does not sink, because it is sustained by the strong hands of the teachers. . . ." [13]

The persistent efforts to defame the sect are inseparable from this

★ The present chapter was written long before the appearance of the work of Robert E. Lerner, *The heresy of the Free Spirit in the later middle ages*, University of California Press, 1972; but it is gratifying to note that Professor Lerner (pp. 25 *seq.*) reaches the same conclusion, i.e. that all these groups of "Luciferans" were in fact Waldensians. The identity of the two was indeed perceived already by Hermann Haupt in 1888. In the case of the Brandenburg heretics it has been conclusively demonstrated by Dietrich Kurze. For references see Note 12.

fantastic over-estimation of its power. The Waldensians were imagined as Devil-worshippers, and as themselves quasi-demonic. This meant that they must be almost irresistible in their work of undermining and destroying the Christian religion, identified with the Catholic Church. It also meant that whatever was felt to be most anti-human, such as blindly promiscuous orgies and incest between parent and offspring, must be an essential part of their world. And during the fourteenth century this stereotype came to be widely accepted even by professional inquisitors. The account of the Waldensians which the inquisitor for Aragon, Nicolas Eymeric, gave in his manual, the *Directorium Inquisitorum*, around 1368, is on the whole well informed and objective—yet even here the following turns up, as one of the Waldensian articles of faith: "It is better to satisfy one's lust by any kind of evil act than to be harassed by the goadings of the flesh. In the dark it is lawful for any man to mate with any woman, without distinction, whenever and as often as they are moved by carnal desires. This they both say and do." [14]

In France and Italy the Waldensians were originally a more considerable force than in Germany; but there too they were persecuted so fiercely that their heyday was already over by the fourteenth century. By that time, most of the survivors had withdrawn into the Cottian Alps, which straddle the French-Italian border, roughly between Gap and Turin. There they formed a solid colony, under Italian leadership. Inquisitors penetrated into those remote valleys at their peril; two are known to have been killed by the embattled Waldensians. Nevertheless from time to time a few Waldensians were caught, and at some of the resulting trials mention was made of the same fantastic beliefs and deeds as had been ascribed to the German Waldensians generations earlier.

Early in 1387 a Dominican inquisitor called Antonio di Setto, of Savigliano, began investigations in the area around Pinerolo, in the Italian foothills of the Cottian Alps. The results were meagre until, some time in the same year, he laid hands on a religious layman, a member of the Third Order of Saint Francis, called Antonio Galosna of Monte San Raffaello. He kept the man in prison for many months, until May 1388, when he produced him before the tribunal which he had set up in Turin. It now appeared that this Tertiary was really a Waldensian. He had often attended nocturnal meetings of the sect, and was able to give most detailed accounts of what went on. [15]

The meetings were commonly held at the home of a Waldensian, or else at an inn, at an hour when the neighbours were safely asleep. The company consisted of artisans and small tradesmen—innkeepers, bakers, cobblers, tailors, haberdashers, fruiterers. It could vary in size from a

mere dozen to forty or so; but it always included both sexes. The
proceedings opened with a sort of Eucharist. The preacher would distri-
bute bread, explaining that it was worth more than the Catholic faith,
and indeed more than God's grace. An old woman would pour out
drink from a special flask in her keeping. This drink was a foul beverage
which, if taken in any large quantity, made the body swell up and could
even lead to death; but even a sip of it would bind a person to the sect
for ever. It was said to contain the excrement of a huge toad which the
woman kept for that purpose under her bed; and it was always brewed
on the eve of Epiphany. Unappetizing though the fare might be, those
present banqueted "with great joy". So fortified, they promised to obey
the preacher in all things, and never to reveal what happened at the
meetings. They also promised to worship the dragon which wages war
on God and his angels (meaning the dragon in the Book of Revelation,
which is Lucifer or Satan). Thereupon the lights were extinguished and
the cry went up: "Let him who has, keep hold." The orgy began, and
continued until dawn; and here too it is particularly mentioned that the
closest relatives had intercourse. But sometimes things were arranged in
more orderly fashion: the men drew lots for the women.

Antonio Galosna named more than a dozen villages around Turin
where these performances were supposed to take place—and not just
occasionally but once or twice in each month (except, he added, when
the weather was wet). He also named dozens of men and women who
were supposed to participate in them. But, circumstantial though his
confession was, in the end it helped him not at all. At one point the
secular authorities intervened to remove him from the inquisitor's
power—whereupon he promptly denied everything, as having been
extracted by fear of torture. But the inquisitor reasserted his claims;
and though Antonio reverted to his original confession, he was burned
nevertheless. And in 1451 another Dominican inquisitor, also at
Pinerolo, induced another Waldensian to confirm that the sect did
indeed indulge in promiscuous and incestuous orgies. In these Italian
trials there are hints that the original Waldensian doctrine may have
absorbed some elements of Catharist origin; but that does not make the
accusations any more plausible. [16]

Meanwhile the French Waldensians were a constant source of vexation to the archbishops of Embrun, in whose see they were concentrated. Not that they ever were a power in the land—on the contrary,
they were mostly poor peasants and shepherds, living in small compact
communities in the high, remote valleys of Fressinière, Argentière,
Valpute and Valcluson, and seldom venturing outside. But the very fact

that such communities existed and persisted was felt by successive archbishops and inquisitors as an intolerable offence—and not by them alone. The example set by Emperor Frederick II in 1231, when he joined forces with Pope Gregory IX in an effort to stamp out heresy within the Empire, had since been imitated by many rulers; and from 1365 onwards the governor of Dauphiné and the council of Dauphiné (later the *parlement* of Grenoble) repeatedly sent armed expeditions against the mountain villages. In effect it was an intermittent crusade; and like other crusades it enjoyed papal blessing. Desiderated already by John XXII and Benedict XII, the campaign against the Waldensians of Dauphiné was actively supported by Clement VI, Alexander V, Eugenius IV and Innocent VIII.

It reached its height in the years after 1486, when a particularly resolute archbishop, Jean Baile, made a supreme effort to extirpate the sect.[17] He appealed to the Waldensians to return to the Church; and as not a single Waldensian came forward, turned to Pope Innocent VIII for help. The pope responded by replacing the regular inquisitor for Dauphiné, who was elderly, by an Italian called Alberto Cattaneo, who seems to have been only twenty-two years old. Normally an inquisitor was appointed by the provincial of his order, Dominican or Franciscan as the case might be, and was chosen largely for his familiarity with local conditions. Cattaneo, however, was an extraordinary commissioner, appointed directly by the pope; and he proved a bad choice. Though not lacking in attainments—he was archdeacon of Cremona and a doctor of canon and of civil law—he was quite unequipped to act as a judicious inquisitor. Knowing not a word of French, wholly ignorant of conditions in Dauphiné, he was unable to control the secular officials who were his assistants. During his time torture and threats of torture were used far more freely than was usual; Waldensians are known to have died while being tortured by the officials of Embrun.[18]

Cattaneo's first step was moderate enough: like the archbishop before him, he summoned the inhabitants of the valleys to give themselves up, to accept absolution, to be reconciled with the Church. But when he in his turn met with no response, he pressed for a military invasion of the valleys where the Waldensians had their stronghold; and his request was granted. By order of the *parlement* of Grenoble, and under the command of the lieutenant of the governor of Dauphiné, an expeditionary force set out in March 1488. Those who took part in it could look forward both to a plenary indulgence—which was promised by the pope—and to a share in the property of the heretics; and they were correspondingly zealous. The Waldensians were forced back to

the icy mountain peaks, where after a gallant resistance they were
overwhelmed. Scores were put to the sword or thrown from the
rocks.

Many more were taken prisoner or gave themselves up; and while a
few were burned as impenitent or relapsed heretics, the majority were
received into the Church. Some fifty of these were interrogated by
Cattaneo with the assistance of secular lawyers, including the chief
magistrate of Briançon. Doctrinally these Waldensians turned out to be
as close to Catholicism as their precursors two and three centuries
earlier—professing all the principal Catholic dogmas, including the real
presence in the Eucharist, and rejecting only the hierarchy of the Roman
Church. Nevertheless the old slanders against the sect not only persisted but were reinforced. Already before the expedition some captured Waldensians, under interrogation, had talked of nocturnal orgies;
and some amongst the new batch of prisoners spoke in similar vein. [19]
While many indignantly denied that such things occurred at all, others
were more forthcoming. In particular, they had much to say about the
Waldensian preachers, or "barbes" (so called from the Piedmontese
word for "uncle"). They stated that the "barbe" would commonly
launch the orgy by crying out, "Let him who has, have. Let him who
holds, hold. Whoever puts the light out shall have life eternal." [20] This
curious notion was not new—Antonio Galosna had produced it a
century earlier—and its factual basis is known: at the end of a Waldensian service the preacher would say, "Let him who has grasped (the
meaning), retain it"; after which the congregation would meditate for
a few minutes in darkness before dispersing. [21]

The "barbes" were simple, uneducated men, mostly of Italian origin.
They functioned not as resident priests but—like Catholic friars—as
itinerant preachers. Disguised as merchants or pedlars, they were
constantly on the move and covered vast distances on foot. It was a
dangerous, nerve-racking existence; and though the Waldensian communities sheltered them loyally, from time to time one of them would
be captured. It seems that four perished at Grenoble in 1492; [22] and in
the same year two more were caught in the mountains north of
Briançon. One of these, an Italian from Spoleto called Francis of
Girundino, otherwise known as the "barbe" Martin, was tried at Oulx
(now on the Italian side of the frontier). His interrogation, which was
carried out not by an inquisitor but by a canon of the abbey of Oulx,
assisted by a councillor of the governor of Dauphiné and the chief
magistrate of Embrun, provided new and picturesque details concerning the imaginary orgies. [23] Now it appeared that the orgy or "syna-

gogue"* was held only once a year, always in a different region; but it was very incestuous indeed. If the presiding "barbe" was not a local man, he had to withdraw after delivering his sermon, before the orgy began; for only a local man would have relatives available to mate with. One is reminded of Tertullian's ironic comment some thirteen centuries earlier: "Be sure to bring your mother and sister. But what if . . . the convert has none? I suppose you cannot become a regular Christian if you have neither mother nor sister?" Martin added that a male child conceived at this incestuous orgy was regarded as pre-eminently suited to become a "barbe" in due course. As for Martin's companion, the "barbe" Pietro de Jacopo, he was interrogated separately, by the episcopal commissary at Valence. He agreed about the orgies—and added that at these gatherings the Waldensians worshipped an idol called Bacchus!

Incredibly, the very transcript of Martin's interrogation contains a phrase which makes nonsense of the whole story: in the Waldensian view the Catholic clergy, from the pope downwards, were no true clergy precisely because they broke their vows of virginity and chastity. Other prisoners, interrogated in other places, are recorded as maintaining that the sacrament of matrimony is to be faithfully and firmly kept. And indeed the moral strictness of the Waldensians, even at this late stage, is beyond all doubt.

The statements about orgies nevertheless served their purpose. Widely publicized, they brought the Waldensians into general disrepute, so that the sectarians came to be regarded as the worst enemies of society, against whom fresh pursuits could be launched with general approval. Moreover, as so often, economic motives contributed to the dynamism of the persecution. A Waldensian who recanted and was absolved could still see anything up to a third of his property confiscated; a Waldensian who refused to recant was either burned or imprisoned for life—and in either case all his property was confiscated. The total confiscations were massive—in some valleys the land confiscated amounted to a third of all taxable land. It is not surprising that the beneficiaries—the archbishop of Embrun in the first place, but also the various local lords—did everything possible to keep their gains.[24]

Viewed from Paris things looked different. When Louis XII succeeded to the throne in 1499 he was not convinced that small groups of Waldensians in remote Alpine valleys really constituted a threat to French society; and with the pope's agreement he sent his own confessor, the bishop of Sisteron, Laurent Bureau, to carry out an enquiry on

* On the significance of this term see below, p. 100.

the spot. It was the beginning of a gradual rehabilitation. In 1509 the grand council, sitting in Paris, annulled all the sentences passed by the late archbishop Jean Baile, the inquisitor Alberto Cattaneo and his successor François Plouvier, and restored all confiscated properties to the original owners or their heirs. This came about not because the persecuted were able to prove their orthodoxy—most of them certainly were Waldensians, not Catholics—but because the king had an over-riding interest in establishing peace and unity within the kingdom, and was unimpressed by an inquisitorial institution which had lost almost all the power and prestige it had once possessed. Thereafter no more was heard of Waldensian "synagogues".

For at least two and a half centuries tales of promiscuous and inces-tuous orgies and of Devil-worship had pursued this purely—indeed naïvely—Christian sect. Yet it so happens that in no single instance can one fill in all the details—who first voiced the charges, what sources he drew on, how much pressure was needed to obtain substantiation. However, the lacuna can be filled: one has only to examine the case of another group of poverty-loving Christians, the Fraticelli "de opinione" in fourteenth-century Italy.

–2–

In 1466 a score of Fraticelli "de opinione" were subjected to inquisi-torial investigation in the papal prison in Rome, the Castel Sant' Angelo.[25] Some of the accused made horrifying confessions; and down to the present day there have been serious and eminent historians, including specialists in this particular field, who have accepted these confessions at their face value.[26] For some five centuries, a cloud has hung over the reputation of the Fraticelli. In the following pages the case will be investigated afresh.

The Fraticelli can be understood only in terms of the Franciscan movement and its development.[27] The original confraternity which St Francis gathered around him, from 1209 onwards, was wholly unworldly and lived in absolute poverty. Members had to dispose of all their possessions before joining; they aimed to own nothing but the barest necessities of life; they earned their bread from day to day, by manual work; they were not permitted to receive or to handle money. All the energies of these first Franciscans were devoted to nomadic preaching amongst the poor, and to caring for lepers and outcasts. But within a few years the little confraternity grew until it numbered thousands of members; and in 1220 a papal bull constituted it as a monastic order.

Francis died in 1226, and by the 1230s the Franciscan Order had already departed far from his ideal. It was now a great organization extending throughout western Christendom; seeking and wielding influence in church and state; active in teaching theology and canon law in the universities; and—like other monastic orders—owning vast properties in land and buildings. But many Franciscans could not reconcile themselves to these transformations and strove to restore the hard, simple way of life that had prevailed in the earliest years. At first these zealots—or Spirituals, as they called themselves—formed a minority within the order; and at times they were even able to set the tone for the order as a whole. The most extreme amongst them, however, chose another course.

Already in the thirteenth century some of the Spiritual party left first the official order and then the Church itself. Inspired by apocalyptic writings which were falsely ascribed to the Calabrian abbot Joachim of Fiore, these men regarded the Church of Rome as the Whore of Babylon and the pope as Antichrist; while regarding themselves as the one true church, an elite appointed by God to lead the whole world to a life of voluntary poverty. Inevitably they were condemned as heretics and persecuted accordingly; which in turn increased their fury against the Church.

The Fraticelli were the successors, in the fourteenth and fifteenth centuries, of these heretical Spirituals. In the fourteenth century they had a certain importance, especially in Italian life. At that time they enjoyed the support of the political enemies of the popes: the Ghibellines welcomed and protected them. Many others, who were simply dissatisfied with the Church because of its wealth and worldliness, were also attracted by these poverty-loving rebels.

The most radical of the Fraticelli were known as the Fraticelli "de opinione"; a term which requires some elucidation. At one time, very many Franciscans had believed that Christ and the apostles had lived in absolute poverty, owning no property at all, whether as individuals or in common. A general chapter of the order, held at Perugia in 1322, had even accepted a proposition to that effect. But the papacy had always recognized the dangerous implications of the belief. The chapter at Perugia was held in the pontificate of John XXII—the great financial administrator who, in his determination to restore the papacy to its former independence of secular monarchs, concentrated above all on increasing its wealth. In 1323 John declared that to affirm the absolute poverty of Christ and the apostles was to fall into heresy; and this view of the matter was maintained by subsequent popes. It was also accepted, however reluctantly, by the Franciscan order as such. For the Fraticelli "de opinione", on the other hand, the absolute poverty of Christ and the apostles was an article of faith. In response to papal condemnations they retorted that John XXII and all popes following him were themselves heretics; that the Catholic clergy, in so far as they obeyed the popes, had forfeited all authority; and that sacraments administered by such clergy were worthless. These views on the poverty of Christ and the apostles, and on the illegitimacy of the Catholic hierarchy, constituted the "opinion" after which the sect was named.

The Fraticelli "de opinione" were never very numerous, nor did they evolve a unified organization. Nevertheless, the popes felt these dissidents to be a menace, both on doctrinal and on social grounds. They made repeated efforts to eliminate them, by conversion if possible, by physical extermination if necessary; and in the end they succeeded. By the middle of the fifteenth century the sect had been reduced to a few obscure, clandestine groups, and the heresy had lost most of its importance. The papal onslaught of 1466 was directed against an already defeated foe.

The pope at that time, Paul II, was a man whose enthusiasm was more easily engaged by his magnificent collection of antiquities and works of art, and by the jewels which he assembled for his personal adornment, than by the ideal of absolute poverty. In 1466 it came to his ears that many Fraticelli "de opinione" would be making their way to Assisi, to attend the festival of Portiuncula that was to be held there in July. The little chapel of St Mary of the Angels, known as the Portiuncula, was the place where St Francis had received the revelation which determined his vocation; now it had become a favourite place of pilgrimage for the Fraticelli—and also a place where, amongst the crowds of pilgrims, they could meet without attracting notice. Not so, however, on this occasion: investigators sent specially by the pope seized a score of them, of both sexes and the most various ages.

It turned out that the prisoners had come a long way to Assisi: some from the area around Poli, not far from Rome; others from the area around Maiolati, in the mountainous, inland part of the March of Ancona. All were obscure inhabitants of obscure villages; but despite this, it was thought worthwhile to transport them all the way to Rome and to incarcerate them in the papal fortress itself. Moreover, the ecclesiastics who interrogated them there included an archbishop and two bishops, as well as the commandant of the fortress; and torture was used freely. Clearly, great expectations were attached to this mass interrogation and the confessions it might produce. They were not disappointed.

The first prisoner to be interrogated was a "priest" of the sect, called Bernard of Bergamo. His answers give a lively and convincing picture of Fraticelli life.[28] Bernard had spent his noviciate in Greece; for the Fraticelli, in flight from persecution in Italy, had established monasteries across the water, outside the bounds of Latin Christendom. After ordination Bernard had returned to Italy, to teach the doctrine of the Fraticelli at Poli: preaching against the errors of John XXII, condemning the Catholic clergy, exalting absolute poverty. Though his activity was clandestine, it evidently found some response. Even great nobles were favourably disposed. The overlord of the village, Count Stefano de Conti, protected the Fraticelli and treated Bernard as his father confessor—and in due course was imprisoned by the pope in the fortress of Sant' Angelo for so doing. Bernard recalled, too, how a great lady of the Colonna family summoned him to her castle, so that she could make her confession to him instead of to a Catholic priest; she has been identified as Sueva, the mother of Stefano Colonna, count of Palestrina.

Such situations, where poverty-loving heretics were secretly patronized by rich and powerful families, were not uncommon in the fourteenth and fifteenth centuries. But the majority of Bernard's flock consisted of ordinary villagers. He reckoned that twenty or thirty men and women of Poli attended when, secretly, he celebrated mass. One inhabitant had bequeathed his house so that Fraticelli "priests" could celebrate mass, hear confessions and ordain new "priests" in security. Even the Catholic priest of the parish seems to have been implicated to some extent; for when a Fraticelli "bishop" died, he allowed him to be buried in consecrated ground. (In the light of Bernard's confession, the body was disinterred and burned.)

All this rings true, and it was confirmed and completed by the evidence of the "lay" prisoners. These people called themselves "the poor of Christ" and regarded themselves as God's elect. Indeed—exactly like the Waldensians—they held that they were the only true Christians, for they alone imitated Christ and the apostles in their absolute poverty. Whole families lived and died in this faith, and had done for generations; children were born into it. From time to time inquisitors would descend on these remote villages and scare those whom they did not imprison or burn into abandoning their faith. But sooner or later the renegades were apt to decide that the poverty-loving brethren offered a surer way to salvation than a Church weighed down with possessions and riddled with simony; and they would drift back. So the Fraticelli communities survived, minute islands of asceticism in a sea of worldliness.

But if the first confession at the Castel Sant' Angelo yields a perfectly coherent picture, the second reveals some strangely incongruous features. For the statements by the next prisoner, Francis of Maiolati, include the following:

"Interrogated concerning the matter of the *barilotto*, he said that when he was young, ten or twelve years of age, he twice found himself in the crypt of a church which has since been destroyed, at a spot near Maiolati. After mass had been celebrated at night, just before dawn, the lights were put out and the people cried, 'Put out the light, let us go to eternal life, alleluia, alleluia; and let each man take hold of his woman.'"

Asked what he did himself, and whether he had sexual intercourse with any woman, he replied that he was young at that time, and the young people left the church; the adults stayed behind and had intercourse with the women present. They made a stamping noise, like the noise on the holy day of Venus.

Interrogated concerning the powders, he replied that, from the babies born, they take one little boy as a sacrifice. They make a fire, around which they stand in a circle. They pass the little boy from hand to hand until he is quite dried up. Later they make powders from the body. They put these powders in a flask of wine. After the end of mass they give some of this wine to all taking part; each drinks once from the flask, by way of communion. And he, Francis, was there twice, and drank twice, when attending mass. He also said that for thirty years he had not belonged to the sect, because he had had no occasion. He joined again after the arrival of Brother Bernard, who brought him back to it by his preaching; and he had made confession four times to the same Bernard.[29]

Such was the story told by Francis of Maiolati. To understand it, two facts have to be borne in mind. As in all inquisitorial trials, the tribunal was empowered to use torture; and again and again the record of the enquiry expressly states that torture was in fact used. Francis may not have been tortured, but he certainly knew that he could be. Secondly, the prisoners incarcerated in the Castel Sant' Angelo included a Fraticelli "bishop", Nicholas of Massaro. This man did not figure at all in the first series of interrogations; but there are strong indications that Francis's statement was intended to prepare the way for his appearance later. Interrogated afresh, Francis stated that he knew of the ritual infanticide only from senior members of the sect.[30] Another prisoner, Angelo of Poli, was more precise: the first time he had ever heard of the *barilotto* was now, in prison, when the "bishop" Nicholas had told him of it.[31] It is impossible to tell whether these laymen were forced to incriminate their "bishop" or whether, on the contrary, the "bishop" was forced to mislead his followers; but it is also immaterial. By whatever means, the scene was set for a dramatic confession by a leader of the Fraticelli.

The enquiry began in August 1466, and in October the commission laid its report before Pope Paul. The pope insisted that the enquiry should be resumed forthwith, and the prisoners interrogated afresh.[32] This time Nicholas of Massaro was at the head of the line; a venerable figure, it would seem, for he had been a bishop for some forty years. He at once confessed to everything—to taking part in the orgies and in the infanticides; also to handing out the wine with the ashes of the incinerated baby "nine or ten times". He had only one correction to make: the orgies were not wholly promiscuous, the men usually chose women they knew, and he himself usually took Catherine of Palumbaria.[33] Catherine, being summoned, failed to confirm this—she could recall having intercourse with the elderly Nicholas only once or twice. On the other hand, she knew all about the infanticides and the making of the powders; indeed, these things were frequently done in her very house.[34]

This is the sum total of evidence concerning orgies, infanticides and cannibalistic beverages amongst the Fraticelli: for the rest, the records of the interrogations, which are unusually full and vivid, show only how utterly strange these stories seemed to the ordinary lay members of the sect. The reaction of one exceptionally strong character, Antonio of Sacco, is revealing. In August and again in October this man stood by his faith.[35] He refused to abjure, and he refused to kneel before the tribunal. Told that the "bishop" Nicholas himself had abjured, he remained unshaken; in that case, he replied, he would subordinate himself not to a heretical pope but to God alone. He admitted, and gloried in, every article of faith of the Fraticelli. At the same time he denied all knowledge of the *barilotto*. So, at the renewed enquiry in October, Antonio de Sacco was tortured in the usual way; being hauled up by a rope around his wrists, which were tied behind him, and then suddenly dropped—a proceeding calculated to tear the muscles and dislocate the joints. After several applications of this torture Antonio admitted to taking part in the *barilotto*—but as soon as he was taken off the rope, he denied it. Tortured again, he confirmed his first statement—but when he was brought before the tribunal, he again denied everything.[36]

In the end Antonio capitulated, like all the other accused, to the extent of abjuring his faith, asking to be received back into the Church, and promising to accept the pope as the true vicar of God on earth.

Coming close up to the commissioners he said humbly: "My lords, forgive me." But he also said: "My lords, you saw how yesterday, when I was being tortured, I said I had twice attended the *barilotto*. It's not true. I have a young wife and a beautiful daughter, who are detained here in the prisons of Sant' Angelo. I would never have permitted such things." (37)

The rest of the accused were no more helpful. Unlike Antonio of Sacco they all abjured very quickly, during the first series of interrogations—but even so, nobody supported Francis of Maiolati in his allegations. It was not simply that nobody confessed to taking part in such sinister practices—nobody knew anything at all about them. And the same happened when the interrogations were resumed in October. Apart from Nicholas, Catherine and Francis, nobody could throw any light on the matter—and Francis himself insisted that he had never seen any of these things himself. Indeed, as the proceedings continued he could no longer even recall the age at which he had heard, from outside a church, what he thought was a *barilotto*—perhaps it was ten, but then again perhaps it was fifteen. (38)

The final picture, then, is paradoxical in the extreme. The tribunal really had investigated two groups of Fraticelli "de opinione". It had found them to hold all those views—on the all-importance of absolute poverty, on the sublime merits of the Fraticelli, on the depravity of the Church of Rome—which were commonly attributed to them. That much can be regarded as established; and it was enough, by itself, to get the prisoners condemned as heretics. But beyond that point the case is submerged in a welter of implausibilities and contradictions. In the end the tribunal was left with two leading personalities—the "bishops" Nicholas of Massaro and his friend Catherine of Palumbaria—who admitted to organizing orgies and infanticides and cannibalistic communions on a massive scale; but not one member of the rank and file who had ever taken part in, or even witnessed, any of these activities. A couple of generals, in short, with no troops at all.

Moreover, the behaviour of the tribunal itself was full of paradoxes. With the means at its disposal, it certainly could have extracted confessions from the other prisoners, some of whom were adolescent boys and girls; but it did not insist. And when it came to sentence the prisoners, it revealed a similar uncertainty. It sentenced them for their real beliefs—banishing some for seven years, imprisoning others for life; but it also described them collectively as "murderers, adulterous, incestuous". The explanation must surely be that the tribunal had a double task. In the first place it was concerned, as the Inquisition normally was,

to reclaim repentant heretics for the Church and to punish the impenitent or relapsed. But it was also concerned to establish that the movement of the Fraticelli was a monstrous, anti-human conspiracy.

Yet it does not follow that the commission was a mere pack of cynics.
It is quite possible that the eminent ecclesiastics who guided the interrogation believed that they were simply uncovering the truth. For by the
time of the trial in 1466 these particular accusations formed part of the
clergy's stereotype of the Fraticelli. The story of how this came about
has never been told, and it deserves to be.

The activities described by Francis of Maiolati include one very
curious feature. The Fraticelli were said not simply to kill babies but to
do so in a particularly bizarre manner—by passing them from hand to
hand until they died. Now this strange fantasy had a long history
behind it. As early as the eighth century the head of the Armenian
church, John of Ojun, had described how the Paulician heretics killed
the fruit of their orgies in just that way.[39] And in the twelfth century
the French chronicler Guibert de Nogent had said of the heretics of
Soissons almost exactly what Francis of Maiolati said of the Fraticelli:
"They light a great fire and all sit around it. They pass the child from
hand to hand and finally throw it on the fire, and leave it there until it
is entirely consumed. Later, when the child is burned to ashes, they
make those ashes into a sort of bread; each eats a piece by way of communion." [40] So, behind the grim and solemn procedures of interrogation and torture, we discover a literary tradition. More precisely, we
discover an age-old fantasy enshrined in theological tracts and monastic chronicles.

It is possible to trace the route by which this fantasy reached the
tribunal of bishops in Rome. In the mid-fourteenth century the Franciscan Order produced a reform movement from within its own ranks,
the Observants. Like the Franciscan Order itself, the Observant reform
started in central Italy and quickly spread through the whole of Italy
and into other lands. The basis of the reform was the "poor and scanty
use" of worldly goods; and many of the Observants were as ascetic in
their way of life as the Fraticelli themselves.

An early promoter of the Observant movement was St Bernardin of
Siena, who was active during the first half of the fourteenth century.
For some thirty years he travelled throughout Italy, preaching in a style
which was both eloquent and pithy and which evoked immense popular response. And a sermon which he delivered in the Piazza del Campo
at Siena in 1427—that is, some forty years before the trial in the Castel
Sant' Angelo—includes an account of the barilotto; an account which

incidentally explains the origins of the term itself. Bernardin gives the usual account of the promiscuous nocturnal orgy, of the tossing to death of the baby boy, of the making of the powders; but he also has something new to say. The sect which performs these rites calls itself "the people of the barilotto"; and the *barilotto* is really the little barrel, or flask, in which the mixture of powdered ashes and wine is kept, and from which the members of the sect ceremonially drink.[41]

In all this there is not a word about the Fraticelli. Indeed, no particular sect is named at all; and the one indication given—that some of the people are to be found in Piedmont, where they make a practice of killing inquisitive inquisitors—would point to the Waldensians rather than to the Fraticelli. But Bernardin had a devoted friend and collaborator, who often accompanied him as he travelled from town to town—and who, in due course, was to procure his canonization. This was St John of Capestrano; and it was he who turned Bernardin's quite unspecific story into an accusation against the Fraticelli.

In personality John of Capestrano in some ways recalls Conrad of Marburg; though he lived some two centuries later and played a far greater part in the life of his time.[42] Up to the age of twenty-nine he lived a wholly secular life; being married, a successful magistrate, and deeply involved in the political and military struggles between the small Italian states. The turning-point came when he was captured and imprisoned, broke a leg in trying to escape, and then, while lying chained and in agony in a dungeon, saw repeated visions of St Francis. Liberated by his captors, he renounced all his possessions and became an Observant Franciscan. In the end he was to do more than anybody to make the Observants into the dominant branch of the Order, and an important factor in European life. Canonized in 1690, he is known as "the apostle of Europe".

In his lifetime Capestrano was a legendary and formidable figure. Journeying incessantly, preaching almost daily, he enjoyed a prestige equalled only by Bernardin. Successive popes favoured and employed him, sometimes as legate, sometimes as inquisitor. Extraordinarily ascetic in his way of life, he was also extraordinarily relentless in his pursuit of dissidents. He constantly urged princes, towns and even popes to sharper action against the Jews; while as inquisitor he became the scourge of the Italian Fraticelli.

As early as 1418 Pope Martin V appointed Capestrano inquisitor, with the special task of tracking down the Fraticelli. It proved a shrewd move, not only because Capestrano brought enthusiasm to the work but because, as a true ascetic himself, he was able to undermine the appeal of these unorthodox ascetics. But Capestrano was by no means a full-time inquisitor; the persecution was intermittent, and thirty years were to pass before it reached its triumphant conclusion.

In 1449 plague was raging in Rome; and to escape it the pope, Nicholas V, moved for the summer to Fabriano, a small town in the inland, mountainous part of the March of Ancona. Capestrano followed him, partly to further the interests of the Observants, partly to press for the canonization of his friend Bernardin, who had died in 1444. But the March of Ancona had long been one of the main centres of the Fraticelli, and remnants of the sect were still hiding there. Before returning to Rome, Pope Nicholas bestowed unrestricted inquisitorial powers on Capestrano for the specific purpose of pursuing the local Fraticelli. A collaborator was also nominated: St James of March, who was also an Observant and had also been concerned with the Fraticelli for many years—and who moreover was operating on his home ground. [43]

As the area around Fabriano was papal territory there was no authority, ecclesiastical or secular, to hinder the two men from using their powers to the utmost. Capestrano was in a state of high excitement. On 8 November he wrote from Massaccio to the pope's brother, who was the apostolic legate in Bologna, urging him to fresh zeal against the heretics. The defence of the faith, he insisted, must take precedence over all other work; as for his own activity, something extraordinary was about to happen: within the next three days more would be accomplished than in the last six years. And his campaign against the Fraticelli did in fact prove immensely successful. The villages of Massaccio, Poggio and Meroli were purged; and so was Maiolati, which was to figure again in the trial of 1466. Many Fraticelli recanted; those who stood firm were burned—Fabriano itself witnessed the burning of a Fraticelli "pope" together with some of his faithful flock. [44]

The lives of Capestrano in the great hagiographical collection, the *Acta Sanctorum*, contain further details, which are plausible in themselves and which probably likewise apply to this episode in his career. [45] They tell how the Fraticelli repeatedly tried to assassinate him; how he had thirty-six of their settlements burned to the ground; and how the remnants of the Fraticelli fled to Greece. At the trial of 1466 the "priest" Bernard was to describe how in Greece new centres were founded and new clergy trained, to be sent back to Italy as missionaries. [46] But this was only a last faint flicker of life: the persecutions of 1449 had effectively broken the Fraticelli movement.

Now there exists an account, written within three or four years of these events, which shows that all the infamies with which the Fraticelli were to be charged in 1466, in Rome, were already attributed to them in 1449, at Fabriano. The well-known humanist Flavio Biondo was apostolic secretary at that time. In his book describing the various provinces of Italy, called *Italia Illustrata*, he mentions the sojourn of Pope Nicholas at Fabriano, and then goes on to give an account of the Fraticelli.[47] All the familiar features are there: the promiscuous orgies, the killing of a child by throwing it from hand to hand, the incineration of the corpse, the mixing of ashes in wine which is then used to initiate new members. The term *barilotto* turns up, in its Latin form, and is explained just as St Bernardin explained it: the whole performance is named after the little barrel of wine-with-ashes.

But the most instructive part of Biondo's tale is the piece of personal reminiscence at the end:

> John of Capestrano, a most religious and indubitably holy man, related to us how, when he was in charge of persecuting this sect of people, a most wicked woman voluntarily confessed to him, as follows. When, as a result of this diabolic copulation, she had given birth to a child, she carried it to the cave, in a casket lightly decorated for the purpose. Her state of mind was joyful; she brought a most precious gift. And she stayed to watch her son, who was screaming most piteously, being roasted. She did this not only dry-eyed, but with a happy mind. When, therefore, some twelve members of that most cruel sect came to Fabriano, where the court was, they were very thoroughly investigated; and as they obstinately refused to come to their senses, were burned, as they deserved.[48]

Biondo wrote under the very eyes of the pope, indeed in *Italia Illustrata* he often addresses him directly: "tu, Pater Sancte . . .".[49] So what he says of the pope's friend and emissary can be relied on: Capestrano must indeed have told these tales about the Fraticelli. And this is confirmed by an unpublished sermon of Capestrano's. In 1451 the fiery preacher was sent to Germany; and the following year at Nuremberg he included, in his preaching, a story about certain cruel heretics who held incestuous orgies in caves.[50] But Capestrano's responsibility does not end there. The Fraticelli had been persecuted for a century before the episode at Fabriano, yet no such charges had ever been brought against them. Bernardin of Siena, who was familiar with such stories, never connected them with the Fraticelli. Everything suggests that Capestrano was the first to ascribe the *barilotto* to the Fraticelli; and that he did so in the heat of the persecution at Fabriano.

Once voiced, the accusations had to be answered by confessions, which legitimated renewed accusations, which produced further confessions. It is clear from Biondo's account that at least some of the dozen Fraticelli who were burned at Fabriano had been forced to confess to practising the *barilotto*. Nearly twenty years later, in the interrogations of Francis of Maiolati in the Castel Sant' Angelo, the phrases "interrogated concerning the matter of the *barilotto*", "interrogated concerning the powders", appear without previous explanations. Clearly, the interrogators were following an established pattern; and sure enough, the "bishop" Nicholas of Massaro hastened to confirm their preconceptions.[51] It seems, too, that by that time the slanders had penetrated to the common people. Prisoners described how peasant youths around Maiolati would mock the Fraticelli "de opinione" by calling them "fratri de *barilotto*", and how boys would shower one another with insults such as, "You were born from the *barilotto*." And that, at least, sounds convincing.

The trial of 1466 was the end of the Fraticelli as an organized sect; but the defamation continued and increased, until it distorted the whole history of the movement. In the following century a Spanish scholar, Juan Ginez de Sepúlveda, wrote a biography in which he had occasion to mention the activities and fate of some quite different Fraticelli—people who had lived neither near Fabriano nor near Rome, and in the mid-fourteenth century instead of the mid-fifteenth. And he, too, tells blithely how these Fraticelli indulged in nocturnal orgies, killed and incinerated babies, mixed the ashes in their communion wine—all things of which no contemporary had ever accused them.[52] The evil repute of the Fraticelli has lingered on, down to the present day.

In the above account that evil repute has at last been traced to its true source. This was found to lie not in anything the Fraticelli really did, nor even in popular rumour, but in a literary tradition which was known only to educated men.* Tales told long before, about quite different

---

* This literary tradition must have had even greater continuity than appears from the above account. The story as told by Biondo in the fifteenth century, and as repeated by Sepúlveda in the sixteenth, contains the following curious detail: "He in whose hands the baby expires, is held to be appointed supreme pontiff by the divine spirit." This detail does not appear in the earlier western sources known to us, such as Bernardin of Siena and Guibert de Nogent. On the other hand, it was known in Armenia seven centuries earlier. John of Ojun's treatise against the Paulicians says: "They venerate him in whose hands the child expires, and promote him head of the sect." So far as is known, John of Ojun's treatise first became accessible in the West when an Armenian manuscript, buried in a monastery in Venice, was translated into Latin in 1834. Yet the resemblance is surely too close, and too bizarre, to be explicable by coincidence. There must have been more links in this literary tradition than are now discernible.

sects, and recorded in Latin writings, were applied by St John of Capestrano to the Fraticelli. And just as, in earlier centuries, Pope Gregory IX and Pope John XXII had been led, by Conrad of Marburg and Henry of Schönberg, to accept the most monstrous fantasies concerning the Waldensians, so Pope Nicholas V and Pope Paul II were led by Capestrano and his successors to accept these accusations against the Fraticelli. Both these fifteenth-century popes were cultured men—Nicholas indeed was one of the most learned scholars of his day.

The defamation of the Fraticelli, then, was the work of intellectuals in positions of authority. Also, it was carried out at a time when the Fraticelli no longer had any appreciable influence or importance. We have met this pattern before, and we shall be meeting it again.

−3−

Again and again, over a period of many centuries, heretical sects were accused of holding promiscuous and incestuous orgies in the dark; of killing infants and devouring their remains; of worshipping the Devil. Is it conceivable that no sect ever did such things at all? In the past, historians have diverged over that question. But here the matter must be settled once and for all; for otherwise the whole argument of this book hangs in the air.

One of the charges can be dismissed without more ado. Normally, when heretics were tried and interrogated by inquisitors, transcripts of the proceedings were kept. Hundreds of these transcripts have survived, and they offer no evidence for the killing and eating of babies or children. Indeed, only one sect ever seems to have been formally charged with such offences—the Fraticelli "de opinione" at Fabriano and Rome; and as we have seen, the "evidence" produced even in that belated instance turns out to have been taken almost verbatim from polemical tracts and monastic chronicles, written centuries before. All the other accounts of child-eating derive from the same literary tradition. Weighed against the silence of the inquisitors, they have no authority whatever.

At first glance, the charge of holding promiscuous and incestuous orgies might seem to have rather more basis in real happenings. It is certain, for instance, that some of the heretical mystics known as the Brethren of the Free Spirit did claim to have attained a state of total oneness with God, in which all things were permitted to them; and it was widely believed at the time that they gave expression to this conviction by practising free love amongst themselves. There is also the case of the Dualist heretics known as Cathars. According to Catharist doctrine, all matter was evil, and human bodies were prisons from which human souls were struggling to escape; whence it followed that procreation was an abomination. Catholic polemics pointed out the logical consequences of such a view. If all procreation was utterly evil, no form of sexual intercourse was more reprehensible than any other; incest between mother and son was no worse than intercourse between man and wife. So long as no more souls were incarcerated in flesh, no harm was done; and to avoid that, abortion or even infanticide were legitimate.

However, on closer examination none of this really provides an explanation for the tales of promiscuous and incestuous orgies. There is no firm evidence that in practice Cathars ever drew libertine consequences from their hatred of the flesh.[53] Catharist morality was only meant to be followed by the elite of the sect, the *perfecti*; and in general even the Catholic clergy, while attacking Catharist doctrine, paid tribute to the chastity of these people.[54] Nor is there any reason to think that the Brethren of the Free Spirit indulged in collective orgies; if any of them did indeed practise free love, they did it in private. Indeed, of all the innumerable stories of nocturnal orgies only one, concerning an incident which is supposed to have taken place in Cologne in 1326, could possibly refer to the heretical mystics of the Free Spirit; and even that has now been shown to be mythical.*

Above all, there are the brute facts of chronology. Stories of heretics and their orgies were circulating in France already in the eleventh century—but there were no Cathars in the West before the middle of the twelfth century, and the Brethren of the Free Spirit are first heard of in the thirteenth. The beliefs and activities of these sectarians can no more account for the defamation of the Waldensians or the Fraticelli than the activities of the Carpocratians can account for the very similar tales told of the early Christians.[55]

And of course it is to those ancient tales that we must look for an explanation. After all, both the accusations of promiscuous orgies and the accusations of child-eating belong to a tradition dating back to the

---

* On the Free Spirit see Robert E. Lerner, *The heresy of the Free Spirit in the later middle ages*, University of California Press, 1972, which is not only the most recent but also the most thorough survey of this difficult field. Lerner doubts whether the Brethren ever practised free love at all. In view of what is known about the English Ranters of the seventeenth century, who professed very similar doctrines, this scepticism seems excessive. But however that may be, Lerner demonstrates conclusively (pp. 29–31) that the orgy at Cologne was imaginary—a conclusion which I reached independently when I came to revise *The Pursuit of the Millennium* for the 1970 edition.

second century. The Fathers who first defended the Christians against these accusations also, by the very act of putting them in writing, perpetuated the accusations. Embedded in theological works which were preserved in monastic libraries and which moreover were frequently recopied, these tales must have been familiar to many monks. It was only to be expected that, when it came to discrediting some new religious out-group, monks would draw on this traditional stock of defamatory clichés. Moreover, it is known that by the fourteenth century certain chroniclers deliberately inserted such stories into their narratives in order to provide preachers with materials for their sermons against heresy.[56]

More serious consideration has to be given to the idea that heretics worshipped the Devil. This charge cannot simply be derived from what pagan Romans said about the Christian minority in their midst. Did it, then, reflect what some group or sect of medieval heretics really believed or practised? Few people nowadays are likely to accept that demonic cats descended miraculously from on high [57]—but perhaps some reality lurks behind these fantasies, perhaps there really was a cult of Lucifer or Satan? Even so sceptical (and anticlerical) a historian as Henry Charles Lea thought so,[58] and today it is still widely assumed that such a cult must have existed.

Three arguments have been advanced in support of this view. It has been pointed out that some medieval sources describe a coherent and conceivable doctrine, which they attribute to a sect of "Luciferans". It has been suggested that the Dualist religion, pushed to its logical conclusion, could very well lead to Devil-worship. And it has also been said that the intelligent, educated and devout men—including some popes—who accepted that a cult of Satan existed, would not have done so without solid evidence. These arguments have to be examined.

It is true that accounts of a Luciferan doctrine are to be found not only in the bull which Pope Gregory IX fulminated at the prompting of Conrad of Marburg in 1233,[59] but in half a dozen other German and Italian sources.[60] The Luciferan doctrine, it appears, taught that Lucifer and his demons were unjustly expelled from heaven, but will return there in the end, to resume their rightful places and to cast God, Michael and his angels into hell for all eternity. Meanwhile the Luciferans must serve their master by doing everything in their power to offend God; their reward will be everlasting blessedness with Lucifer. The accounts agree with one another and are not, on the face of it, implausible. But how reliable are they?

Internal evidence shows them to be wholly unreliable. Each one is accompanied by statements which are anything but plausible. In one case we hear of demons who vanish into thin air when the Luciferan rite is interrupted by the appearance of the Eucharist. Another source blithely states that in Austria, Bohemia and the neighbouring territories alone the worshippers of Lucifer number 80,000. Another—a confession attributed to a heretic called Lepzet, of Cologne—proclaims that the man himself, in his zeal to serve Lucifer and offend God, has committed more than thirty murders! Yet another speaks of a magic potion containing the excrement of a gigantic toad; while in the bull *Vox in Rama* both a demonic toad and a demonic cat receive kisses of homage. Moreover, most of the sources contain references to those promiscuous and incestuous orgies which we have just shown to be unreliable. But where a source contains untrustworthy or demonstrably false statements it should be treated with scepticism throughout; and that is the case with all the sources that tell of a Luciferan doctrine.

In any case, these accounts of a particular Luciferan doctrine are simply very belated additions to the traditional tales about a Devil-worshipping sect, which can be traced back some four centuries earlier; and it is the tales themselves that present the problem. Is it possible that a Devil-worshipping sect really did develop out of the Dualist religion?

One has only to examine the stories one by one to see how groundless this supposition is. Until recently it was thought that the Paulicians of Armenia, whom John of Ojun accused of Devil-worship in the eighth century, were Dualists; but the latest research has shown that at that date they were nothing of the kind.[61] The Bogomiles accused in the eleventh century were indeed Dualists—but not a word, in the couple of paragraphs allocated to them, suggests that Psellos was aware of the fact. Psellos was in Constantinople, the Bogomiles were in Thrace, and he knew so little about them that he even got their name wrong.[62] And in the West too accusations of Devil-worship were hurled at sects which knew nothing of Dualism. Already the heretical group discovered at Orleans in 1022 was so accused; and the stereotype of the Devil-worshipping sect was fully developed, in every detail, by 1100. But historians are generally agreed that the Dualist religion was unknown in the West before 1140 at the earliest.[63]

Between the middle of the twelfth and the middle of the thirteenth century that form of the Dualist religion known as Catharism did flourish in the West, and it was widely interpreted as a cult of Satan— witness the preposterous etymology which derived the very name "Cathar" from the worship of the demonic cat.[64] Is it possible that Catharism, at least, sometimes involved Devil-worship?

Towards the close of the twelfth century a French monk called Rudolf Ardent summarized the belief of the Cathars. According to him, they held that, whereas God created all invisible things, the Devil created all visible ones; so they worshipped the Devil as the creator of their bodies.[65] About the same time a French chronicler recorded the confession which two Catharist leaders were supposed to have made after spending some months as captives of the papal legate: "they said that Satan and Lucifer is the creator of heaven and earth, of all things visible and invisible . . .".[66] No doubt it was such reports as these that gave rise to the notion of a Luciferan doctrine. They must also have lent fresh credibility to the age-old tales of a Devil-worshipping sect. But as evidence for the existence of a Luciferan doctrine or a Devil-worshipping sect they are valueless, for they grossly distort what Cathars really believed.

We have reliable information concerning the real beliefs of the Cathars—including some Catharist writings.[67] Like other Dualists, they were convinced that the material universe was created by an evil spirit—in effect, the Devil—who still dominated it. But so far from worshipping the Devil they were passionately concerned to escape from his clutches. That aspiration was the very heart of their religion. For souls were not created by the Devil but by God. Indeed, in the Catharist view souls are the angels who fell from heaven; they have been imprisoned in one body after another, and they yearn to escape from the material world and re-enter the heaven of pure spirituality. The morality of the Catharist *perfecti*—their condemnation of marriage, their horror of procreation, their vegetarianism and fasting—reflects their total rejection of the material world, imagined as a demonic creation. To come to terms with the flesh, to accept the world of matter—that is to reveal oneself as a servant of the Devil; and to be a servant of the Devil is to be incapable of salvation.

There is, then, no reason to think that, even in the twelfth and thirteenth centuries, tales of a Devil-worshipping sect reflected something that really existed amongst the Cathars. Moreover in the fifteenth century, long after the Cathars had been exterminated those Bible-studying Christians the Waldensians were still being persecuted as "Luciferans".

Finally, we must ask ourselves whether intelligent, educated and devout men could have accepted that a cult of Satan existed, if they had not had good grounds for thinking so. Several modern historians have argued, and have convinced many readers, that such a thing is inconceivable. But they are in error. The same people who accepted that a cult of Satan existed, also accepted that Satan miraculously materialized at the celebration of his cult, usually in the form of a gigantic animal. The two beliefs were practically inseparable; and if the one seems to lack evidential value, so should the other.

There is in fact no serious evidence for the existence of such a sect of Devil-worshippers anywhere in medieval Europe. One can go further: there is serious evidence to the contrary. Very few inquisitors claimed to have come across these Devil-worshippers, and most of those few are known to have been fanatical amateurs, of the stamp of Conrad of Marburg. We may be sure that if any sect really had held such beliefs, it would have figured in one or other of the two standard manuals for inquisitors: that by Bernard Gui or that by Nicolas Eymeric, both dating from the fourteenth century, when the Luciferans are supposed to have been at the height of their influence. But it does not. As we shall see in a later chapter, the only kind of "demonolatry" known to Eymeric lay in the efforts of individual practitioners of ritual or cere-monial magic to induce demons to do their will—which is a different matter altogether.[68] Gui's comments have even less bearing on the matter. In fact, neither Eymeric nor Gui even hint at the existence of a sect of Devil-worshippers; and that should settle the question.

To understand why the stereotype of a Devil-worshipping sect emerged at all, why it exercised such fascination and why it survived so long, one must look not at the belief or behaviour of heretics, Dualist or other, but into the minds of the orthodox themselves. Many people, and particularly many priests and monks, were becoming more and more obsessed by the overwhelming power of the Devil and his demons. That is why their idea of the absolutely evil and anti-human came to include Devil-worship, alongside incest, infanticide and cannibalism.

But how did this preoccupation with the Devil ever start? How did it turn into such a terrifying obsession? How, above all, could it be believed that Christendom was threatened by a conspiracy of human beings under the Devil's direct command? This chapter in the history of the European psyche deserves more than a passing glance.

CAMROSE LUTHERAN COLLEGE
LIBRARY

4

CHANGING VIEWS OF THE DEVIL AND HIS POWER

-I-

The Old Testament has little to say about the Devil and does not even hint at a conspiracy of human beings under the Devil's command.

For the early Hebrews Yahweh was a tribal god, they thought of the gods of the neighbouring peoples as antagonistic to them and to Yahweh, and they felt no need for any more grandiose embodiment of evil. Later, of course, the tribal religion developed into a monotheism; but then the monotheism is so absolute, the omnipotence and omnipresence of God are so constantly affirmed, that the powers of evil seem insignificant by comparison. The desert demon Azazel in Leviticus, the night demon Lilith and the goat demons in Isaiah—these are all residues of pre-Yahwistic religion and they remain outside the bounds of the religion of Yahweh; they are hardly brought into relation with God at all and they are certainly not powers standing in opposition to him. As for the dragon which appears in the Old Testament under the names of Rahab, Leviathan and Tehom Rabbah—that is taken over from the Babylonian creation myth, and symbolizes primeval chaos rather than evil at work in the created world. Nor does the Old Testament know anything of Satan as the great opponent of God and the supreme embodiment of evil. We are accustomed to regard the serpent, which deceived Eve in the Garden of Eden, as being Satan at war with God; but there is no warrant for this in the text. On the contrary, on the few occasions when Satan appears in the Old Testament, he figures less as the antagonist of Yahweh than as his accomplice.

Satan, in fact, developed out of Yahweh himself, in response to changing ideas about the nature of God.[1] When Yahweh ceased to be a tribal god and became the Lord of the universe, he was at first regarded as the author of all happenings, good and evil. Thus we read in Amos (eighth century B.C.): ". . . shall there be evil in a city and the Lord hath not done it?" [2] Even Deutero-Isaiah (sixth century B.C.) can still make Yahweh say: "I form the light, and create darkness: I make

peace and create evil: I the Lord do all these things." [3] But gradually
the religious consciousness changed until it was felt as an incongruity
that God should be directly responsible for evil. At this point the
threatening, hurtful functions of God detach themselves from the rest
and are personified as Satan. [4]

In the prologue to the Book of Job (probably fifth century B.C.)
Satan appears as a courtier in the court of God, and his achievement is
that he induces God to inflict suffering on a blameless man. Earlier, God
would have been perfectly capable of doing this without inducement,
and moreover the very idea that God could be induced or influenced
to do anything at all would have been theologically intolerable. This
older view pervades the story of Job itself, as distinct from the prologue;
in this ancient folk-tale Job has no hesitation in ascribing his misfortunes to Yahweh, and he knows nothing of Satan. A similar development can be observed if one contrasts a story in the Second Book of
Samuel, which may date from as early as the tenth century B.C., with
the same story as it is told in the Book of Chronicles, which is no older
than the fourth century B.C. II Samuel 24 tells how the Lord tempted
David to number the people, and with what results. Any census was
regarded as an infringement of divine power because it made a human
being conscious of his own power. So, to punish David for carrying
out the census, the Lord sent a plague to reduce the population; after
which the Lord "repented him of the evil". Six or seven centuries later
such behaviour was felt to be incompatible with the divine nature. In
I Chronicles 21, the same story is told, and in exactly the same words,
save for one vital difference: the responsibility for tempting David is
transferred from God to Satan.

This story in Chronicles seems to be the one instance in the whole of
the Old Testament which in any way suggests that Satan exists as a
principle of evil; it is also the one instance where the noun "Satan"—
meaning "adversary"—is used without an article, so that it becomes a
proper noun. No longer a function of the divine personality, Satan
emerges here as an autonomous being, a power which tempts men to
sin against God. It was indeed a turning point; for during the following
three centuries the Jews produced a new, complex and comprehensive
demonology. From the second century B.C. to the end of the first
century A.D. there grew up a body of literature which is sometimes
called apocalyptic, because it is full of allegedly supernatural revelations
about the future, and sometimes apocryphal, because the separate
works carry spurious attributions ascribing them to such Old Testament figures as Enoch, Ezra and Solomon. This literature abounds in

references to evil spirits working to thwart and undo God's plan for the world.(5)

Although such a notion is quite foreign to the Old Testament, it had somehow to be sanctioned by the authority of the Old Testament. This was achieved by invoking a couple of sentences in Genesis 6: "And it came to pass . . . that the sons of God saw the daughters of men that they were fair; and they took them wives of all which they chose. . . . There were giants in the earth in those days; and also after that, when the sons of God came in unto the daughters of men, and they bore children to them, the same became mighty men which were of old, men of renown." This mysterious passage seems to reflect a popular legend concerning giants and their origin; and considerable ingenuity must have been required to relate it to evil spirits and *their* origin. But the Apocrypha manage it.

The *Book of Enoch*, or *I Enoch*, tells how the angels, led by Semjaza and Azazel, fell from heaven through lusting after the daughters of men; from their miscegenation came the evil and destructive race of giants. Impiety spread through the earth until, in an effort to restore order, God sent the Flood to destroy most of mankind and at the same time chained the angels in the dark places of the earth—there to await the Last Judgement, when they will be cast into fire.(6) But the giants themselves remained on earth, and in due course they produced evil spirits. Just how this happened is unclear, but the point is immaterial; what matters is that the evil spirits "rise up against the children of men and against the women".(7) In other words they are demons, who torment human beings on this earth. They also lead them astray into sacrificing to pagan gods (8)—a role which was to persist under Christianity, as one of the main and most sinister activities of demons.

This account in *I Enoch* dates from the second century before Christ; and later Apocrypha were to elaborate on it. Many of them treat of these demons and the nefarious activities which they carry on under the command of their leader, who is called now Mastema, now Belial or Beliar, now Satan. In the *Book of Jubilees* (c. 135–105 B.C.) Mastema commands a tenth part of the evil spirits, the other nine-tenths being bound in "the place of condemnation". Within the limits prescribed by God the evil spirits or demons wreak destruction on the earth—but they are also seducers, they tempt human beings to every kind of sin.(9) This is still plainer in the *Testaments of the Twelve Patriarchs* (109–106 B.C.). Here the chief of the fallen angels, Belial, emerges as the antagonist and rival of God, with whom he competes for the allegiance of men: "Do you choose darkness or light, the law of the Lord or the works of

Belial?" [10] His subordinates tempt men to fornication, jealousy, envy, anger, murder—and also to idolatry, or the worship of the pagan gods.

Some of the Dead Sea Scrolls present a very similar picture. Whatever the sect that produced them, it clearly subscribed, at least at certain times, to much the same demonology as the Jews who wrote or read the Apocrypha. Moreover in some of its writings one finds an idea which was to undergo a spectacular development in later centuries: the idea that the Devil (Beliar, Satan or whatever) has his servants amongst living men and women—human collaborators, as it were, of the host of evil spirits. In the document known as *The war of the Sons of Light and the Sons of Darkness*, which dates from about the time of Jesus, the sect is looking forward to a fifty years' war in which its members, as "the sons of light", will exterminate the heathen, who are called "the sons of darkness" and also "the sons of Belial". "This shall be a time of salvation for the people of God, an age of dominion for all the members of His company, and of everlasting destruction for all the company of Satan . . . (for the sons) of darkness there shall be no escape." [11] And again, "Cursed be Satan for his sinful purpose and may he be execrated for his wicked rule! Cursed be all the spirits of his company for their ungodly purpose and may they be execrated for all their service of uncleanness! Truly they are the company of Darkness, but the company of God is one of (eternal) Light." [12] In other words, the Devil and his servants, human and demonic, form a single host and are all alike doomed to be overthrown and annihilated.

–2–

The demonology which figures in some of the Jewish Apocrypha and some of the Dead Sea Scrolls is also present, in a modified form, in the New Testament. [13] For unlike Yahweh in the Old Testament, God in the New Testament has formidable antagonists in Satan and his host of subordinate demons; the Gospels, Acts, the Pauline Epistles, the Book of Revelation, are full of references to the prodigious struggle. Now Satan's role is to oppose the new religion which was to become Christianity; he is the relentless enemy of Jesus, and of those who follow Jesus, he is forever plotting to seduce these followers from their allegiance and to ruin them in body and soul. Indeed the whole world is pictured as divided into two kingdoms, the kingdom of Christ and the kingdom of the Devil. Over against the kingdom of Christianity, which being the kingdom of God is full of light and radiance, stands the kingdom of Satan, where the powers of darkness prevail. Satan strives to prevent the extension of Christ's kingdom; while Christ's mission is to destroy the kingdom of Satan.

The Devil's power is manifested in whatever draws men away from God, and above all in any and every form of resistance to Christian teaching. It is, therefore, manifested in the Jewish religion; writing around the end of the first century, John makes Jesus say to the Jews who reject him, "Ye are of your father the devil, and the lust of your father ye will do." [14] More emphatically, it is manifested in paganism. Indeed for Paul, writing between A.D. 50 and 70, Satan is the ruler of the whole world in so far as it has not, or has not yet, turned to Christ: "The God of this world hath blinded the minds of them which believe not, lest the light of the glorious gospel of Christ, who is the image of God, should shine unto them." [15] His own task is to go to the Gentiles, "to open their eyes, that they may turn from darkness to light, and from the power of Satan unto God". [16]

As in the Jewish Apocrypha, the Devil in the New Testament is aided by multitudes of lesser demons, who both tempt people to reject Jesus and harass them physically. As tempters they operate above all through the official Roman religion. For the gods of that religion are really demons in Satan's service; Paul is quite clear that "the things which the Gentiles sacrifice, they sacrifice to the devils, and not to God". [17] But at their master's command demons also "possess" people, i.e. cause such disorders as epilepsy and hysterical paralysis and numbness. Most of the miracles of Jesus consist in curing just such disorders, and are therefore understood as weakening Satan—each miracle an inroad on Satan's dominion.

There is, admittedly, some uncertainty as to the precise stage which has been reached in the struggle between Jesus and Satan. Sometimes it seems that the crucifixion of Jesus has already effectively overthrown Satan. John makes Jesus say of his impending death, "now shall the prince of this world be cast out", [18] and "the prince of this world is judged"; [19] and Paul too holds that through his death Jesus has destroyed the power of the Devil. [20] But in other passages Satan is shown as still fully active: "your adversary, the devil, as a roaring lion, walketh about, seeking whom he may devour". [21] And the Book of Revelation is quite clear that the struggle can never be finally decided until the second coming of Christ; it is only at the Last Judgement that Satan will be cast into the lake of fire and brimstone. [22] Yet these seeming inconsistencies are little more than differences of emphasis; they cannot obscure the great optimism, the overwhelming certainty of victory, which inspired Christians in the first century. It is always clear that Satan and his hosts are utterly subordinate to God and power-less when confronted by the Messiah. It is the faith of a young and mili-tant church.

−3−

Throughout the history of the early church Satan and the lesser demons continued to be imagined very much as they were in the New Testament; save that with the elaboration of a Christian theology, their theological significance became more clearly defined. Gradually they were integrated into the central doctrine of Christianity, the doctrine of the fall of man, original sin, and man's redemption through the cruci-fixion of Christ.

Already in the first century before Christ, the *Book of Enoch* hinted that it was one of a number of "Satans", conceived as followers of a chief Satan, who had led Eve astray.[23] In the first century after Christ, Satan was at last brought explicitly into relation with the serpent in the Garden of Eden; either the serpent was Satan disguised, or Satan acted through the serpent. The connection was first clearly established in a number of first-century Apocrypha, all of them either Christian in origin or else strongly coloured by Christianity. In particular the *Books of Adam and Eve*, which were composed in the last quarter of the century, elaborate on the part played by Satan in the fall. To deceive Eve he hung himself on the walls of Paradise, looking like an angel and singing hymns like an angel; and he also persuaded the serpent to let him speak through its mouth.[24] This same Satan was once one of the angels of God, but he disobeyed God's commands and led other angels to disobey; with the result that he and his followers were cast out of heaven.

In the main, this view of the fall of Satan and the fall of man was adopted by the Fathers of the Church, from the second-century apolo-gist Justin Martyr onwards. The only point of dispute concerned the fall, not of Satan himself, but of the lesser angels. Whatever the *Books of Adam and Eve* might say, most of the Fathers could not overlook the doctrine of more venerable Apocrypha. The *Book of Enoch*, as we have seen, held that these angels had fallen because they desired the daughters of men; from which it followed that, unlike Satan, they had not fallen until well after the fall of man. But in the third century this difficulty was circumvented by that pre-eminent theologian, Origen. He pro-claimed that the passage in Genesis concerning the sons of God and the daughters of men was to be taken allegorically; the true fall of the angels had taken place before the creation of man, indeed before the creation of the world. The Greek Church followed Origen at once; somewhat later St Jerome (c. 340–420) and St Augustine of Hippo (354–430) implanted the same idea in the Latin Church. By the end of the fourth century it was generally accepted in East and West alike that the fall of man was part of a prodigious cosmic struggle which had begun when some of the heavenly host had revolted against God and had been cast out of heaven.

As for the present habitat of the demons, there was never, in those centuries, any doubt about that. Whereas the angels dwelt in the highest heaven, near the throne of God, the demons were confined to the dark air immediately above the earth. This is the original meaning of Paul's famous phrase about "spiritual wickedness in high places",[25] and the Fathers shared his view. Augustine, for instance, maintained that "the Devil was expelled, along with his angels, from the lofty abode of the angels, and was cast into darkness, that is to say into our atmosphere, as into a prison".[26] It was also agreed that, since angels possessed ethereal bodies, composed of air and light, demons must be similarly equipped. According to Augustine, these ethereal bodies give demons extraordinary powers of perception and enable them to transport themselves through the air with extraordinary speed.[27]

From their airy habitat Satan and his demons wage incessant war upon the Christians. That is how Paul imagines them;[28] and the Fathers expatiate at length on the various ways in which they persecute the new faith and its adherents. For the Devil, who never knows peace, cannot leave men in peace;[29] together with his demons he causes both the sickness of individuals[30] and collective disasters such as drought, bad harvests, epidemics amongst men and beasts.[31] Moreover the demons have now devised new ways to afflict the Church. On the one hand they inspire Roman officialdom to persecute Christians,[32] and on the other hand they seduce Christians to abandon the true faith, to fall into schism and heresy.[33] St Cyprian even holds that but for the activity of devils there would be no heresies or schisms at all.[34]

For the Fathers, as for Paul, the demons are also present in the deities of the ancient world. As they see it, if a Christian ventures to criticize new practices or beliefs, after they have received the official sanction of the Church, this must be instigated by a pagan deity, operating as a demon. When a monk called Vigilantius writes against the growing cult of the bones of the martyrs, Jerome retorts: "The unclean spirit who makes you write these things has often been tormented by this humble dust (of the bones of the martyrs). . . . Here is my advice to you. Go into the basilicas of the martyrs, and you will be cured. Then you will confess, what you now deny, that it is Mercury who speak through the mouth of Vigilantius." [35] The surest proof of the truth of Christianity lies in the ability of Christians to exorcize demons from the human beings whom they have possessed; for each such exorcism represents a victory of Christ over a pagan deity. This is the view of Tertullian and Cyprian early in the third century, [36] and it is still the view of Sulpicius Severus in his life of St Martin of Tours, written early in the fifth century: "Each time Martin came to the church, the demoniacs who were there howled and trembled as criminals do when the judge arrives. . . . When Martin exorcized the demons . . . the wretched demons expressed in various ways the constraint they were under. . . . One would admit he was Jupiter, the other Mercury." [37]

Satan's greatest offence, in fact, lay in the persistence of the pagan religion itself; for all who adhered to it were in effect worshipping demons. Such an interpretation of the ritual of Graeco-Roman religion is like a foretaste of those fantasies of Satan-worship which medieval clerics were to weave around the activities of dissenting sects, a thousand years later.

Nevertheless, the similarities between early Christian and medieval Christian attitudes should not be exaggerated. The atmosphere of morbid fascination which fills the medieval descriptions is quite lacking in the polemics of the early Fathers; and it is easy to see why. In the days of the Fathers the Church was still full of optimism, still sure of its faith and of the triumph of that faith. Satan might be strong, but it was within the power of any Christian to resist him. The work known as *The Shepherd of Hermas*, which dates from the first half of the second century, is emphatic on the point: he who fears God cannot be affected by the Devil; Satan himself takes flight when he comes up against strong resistance, so only those without the Christian faith need fear him. [38] In the second half of the second century Irenaeus maintains that the Devil flees before the prayers of Christians, [39] while Tertullian is convinced that it is enough simply to pronounce the name of Christ. [40] If God allows demons to tempt a Christian, it is in order that the Christian may put them to shame and at the same time strengthen his own faith. And in Origen's view the power of Satan and his hosts is already declining; each time a demon is successfully resisted by a Christian, he is thrust into hell and loses the right to tempt. As a result, the number of demons on active service is diminishing, the power of the pagan gods dwindles, and pagans find it ever easier to become Christians. [41]

This sublime self-confidence still inspired the Church which christianized the Germanic and Celtic peoples of Europe. But gradually over the
centuries new and terrible anxieties began to make themselves felt in
Christian minds, until it came to seem that the world was in the grip of
demons and that their human allies were everywhere, even in the
heart of Christendom itself.

– 4 –

Satan and his demons, as they were known to the early Christians,
were already products of a long and complex evolution; and they continued to change during the following centuries. By the later Middle
Ages they had become far more powerful and menacing, and they were
also far more closely involved in the lives of individual Christians.

They also shed their ethereal bodies. As early as the fifth century, the
religious philosopher known as Pseudo-Dionysius or the Pseudo-
Areopagite propounded the theory that the angels were purely spiritual
beings, organized in an elaborate hierarchy; and the same applied to
fallen angels, or demons. The book containing these speculations,
entitled *The Celestial Hierarchy*, was translated from Greek into Latin
by Joannes Scotus Erigena in the ninth century; and in the twelfth
century the mystic Hugh of St Victor, in Paris, wrote a commentary
on it, in which he argued powerfully for the absolute spirituality of the
demonic as of the angelic hosts. Hugh's disciple, Richard of St Victor,
pointed out that if, as is stated in the New Testament, a man can contain
a legion of demons, demons must indeed be incorporeal, for a legion
comprises 6,666 individuals. The great scholastics followed in the footsteps of these mystics, until in the thirteenth century St Thomas
Aquinas established the spiritual nature of angels and demons as an
unshakeable part of Roman Catholic doctrine.

Yet these speculations were of limited relevance, for demons retained
their capacity to take on a bodily form at will. Early in the fifth century Jerome insisted that demons were able to take on grotesque forms,
and to be seen, heard and felt by human beings. About the same time
the ecclesiastical historian Theodoret told how in the preceding century
Bishop Marcellus of Apamea in Syria had tried to burn down a temple
of Jupiter; he was constantly impeded by a black demon, who kept
extinguishing the fire.[42] Around 600 Pope Gregory the Great introduced Satan or some lesser devil into many of his stories about monks
and bishops. He describes, for instance, the curious adventure of a Jew
who happened one night to find himself in a temple of Apollo. A
throng of demons were in the temple, and they were reporting to their

leader on the various tricks they had played on pious Christians. One of them had even induced a bishop to pat a nun tenderly on her back.[43] The biography of St Afra, which belongs to the period between 700 and 850, already shows Satan in the form that was to become standard in the later Middle Ages: pitch-black, naked and covered with a wrinkled skin.[44]

As spiritual beings who were yet capable of appearing physically on earth, and as enemies of Christ who operated through the moral weakness of Christians, the demons of medieval Europe were powerful indeed. In the tenth century Ratherius, bishop of Verona, felt it necessary to point out that Satan and his hosts were still subject to an omnipotent God. This should have been clear to the clergy at least; yet it was the clergy who constantly stressed Satan's near-omnipotence. To appreciate just how obsessive their preoccupation had become by the thirteenth century one has only to consider some of the anecdotes told by two German monks, Caesarius, of the monastery of Heisterbach in the Rhineland, and Richalmus, abbot of the monastery of Schönthal in Württemberg.

Caesarius, who entered his monastery towards the year 1200 and died between 1240 and 1250, has sometimes been regarded as a mere joker, a connoisseur of tall stories; but he was nothing of the kind. The very form of his best-known book, the *Dialogus Miraculorum*, shows how serious his intention was; for it consists of a series of dialogues in which Caesarius, as an experienced man, instructs a novice of his monastery. It was a monastery noted for its strict discipline; and the monks who were Caesarius's colleagues, and who no doubt read and criticized his writings, would never have tolerated a frivolous treatment of matters touching so nearly on the salvation and damnation of souls. Caesarius's tales are in fact *exempla*, cautionary tales designed to be used in sermons; and many of them are to be found in other well-known collections of *exempla* from the same period.

In Caesarius's book Satan and the lesser demons appear as obstinate rebels against God. We hear how once a demon went to confession. Appalled by the number of his sins, the father confessor remarks that they must have taken more than a thousand years to perform; to which the demon replies that he is older than that, for he is one of the angels who fell with Satan. Yet, having seen how penitents are granted absolution even for grievous sins, he hopes for the same relief. So the priest prescribes a penance: "Go and throw yourself down three times a day, saying: 'Lord God, my Creator, I have sinned against you, forgive me.' And that shall be your whole penance." But the demon finds this too hard, for he cannot humble himself before God; and so he is sent packing. (45)

This particular demon appears in human form, and that is not uncommon. Other tales of Caesarius show a demon in the guise of a big, ugly man dressed in black; (46) or, when he is set on seducing a woman, as a fine, smartly dressed fellow or a handsome soldier. (47) It is not uncommon for a demon to appear as a Moor. (48) And the demons who sit on the stately train of an ostentatious lady are like tiny, black Moors, who giggle, clap their hands and jump about like fish in a net. (49) But demons can also manifest themselves as oxen, horses, dogs, cats, bears, apes, toads, ravens, lambs.

Both Caesarius and the novice know that demons are exceedingly numerous—it seems that no less than a tenth of all the hosts of heaven fell with Satan. Because of this, one human being can be tormented by the attentions of more than one demon. Caesarius proves this by the story of a French nun whom a demon tormented grievously with the temptation of lust. She prayed ardently to be relieved of this temptation; whereupon her good angel appeared and recommended a verse from a psalm as a certain cure. But as soon as the nun escaped from the temptation of lust, another demon afflicted her with an irresistible urge to blaspheme. Again the angel suggested a helpful verse—but added that, once cured of blasphemy, she would be tortured again by lust. The nun chose lust, for it is better that one's flesh should suffer than that one's soul should be damned. (50)

Caesarius recognizes that God imposes certain limits to the powers of demons: nobody can be forced to sin, and holy men are capable of resisting any temptation. And nevertheless the accent has shifted, unmistakably, since the days of the early Church. Now the stress is all on the ubiquity and resourcefulness of the demons, the relative helplessness of human beings. Demons are always around us and in our midst, and their cunning is infinite; (51) they lead people astray by false promises or even by false miracles, (52) they undermine their faith. (53) No trouble is too great if they can damn a soul; a demon has been heard to say that he would rather accompany a soul to hell than go alone to heaven. (54) Indeed, a demon is such a dangerous being that only an exceptionally virtuous person can see or touch one without suffering serious harm. (55) Caesarius tells of an abbot and a monk who nearly died after seeing a demon, and of two youths who fell sick after seeing a demon in the form of a woman. (56) A woman pressed the hand of a man-servant whom she thought she knew; it proved a bad mistake, for the servant was really a demon, and within a few days the woman was dead. (57)

A soldier who played cards with a demon at night had his entrails torn out.[58]

Most disturbing of all, a demon can enter a person's body and take up residence in its bowels and hollow places, where the excrement is. Caesarius illustrates the point with a story of a five-year-old boy who swallowed a demon while drinking milk; it continued to torment him until he was a grown man, when the apostles Peter and Paul were moved by his piety to expel it.[59] But sometimes what appears as possession is really a still more sinister phenomenon. There was once a priest whose singing was a joy to all—until one day another priest heard it, and realized that such perfection must come not from a human being but from a demon. So he exorcized the demon, which promptly departed—whereupon the singer's body fell lifeless to the ground, showing that for some time it had been animated by the demon alone.[60]

Around 1270 a whole book was composed from the discourses of Richalmus, abbot of Schönthal, concerning the plots and wiles which demons use to ensnare human beings.[61] He too addresses his hints to a novice in the monastery, and unlike Caesarius he takes his material chiefly from the monastic life; his special concern is with the temptations and obstacles with which demons try to divert monks from their quest for sanctity. Within these limits he presents much the same picture as the Rhenish monk.

It was always understood that angels are organized hierarchically, and according to Richalmus the same applies to demons. The finest and most cunning demons dwell permanently in the air just above the earth, and it is they who issue instructions to demons of the cruder sort, who patrol the earth itself;[62] there is in fact a constant mutual incitement to evil-doing, with the superior demons setting the pace.[63] But hierarchy obtains even amongst demons occupied with a particular job on earth; for instance, in each monastery a staff of demons is employed, and those operating at the top level are themselves known as "the abbot" or "the prior".[64] But from the point of their human victims it is the sheer numbers that impress: "It is untrue what some people say, that each human being is pursued by only one demon, for several demons pursue each human being. Just as a man who plunges into the sea is wholly surrounded by water, above and below, so demons too flow around a man from all sides."[65] Indeed there are times when demons "surround a man like a thick vault, so that there is no air-hole between them".[66] When Richalmus shuts his eyes he often sees the tiny bodies of the demons surrounding him and every human being, thick as specks of dust in the sunlight.[67]

Demons are filled with such hostility towards mankind that it is a miracle that any human being survives; in fact, but for the protection afforded by God's grace, nobody would. Not for a moment do demons cease from their plaguing and tempting of mortals, and particularly of the pious. "Just as one watches the hand on a pair of scales, to see whether it rises or falls, so do demons ceaselessly observe a man. And the more Christian charity there is in a man, the more violently they attack him. . . . If he is less charitable, they pause and cease from tormenting." [68] From this it follows that they concentrate particularly on priests and monks. Richalmus is well equipped to describe the demonic persecutions which he and his brethren have to endure, for he can hear demons talking together. The song of birds, the coughing of human beings, indeed every sound that breaks the silence of meditation—all is demons' talk; and Richalmus has the gift of understanding it. [69]

Demons specialize in sending afflictions that lead monks into indecorous or irreverent behaviour. Often at holy communion Richalmus has had to rush from the church and vomit up the host he has just received. [70] Fortunately he has found a partial remedy in the sign of the cross; but even this is of limited use against the infinite resourcefulness of demons. One day demons provoked an attack of giddiness to prevent the abbot from celebrating mass; and the following night he overheard two demons plotting together: "One demon asked another to make me hoarse. The latter replied that he lacked the opportunity for that, but could arrange for flatulence." [71] This is a special skill of theirs: "Often they make my belly swell so much that, contrary to custom, I have to loosen my belt. Later when they stop—perhaps from forgetfulness—I tighten the belt again in the usual manner. But if they return and find it like that, they torment and harass me so that I really suffer." [72] They also tempt him to sleep at unsuitable times. As he sits over holy books he begins to doze; if, to wake himself up, he takes his hands from under his habit and holds them out to the cold air, the demons promptly send a flea into his habit, so that he has to put his hands in again. [73] When he sits in the choir, demons tempt him to sleep—although, as he hastens to assure the novice, they fail in this, and the snores that come from him are really the work of the demons themselves. [74] Demons will also make a monk sing feebly, or even out of tune, during the service. [75]

In every way demons strive to prevent the proper discharge of religious duties. When a priest is preparing to celebrate mass, they will send unsuitable thoughts to confuse and irritate him. [76] They will put a plaster on the ears of a lay brother just when he should be having the rule of the order explained to him. [77] The abbot would like to keep his head covered by his cowl, for the outer light extinguishes the inner light; but demons make his head itch, so that he has to uncover it to scratch.[78] When there is heavy work to be done, such as building a wall, demons make the monks unwilling to do it. They will pretend to sympathize: "You poor people! You have to work like slaves! What unbearable work! Isn't it a shame to have to work so hard!"[79]—with the result that the monks start complaining. It can even happen that demons will lead a monk out of the monastery and into the nearest town, where they will saddle a horse and send him riding off.[80]

Brooding on all these demonic strategems, Richalmus has little help or hope to offer. He knows, of course, that good spirits surround us as well as evil ones, and that each of us has, in addition, a special guardian angel; but he has little confidence in their powers, and insists that when good spirits help or warn us, the evil ones promptly redouble their efforts.[81] As for self-help, the only counter-measure that he recommends is the sign of the cross. When a monk lost his voice while singing the response, the abbot made the sign of the cross—and watched how the demons scuttled off, in great indignation, as the singer regained his voice.[82] The fleas and lice that torment a man are really demons; and the abbot, on the strength of his own experience, advises the novice to use the sign of the cross against them too.[83] The sign of the cross is indeed powerful, particularly if it is made properly and not scamped; yet there are strict limits to what even this remedy can achieve. It has little or no effect when many demons are acting in concert.[84] And in any case its power is short-lived—the demons soon return to the struggle "like a brave warrior, who has to be wounded and pierced through, before he will give way".[85]

It is a far cry from the self-confidence of the early Christians. Now demons are no mere external enemies, doomed to be defeated again and again, and finally cast down for ever, by the bearers of a militant faith. They have penetrated into every corner of life, above all they have penetrated into the souls of individual Christians. No longer imagined as causing drought or bad harvests or epidemics, demons have come to represent desires which individual Christians have, but which they dare not acknowledge as belonging to themselves. People feel themselves victims of forces which they are quite unable to master—and the more concerned with religion they are, the more grievous their afflictions: monks and nuns suffer most of all. These menacing forces are, above all, temptations to irreverence and sacrilege, indiscipline and rebellion. Often the psychic tensions and conflicts which they generate express themselves in such physical symptoms as giddiness and indigestion. But at the same time these forces take on the appearance of external beings, demons endowed with what look like bodies, animal or human. Ritualistic gestures seem the only means of resisting them—the inner resources of faith are not available, or not in sufficient abundance.

It is not surprising that in such an atmosphere people should have elaborated the fantasy of a secret society of Devil-worshippers. The source of the fantasy lay less in the existence of the Dualist religion than in the anxieties that haunted the minds of Christians themselves. It was because Christians, and particularly monks, were so obsessed by the power of Satan and his demons that they were so ready to see Devil-worship in the most unlikely quarters.

We have seen how, in the 1230s, Conrad of Marburg was moved by these fantasies to torture and kill not only heretics but also a number of perfectly orthodox Catholics; and how the pope himself was influenced into supporting this killing. At the beginning of the fourteenth century very similar fantasies were to be used to legitimate a far larger and more celebrated judicial killing, this time in France. The episode has entered history as "the affair of the Templars".

5

THE CRUSHING OF THE KNIGHTS TEMPLARS

-I-

The capture of Jerusalem in the First Crusade, in 1099, greatly stimulated the movement of pilgrims to Palestine. Many of these people arrived in a sorry state, sick or penniless or both; and the Order of the Hospital of St John of Jerusalem was developed to supply them with alms and medical care. But pilgrims were also exposed to armed attack by the Moslems. Around 1118 a knight from Champagne called Hugues de Payens, inspired by the example of the Hospitallers, founded a new fellowship, this time for the purpose of giving military protection to the pilgrims as they toiled towards the Holy City. Like the Hospitallers, this new body resembled a monastic order in that its members vowed to live in chastity, obedience and self-denial. But it was also a fraternity of warriors, pledged to fight for the King of Heaven. As headquarters it was granted a dwelling near the Dome of the Rock, which stands on the site of the Temple, and so acquired the name which was soon to become famous throughout Christendom. At first these fighting monks called themselves "Poor fellow-soldiers of Christ and of the Temple of Solomon"; but soon they were known simply as the Knights Templars, and their organization as "The Temple".[1]

The fraternity quickly expanded its field of activity. Instead of merely providing armed escorts for pilgrims it turned into a standing army committed to perpetual struggle against the forces of Islam. As such, it was carrying out what all western Christians regarded not only as a vital but as a holy task; and recognition came quickly. At the synod of Troyes in 1128 that uniquely prestigious personality, St Bernard, recommended that the fraternity should be officially recognized as a monastic order; and this was done. The pope gave his sanction, so that the Church could, through the Templars, make its contribution to the security of the Holy Land. St Bernard lent his assistance in drawing up an appropriate monastic rule. A new kind of organization had come into being—a fighting force sworn to the service of the Church, a religious order which offered salvation as a reward for valour in war. The dual nature of the Temple was symbolized by its banner, which was piebald—the white signifying gentleness towards the friends of Christ, the black ferocity towards his enemies.

Down to the final evacuation of Outremer (as the Christian kingdom in the Holy Land was called) in 1291, the Templars were its valiant defenders. Crusades came and went, but the Templars were always there, as outposts of Christendom in the alien and hostile world of Islam. Their only permanent allies were the Hospitallers, who had transformed themselves into a military order on the model of the Templars. For the greater part of the time—indeed, from the fall of Edessa in 1144 onwards—these two military orders were carrying on, against overwhelming odds, a struggle which in the end they were bound to lose. Their courage and devotion were unrivalled. That the Franks were able to keep their foothold in the East for nearly two centuries was mainly due to the fighting qualities of the Templars and Hospitallers.

But in the West too the Temple was a power to be reckoned with. As was the case with other monastic orders, the rule forbade individual members to own property but permitted the order to do so. Immediately after the synod of Troyes in 1128 the king of France made gifts of land, and thereby launched the order on its career as a landed proprietor. Monarchs and nobles all over western Europe followed suit, and within fifteen years the Temple owned lands in Castile, Brittany, England, Languedoc, Apulia, Rome, Germany and Hungary. With the increase in trade during the twelfth and thirteenth centuries these properties grew in value. Moreover every knight who joined the order for life surrendered all his wealth to it. Inevitably the order became very rich.

During the disastrous Second Crusade, in 1147, Louis VII was deeply impressed by the unfailing military and financial support which he received from the Templars. But for their help, he admitted, he could not have survived for a moment. He borrowed heavily from them; and on his return to France he repaid the loan by giving the order land on the outskirts of Paris. Very soon a huge fortress had sprung up there—a great tower and four lesser towers, equipped with a wharf of its own, equipped also with its own police force and its own jurisdiction. The privileges it enjoyed were such that it attracted immigrants from other parts. The Paris Temple was in effect an autonomous township, and it became the headquarters of the whole order in the West.

The original purpose of the order in the West was to support the fighting forces in the East. The houses scattered over the face of Europe dispatched the excess revenue from their estates to the head-quarters in the Holy Land; and they also served as depots for recruiting and training men for war against the infidel. But the order soon acquired other functions, undreamed of by its founders and unconnected with the struggle against Islam. The Templars' houses—which were really castles—were regarded as models of safety. Popes and monarchs travelling abroad were happy to be accommodated in them. Both in France and in England the Templars' headquarters were frequently used as safe deposits for the crown jewels and even for public monies.* All monies collected for the Holy Land were entrusted to the Temple for conveyance, and so were tithes destined for the papal curia.

The Temple went into banking. Trade was growing, and with it the demand for currency; but it was difficult and expensive to transport large quantities of gold. The Temple seized the opportunity to establish a credit system. It began by arranging the transfer of deposits for the convenience of pilgrims, so that on their arrival in the Holy Land they would no longer find themselves penniless; and soon it extended similar services to merchants. With its far-flung organization and its reputation for probity, the order was able to issue letters of credit which were accepted by traders in every Christian country. Before even the Italian banks had entered the scene, the Temple had developed a system of international banking. It even lent money for the crusades—and lent it, moreover, at interest. The Church might condemn "usury"—the Temple circumvented the ban by collecting interest under the guise of rents.

The Paris Temple in particular became the centre of European finance. For France it also became an unofficial ministry of finance, which again and again tided the kingdom over financial crises. For the French monarchy the Temple could always raise a loan, whether for a royal dowry or for a war. At the beginning of the fourteenth century, on the very eve of the catastrophe which was to destroy it, the Temple advanced the full dowry for the daughter of Philip the Fair on her betrothal to the heir of England. At the same time the treasurer of the Paris Temple, Hugues de Pairaud, was appointed receiver and warden of all the royal revenues.

Other Templars before Hugues de Pairaud had been deeply involved in affairs of state. Templars were indeed often men of great worldly wisdom, widely travelled, experienced, shrewd; and monarchs and

* In London the Inns of Court known as the Inner and Middle Temple owe their names to the fact that they occupy the site of the Templars' headquarters.

prelates were happy to give them leading appointments in their house-
holds and to employ them as confidential envoys. The chamberlain at
the papal curia was almost always a Templar, Templars often functioned as almoners at royal courts, some Templars spent years travelling
between East and West on diplomatic and political missions. As for the
chief officers of the order—not only the grand master, who was always
in the Holy Land, but also the grand preceptors of the various western
provinces, and under them the preceptors or priors, who themselves
often had jurisdiction over dozens of houses—they were great digni-
taries in church and state. At court they took precedence as ecclesiastics,
and in the councils of the Church they were respected as leaders of
warriors.

The order as a whole enjoyed extraordinary prerogatives. The papacy
in particular expressed its good will in a series of privileges, culminating
in 1163 in the bull *Omne datum optimum*. The Temple had supported
Pope Alexander III against rival candidates for the papacy; and this bull
shows the extent of the pope's gratitude. For it turned the Temple into
an autonomous institution, subject to no authority, secular or ecclesiastical, save only the pope himself. The order and all its possessions were
declared to be, in perpetuity, under the safeguard and protection of the
Holy See. Moreover the order was entitled to build its own churches,
and to appoint its own confessors. The Temple had always cultivated
secrecy, no doubt in the first place for military reasons; but this bull
encouraged the habit. Chapter meetings from which all outsiders were
rigorously excluded, and where every crack in door or wall was carefully blocked, symbolized the Templars' sense of being a race apart.

Inevitably the Temple attracted hostility, and from many different
quarters. As an ecclesiastical order it was hated by many elements in the
Church. Much of the land bestowed on the order was taken from
ecclesiastical estates; parish priests and monasteries saw their tithes
reduced, and resented it bitterly. And that was not all: only too aware
of its privileges and exemptions, the Temple itself constantly infringed
the rights of other religious institutions. It claimed tithes which rightly
belonged to others; it acquired churches which were not intended for
its use; it installed and removed priests in the churches that came under
its control. Above all, the concessions which the order had received
from the papacy removed it from effective control by the bishops, for
whom Templars often showed open contempt. Sometimes they arranged for their priests to administer the sacraments to persons whom
bishops had excommunicated. Even popes had occasions to protest
about this. The history of the Temple in the West was punctuated by

disputes with ecclesiastics and ecclesiastical bodies, both about money and about rights.

Through its involvement in finance and trade the order also came into conflict with secular interests. In France we find vintners protesting about unfair competition from the Templars, who were entitled to sell wine tax-free; and cloth-merchants complaining that the Templars were killing their trade by exorbitant levies. The Temple even acquired a fleet of its own and appropriated much of the pilgrim traffic to the Holy Land; thus earning the enmity of the shipping houses of Marseilles and the Italian merchant republics.

In pursuit of its own interests the Temple was ruthless. Filled with a conviction of their own superiority, trained to regard themselves as the fighting elite of Christendom, Templars had little sympathy for the sufferings of others and little regard for their feelings or opinions. Early in the thirteenth century Pope Innocent III, who was a friend of the order and had once been a Templar himself, issued a bull entitled *De insolentia Templariorum*; and the term was justified. Protected from the ban of any ecclesiastic other than the pope, set almost above the secular law as well, the Templars were bound to become a singularly arrogant body of men. Ruthlessness and arrogance are in any case normal characteristics of a warrior aristocracy. In the case of the Templars they were reinforced by the privileges and exemptions bestowed on the order. In a dispute with its neighbours, a house of Templars was as capable as any other noble household of employing arson and murder; but it was less likely to be visited with commensurate penalties.

In other respects too the Templars resembled and outdid other members of the aristocratic caste. Although officially only the order was rich and individual Templars were propertyless, it did not always look like that. Amongst the great officers of the Temple display was often accepted as a business asset; and some of them, in their public appearances, made the same magnificent showing as secular lords and princes. But people did not forget that the Temple was a religious order; and ruthlessness, arrogance, violence against neighbours, pomp and luxury were not held to its credit.

Yet these things would never have led to the persecution, let alone the destruction, of the order. Many other monastic orders enjoyed extensive exemptions and privileges, and were correspondingly unpopular. In the thirteenth century the mendicant orders of Franciscans and Dominicans were envied and attacked most bitterly by the secular clergy. Above all the other great military order, the Hospital of St John, was criticized on precisely the same grounds as the Temple, and with just as much cause. In addition, the Hospital was frequently involved in scandals—popes chided it severely for sexual incontinence, for protecting pilgrim-killers instead of pilgrims, even for straying into heresy. Such complaints as popes voiced from time to time against the Temple were far milder. But the Hospital survived unscathed while the Temple went under. Why?

To fight the Saracens, to defend the Holy Land—that was the purpose of both the great military orders (as well as the smaller and newer order of Teutonic Knights); and much was forgiven them so long as they were manifestly fulfilling it. But the Christian kingdom in the Holy Land could survive only so long as Islam was divided, and the time was bound to come when this tiny outpost of an alien civilization would be finally overwhelmed. In 1290 Acre, the last Christian stronghold, fell to the Moslems. The Templar force went down fighting, and the few who survived were the last Christians to quit Palestine. The remnants of the Christian colony congregated on the island of Cyprus, and a period of reconsideration began. Despite their heavy losses in the East, the military orders still had by far the greater part of their personnel and possessions intact, on the mainland of Europe; and now they had to find new roles. The Hospitallers took to the sea; from Cyprus and later from Rhodes they policed the Mediterranean and combated Moslem piracy. The main body of Teutonic Knights had long been engaged in extending the area of German rule at the expense of the Slavs; the remainder now joined them. Only the Templars failed to find themselves a new field of military activity.

In Spain the Templars continued to fight the Moors, as they had always done; but in other countries they merely protested their undying fidelity to the Holy Land, and stayed at home. The leaders of the Temple seemed to assume that Christendom owed the order a living for its past achievements. It proved a dangerous assumption. Lacking a positive policy of its own, the Temple became a passive object of other people's policies. It had always been primarily a French order; the one way in which it could be destroyed was through an attack on the French branch; and the one person capable of carrying through such an attack successfully was the king of France. At the beginning of the fourteenth century King Philip IV of France, known as "the Fair", found it convenient and profitable to destroy the Temple, and acted accordingly.

Philip was both a shrewdly calculating politician and a bit of a religious megalomaniac. The realm to which he succeeded in 1285 was already larger and more unified than it had ever been, with a single currency issued by the royal mint, a uniform and codified system of law, an efficient civil service staffed no longer by clerics but by lawyers. Philip was wholly devoted to consolidating the unity and increasing the power of this emergent national state. In his eyes this was a holy duty: in furthering the cause of the state and of his dynasty, he was serving God and the Christian faith. Iron-willed, relentless, merciless, he never doubted for a moment that he was acting on God's behalf, indeed that God was acting through him. To augment the power of the king of France was to carry out the divine intention.

In the main Philip's policy faithfully continued that of his whole dynasty; but, precisely because he was a genuine fanatic who felt himself to be under God's special protection, he could at times embark on projects of quite unrealistic scope. The situation that arose after the final collapse of the Christian venture in the Holy Land lured him on. From 1292 onwards the Catalan mystic Ramon Lull, who had long interested himself in the possibility of converting Islam to Christianity, propagated proposals for combined missionary and military action. Missionaries equipped with a sound knowledge of Arabic were to be supported by a new crusading army; the core of this army was to consist of the Temple and the Hospital, amalgamated, and the whole was to be commanded by a particular king, who would take the title of *Bellator Rex* and would in the end become king of Jerusalem. At first, it seems, Lull was thinking of inducing James II of Aragon to undertake a crusade against Moslem Granada; but he expounded his ideas in Paris, and found ready listeners at the French court. [2]

Philip the Fair fancied himself for the role of *Bellator Rex*; and his interpretation of that role was grandiose. He outlined it in a programme of 80 points; and although only fragments survive, they are startling enough. [3] They show that he thought of abdicating the French throne in favour of his eldest son, to become instead grand master of the combined military orders. The orders were to be renamed Knights of Jerusalem, and the grand master was to take the title of King of Jerusalem. After Philip's death the eldest son of the king of France was always to be grand master. All prelates, including archbishops and bishops, were to surrender their incomes, above a small salary, to the grand master, for the conquest of the Holy Land; and the monastic orders were to do likewise with their revenues. Moreover the grand master, or *Bellator Rex*, was to have a powerful say in papal elections. These aims were of course utterly unrealistic—yet we are told that they represented only a small part of Philip's total ambitions. The lawyer and publicist Pierre Dubois, in his book *De Recuperatione Terre Sancte*, gives some indication of what the king may really have had in mind.[4] The king of France was to become Roman emperor and reconquer the Holy Land; thereafter, from Jerusalem, he was to rule over a vast federation of nations, and so establish the reign of universal peace.

Meanwhile Philip had to cope with the very real and urgent financial problems which he had inherited. On his succession he had found his realm almost bankrupt, and costly wars further weakened its finances. Philip resorted to a whole series of expedients. In 1294 and 1296 he imposed tithes on the Church in France, and in 1296 he also forbade the export of gold, including the customary contributions to the Holy See—moves that led to the first of his many conflicts with the papacy. He took gold and silver vessels from his richer subjects, against a fraction of their value, and had them melted down and recast as coins. He imposed levies on trade and property, such as had never been known before, and above all he repeatedly debased the currency. All this brought him into conflict with his own subjects. After a particularly heavy devaluation, in June 1306, the king had to flee from the enraged populace of the capital and take refuge (ironically enough) in the Paris Temple, for three whole days.

The following month Philip turned on the Jews: on one and the same day, 22 July 1306, Jews throughout France were arrested and imprisoned. The Jews' money was seized by the royal exchequer, their goods auctioned for the benefit of the exchequer, their businesses transferred to the Italian banks which were deep in Philip's confidence; while the Jews themselves (those who survived) were expelled from the kingdom. The royal publicists presented this last expedient as a great victory for Christ. They were to say the same, a couple of years later, of the destruction of the Temple.

To Philip the religious megalomaniac the existence of the Temple presented an infuriating obstacle, while to Philip the politician the destruction of the Temple offered financial relief. For the great officers of the Temple were rigidly opposed to any amalgamation with the Hospital. The two orders had always competed—for endowments, for recruits, for renown. In the Holy Land they had of necessity collaborated in fighting the Saracens—yet even then the rivalry between them had often led to bloody clashes. With the loss of the Holy Land, the only bonds between them snapped. When Pope Clement V asked the last grand master of the Temple, Jacques de Molay, for his views on amalgamation, the response was decidedly negative.[5] Clement passed Molay's memorandum to the royal officials; so Philip knew that so long as the Temple survived as an autonomous institution, it would block even the first steps to his becoming *Bellator Rex*. This happened in 1306, the same year in which Philip despoiled and expelled the Jews. And Philip knew that the Temple in France was vastly richer than the Jews.

Up to that time, relations between the king and the French Templars had been excellent. As we have seen, the Paris Temple acted as unofficial ministry of finance, its treasurer was warden of the royal revenues. During 1303-4 Philip's financial needs resulted in particularly close dealings with the order; and as a reward for services rendered he published a most flattering proclamation in which he praised the Templars for their piety, their charity, their liberality, their valour—and substantially increased their already extensive privileges in his kingdom. Jacques de Molay stood godfather to Philip's infant son.

On 12 October 1307 the grand master received a further honour; for on that day he acted as pall-bearer at the funeral of the wife of the king's brother, Charles of Valois. Early in the morning of 13 October the Templars throughout France were arrested by officers of the crown. The torturers began their work, and within a few days confessions began to accumulate. Most of the offences to which the Templars confessed mirror the age-old fantasies with which this book is concerned. The work of Conrad of Marburg was being resumed, under the auspices of the king of France.

–2–

Early in 1304 or (more probably) 1305 a Frenchman called Esquiu de Floyran made his way to Lerida, where King James II of Aragon was accustomed to pass the spring months.[6] He obtained an audience of the king and, in the presence of the king's confessor, made certain horrific revelations concerning the Order of the Knights Templars. But the situation of the Temple in Aragon was very different from its situation in France: it had no autonomy but was wholly dependent on, and devoted to, the monarch. James II had little incentive to turn against his faithful Templars, and refused to take the revelations seriously without real proof.

Esquiu returned to France. Did he already then make contact with the chief of the new-style civil servants, Guillaume de Nogaret, who was to play such a large part in the destruction of the Temple? Did Nogaret plan everything that followed? It has never been proved, but it does seem likely. Somehow Esquiu got access to King Philip. According to one not improbable story, he had himself imprisoned along with a criminal who had once been a Templar. Both were under sentence of death, and they confessed their crimes to one another. The ex-Templar confessed to having performed such extraordinary iniquities, during his years in the order, that Esquiu felt it his absolute duty to pass the information on to the king, and bullied the prison officers until he got his way. However that may be, Esquiu de Floyran certainly provided the "information" which enabled Philip to proceed against the order. He reappears later in the story too. He took an active part in torturing Templars under interrogation, and by 1313 was comfortably in possession of a piece of land which had belonged to the Temple. He also wrote to King James of Aragon, claiming a share in the property of the Aragonese Templars.

It seems that Esquiu's revelations reached the ears of Philip the Fair in the autumn of 1305, and that the king passed them on to the pope that winter. As a religious order, the Temple came under papal, not royal, jurisdiction, and any investigation ought by rights to have been carried out under papal auspices. But, as we have seen, the usually harmonious relations between king and Temple became less harmonious in the course of 1306, and Esquiu's story acquired a new value for the king. It may also have acquired a new credibility. There was in Philip at least as much of the fanatic as of the cynic, and he may well have persuaded himself that an organization which was capable of thwarting his aims was capable of any iniquity. It is said that he even planted a dozen spies in the various French provinces of the Temple, in an effort to obtain confirmatory evidence—a vain effort as it turned out, for not one of these men was even called as a witness against the Temple.

However that may be, once Philip had decided to use Esquiu's revelations to destroy the Temple, he took no chances. Late in August 1307 Pope Clement informed him that he proposed to carry out an investigation. Philip realized that a papal investigation, carried out while the Templars were still at liberty and able to conduct their defence, would be unlikely to result in the condemnation and suppression of the order. His misgivings must have been reinforced by the unperturbed behaviour of the grand master. Jacques de Molay knew of Esquiu's charges, and his response was to urge the pope to investigate, so that the order could clear its name. On 11 September he visited the pope at Poitiers, where the two men discussed not the affairs of the Temple but plans for a possible new crusade. Clearly, if the order was to be destroyed, the king must take charge of the proceedings: the Templars must be got into the hands of the royal officials, without hope of escape. When Philip struck, he did so without asking the pope; and several weeks were to pass before he communicated with him at all.

The order for the arrest of the Templars was drawn up on 14

September and dispatched, in the king's name, to officers of the crown throughout the kingdom. It is a model of the dehumanizing use of language. Each word is chosen with the object of setting the Templars outside the bounds of humanity: [7]

> A bitter thing, a thing to weep over, a thing horrible to think of and terrible to hear, a detestable crime, an abominable act, a fearful infamy, a thing altogether inhuman, or rather, foreign to all humanity has, thanks to the report of several trustworthy persons, reached our ears, smiting us with grievous astonishment and causing us to tremble with violent horror; and, as we weigh its gravity, an immense pain rises in us, all the more cruelly because we cannot doubt that the enormity of the crime makes it an offence to the divine majesty, a shame for mankind, a pernicious example of evil and a universal scandal. . . . (These people) are like beasts of burden which have no understanding, indeed they surpass unreasoning beasts in their astounding bestiality, they expose themselves to all the supremely abominable crimes which even the sensuality of unreasoning beasts abhors and avoids. . . . Not only by their acts and their detestable deeds but even by their hasty words they defile the earth with their filth, they undo the benefits of the dew, they corrupt the purity of the air and bring about the confusion of our faith.

The royal missive goes on to detail the offences to which the Temple is supposed to be addicted, and concerning which the Templars are to be interrogated. These can be summarized as follows:

When a new member is received into the order, a secret ritual follows the ceremony of reception in the chapel. The commander takes the newcomer aside, for instance behind the altar or into the sacristy. There he shows him a crucifix, and the newcomer has to deny Christ thrice, and to spit thrice on the crucifix. Next he has to strip naked. The commander gives him three kisses, one at the base of the spine, one on the navel, one on the mouth. He also tells him that if a fellow-Templar should desire to commit sodomy with him, he must let him do so, for that is required by the statutes of the Temple. Many Templars do in fact practise sodomy together, each wearing a belt which is part of his permanent uniform. It is said that these belts have previously been placed around the neck of a great idol, in the form of a man's head with beard, and that at the meetings of the provincial chapters, the chief officers of the order kiss and worship this head—though the ordinary knights know nothing of this cult. Moreover, the priests of the order refrain from consecrating the eucharistic wafer for the mass.

Such were the charges on which the Templars were tried and to which many of them confessed, and such were the grounds on which, in the end, the Temple was suppressed. For five centuries thereafter these charges were accepted by historians at their face value—the first to cast doubt on them was Raynouard, in 1813. Since then serious historians have refused to accept them *en bloc*—yet only a few have been willing to reject them *en bloc*, either.[8] Most people have always found it difficult to believe that even the most autocratic ruler could or would fabricate an entire body of accusations out of nothing, and then compel great numbers of innocent victims to substantiate them. With the example of Stalin's trials before our eyes, we should have no such difficulty. It is time to reaffirm the conclusion which Heinrich Finke pronounced in 1907: the charges against the Templars were absolutely without foundation.

There is no mystery about the ritual by which new recruits were received into the Temple. There exists a detailed prescription for the ceremony; and nothing could be more sober.[9] The commander of the house warns the candidate of the hardships he will have to endure as a Templar. The candidate in his turn swears before God and the Virgin to obey the grand master; to live in chastity and without personal property; to maintain the good customs of the order; and to fight for the Holy Land. The ceremony ends with the formula of reception: "And so we promise you bread and water and the poor robe of the house and much hardship and labour." This prescription is incontestably genuine, and there is no reason to think that initiations were ever conducted in any other way.

An initiation in these terms would have been perfectly acceptable to the young men—many of them from the noblest houses, many of them deeply pious—who presented themselves as candidates. But how could they possibly have submitted to rituals which, being obscene and blasphemous, were a denial of everything that had attracted them to the order? Did no recruit ever protest at such a gross imposture? The indictments argue that those who protested were killed or imprisoned— but in that case, why did none of their powerful kinsmen take action? And why did noble families continue to send their young men as recruits? Or are we to suppose that scores of young Templars simply vanished, without anyone ever noticing?

The impression of implausibility grows when one comes to examine the charges in detail. We know that on his reception into the order the new recruit had to take a vow of chastity. Is it conceivable that the commander who had just demanded and received such a vow would go on to explain that the statutes of the order encouraged sodomy? We know that the Templars were always ready to give their lives fighting for Christ against the infidel, and that many of them, rather than deny their Lord, spent long years in the prisons of Syria and Egypt. Is it likely that, by way of fortifying them for such sacrifices, their own leaders would make them deny Christ and spit on the crucifix? As for the curious ritual of the three kisses, even the interrogators became confused about that; for whereas some of their victims duly confessed that they had received such kisses from the commander, the majority said that they had given the kisses to their commander. From the trial records it is obvious, too, that in some cases Templars imprisoned together agreed on a non-committal confession: many stated that, while such things were undoubtedly the rule, at their own initiation the whole performance had had to be broken off—whether because a horde of Saracens had suddenly appeared on the horizon, or simply because it was time for dinner! [10]

There remains the story of the belts and the idol. The statutes of the order did in fact stipulate that a Templar must, even when asleep at night, keep on his shirt and hose, and over these a belt, buckled up. No doubt the intention was to discourage any form of sexual activity. The charge brought against the Templars therefore represents a neat inversion of the rule: the belt appears as being somehow an incitement to sodomy, because it mysteriously keeps the wearer in thrall to the head-shaped idol which it has touched. And this idol provides the key to the whole matter. When it reappears in the Templars' confessions it assumes the most varied shapes. All agree, as required, that it consisted of a head, but there agreement ends. Some describe it as having three faces, others as having four feet, others as being simply a face with no feet. For some it was a human skull, embalmed and encrusted with jewels; for others it was carved out of wood. Some maintained that it came from the remains of a former grand master of the order, while others were equally convinced that it was called Baphomet—which in turn was interpreted as "Mohammed". Some saw it as having horns. From all this two things emerge quite clearly: in reality, there was no idol; but in the context of the interrogations and trials it had to exist, as an embodiment of Satanic power.*

* On the idol(s) see J. H. Probst-Biraben and A. Maitrot de la Motte-Capron, "Les idoles des chevaliers du Temple", in *Mercure de France*, vol. 294 (August–September 1939), pp. 569–90. The authors point out that all that was actually found in the Templar houses was a single reliquary in the form of a bust of a woman, such as often figured in perfectly orthodox Catholic devotions directed

The Satanic nature of the idol is hammered home in a series of confessions where it figures in company with our old acquaintance, the Satanic cat.[11] This cat appeared alongside the idol in a sort of cloud, lingered there throughout the ceremony and then disappeared, never to be seen again; nobody could explain it, except by saying that it came from the Devil or was itself the Devil. The Templars present revered it, removing their hats, bowing low before it, finally kissing it beneath the tail. For the rest, the cat was as variable as the idol, in that some saw it as black, some as grey, some as brindled and some as red.

After all this, it comes as no surprise to learn, from some of the confessions, that the idol was anointed with the fat of roasted infants; and that the bodies of deceased Templars were burnt and their ashes mixed into a powder which was administered to newcomers as a magical potion, to make them hold fast to their abominable ways.[12] Nor are we astonished to hear that the worship of the idol and the cat was sometimes attended by demons in the form of beautiful young girls, whose arrival was all the more remarkable because every window and crevice was sealed, but with whom the assembled Templars were happy to make love.[13]

We are on familiar ground. Clearly the charges against the Templars were simply a variant of those which, as we have seen, had previously been brought against certain heretical groups, real or imaginary. Moreover as the interrogations proceeded, the tortured Templars supplied fresh evidence to show how deeply heretical the order was. Now it appeared that the newcomer to the order was required not simply to deny Christ but to assert that Christ was a criminal who had been executed for his crimes; and he had also to deny the Virgin Mary and all the saints. It was not enough to spit on the crucifix, one had to drag it about the room, trample it under foot, urinate on it; and this not simply at the time of one's reception but also during Holy Week. No Templar believed that the sacraments had any efficacy, or indeed that there was any salvation in Christ. Their only god and saviour was the Devil, represented by the idol and the cat; and the Devil could do wonderful things for his followers.[14]

---

to a female saint or martyr. The notion that the Templars possessed "idols" belonging to a Gnostic cult is an invention of the nineteenth-century Austrian Orientalist von Hammer-Purgstall. The original persecutors of the Temple never suggested it. And of course, as Mohammed is never worshipped by Moslems, and as Islam strictly forbids all forms of idolatry, the Templars cannot have possessed idols representing Mohammed, either. How, in the course of the interrogations, the idol(s) turned into a magical head is described in S. Reinach, "La tête magique des Templiers", in *Revue de l'histoire des religions*, Paris, 1911, pp. 252–66.

The explanation of all this is clear enough. King Philip's aim was to ensure the suppression of the Temple and to secure its property for himself and his descendants. To achieve this he had to demonstrate not that individual Templars had transgressed the rule of the order (which would not have helped at all) but that the order itself was a heretical sect. The heretical doctrines which really were circulating in western Christendom—whether those of the Cathars, or of the Waldensians, or of the Franciscan Spirituals—were all obviously inappropriate to an order of warriors. The one remaining possibility was to invoke the conventional image of a heretical sect: the Temple had to be presented as the embodiment of what was generally felt to be abominable. It was natural that a body of warrior monks should be accused of homosexual sodomy rather than of promiscuous and incestuous orgies; but even here a shift can be observed as the interrogations progress—in one whole series of interrogations sodomy is never mentioned, being replaced by orgies with female demons. As for the other accusations—denial of Christ, Devil-worship, obscene kisses and the rest—they all belong to the traditional stereotypes whose development we have been tracing in previous chapters.

Nevertheless it was not easy to prosecute the Temple as a heretical sect. By rights the tracking down and prosecution of heretics pertained not to the secular authorities but to the Church; and the Temple was in any case protected, in that various papal privileges placed it directly under the jurisdiction of the Holy See. To proceed directly against the Temple meant to infringe the prerogative of the pope twice over. Philip could risk it only because the reigning pope was unable to stand up to him. Clement V was a Frenchman, he and his court were resident not in Rome but in France, he owed his very election to Philip's influence, his freedom of action was largely dependent on Philip's goodwill. Such a situation would have hampered even a vigorous and strong-willed pope; but Clement was compliant by nature, and he was also weakened by a grave internal malady which often incapacitated him for months on end. The arrest of the Templars opened a struggle between king and pope; but it was an unequal struggle, and in the end Philip secured most of his aims.

Philip could not however rely on the operation of ordinary criminal law to produce the desired result; for that, he had to have recourse to the "inquisitorial" procedure which had been developed for dealing with heretics and which had been perfected by the Inquisition during the preceding century.* As we have seen, under this procedure the odds

* The nature and development of this procedure are described at pp. 23-4 above.

were in any case weighted against the accused; but at least the inquisitors usually concentrated on discovering real heretics and eradicating real heresies, and went soberly about the business. But the inquisitorial procedure could also, at times, be shamelessly abused: the victims of Conrad of Marburg were forced to confess to wholly imaginary offences, and so were the Templars. In the proceedings against the Temple the Inquisition was subordinate to the royal power—a situation without parallel in the history of medieval Europe.[15] The first interrogation was actually carried out by the royal officials; only after it was satisfactorily completed were the inquisitors called in, to hear the confessions elaborated and confirmed. Moreover the inquisitors themselves acted under the instructions of a man styled general inquisitor for the whole of France—but he too was in effect a servant of the state. The office appears to have been invented for the purpose by King Philip; at any rate its incumbent, the Dominican friar Guillaume Imbert of Paris, was Philip's own confessor and was far more closely connected with him than with Pope Clement. The task given him by his royal patron was to legitimate the suppression of the Temple, as a heretical sect of the most sinister kind. He did his best, to the delight of the king and the intense vexation of the pope.

The Templars were in a helpless position. In the first place they were numerically far weaker than is often supposed—there were probably less than 4,000 in the whole of Europe, and only about half of those were in France; the knights amongst the French Templars numbered only a few hundred. Then they were quite unprepared, organizationally and psychologically, to stand up to the onslaught which the king had so carefully planned. They lived scattered, in their many houses, through the length and breadth of the land. Seized suddenly, without any warning, kept in complete ignorance concerning their fellows in other areas, and often in solitary confinement, they were told that countless Templars had already confessed to all the charges. If they confessed in their turn, they would be spared, set at liberty, reconciled to the Church; if not, they would be executed.[16] If this failed to produce the desired effect, torture was applied—and the tortures could include having one's feet roasted until the bones fell from their sockets (one Templar actually exhibited a handful of his bones at a later enquiry).[17] In such circumstances it is hardly surprising that, in the first interrogations, in Paris, only four Templars out of 138 refused to confess to any of the offences.

All levels of the order were involved: great officers who were famed throughout Christendom; knights who had proved themselves in battle; heads of preceptories great and small; but above all the smaller fry—sergeants, husbandmen from the estates, even shepherds. Confessions poured forth, but the content of the confessions varied greatly.[18] All except six admitted to spitting on the cross at their reception—but they differed as to whether the cross was a crucifix or a painted cross or a picture in a missal or even the cross which all Knights Templars wore on their robes; also, as to whether the act had been performed in front of the altar or behind it or in a secret room, in the presence of many or alone. Three-quarters confessed to some "indecent" kisses at their reception—but differed as to whether they had given or received them; and only a third knew anything about a kiss at the base of the spine. Some seventy said that they had been instructed to commit sodomy—but all save two or three denied having committed it. On the other hand, few had anything to say about the mysterious idol—though Hugues de Pairaud, the second most important personage in the order in France, admitted that he had seen, touched and adored it.[19] This was quite in order: the royal instructions made it plain that only the greatest officers were supposed to know about it. Nevertheless in some later interrogations all such limitations were dropped, and the idol turned out to be known to everyone, after all.[20]

Meanwhile a massive propaganda campaign was launched against the order. Franciscan and Dominican friars, who had always been bitterly hostile to the Temple, acted as the king's spokesmen and carried the officially sanctioned slanders into every corner of the land. Moreover, at least some of the Templars were compelled to appear in public and condemn themselves—just like the accused in Stalin's show trials six centuries later. One of the surviving documents tells how, on 26 October—that is, a fortnight after the arrests—32 of the Paris Templars appeared before a brilliant assembly of clergy and university doctors and confirmed the accuracy of their confessions.[21] Even the grand master was involved in these performances. Jacques de Molay was first interrogated on 25 October when, without being tortured, he confessed that at his reception, many years before, he had denied Christ and had spat near the crucifix. On the very same day this great dignitary was called upon to repeat his admission before an audience of leading personalities, clerical and lay. With a show of deep remorse he declared that the Temple, though founded to defend the Holy Land, had long since been seduced by Satan. Now God in his mercy had, through his servant Philip the Fair, uncovered these enormities; and the grand master could only implore the assembly to pardon him and his companions, and to plead their cause before the pope and the king.[22]

Pope and king: Philip had managed to convey, not only to the grand master but to the general public, the impression that the arrest of the Templars had been carried out with the knowledge and consent of Pope Clement. The reality was very different. Clement was outraged to see his own prerogatives disregarded and his name taken in vain; and he was not convinced, either, of the Templars' guilt. But there was little he could do about it. However indignant he might feel, and whatever efforts he might make to assert his independence, he remained a weak man in a weak position, and no match at all for the astute and ruthless Philip. During the following months the king was to reduce the pope, by a mixture of bullying, cajolery and trickery, to the position of a mere accomplice.

Clement's first reaction to the arrests was to hold a series of secret consistories of cardinals, and to assure the Templars in his entourage that they could rely on his protection. Almost immediately something happened to shake him: a prominent Templar, who was one of his own personal attendants, came forward to confess that at his reception he had denied Christ—and not privately, either, but in front of a great assembly of the order, under the grand master himself.[23] Apparently it did not strike the pope as odd that this particular Templar had been received into the order at the age of eleven; or occur to him that the king might have had a hand in this strange declaration. In a bull issued on 22 November, entitled *Pastoralis praeeminentiae*, he summoned the monarchs of western Europe to arrest the Templars in their territories and to secure their properties in the name of the Church.[24] But then doubts overcame him again. Two cardinals whom he had sent to Paris to investigate returned full of misgivings; for in their presence some of the imprisoned Templars, including Jacques de Molay and Hugues de Pairaud, had withdrawn their confessions.

Early in 1308 Clement made his one real attempt at resistance. He refused to condemn the order; he suspended the inquisitorial powers of inquisitors and bishops; and he explicitly reserved to himself all decisions concerning the fate of the Temple and its possessions. Philip's answer was to intensify the propaganda campaign against the Temple and to launch one against the pope. In May 1308 the Estates General met at Tours to consider the matter—a huge assembly, to which the third estate alone sent some 700 delegates. The summons, written by Nogaret, already declared the Temple guilty: "Oh grief! The abominable error of the Templars, so bitter, so lamentable, is not hidden from you. . . ." All the accusations—denying Christ, spitting and trampling on the cross, worshipping idols, indecent kisses, sodomy—are solemnly listed as proven offences, which together represent a threat to the very cosmos: "Heaven and earth are agitated by the breath of so great a crime, and the elements are disturbed. . . . Against so criminal a plague everything must rise up: laws and arms, every living thing, the four elements. . . ." [25] No wonder that the Estates General voted almost unanimously for the execution of the Templars.

Next came a great consistory of clergy and laity at Poitiers, where the pope lived; stage-managed by the king, with the king himself present and with royal officials as the chief speakers. Speeches prepared by Nogaret were declaimed for the pope's benefit. "Christus vincit, Christus regnat, Christus imperat"—the opening words of the coronation anthem provided the text for the first oration, and were given a new significance. [26] Never, since he first triumphed over the Devil in the crucifixion, had Christ won such a swift and wonderful victory as now, when his delegates had miraculously uncovered the heresy of the Templars—a heresy which had long been working in secret, to the peril of souls, the overthrow of the faith and the destruction of the Church. In its beginnings the struggle had been a terrible one, for the accusers were weak, the accused immensely strong (one recognizes a perennial paranoid theme . . .). But its development had been most gladsome; for, once delivered into the hands of the king and his officers (men devoid of cupidity and ambition, true servants of Christ), some of the Templars had hanged themselves or hurled themselves to their death while almost all the remainder had willingly confessed; one had even given up the ghost while confessing.

Through the pompous phrases the horrors of the torture chamber can be divined easily enough; but the orator knew how to divert attention from that thought. The Templars, he pointed out, had long been suspect, because "they held their chapters and their meetings at night, which is the custom of heretics, he who does evil flees the light". Down the centuries this argument had never changed, and had never lost its force.

In all this the king's spokesman was concerned not simply to discredit the Temple but also, and above all, to intimidate the pope; and he ended his speech with an unmistakable threat. The fact of the Templars' guilt neither could nor should be questioned by any true Catholic; nobody—least of all the pope—should worry about how the truth had been discovered, by what means or in whose presence. All that mattered was that the facts had come to light and were now notorious; to doubt them would be tantamount to aiding and abetting heresy. In other words, if Clement questioned Philip's right to imprison and torture the Templars, he would lay himself open to a charge of heresy. He would also be setting himself against the will of the French people. Pamphlets and orations from the pen of the royal publicist Pierre Dubois hammered the point home: the aggressor is regaining his strength, he will counterattack, he may be victorious; if the pope will not take action to forestall this, the people of France will take the law into their own hands. The pope must do his duty: he must formally condemn the Temple, and he must set the inquisitors free to continue their work. [27]

For a time Clement stood firm; but his resolution, never very strong, collapsed when some captive Templars, carefully chosen by the royal officials, were brought before him and renewed their confessions. Pope and king entered on secret negotiations; and early in July they reached an agreement. In effect, Clement capitulated, but—as weak, well-meaning men commonly do in such situations—he also set about salving his conscience and saving his face. On the one hand he persuaded himself that some Templars, at least, were guilty; this justified him in ordering the bishops to use inquisitional procedure, including torture, against the Templars in their dioceses. On the other hand he set up papal commissions in the various countries to investigate the extent to which the order, as distinct from individual Templars, was involved in the alleged offences; this enabled him to pretend that papal rights had been respected.

The French bishops had always hated the Templars, and their inquisition proved merciless—in Paris alone thirty-six prisoners died under torture. [28] But few in any age are equipped to endure such martyrdom; so confessions came in plenty, to confirm and amplify those previously extorted by the royal officials. However, the pope's command was addressed not simply to the French bishops but to the episcopate throughout western Christendom; and in countries other than France it produced quite different results. In Portugal the king simply refused to sanction the arrest of his Templars; in Castile an investigation was begun, but petered out; in Aragon the bishops carried through an investigation, but remained unconvinced of the Templars' guilt; in England a face-saving compromise was devised; in Germany, it seems, the Templars were acquitted; and that was certainly the case in Cyprus, where there were Templars from all over Europe. The reason is plain: in none of these countries were the authorities interested in destroying the order. Only in France and in those parts of Italy and Sicily which were controlled either by Philip or by Clement was torture used ruthlessly; and only there were confessions forthcoming.

As for the papal commissions—even the commission operating in France—these came up with results which must have surprised Pope Clement and which were certainly unwelcome to King Philip. By the time the commissions started work, in September 1309, inquisitorial interrogations had been going on for nearly two years and many hundreds of confessions had been extorted; and this naturally made any fresh investigation of the order very difficult. Moreover, the king had considerable influence in deciding the membership of the commissions. Yet despite all this, truth would out. When the commission announced that it would hear any Templars who would volunteer to give evidence, more than 500 at once came forward. Though they were still prisoners of the king, worn with hardship, hunger and torture, these men took on new life at the prospect of defending the honour of the Temple. In Paris in 1307, 134 Templars had affirmed the guilt of the order; in 1310, 81 of those same 134 appeared as defenders. In Bayeux, 12 Templars had confessed; now 10 of those 12 appeared as defenders.

A defence submitted in writing by a group of Templars has survived, and it overflows with innocence, indeed with naïvety.[29] Why, it asks, will nobody listen to those who tell the truth, even though they die under the torture and so earn the palm of martyrdom? How does it come that former Templars, who have been expelled from the order, can now earn money and privilege by slandering it? Quite unaware of the part played by King Philip, the defenders argue that he must have been deceived by those lying witnesses. Until the arrests, no hint was ever heard of the scandalous accusations. But now their captors keep telling them that, if they go back on their confessions, they will be burned alive. Therefore they ask that while they or any of their brethren are giving evidence, laymen (meaning the royal officials) shall not be allowed to hear it; for "in general the brethren are so struck with fear and terror that it is astonishing, not that some have lied, but that any at all have sustained the truth".

Their fears were only too well founded. Under inquisitorial procedure, any heretic who withdrew his confession was due for burning. And although the papal commission had assumed that those who appeared before it would be safe, at least until it had completed its investigation, there was no formal agreement to that effect. The evidence accumulating before the commission was endangering King Philip's whole plan; and he intervened ruthlessly. He forced the pope to appoint a young man of twenty-two, who was also the brother of his superintendent of finances, to the archbishopric of Sens, which included Paris. The new archbishop, acting in council, at once seized fifty-four Templars who had withdrawn their confessions and offered them the choice of either going back on their recantation or else of being handed over to the secular arm for burning. All fifty-four stood firm, and even in the flames continued to proclaim their innocence and the purity of the order. Others stood firm also: in all, some 120 perished in Paris, as against a mere two who chose the easier course.

The burnings achieved their purpose nevertheless. As one Templar put it, on the day after the burning of the fifty-four, rather than be burned he would swear not only that all the accusations against the order were true but also, if required, that he himself had killed Jesus Christ.[30] Defenders stopped coming forward. The papal commission, though reduced to a farce, solemnly continued its work; but of the Templars who remained to be heard, none was prepared to withdraw the confession which had previously been extracted by torture or the fear of torture.

King Philip had still to secure what had been his aim throughout: the suppression of the Temple. The pope lacked the nerve to perform this final act; so, in an effort to provide at least a semblance of legitimacy, an œcumenical council was convened at Vienne, near Avignon, during the winter of 1310–11. But things did not turn out as hoped. By five or six to one, the assembled prelates refused to condemn the order without first examining some of its members. Moreover, nine Templars suddenly presented themselves and demanded the right to defend the order before the council. Once more it looked as though the long tale of torture, terror and perjury would be revealed, this time to an international audience of princes of the Church. The pope had the nine Templars arrested and imprisoned, but he was unable to move the council from its decision. Again it was Philip who took the decisive step. Since it was impossible to get the order formally condemned without the council's participation, he persuaded the pope to suppress it himself, by papal decree. The deed was done on 22 March, while the council stood adjourned; and the reassembling cardinals could only register, with vexation, the very thing they had tried to prevent.

Not everything went Philip's way. His fantasy of himself and his descendants as hereditary grand masters of a new crusading order—this proved indeed mere fantasy. For after much discussion, pope and council decided against the creation of a new order; and in this matter Philip had to give way. On the other hand, he succeeded in holding on to the wealth of the suppressed order. Pope and council decided to transfer the Temple's property to its old rival, the Hospital; but in France the decision remained a dead letter. There much of the order's wealth had already vanished into the royal coffers; and the Hospital never managed to wrest the remainder from Philip or his successors.

In May 1312 the pope pronounced on the fate of the surviving Templars. Except for the relapsed heretics—those who had confessed and subsequently withdrew their confessions—they were to be sent in small groups to various monasteries, there to pass the remainder of their days. Thereafter the mass of individual Templars vanish into obscurity. It was another matter with the four great officers of the Temple in France, and particularly with the grand master, Jacques de Molay. It would have been too dangerous to set these men free, so they were sentenced to imprisonment for life.

On 18 March 1314 the four leaders appeared on a scaffold in Paris, to hear their sentences read out. Two listened in silence; but two—Jacques de Molay and the preceptor of Normandy, Geoffroi de Charnay—did not. The grand master had not always shown himself a hero: in 1307 he had produced a confession without being tortured, and had even sent a circular letter throughout France instructing his subordinates to do likewise. But now, at the last moment when he could still have done so, he spoke up. He solemnly declared that the rule of the order had always been holy and righteous and Catholic, and that the order was altogether innocent of the heresies and sins of which it had been accused. As for himself, he indeed deserved to die, because, from fear of torture and under pressure from pope and king, he had falsely subscribed to some of the accusations.[31]

King Philip reacted as was to be expected: without waiting for ecclesiastical authority of any kind, he had Jacques de Molay and Geoffroi de Charnay burned at the stake.

So ended "the affair of the Templars". In the context of our story it is a most significant event. In it we see, for the first time since the days of the Roman Empire, secular authorities invoking and exploiting those dehumanizing fantasies whose history we have been tracing. But we can also observe how the fantasies themselves were changing. Now for the first time apostasy, the deliberate renunciation of Christ and of Christianity, moves into the middle of the picture.

This is no matter for surprise. We have noted in previous chapters the change that was taking place in the very texture of religious feeling: how the power of the Devil and his demons seemed ever greater, men's resources of faith ever less adequate. Somewhere at the back of people's minds the urge to apostasy was beginning to make itself felt. It suited the purposes of King Philip that the Templars should be regarded, and treated, as incarnations of that urge—even though in reality those devout and unsophisticated warriors would have been the last to feel it.

Not that the Templars were the only ones to be cast in that role. In those same years individual allies of the Devil were being sought, and found, in even more unlikely quarters.*

* See Chapter Ten, sections 1 and 2.

6

THE NON-EXISTENT SOCIETY OF WITCHES

Hundreds of books and articles have been written about the great European witch-hunt of the fifteenth, sixteenth and seventeenth centuries, and during the last few years the subject has received more attention from historians than ever before. But that does not mean that nothing remains to be said. On the contrary, the more is written, the more glaring the disagreements. Were there people who regarded themselves as witches? If so, what did they do, or believe themselves to do? Were they organized, did they hold meetings? What are we to make of covens and sabbats? Again, when and where did the great witch-hunt begin? Who launched it, who perpetuated it, and for what motives? And just how "great" was it—did the numbers of those executed run into thousands, or into tens of thousands, or into hundreds of thousands? On most of these questions there is still no consensus amongst historians—and even where consensus exists, it is not necessarily correct. The remaining chapters of this book will be devoted to examining the matter anew.

We may start with the stereotype of the witch as it existed at the times when, and the places where, witch-hunting was at its most intense. The profile of that stereotype at least is established beyond all dispute. We possess not only the records of innumerable witch-trials, but also memoirs and manuals by half a dozen witch-hunting magistrates; and the figure of the witch that emerges could not be clearer or more detailed.

A witch was a human being—usually a woman but sometimes a man or even a child—who was bound to the Devil by a pact or contract, as his servant and assistant.

When the Devil first appeared to a future witch he was clad in flesh and blood; sometimes his shape was that of an animal but usually it was that of a man, fully and even smartly dressed. Almost always he appeared at a moment of acute distress—of bereavement, or of utter loneliness, or of total destitution. A typical pattern was that an elderly widow, rejected by her neighbours and with nobody to turn to, would be approached by a man who would alternatively console her, promise her money, scare her, extract a promise of obedience from her, in the end mate with her. The money seldom materialized, the copulation was downright painful, but the promise of obedience remained binding. Formally and irrevocably the new witch had to renounce God, Christ, the Christian religion, and pledge herself instead to the service of Satan; whereupon the Devil set his mark on her—often with the nails or claws of his left hand, and on the left side of the body.

If becoming a witch rarely brought either wealth or erotic pleasure, it had other rewards to offer. A witch was able to perform *maleficium*, i.e. to harm her neighbours by occult means. The pact meant that the Devil would demand this from his servant, but it also meant that he would supply her with supernatural power for the purpose. With the Devil's aid a witch could ruin the life of anyone she chose. She could bring sudden illness, or mental disorder, or maiming accidents, or death, on man, woman or child. She could bedevil a marriage by producing sterility or miscarriages in the woman, or impotence in the man. She could make cattle sicken or die, or cause hailstorms or unseasonable rain to ruin the crops. This was her reward; for a witch's will, like her master's, was wholly malignant, wholly set on destruction.

Witches were believed to specialize in the killing of babies and small children. More than mere malice was at work here—witches needed the corpses for all sorts of reasons. They were cannibals, with an insatiable craving for very young flesh; according to some writers of the time, to kill, cook and eat a baby which had not yet been baptized was a witch's greatest pleasure. But the flesh of infants was also full of supernatural power. As an element in magical concoctions it could be used to kill other human beings, or else to enable a captured witch to keep silent under torture. It could also be blended in a salve which, applied to a witch's body, enabled her to fly.

At regular intervals witches were required to betake themselves to the sacrilegious and orgiastic gatherings known first as "synagogues", later as "sabbats". There were ordinary sabbats, which were usually held on Fridays and were small affairs, involving only the witches of a given neighbourhood; and there were œcumenical sabbats, held with great ceremony three or four times a year, and attended by witches from all quarters. A sabbat was always a nocturnal happening, ending either at midnight or, at the very latest, at cockcrow. As for the locality, it might be a churchyard, a crossroads, the foot of a gallows; though the larger sabbats were commonly held at the summit of some famous mountain in a faraway region.

To attend the sabbat, and in particular to attend the œcumenical sabbat, witches had to cover great distances in very little time. They did so by flying. Having anointed themselves with the magic salve they would fly straight out of their bedrooms, borne aloft on demonic rams, goats, pigs, oxen, black horses; or else on sticks, shovels, spits, broomsticks. And meanwhile the husband or wife would sleep on peacefully, quite unaware of these strange happenings; sometimes a stick laid in the bed would take not only the place but also the appearance of the absent spouse. Thanks to this arrangement, some witches were able to deceive their mates for years on end.

The very numerous accounts of the sabbat differ from one another only in minor details, so it is easy to construct a representative picture. The sabbat was presided over by the Devil, who now took on the shape not of a mere man but of a monstrous being, half man and half goat: a hideous black man with enormous horns, a goat's beard and goat's legs, sometimes also with bird's claws instead of hands and feet. He sat on a high ebony throne; light streamed from his horns, flames spouted from his huge eyes. The expression of his face was one of immense gloom, his voice was harsh and terrible to hear.

The term "sabbat", like the term "synagogue", was of course taken from the Jewish religion, which was traditionally regarded as the quintessence of anti-Christianity, indeed as a form of Devil-worship. For the sabbat was above all an assertion of the Devil's mastery over his servants, the witches. First the witches knelt down and prayed to the Devil, calling him Lord and God, and repeating their renunciation of the Christian faith; after which each in turn kissed him, often on his left foot, his genitals or his anus. Next delinquent witches reported for punishment, which usually consisted of whippings. In Roman Catholic countries witches would confess their sins—for instance, attending church—and the Devil would impose whippings as a penance; but everywhere witches who had missed a sabbat, or who had performed insufficient *maleficia*, were soundly whipped. Then came the parody of divine service. Dressed in black vestments, with mitre and surplice, the Devil would preach a sermon, warning his followers against reverting to Christianity and promising them a far more blissful paradise than the Christian heaven. Seated again on his black chair, with the king and queen of the witches on either side of him, he would receive the offerings of the faithful—cakes and flour, poultry and corn, sometimes money.

The proceedings ended in a climax of profanity. Once more the witches adored the Devil and kissed his anus, while he acknowledged their attentions in a peculiarly noxious manner. A parody of the Eucharist was given, in both kinds—but what was received was an object like the sole of a shoe, black, bitter and hard to chew, and a jug full of nauseous black liquid. After this a meal would be served; and often this too would consist of revolting substances—fish and meat tasting like rotten wood, wine tasting like manure drainings, the flesh of babies. Finally, an orgiastic dance, to the sound of trumpets, drums and fifes. The witches would form a circle, facing outwards, and dance around a witch standing bent over, her head touching the ground, with a candle stuck in her anus to serve as illumination. The dance would become a frantic and erotic orgy, in which all things, including sodomy and incest, were permitted. At the height of the orgy the Devil would copulate with every man, woman and child present. Finally he would bring the sabbat to a close by sending the participants off to their homes, with instructions to perform every conceivable *maleficium* against their Christian neighbours.

That is how witches were imagined when and where witch-hunting was at its height. It will be observed that they were thought of as a collectivity: though they perform *maleficium* individually, they are a society, assembling at regular intervals, bound together by communal rites, subject to a rigid, centralized discipline. In every respect they represent a collective inversion of Christianity—and an inversion of a kind that could only be achieved by former Christians. That is why non-Christians, such as Jews and Gypsies, though they might be accused of *maleficium*, were never accused of being witches in the full sense of the term. Witchcraft was regarded as apostasy—and apostasy in its most extreme, most systematic, most highly organized form. Witches were regarded as above all a sect of Devil-worshippers.

–2–

How did this strange stereotype come into being? Ever since historical research into these matters began, in the second quarter of the nineteenth century, two principal explanations have been offered. Some scholars have argued that a sect of witches really existed, and that the authorities who pursued and tried witches were in effect breaking the local organizations of that sect. Others have argued that the notion of a sect of witches first developed as a by-product of the campaign of the Inquisition against Catharism, and that the stereotype was first used in a massive inquisitorial witch-hunt that claimed hundreds of victims in southern France during the fourteenth century.

When it was first propounded, the first of these two theories represented a radical innovation. In the eighteenth and early nineteenth centuries practically no educated person believed that there had ever been a sect of witches; it is only since around 1830 that this has gradually ceased to be taken for granted. Not, of course, that those scholars who have maintained that there really was a sect of witches have claimed that the sect did all those things it was originally believed to do. They have not argued that witches flew through the air to the sabbat, or that the Devil presided over it in corporeal form. But they have argued, and very forcibly, that witches were organized in groups under recognized leaders; that they adhered to a religious cult that was not only non-Christian but anti-Christian; and that they assembled, under cover of night, at remote spots, to perform the rituals of that cult. On this view, what we find in the witch-trials and the writings of witch-hunters represents a distorted perception of groups that really existed, of meetings that physically took place. Propounded by academics at leading universities in Europe and North America, often in works published by university presses, this interpretation has been taken on trust by multitudes of educated people. It still is: when conversation turns to the great witch-hunt, it is assumed more often than not that the hunt must have been directed against a real secret society.

The founding of this school of thought has sometimes been ascribed to the Italian cleric Girolamo Tartarotti-Serbati, who published *Del Congresso Notturno delle Lamie* in 1749, or else to the great German folklorist Jacob Grimm, on account of certain passages in his *Deutsche Mythologie*, first published in 1835; but in both cases wrongly. Tartarotti and Grimm merely drew attention to the fact that folk beliefs dating from pre-Christian times had contributed something to the stereotype. Neither even hinted that the great witch-hunt was directed against an anti-Christian sect. The first modern scholar to advance that view seems to have been Karl Ernst Jarcke. In 1828, when Jarcke was a young professor of criminal law at the University of Berlin, he edited the records of a seventeenth-century German witch-trial for a legal journal, and appended some brief comments of his own. He argued that witchcraft was above all a nature religion that had once been the religion of the pagan Germans. After the establishment of Christianity this religion survived, with its traditional ceremonies and sacraments, as a living tradition amongst the common people; but it took on a new significance. The Church condemned it as Devil-worship, and in the end this view of the matter was adopted even by those who, in secret, still practised it. At the core of the old pagan religion were secret arts for influencing the course of nature—arts which, in the view both of the adherents of that religion and of the Christian clergy, depended on the Devil for their efficacy. As the Christian religion became the religion of the common people, the practice of those arts came to be regarded, and experienced, as a conscious, voluntary service of the evil principle; to be initiated into them was to choose the Devil's service. That explains why, in the later form of witch-belief, anyone adept in those arts was expected to employ them for the purpose of harming others, i.e. was expected to perform *maleficia*.[1]

In 1839 a variation on the theme was produced by the historian Franz Josef Mone, who after a brilliant academic career was at that time director of the archives of Baden. He too saw witchcraft as a cult deriving from pre-Christian times—only in his view its origin lay not in the religion of the ancient Germans as such but in an underground, esoteric cult practised by the lowest strata of the population. The Germanic peoples who sojourned on the north coast of the Black Sea came in contact with the cult of Hecate and the cult of Dionysos, and the slave elements in the population adopted these cults and fused them into a religion of their own. This religion was characterized by the worship of a goat-like god, the celebration of nocturnal orgies and the practice of magic and poison. As the Germanic peoples moved west, the religion came with them; but free-born men and women regarded it with contempt. At all times it stood in opposition to the official religion of society, and it continued to do so when that religion was Christianity. The underground religion was witchcraft. Witches were therefore members of "a fully organized secret society" with roots in the distant past; and the Devil who presided over the sabbat was a distorted version of Dionysos. Even the *maleficia* against domestic animals, which bulk so large in the trials, might well reflect the fact that the Bacchantes, in their frenzy, used to kill roes and fawns.[2]

Neither of these theories is convincing. Neither Jarcke nor Mone can show that the worship of ancient gods, whether Germanic or Greek, was in fact practised by organized, clandestine groups in the Middle Ages. Nor do they even try to explain why such groups, after passing unnoticed for the best part of a thousand years, should have attracted ever increasing attention in the fifteenth, sixteenth and seventeenth centuries. Yet both men were serious scholars, and between them they started a hare which other scholars, some of them equally serious, have continued to pursue at intervals right down to the present day.

Jarcke and Mone were ardent Roman Catholics—in fact both of them at times acted as journalistic spokesmen for the clerical interest. Moreover they propounded their theories in the midst of the reaction against the French Revolution and its consequences, when a horrified obsession with secret societies was very widespread in conservative circles.[3] They had no sympathy at all for the secret society of witches that they supposed to have existed: in their eyes it was a thoroughly evil conspiracy against the true religion and the true Church. But the opposite view also found a spokesman, in Jules Michelet. In *La Sorcière* (1862) he portrays witchcraft as a justified, if hopeless, protest by medieval serfs against the social order that was crushing them.

Michelet imagines serfs coming together secretly, at night, to perform ancient pagan dances, with which they blended satirical farces directed against lord and priest. This, he thinks, happened already in the twelfth and thirteenth centuries; in the fourteenth, when both the Church and the nobility were largely discredited, the sabbat turned into a ritualized defiance of the existing social order, epitomized by the Christian God. Michelet calls it "the black mass"; and at its centre he puts not the Devil, nor a man impersonating the Devil, but a woman—a female serf in her thirties "with a face like Medea, a beauty born of sufferings, a deep, tragic, feverish gaze, with a torrent of black, untamable hair falling as chance takes it, like waves of serpents. Perhaps, on top, a crown of vervain, like ivy from tombs, like violets of death."[4]

This romantic figure is the priestess of the cult; indeed, Michelet credits her with inventing, organizing and staging the entire sabbat. She induces peasants to give food for the communal meal—knowing that those who do so will find themselves committed to a conspiracy. She sets up a giant wooden figure, hairy, horned, with a great penis. It represents Satan, imagined as "the great serf in revolt", a rebel against the God who unjustly cast him out of heaven, but also himself a sort of nature god, "who makes plants germinate", who even "found Nature prostrate, cast out by the Church like a dirty baby, and picked Nature up and put it in his breast".[5]

At the sabbat the priestess ritually mates with Satan: before the assembled multitude, she seats herself on his lap and, in a simulated copulation, receives his spirit. Later, after the banquet and the dance, she turns herself into an altar. A man disguised as a demon makes offerings on her prostrate body: corn is offered to Satan to ensure a good harvest, a cake is cooked on her back and distributed as Eucharist. Finally the priestess shouts defiance at the Christian God; while a horde of "demons" rush out and jump over fires, to cure the assembled peasants of their fear of hell-fire.

Now, none of this figures in any contemporary account of the witches' sabbat. Not one mentions a priestess, or so much as hints that a single woman dominates the ritual. As for the "black mass" celebrated on a woman's back—that notion was born in an entirely different historical context: the "affair of the poisons", which took place in Paris around 1680.[6] Nor was the sabbat, even at its first appearance, imagined as a festival of serfs—already in 1460, at Arras, rich and powerful burghers were accused of attending it, along with humbler folk.[7] To give his account even a shadow of plausibility, Michelet has to pretend that all extant accounts of the sabbat date from the period of its decadence; the true, original sabbat being something quite different. The argument is not likely to commend itself to historians.

Even so, the accounts of the sabbat that we do possess confront Michelet with some pretty problems. Some stock features are simply passed over in silence—not a word is said, for instance, about *maleficium*; but with others he copes as best he can. He is exercised by the tales of erotic orgies, with their stress on incest. There cannot, he assures us, have been any open promiscuity, as young children were present. On the other hand, he admits that incest may have occurred, discreetly, and he even offers two mutually exclusive explanations to account for it. Perhaps incest is to be understood in terms of a medieval law which extended the forbidden degrees to include cousins six times removed. Or perhaps, on the other hand, the priestess, being a woman and sympathizing with women, encouraged sons to mate with their mothers, so that mothers could be assured of a roof over their heads in old age. Again, innumerable contemporary accounts refer to the fact that Satan's seed, when received by the witches, felt cold. Michelet suggests that whatever mating took place at the sabbat must have been followed by an icy "purification", to prevent conception. As for the babies which were supposedly eaten at the sabbat, these were simply models of babies, made to look like meat. Placed on the back of the priestess, they represented the People; and when serfs partook of them —or went through the motions—the People were simply worshipping the People, in truly democratic spirit.

That is what *La Sorcière* has to say about the sabbat; and despite the special pleading, the suppression of texts and the fatuities of exegesis on which the interpretation depends, it was not without influence. For in *La Sorcière* Michelet deployed all those visionary and poetic gifts that make him so compelling a historian. Though he protested that the book was free from emotional romancing, was indeed the most unquestion-ably true of all his works, the opposite is the case. *La Sorcière* was written when Michelet was sixty-four, and it was written fast: the two chapters on the sabbat took a day each, almost the whole book was finished in two months.[8] Driven by a passionate urge to rehabilitate two oppressed classes—women, and the medieval peasantry—the aging romantic radical had neither time nor desire for detailed research. The result was an imaginative creation of such power that it has continued to be reprinted, and read, and taken seriously, for generation after generation. In a general sense it seems to have influenced even some highly sophisticated French historians of today. Professor Emmanuel Le Roy Ladurie, for instance, in his monumental work *Les paysans de Languedoc* (1966), still presents sabbats as real meetings in which the peasant urge to revolt found symbolic expression.[9]

But *La Sorcière* also contains hints of a different interpretation. In passing, Michelet suggests that the sabbat was really the celebration of a fertility cult, aimed at securing abundance of crops. At the hands of later scholars this notion was to undergo some startling elaborations.

In his notes to *The Waste Land*, T. S. Eliot lists, as one of the works to which he was most indebted, *The Golden Bough* by Sir James Frazer—"a work of anthropology . . . which has influenced our generation profoundly". Unlike some of Eliot's other notes, this one was per-fectly serious: first published in 1890, reissued with enlargements in twelve volumes between 1907 and 1915, *The Golden Bough* had indeed launched a cult of fertility cults. At least in the English-speaking world it became fashionable to interpret all kinds of rituals as derivatives of a magic originally performed to encourage the breeding of animals and the growth of plants, and to see in the most diverse gods and heroes so many disguises for the spirit of vegetation. It was to be expected that this kind of interpretation would be applied also to the history of European witchcraft; and so it was, in *The Witch-Cult in Western Europe*, by Margaret Murray. The year was 1921, and the influence of *The Golden Bough* was at its height. (*The Waste Land*, with Eliot's comment, appeared the following year.)[10]

The impact of *The Witch-Cult in Western Europe* has been extra-ordinary. For some forty years (1929–68) the article on "Witchcraft" in successive editions of the *Encyclopædia Britannica* was by Margaret Murray and simply summarized the book's argument, as though it were a matter of established fact. By 1962 a scholar was moved to comment with dismay: "The Murrayites seem to hold . . . an almost undisputed sway at the higher intellectual levels. There is, amongst educated people, a very widespread impression that Professor Margaret Murray has discovered the true answer to the problem of the history of European witchcraft and has proved her theory." [11] Since that was written the Murrayite cause has received formidable reinforcements. The Oxford University Press, the original publishers of the Witch-Cult, re-issued it in 1962 as a paperback, which has been frequently reprinted since and is still selling well. In a foreword to this new edition the eminent medievalist Sir Steven Runciman praises the thoroughness of the author's scholarship and makes it plain that he fully accepts her basic theory. Some leading historians of seventeenth-century England have shown themselves equally trusting. Even amongst scholars specializing in the history of witchcraft the book has exercised and—as we shall see—continues to exercise considerable influence. It has also inspired a whole library of new works, which have disseminated the doctrine amongst more or less serious readers. It is significant that in Britain even that respectable series, Pelican Books, having published an anti-Murrayite work on witchcraft by Professor Geoffrey Parrinder in 1958, replaced it in 1965 by the Murrayite work of the late Pennethorne Hughes. More dramatically, the Witch-Cult and its progeny have stimulated the extraordinary proliferation of "witches' covens" in Western Europe and the United States during the past decade, culminating in the foundation of the Witches International Craft Association, with headquarters in New York. In 1970 the association, under the leadership of Dr Leo Martello and his "high priestess" Witch Hazel, held "the world's first public Witch-In for Halloween" in Central Park. Even Margaret Murray, one imagines, would have been surprised by the development of the Witches' Liberation Movement, with its plans for a Witches' Day Parade, a Witches News Service, a Witches' Lecture Bureau and a Witches' Anti-Defamation League. [12]

The argument presented in the Witch-Cult and elaborated in its successor The God of the Witches (1933) can be summarized as follows:

Down to the seventeenth century a religion which was far older than Christianity persisted throughout Western Europe, with followers in every social stratum from kings to peasants. It centred on the worship of a two-faced, horned god, known to the Romans as Dianus or Janus. This "Dianic cult" was a religion of the type so abundantly described in The Golden Bough. The horned god represented the cycle of the crops and the seasons, and was thought of as periodically dying and returning to life. In society he was represented by selected human beings. At national level these included such celebrated personages as William Rufus, Thomas à Becket, Joan of Arc and Gilles de Rais, whose dramatic deaths were really ritual sacrifices carried out to ensure the resurrection of the god and the renewal of the earth. At village level the god was represented by the horned personage who presided over the witches assemblies. Hostile observers, such as inquisitors, naturally took this personage to be, or at least to represent, the Devil; so that to them witchcraft seemed a form of Satan-worship. In reality, the witches were simply worshipping the pre-Christian deity Dianus; and if they appeared to kiss their master's behind, that was because he wore a mask which, like the god himself, had two faces.

The preservation of the Dianic cult was largely the work of an aboriginal race, which had been driven into hiding by successive waves of invaders. These refugees were of small stature—which was the reality behind stories of "the little people", or fairies. Shy and elusive, they nevertheless had sufficient contact with the ordinary population to transmit the essentials of their religion. The witches were their disciples and intellectual heirs.

The organization of the Dianic cult was based on the local coven, which always consisted of thirteen members—twelve ordinary members, male and female, and one officer. The members of a coven were obliged to attend the weekly meetings, which Dr Murray calls "esbats", as well as the larger assemblies, or sabbats proper. Discipline was strict: failure to attend a meeting, or to carry out the instructions given there, was punished with such a beating that sometimes the culprit died. The resulting structure was remarkably tough: throughout the Middle Ages the Dianic cult was the dominant religion, Christianity little more than a veneer. It was only with the coming of the Reformation that Christianity achieved enough hold over the population to launch an open attack on its rival—the result being the great witch-hunt.

Margaret Murray was not by profession a historian but an Egyptologist, archaeologist and folklorist. Her knowledge of European history, even of English history, was superficial and her grasp of historical method was non-existent. In the special field of witchcraft studies, she seems never to have read any of the modern histories of the persecution; and even if she had, she would not have assimilated them. By the time she turned her attention to these matters she was nearly sixty, and her ideas were firmly set in an exaggerated and distorted version of the Frazerian mould. For the rest of her days (and she lived to 100) she clung to those ideas with a tenacity which no criticism, however well informed or well argued, could ever shake.

There has been no lack of such criticism. George Lincoln Burr, Cecil L'Estrange Ewen, Professor Rossell Hope Robbins, Mr Elliot Rose,

Professor Hugh Trevor-Roper, Mr Keith Thomas are amongst those who, from the 1920s to the 1970s, have either weighed the theory and found it wanting, or else have dismissed it as unworthy of consideration. But other scholars have taken a different view and have maintained that beneath its manifest exaggerations, the theory contains a core of truth. The reason is given by Arno Runeberg in his book *Witches, demons and fertility magic* (1947). He points out that some of the accounts of witches' assemblies quoted by Murray have no fantastic features but are perfectly plausible. The witches go to and from the sabbat not by flying but on foot or on horseback; the "Devil" has nothing supernatural about him but sits at the head of the table like an ordinary man; the meal is quite unremarkable; the participants even specify who supplied the food and drink. Runeberg concludes: "That such drinking-bouts should be only hallucinations . . . is indeed curious. Neither is it probable that the persecutors by leading questions would have caused people to tell such stories." [13] According to this view these commonplace happenings, themselves perhaps neither very frequent nor very widespread, represent the reality around which fantasies clustered, gradually building up the whole phantasmagoria of the witches' sabbat as we find it in other and better known accounts. It would be a powerful argument if the accounts quoted by Murray were really as sober as they appear to be—but are they? The only way to find out is to examine her sources in their original contexts—a tiresome task, but one which is long overdue.

The relevant passages in the *Witch-Cult* carry references to some fifteen primary sources, mostly English or Scottish pamphlets describing notorious trials. Now, of all these sources only one is free from manifestly fantastic and impossible features—and even in that one the Devil, though "a bonny young lad with a blue bonnet", has the conventional requirements of a cold body and cold semen, and gladly mates with a witch aged eighty. [14] To appreciate the true import of the other sources one has only to compare, in half a dozen instances, what Murray quotes with what she passes over in silence.

The activities of the Lancashire witches who were tried in 1612 are represented by the following excerpts from a contemporary pamphlet: *

> The persons aforesaid had to their dinners beef, bacon and
> roasted mutton; which mutton (as this witness's said brother said)

---

* In this and the following quotations I have modernized the spelling and replaced a few obsolete words by their modern equivalents. N.C.

was of a wether of Christopher Swyers of Barley: which wether was brought in the night before into this witness's mother's house by the said James Device, this witness's said brother: and in this witness's sight killed and eaten. . . . And before their said parting away, they all appointed to meet at the said Preston's wife's house that day twelve-month; at which time the said Preston's wife promised to make them a great feast.

After which they "went out of the said house in their own shapes and likenesses. And they all, as soon as they were out of doors, got on horseback, like foals, some of one colour, some of another." (15)

The Devil, it will be noted, does not figure at all in this account; and one would never guess how large a part the demonic powers played in the trial as a whole. The key witness was a nine-year-old girl, Jennet Device, who gave evidence against her mother, her grandmother and her brother. Now according to young Jennet a spirit in the form of a brown dog called Ball approached her mother and asked what she wished him to do; and on her instructions killed three men by occult means. She had also listened to a black dog called Dandy having a similar conversation with her brother James; after which Dandy contrived the death of an old woman. (16)

The Somerset trials of 1664 are regarded by Murray as particularly illuminating. She quotes from the evidence of Elizabeth Styles:

"At their meeting they have usually wine and good beer, cakes, meat or the like. They eat and drink really when they meet in their bodies, dance also and have music. The man in black sits at the higher end, and Anne Bishop usually next him. He uses some words before meat, and none after, his voice is audible, and very low." (17)

She does not quote the sentence immediately preceding: "At every meeting the Spirit vanishes away, he appoints the next meeting place and time, and at his departure there is a foul smell." Nor is there any mention of certain other details supplied by the same witness. For Elizabeth Styles said that, while the Devil sometimes appeared to her as a man, he usually did so in the form of a dog, a cat or a fly; as a fly, he was apt to suck at the back of her head. He also provided his followers with oil with which to anoint their foreheads and wrists—which enabled them to be carried in a moment to and from the meetings. On the other hand, Elizabeth added that sometimes the meetings were attended by the witches' spirits only, their bodies remaining at home. (18)

A Scot herself, Murray draws heavily on the records of Scottish trials for her material. A typical source, covering both the feast at the sabbat and the return from it, is the confession of Helen Guthrie, one of the alleged witches tried at Forfar in 1661. The *Witch-Cult* gives the following excerpts:

> They went to Mary Rynd's house and sat down together at the table, the devil being present at the head of it; and some of them went to John Benny's house, he being a brewer, and brought ale from hence . . . and others of them went to Alexander Hieche's and brought aqua vitae from thence, and thus made themselves merry; and the devil made much of them all, but especially of Mary Rynd, and he kissed them all except the said Helen herself, whose hand only he kissed; and she and Jonet Stout sat opposite one to another at the table. [19]

> Herself, Isobell Shyrie and Elspet Alexander, did meet together at a house near to Barrie, a little before sunset, after they had stayed in the said house about the space of an hour drinking three pints of ale together, they went forth to the sands, and there three other women met them, and the Devil was there present with them all . . . and they parted so late that night that she could get no lodging, but was forced to lie at a dike side all night. [20]

All very normal—until one looks at the original source and discovers what those sets of dots represent. With the lacunae filled in the passages read as follows:

> . . . and brought ale from hence, and they (went) through at a little hole like bees, and took the substance of the ale . . .

> . . . and the Devil was there present with them all, in the shape of a great horse; and they decided on the sinking of a ship, lying not far off from Barrie, and presently the said company appointed herself to take hold of the cable tow, and to hold it fast until they did return, and she herself did presently take hold of the cable tow, and the rest with the Devil went into the sea upon the said cable, as she thought, and about the space of an hour thereafter, they returned all in the same likeness as before, except that the Devil was in the shape of a man upon his return, and the rest were sorely fatigued. . . . [21]

After this it comes as no surprise to learn that another member of the group was accustomed to turn herself into a horse, shod with horseshoes, and in that guise transport her fellow witches, and even the Devil himself, to and from the sabbat—with the result that the following day she was confined to bed with sore hands. Nor is it unexpected that the Forfar witches should sometimes have had less ordinary meals than those described above. In the event they confessed to digging up the corpse of a baby, making a pie of its flesh, and eating it; the purpose being to prevent themselves from ever confessing to their witchcraft—

just as, five centuries earlier, the heretics of Thrace and of Orleans were supposed to have been inwardly and irrevocably bound to their sect by consuming the ashes of babies' bodies. In the case of the Forfar witches it was a vain hope, for in Scottish trials torture was commonly employed until a confession was obtained.

Similar use is made of Isobel Gowdie's confession (or rather confessions, for under increasing pressure she made four) at Auldearn, in Nairn, in 1662:

> We would go to several houses in the night time. We were at Candlemas last in Grangehill, where we got meat and drink enough. The Devil sat at the head of the table, and all the Coven about. That night he desired Alexander Elder in Earlseat to say the grace before meat, which he did; and is this: "We eat this meat in the Devil's name" (etc.) And then we began to eat. And when we had ended eating, we looked steadfastly to the Devil, and bowing ourselves to him, we said to the Devil, We thank thee, our Lord, for this.—We killed an ox, in Burgie, about the dawning of the day, and we brought the ox with us home to Aulderne, and feasted on it.[22]

The simple dash between the two stories conceals much, including the following items:

> All the coven did fly like cats, jackdaws, hares and rooks, etc., but Barbara Ronald, in Brightmanney, and I always rode on a horse, which we would make of a straw or a bean-stalk. Bessie Wilson was always in the likeness of a rook. . . . (The Devil) would be like a heifer, a bull, a deer, a roe, or a dog, etc., and have dealings with us; and he would hold up his tail while we kissed his arse.[24]

Isobel Gowdie had much more to say. When she and her associates went to the sabbat they would place in the bed, beside their husbands, a broom or a three-legged stool, which promptly took on the appearance of a woman. At the sabbat they made a plough of a ram's horn and yoked frogs to it, using grass for the traces. As the plough went round the fields, driven by the Devil with the help of the male officer of the coven, the women followed it, praying to the Devil that the soil might yield only thistles and briars.

Murray cites Isobel Gowdie as an example of a witch who rode to and from meetings on horseback; the proof being Isobel's own words, "I had a little horse, and would say, 'Horse and Hattock, in the Devil's name!'" This, however, is the very phrase that fairies were believed to use as they flew from place to place; and the rest of Isobel's account shows that, in a desperate effort to find enough material to satisfy her interrogators and torturers, she did indeed draw on the local fairy lore:

> I had a little horse, and would say, "Horse and Hattock, in the Devil's name!" And then we would fly away, where we would, even as straws fly upon a highway. We would fly like straws when we please; wild-straws and corn-straws will be horses to us, if we put them between our feet and say, "Horse and Hattock, in the Devil's name!" If anyone sees these straws in a whirlwind, and do not bless themselves, we may shoot them dead at our pleasure. Any that are shot by us, their souls will go to Heaven, but their bodies remain with us, and will fly as our horses, as small as straws. I was in the Downie-hills, and got meat from the Queen of Fairie, more than I could eat. The Queen of Fairie is bravely clothed in white linen. . . .[24]

At this point Isobel's interrogators cut her short: she was straying too far from the demonological material they required. After a further three weeks in gaol she produced a version in which the fairies were duly integrated into the Devil's kingdom. The Devil himself, she asserted, shaped "elf-arrow-heads" and handed them over to small hunch-backed elves, who sharpened them and in turn passed them to the witches for shooting. As the witches had no bows, they flicked the arrows from their thumb-nails as they sailed overhead on their straws and bean-stalks; and the arrows killed those they hit, even through a coat of armour.[25] This is the passage that led Murray to her theory about the fugitive aboriginal race; others will interpret it in a different sense. Certainly we are a long, long way from those commonplace feastings at Grangehill and Auldearn.

At the risk of some repetitiousness we may add one further sample, concerning the famous sabbat supposed to have been held at a (non-existent) place called Blokulla, or Blockula, in Sweden, in 1669. Murray quotes the following passages from a contemporary English translation of a German pamphlet:

> Another boy confessed too, that one day he was carried away by his mistress, and to perform the journey he took his own father's horse out of the meadow where it was, and upon his return she let the horse go in her own ground. The next morning the boy's father sought for his horse, and not finding it, gave it over for lost; but the boy told him the whole story, and so his father fetched the horse back again. . . . In a huge large room of this house, they said, there stood a very long table, at which the witches did sit down.

... They sat down to table, and those that the Devil esteemed most, were placed nearest to him, but the children must stand at the door, where he himself gives them meat and drink. The diet they did use to have there, was, they said, broth and colworts and bacon in it, oatmeal, bread spread with butter, milk and cheese. And they added that sometimes it tasted very well, and sometimes very ill. [26]

The reader would hardly divine what followed the meal: the Devil mated with all the women present, and in due course they produced sons and daughters for him, who then married one another, and brought forth toads and serpents. Nor could one guess what other means of transportation were available for that same journey: "For their journey, they said they made use of all sorts of instruments, of beasts, of men, of spits and posts, according as they had the opportunity; if they do ride upon goats, and have many children with them, so that all may have room, they stick a spit into the back-side of the goat, and then are anointed with the aforesaid ointment"—which enables the whole party to fly through the air "over churches and high walls". [27]

Murray is of course aware of these fantastic features—but she never-theless contrives, by the way she arranges her quotations, to give the impression that a number of perfectly sober, realistic accounts of the sabbat exist. They do not; and the implications of that fact are, or should be, self-evident. Stories which have manifestly impossible features are not to be trusted in any particular, as evidence of what physically happened. Since the stories of witches' sabbats adduced by Murray abound in such features, they are to be strongly distrusted. As soon as the methods of historical criticism are applied to her argument that women really met to worship a fertility god, under the supervision of the god's human representatives, it is seen to be just as fanciful as the argument which Michelet had propounded, with far greater poetic power, some sixty years earlier.

If Arno Runeberg had troubled to trace Murray's quotations back to their origins, he would perhaps never have produced *Witches, demons and fertility magic* at all. But once published—by the Finnish Academy of Sciences in 1947—the book lent new credibility to Murray's central thesis. For it is by no means an unsophisticated work. It contains a mass of valuable information about European folk-beliefs, much of it directly relevant to the age-old popular image of the witch. It has no use at all for such fancies as the aboriginal race of dwarfs, or even for the Dianic cult in the sense of a homogeneous religion. Precisely because it avoids such eccentricities it has persuaded some serious historians, right down to the present day, that the witchcraft we hear of at the close of the Middle Ages was indeed derived from a fertility cult.[28]

Runeberg starts from pre-historic times. In a world still dominated by the wilderness, primitive hunters and farmers developed a form of magic which was intended to influence the spirits of forests and rivers and mountains. Popular fertility rites, such as have survived in many peasant communities almost to the present day, are derived from that magic. But apart from these rites, which were celebrated publicly, with the whole village participating, there existed a secret art, known only to specialists, i.e. to professional magicians. These magicians were men and women who had learned how to penetrate into the world of nature-spirits, how to become like those spirits, how to influence them and to partake of their powers. In the primitive world-view, nature-spirits and magicians alike "bestow fertility, wealth and strength on whomever they wish, at the same time that they smite their enemies with sickness and death".[29] The notion of the maleficent magician, or witch, arose from that of the "magical transfer": witches used magic to procure fertility and abundance in their own crops and herds, which implied inflicting a corresponding deprivation on one's neighbours.

The magicians formed associations, which met secretly, at night, to perform communal rites; and by the close of the Middle Ages these associations were being severely persecuted by the Church, for prac-tising a pagan cult. The Cathars were also being persecuted; and it was only natural that the two harassed and outlawed breeds should form an alliance, should indeed amalgamate. Effected in the first instance in the inaccessible valleys of southern France and of the Alps, this alliance or amalgamation gave rise to a new heretical sect, which spread gradually over vast areas of western Europe. This is the sect that we meet in the protocols of the witch-trials and the books of the witch-hunting magistrates. For Cathars and magicians alike, under the pressure of persecution, turned to Devil-worship. Traditional magic was trans-formed: "The participants in the 'sabbath' were no longer made up of primitive people who tried to influence fertility for their own benefit and according to their own conception of nature, but of sensation-mad, degenerated individuals who actually were convinced that they worshipped Satan himself. The incarnated deity of the witches was enacted by adventurers and rogues. . . ."[30]

In support of his view Runeberg lists a number of similarities be-tween, on the one hand, the accounts of the witches' sabbat and, on the other hand, various peasant rites and beliefs connected with fertility. The large sabbats were commonly supposed to be held at Easter, May

Day, Whitsuntide, Midsummer, All Saints' Day, Christmas or Lent; these are also the times for fertility rites. The sabbats were supposed to involve circular dances; these can be compared with the dance around the May-pole. Banqueting and love-making figure in both kinds of ceremony, and so do figures in animal masks. Runeberg points out, too, that the witches' Devil has some very unexpected features: he is often called by a name which is far more appropriate to a wood spirit than to the Devil of Christian demonology. Moreover at the end of the sabbat the Devil sometimes burns himself up—and this also happens to various puppets representing the corn-spirit or the wood-spirit. All this leads Runeberg to the truly Frazerian conclusion: popular fertility rites and the secret fertility rites of the witches have one and the same object—to kill the "old" spirit of nature and then to resurrect the same spirit in a new, youthful guise. Through all the deformations resulting from contact with Catharism and from the pressures of ecclesiastical persecution, this original sub-structure can still be discerned.

On the face of it, a plausible argument. Nevertheless, it does not prove the existence of an organized body of witches. There is simply no evidence that there ever was a secret society of magicians, devoted to fostering or exploiting the fertility of crops or herds; no theological treatise or confessor's guide even hints at such a thing. In his efforts to trace such a society Runeberg turns not to the Middle Ages, when he claims it existed, but to the sixteenth and seventeenth centuries; and not to primary sources but to Margaret Murray. In the end the only evidence he can produce turns out to consist of those very same accounts of witches' sabbats that we have just shown to be spurious. And the parallels between fertility rites and sabbats can all be explained without assuming that sabbats ever took place. A full century before Runeberg, Jacob Grimm established that certain folk beliefs, including beliefs about fertility, entered into the picture of the sabbat; but that proves nothing about the reality of the sabbat. Moreover, some of the features listed by Runeberg have a far more obvious explanation. It is not really surprising that when the Lord of Hell has to vanish, he should do so in flames. And if the times of the year when the large sabbats were supposed to be held were the times for fertility rites, they also coincide with major feasts and saints' days in the calendar of the Church. As witchcraft was imagined as a blasphemous parody of Christianity, it was only to be expected that witches would foregather at times which Christians regarded as particularly sacred. On the other hand, most forms of *maleficium* cannot possibly be explained as Runeberg tries to explain them, in terms of "magical transfer". Witches were supposed to harm their neighbours for the sake of revenge, or out of pure malice, or on the Devil's orders, and only occasionally and incidentally for the purpose of augmenting their own stocks of food.

Elliot Rose's sprightly book, *A Razor for a Goat*, was published by the University of Toronto Press in 1962. No fertility cult here: Margaret Murray is sharply criticized, both as historian and anthropologist, while Arno Runeberg is not even mentioned. But Rose is just as certain as they that an organization of witches existed, and just as ready to explain what it did, and why. He too goes back to pre-historic times. The famous cave-painting in the cave of the Trois Frères in the French Pyrenees, showing what may be a dancer in animal disguise, with great branching horns, is taken to represent the leader of a sorcerer's society. One wonders whether Rose realized that the picture is reckoned to be some 20,000 years old, for the argument moves at one bound to the arrival of Christianity in Northern Europe. Faced with that event, the society of sorcerers transformed itself into a secret sect, worshipping a god who was represented as half man, half animal, and adoring a leader as the god's manifestation. The leader was no longer disguised as a deer but as a goat; and this was interpreted, first by the Church and later by the sectarians themselves, as representing the great adversary of the Christian God, Satan. These sectarians were the witches; they were Devil-worshippers; and their leaders, when they dressed up as goat-like beings, were impersonating the Devil himself.

For Rose the libidinous aspects of the sabbat are all-important: the dancing, the copulation of the leader with his followers and of the followers with one another. They lead him to imagine a cult centering on ecstatic experiences, and specially attractive to women. In this view the witch-cult becomes a successor, in a Christianized Europe, of the Dionysian religion of ancient Greece: "The dancers are clearly Bacchantes or Mænads, and they are honouring the god who sends their frenzy. . . . They are his servants, inspired by him, submerging their individual wills in the inspiration." [31] The "flying ointments" used by the witches were ecstasy-inducing drugs. The leaders of the cult (Rose calls them "horned shamans") possessed the secret knowledge of herbs which temporarily released human beings from the limitations of humanity; they were experts in the concoction of herbal drugs. Once more one feels the *Zeitgeist* at work: just as Murray's *Witch-Cult* appeared when the vogue of *The Golden Bough* was at its height, so *A Razor for a Goat* was published just as the craze for psychedelic experiments and experiences was building up.

Rose accepts without question the reality of sabbat assemblies both large and small. The fact that the large sabbats were held at fixed times of the year has nothing to do with any fertility cult—it simply means that the witches, like their Greek precursors, "celebrated on great occasions of the year the spiritual energy released by the use of certain herbal drugs".[32] Moreover he thinks that originally the rites themselves probably differed from place to place, standardization being first achieved in the thirteenth century. The standardizers were goliards—wandering scholars who, despite their educational qualifications, had failed to find employment in the Church:

> I suggest they were able, by virtue of their superior education and of the knowledge they pooled with each other, to gain acceptance by witches as masters of the craft, in several places where the cult held out; and that they may have organized it and welded it into a ramifying secret society. . . . From this time the regular coven with its regular meetings, its constituted officers and its rigid discipline may have come into being; from this time thirteen is taken as the standard number in a cell. . . . Now uniformity became possible, and now itinerant witch-masters carried out their visits of inspection in their allotted circuits and met together to consult on the affairs of the craft and exchange the fruits of their learning and experience. Any practice that had formerly been purely local might now become the custom of the society as a whole. . . .[33]

In the sixteenth and seventeenth centuries, under the pressure of persecution, formal organization will have become still more important; so that in the end the forces of order did indeed find themselves faced with a massive underground organization of Devil-worshippers.

Rose's book ends with a startling comment. It mentions, as an established fact, that around 1590 the "Grand Coven" of Scotland, controlling "a large and powerful organization of covens" was headed by the Earl of Bothwell.[34] Now, so far from being an established fact, this is sheer fantasy—and the original begetter of the fantasy was none other than Margaret Murray. Ten pages of the *Witch-Cult*[35] are devoted to arguing that Francis Stewart, Earl of Bothwell, took on the role of Devil in an effort to induce Scottish witches to kill James VI by magical means, and so open the way for him to succeed to the throne. When the *Witch-Cult* first appeared a knowledgeable reviewer commented: "I cannot agree with Miss Murray's account of the Bothwell episode. I find no evidence for his having been the Devil except her desire to believe it."[36]; and anyone who reads the record of the trial of the alleged witches can only agree. Moreover, if we are to believe that Bothwell was the "Devil", then we must also believe that this great lord made a hundred or so of his male and female followers kiss his behind in the kirk of North Berwick. For that matter we must believe that he accompanied them through the air as they flew over the sea, to sink ships at his command. The accused, after prolonged and agonizing torture, said all these things of their Devil; only, they never said that he was the Earl of Bothwell.[37]

Clearly the "case" which Rose uses to clinch his argument was taken not from the original sources but from Murray. It is a revealing slip. Though he wrote his book largely in order to combat some of Murray's more glaring fallacies, he remained under her influence. By her selective use of sources Murray had been able to persuade others as well as herself that there really were covens, in the sense of fixed, local groups of witches; this was indeed one of her most original contributions to the misinterpretation of history. Rose adopted the idea of the coven without, it would seem, ever recognizing its origin or questioning its validity. Like Runeberg, he wrote a better book than the *Witch-Cult*. Like Runeberg, he made ingenious suggestions as to what an organization of witches might have been like. But when one asks for proofs that an organization of witches really existed, nothing is forthcoming beyond those sources which Murray had already offered—and which, when examined, turn out to be full of the wildest fantasies.

Less read, perhaps, than they used to be, the works of Montague Summers still deserve mention in this context. Both *The History of Witchcraft and Demonology* and *The Geography of Witchcraft* were originally published, in 1926 and 1927 respectively, in the Kegan Paul series "The History of Civilization", edited by that eminent Cambridge personality C. K. Ogden. Both were republished as recently as 1963–5; and some of their basic contentions continue to be taken seriously by some historians down to the present day. Summers claimed, though with doubtful justification, to be in holy orders. What is certain is that he was a religious fanatic: a Roman Catholic of a kind now almost extinct—obsessed by thoughts of the Devil, perpetually ferreting out Satan's servants whether in past epochs or in the contemporary world; horrified yet at the same time fascinated by tales of Satan-worship, promiscuous orgies, cannibalistic infanticide and the rest. He was also a prolific writer, whose productions included, in addition to the works mentioned above, half a dozen editions and translations of witch-hunters' manuals, three books on werewolves and vampires, a book on the Marquis de Sade and numerous editions of Restoration comedies.

For Summers witches were what the witch-hunters of the fifteenth, sixteenth and seventeenth centuries said they were: members of a conspiracy, organized and controlled by Satan, to bring about the destruction of Christianity and the spiritual and physical ruination of mankind. The confessions given in witchcraft trials and the stories in the manuals and memoirs of witch-hunting magistrates are accepted as true in essentials. "We know," he writes, "that the Continental stories of witch gatherings are with very few exceptions the chronicle of actual fact." (38) And again: "There persists a congeries of solid proven fact which cannot be ignored, save by the purblind prejudice of the rationalist, and cannot be accounted for save that we recognize that there were and are organizations deliberately nay, even enthusiastically, devoted to the service of evil." (39)

Not that Summers himself wholly denies the claims of rationalism, for he follows Murray in playing down the manifestly impossible features in the accounts of the sabbat. Where a sabbat story can be made to look natural by omitting certain details, he omits them. The physical presence of the Devil at the sabbat is interpreted as Murray interpreted it: men impersonated the Devil (and sure enough, one of those men was Francis Stewart, Earl of Bothwell). As for flight through the air, Summers claims that it rarely figures in such accounts (though in fact it is a stock feature). (40) In his basic outlook Summers is utterly opposed to Murray and her disciples: for them witchcraft is a purely human creation, for him it is an extreme manifestation of the unremitting war of Satan against God. But he is just as convinced as they that an organization of witches existed, and held meetings—and just as unable to produce any credible evidence for that view; or rather, any evidence that remains credible if pursued to its source.

The school of thought we have been considering is by no means extinct, even amongst professional historians. On the contrary, it has recently found a new and vigorous exponent in Professor Jeffrey Russell, of the University of California. Professor Russell is a distinguished medievalist who has specialized in the history of religious dissent. His *Witchcraft in the Middle Ages*, published by the Cornell University Press in 1972, is by far the most learned attempt ever made to show that witchcraft really did involve an anti-Christian cult. It could well convince many who have not been convinced by any of the works mentioned above.

As its title indicates, the book deals not with the great witch-hunt of the sixteenth and seventeenth centuries but with its medieval antecedents. More specifically, it aims to show that witchcraft was a cult, indeed a sect, which developed out of medieval heresy: "The development of medieval witchcraft is closely bound to that of heresy, the struggle for the expression of religious feeling beyond the limits tolerated by the Church." [41] Like heresy, medieval witchcraft can be understood only if it is studied in the context in which it flourished— the context of a profoundly Christian civilization. It was a protest against the dominant religion, and this meant that it was also a form of social rebellion: "The witch was a rebel against Church and society at a time when the two were wholly identified." [42] That is why towards the close of the Middle Ages, in a time of economic, political and social crisis, witchcraft increased along with other forms of revolt. [43]

Russell does not, of course, claim that every form of religious dissent, or heresy, contributed to the development of witchcraft; but he does claim that one particular tendency, perhaps even one particular tradition, contributed mightily. The groups which he regards as representative of that tendency or tradition are in the main the groups described in the second and third chapters of the present volume. But whereas in the present volume the stories which were told about those groups are treated as examples of demonization, Russell believes them to have been more truthful than not. In his view the canons of Orleans who were burned in 1022, the victims of Conrad of Marburg in Germany in 1231–3 and various German and Italian groups in the fourteenth and fifteenth centuries did in all probability worship the Devil and hold indiscriminate erotic orgies, even on occasion kill and eat babies. [44] Indeed, he regards these groups as being already, in all essentials, organizations of witches. Writing of the period 1000–1150 he comments: "Through its connection with heresy, witchcraft in this period witnessed the addition of new elements and the further development and definition of older ones: the sex orgy, the feast, the secret meetings at night in caves, cannibalism, the murder of children, the express renunciation of God and adoration of demons, the desecration of the cross and the sacraments. All these had now become fixed elements in the composition of witchraft." [45] And when we come to the thirteenth century the section on Conrad of Marburg's victims is headed simply "heretic witches". By the time of the great witch-hunt new features have appeared, but most of these too are treated as reflecting real practices. Of course witches did not fly through the air, but witches' sabbats took place, and in very much the form traditionally ascribed to them. Instead of being held in a cave or cellar they were held in the open air; the participants were mostly women; and the proceedings were dominated throughout by a being who was understood to be the Devil. Still addicted to their old practices, blasphemous, promiscuous and cannibalistic, the witches nevertheless devoted much of their attention to their master. They kissed his behind and, being mostly women, copulated with him. Russell considers that "the stirrings of feminine discontent" may have contributed to "the orgiastic elements in the witches' revels"; but he also notes that copulation with the Devil was not pleasurable. He advances a number of hypotheses in explanation of this paradox; one being that "we cannot suppose that . . . a woman submitting sexually to a being she believes to be the Devil can be wholly relaxed".[46]

The witches of the fifteenth, sixteenth and seventeenth centuries, then, were adherents of the most extreme of all heresies, members of the most nihilistic of all sects. But this heresy and this sect were the products of a Christian society which insisted on religious conformity, and they drew new strength from every drive to enforce that conformity. The Inquisition was largely responsible for the spread of witchcraft, but only because of all institutions it was the one most directly concerned with repressing dissent. In the last analysis medieval Christian civilization as a whole was responsible.

Yet if that is the main purport of Russell's argument, it is not the whole purport; for, like so many before him, he also believes that witchcraft was partly rooted in folk practices and beliefs connected with fertility. Fully aware of the inadequacies of Margaret Murray's work, he nevertheless takes her central thesis seriously. Like Runeberg, he holds that fertility rites, with dancing, eroticism, banqueting and the rest, were transformed by the pressures of a hostile Christian society into the witches' sabbat.[47] Moreover he considers that "enormous weight" has been lent to Runeberg's view by the researches of the Italian scholar Carlo Ginzburg. As he sees it, Ginzburg's book *I Benandanti*, published in 1966, illustrates how members of a fertility cult were transformed into witches. Up to 1610 a group of peasants in the district of Friuli in northern Italy fought pitched battles at night against "members of the local witch cult"; by 1640, after a generation of inquisitorial trials, they were generally regarded, and even regarded themselves, as being Devil-worshipping witches. In Russell's view "no firmer bit of evidence has ever been presented that witchcraft existed".[48]

Such is the case presented in *Witchcraft in the Middle Ages* for believing that there really was an organization, indeed a sect, of witches. It is presented with great erudition and persuasiveness—and nevertheless it completely fails to stand up.

To deal first with the matter of the fertility cult: the whole argument is based on a misreading of *I Benandanti*. For as described by Ginzburg, the Friuli peasants did not really fight battles with "members of the local witch cult"—they went into cataleptic trances during which they *dreamed* that, mounted on boats and cats, they fought witches. All that happened physically was that they lay motionless in bed, as though dead, for a couple of hours. The true significance of Ginzburg's researches will be considered in a later chapter. Here it is only necessary to note that they do not in any way confirm Runeberg's contention that real gatherings of fertility cultists were transformed, by persecution, into witches' sabbats.

That Russell should so misunderstand the purport of Ginzburg's book is itself significant. It points to a methodological confusion which leads him into other, more serious errors. "What people thought happened," he writes, "is as interesting as what 'objectively did happen', and much more certain." [49] No doubt—but the two things are by no means the same. Thirty or forty years ago great numbers of Germans believed that world affairs were in the hands of the Jews, who in turn were controlled by a secret government known as the Elders of Zion; while great numbers of Russians believed that Soviet society was riddled from top to bottom by followers of Trotsky who were also agents of the "imperialist" powers. In both cases, the prevalence of such beliefs facilitated the destruction of many millions of human beings. The historian's interpretation of those events will differ greatly according to whether he regards the beliefs as having been substantially correct or, on the contrary, grossly misguided. In the case of the great witch-hunt the situation was, as we shall see, more complex than in the modern persecutions; but it is still the historian's task to distinguish between fact and fantasy so far as is humanly possible.

The task is not as insuperable as Russell, in certain passages, makes it sound. My own grounds for not accepting the existence of a sect of orgiastic, infanticidal, cannibalistic, Devil-worshipping heretics between the eleventh and fifteenth centuries have been given in detail in Chapter III and need not be repeated here. Russell himself explicitly states that charges of ritually murdering children and consuming their blood were "absurd" when brought against Jews; [50] had he included the case of the Fraticelli in his study, he might have concluded, as I did, that similar stereotyped accusations were no more justified when levelled against heretics. My grounds for not accepting even in part the tales of witches' sabbats, as they were retailed from the fifteenth century onwards, have been made abundantly clear in the course of the present chapter. In my view, stories which contain manifestly impossible elements ought not to be accepted as evidence for physical events.

There is a further reason why the notion of a secret society of witches cannot be satisfactorily explained by postulating the real existence of such a society. As we shall see in a later chapter, present-day anthropologists have found very similar notions firmly embedded in the world-views of "primitive" societies in various parts of the world. Bands of destructive witches who kill human beings, especially children; who travel at night by supernatural means; and who foregather in remote spots to devour their victims—these crop up again and again in anthropological literature. But anthropologists are agreed that these bands exist in imagination only; nobody has ever come across a real society of witches. And that indeed is the nub: from Jarcke and Mone onwards, the tradition we have been considering has suffered from the same defect, of grossly underestimating the capacities of human imagination.

Taken as a whole, that tradition itself forms a curious chapter in the history of ideas. Over a period of a century and a half, the non-existent society of witches has been repeatedly re-interpreted in the light of the intellectual preoccupations of the moment. The theories of Jarcke and Mone were clearly inspired by the current dread of secret societies; that of Michelet, by his enthusiasm for the emancipation of the working classes and of women; those of Murray and Runeberg, by the Frazerian belief that religion originally consisted of fertility cults; those of Rose and Russell, maybe, by the spectacle of the psychedelic and orgiastic experiments of the 1960s.

But it is time to turn to the other traditional explanation of how the stereotype of a sect of witches came into being in medieval Europe.

7

THREE FORGERIES AND ANOTHER WRONG TRACK

-I-

Most historians who were not persuaded that a sect of witches really existed have accepted that the stereotype came into being during, and as a result of, the Inquisition's campaign against Catharism in southern France and northern Italy. They have also been in agreement about the immediate consequences: in France, the execution of the first living example of the stereotype, a woman burned at Toulouse in 1275; the first mass trial and execution of witches, carried out in 1335, also at Toulouse; other similar trials, resulting by 1350 in the execution of some 400 persons at Toulouse and a further 200 at Carcassonne; in Italy, a woman of Orta, in the diocese of Novara, tried and presumed burned some time between 1341 and 1352; further trials and executions around 1360, in the neighbouring diocese of Como.

These particulars are to be found already in the earliest scholarly history devoted to the witch-trials, that by Wilhelm Gottlieb Soldan, published in German in 1843; [1] they are given very fully in Joseph Hansen's great history, published in German in 1900; [2] and they are still to be found in the most recent histories by the most reputable scholars. They are nevertheless false from start to finish: none of these things really happened. The entire story can be shown to rest on three fabrications, dating respectively from the fifteenth, sixteenth and nineteenth centuries. As what is involved amounts to a major revision of the history of the witch-hunt, the matter calls for detailed exposition—and if detailed expositions can sometimes be tedious, this one has at least the attraction of the bizarre.

Hansen's influence on twentieth-century historians has been so great that it is reasonable to start with him. He mentions the earliest case in three separate passages, the most striking of which can be translated as follows:

(In the year 1275) the Dominican Hugues de Beniols (or de Bajol), who was at that time inquisitor at Toulouse, carried out in the town a persecution of heretics and sorcerers, in the course of which a widely respected woman, Angela de la Barthe, was denounced by her neighbours as suspect of having dealings with the Devil. The 56-year-old woman confessed to the judge that for many years a demon had visited her and had intercourse with her every night. From this intercourse was born a monster, wolf above, serpent below, and human in between. She fed the monster on small children, making nocturnal excursions to catch these. After two years the monster vanished. The woman, who was obviously mentally deranged, was handed over by the inquisitor to the secular arm. On the orders of the seneschal she was burned in the square of St Stephen at Toulouse, along with several other individuals who had confessed to being magicians, necromancers and diviners. . . .[3]

As his sole source for this story Hansen gives the *Histoire de l'Inquisition en France*, by the Baron de Lamothe-Langon, published in Paris in 1829. The relevant passage in Lamothe-Langon, however, turns out to contain no primary source but merely another summary of the story, accompanied by references to two earlier works: the *Histoire ecclésiastique et civile de la ville et diocèse de Carcassonne*, by the Augustinian monk T. Bouges, Paris, 1741; and the Chronicle of Bardin.[4] On examination these two sources melt into one: Bouges has simply translated the story of Angela de la Barthe from a chronicle written around 1455 by a councillor of the *parlement* of Toulouse called Guillaume Bardin.[5] And that chronicle is the earliest known source of the story.

But the chronicle of Guillaume Bardin is highly unreliable. In the seventeenth and early eighteenth centuries it was trusted and used by many historians; but in 1742, the very year after the publications of Bouges's history, the great scholar Dom Joseph Vaissete printed it in the fourth volume of his *Histoire générale de Languedoc*, and at the same time entered a caveat. In his view a chronicle so manifestly inaccurate might well be a fabrication, concocted by some unknown impostor in the sixteenth or seventeenth century. And although Vaissete went too far— Bardin's authorship is not seriously in doubt—his instinct was sound. When Auguste Molinier came to re-edit Bardin at the beginning of the present century, as part of a new edition of the *Histoire générale*, he too insisted that the chronicler was careless, even somewhat unscrupulous, and not above falsifying his documentary sources.[6]

These strictures certainly apply to the passage concerning Angela de la Barthe, for this contains a ruinous blunder. Bardin says nothing of the inquisitor Hugues de Beniols: that detail was added by Lamothe-Langon, who took the name from a standard list of the inquisitors for

Toulouse. [7] Instead, Bardin attributes the whole persecution not to the Inquisition but to a seneschal of Toulouse called Pierre de Voisins; and he goes on: "I have had in my hands, and have read, the sentence pronounced by the seneschal, in which all these things are laid out." [8] But it is known that Pierre de Voisins had ceased to be seneschal of Toulouse by late 1254, and was dead long before 1275; [9] so Bardin cannot possibly have read such a sentence.

The spuriousness of the story is confirmed by the silence of the contemporary sources. The sole contemporary mention of a witch-trial around 1275 says simply that the royal judge of Carcassonne, Barthelemi Dupuy, in 1274 tried a woman accused of simple sorcery. [10] Perhaps this brief comment prompted Bardin to his flight of fancy; but however that may be, it is certain that Angela de la Barthe never existed. And indeed one might have guessed as much from the details of the story itself: the case has no real parallel in any recorded witch-trial, early or late, but represents, rather, an amalgam of various ideas about witches and about monstrous births, such as would have been familiar to a fifteenth-century lawyer like Bardin.

Yet the story as given by Hansen is not entirely the work of Bardin. It was the Baron de Lamothe-Langon who turned Angela into a lady of rank and gave her the age of fifty-six; who transformed her judge from a seneschal into an inquisitor; who located the place of her execution as the square of St Stephen at Toulouse. And one may reasonably ask on what authority this nineteenth-century writer made these additions to the traditional story—had he some source at his disposal other than Bardin and Bouges? The answer is that his source and authority lay simply in his own fertile brain. In 1823, six years before he published his *Histoire de l'Inquisition*, Lamothe-Langon had helped edit a *Biographie toulousaine*. The entry on the fictitious Angela is clearly from his pen— and it contains, in addition to all these new "facts", the curious sentence: "The chronicler Bardin adds that the sentence pronounced on this insane woman was still extant in his time. And truly it is to be found in the archives of the Parlement (of Toulouse); all these facts are given there at great length. . . ." [11] So, like Bardin before him, Lamothe-Langon claims first-hand knowledge of a document which, as we have seen, never existed at all. As for other sources, not a word.

That is only the beginning of the story. The notion of the witches' sabbat, in particular, is supposed to have been generated by the persecution of the Cathars and to have reached its full development as that persecution drew to its close: by 1330–5 the inquisitors at Toulouse and Carcassonne are said to have been trying women on charges of attending the sabbat and of practising Devil-worship as an expression of the Dualist religion. Briefly mentioned by Soldan, these trials are given fifteen pages of Hansen's history.[12] More importantly, in the massive collection of original sources which he published to accompany his history he printed what purport to be records of the trial proceedings, translated into French.[13] In this case the whole of the material is taken from Lamothe-Langon's *Histoire de l'Inquisition*.

The most striking of the trial records consists of the confessions of two witches, Anne-Marie de Georgel, and Catherine, wife of Pierre Delort, both of Toulouse.[14] These confessions, which are explicitly stated to have been extracted by torture, contain lurid descriptions of the sabbat which the women had been attending, and of the *maleficia* which they had been practising, for many years. But they also contain a distorted version of Catharist doctrine:

> Questioned concerning the Apostles' Creed and the faith that every believer owes to our holy religion, (Anne-Marie de Georgel) answered, as a true daughter of Satan, that between God and the Devil there is complete equality; that the first is king of heaven and the second king of the earth; that all souls which the Devil succeeds in seducing are lost for the All-High and remain for ever between earth and sky; that every night these souls visit the houses they used to inhabit, and try to induce in their children and relatives a desire to serve the Devil rather than God.
>
> She also said that this struggle between God and the Devil has lasted from all eternity and will continue for ever; that now one and now the other has been victorious, but that at present things are developing in such a way that Satan's triumph is assured.

Catherine, wife of Pierre Delort, said much the same:

> Questioned concerning the Apostles' Creed and the faith that every believer owes to our holy religion, she answered that between God and the Devil there is complete equality; that the first reigns in heaven and the second on earth; that the struggle between them will never end; that one should choose to serve the Devil, because he is wicked and because he can command the souls of the dead, which he sends against us to disturb our reason; that the reign of Jesus Christ in this world was temporary and is now drawing to its close; and that Antichrist will appear and wage battle on behalf of the Devil, etc.

The implications are weighty. On the strength of this document it has been widely assumed that the inquisitors operating at Toulouse in the 1330s, being familiar both with the facts of *maleficium* and with Catharist doctrine, combined the two, distorting both in the process, and so arrived at the notion of a sect of witches that assembled at intervals to worship the Devil in corporeal form. By the use of torture they were able to force some women of lowly status to produce confessions in which they described these assemblies and denounced the other participants. The immediate result was the first mass witch-hunt; the long-term result, the creation of a new stereotype, which was to legitimate further and larger witch-hunts, extending from the fourteenth to the seventeenth century. All this would indeed follow if the document were genuine; but none of it does, for the document can be shown to be a nineteenth-century forgery.

The context that Lamothe-Langon gives to the confessions—and which Hansen omitted to examine—shows them to be spurious. For in Lamothe-Langon's history the confessions are presented as part of a sermon preached by the inquisitor Pierre Guidonis in the cloisters of St Stephen's at Toulouse, on an occasion when he pronounced judgement on no less than sixty-three persons accused of heresy or witchcraft. Lamothe-Langon lists by name a number of personages, ecclesiastical and lay, who are supposed to have been present on that solemn occasion; they include six "capitouls", or members of the town council of Toulouse. But whereas the six capitouls named really were in office in 1335, the inquisitor was not. This is not to deny that Pierre Guidonis existed—he was in fact the nephew of the famous inquisitor Bernard Guidonis (or Gui). But in 1335 Pierre Guidonis was not an inquisitor at all but was the prior of the Dominican convent at Carcassonne. If he was ever inquisitor at Toulouse at all, it can only have been in 1344; and even this is more than doubtful.[15] Nor can the mistake be due to a mere slip of the pen—by 1344 not one of the capitouls listed by Lamothe-Langon was still in office.[16] It is quite impossible that any contemporary source should have listed these men as being present at an inquisitorial judgement by Pierre Guidonis. From this it follows that the document which Lamothe-Langon claims as his source never existed; and the confessions of Anne-Marie de Georgel and Catherine, wife of Pierre Delort, evaporate into thin air.

Much else evaporates with them. According to Lamothe-Langon, every single one of the sixty-three persons judged on that occasion was found guilty; eight being executed, eleven sentenced to life imprisonment and the rest to twenty years' imprisonment. Elsewhere he states: "Between 1320 and 1350 the inquisition of Carcassonne passed more than 400 sentences for the single offence of magic; more than 200 of these entailed the death penalty. The inquisition of Toulouse was still more severe: 600 persons appeared before it; and two-thirds of these were executed by the secular arm. These abominable executions continued during the last part of the century." [17] And in fact the trials listed extend right down to the 1480s. These statements provide the sole basis for the belief, which has by now become a commonplace, that the Inquisition conducted a massive witch-hunt in the south of France, reaching its height during the fourteenth century and continuing at intervals until late in the fifteenth.

We shall be considering in a later chapter what developments in the fourteenth century really did prepare the way for the great witch-hunt, and what share the Inquisition really did have in those developments. Here there is no need to go into detail—a few simple facts are enough to show that the witch-hunts listed by Lamothe-Langon cannot possibly have taken place.

It is true that in 1320 the inquisitors of Toulouse and Carcassonne were empowered by Pope John XXII to proceed against practitioners of certain types of magic. [18] But neither the pope nor the inquisitors were thinking of anything remotely resembling Lamothe-Langon's witches. The papal instructions contain not a word about assemblies of Devil-worshipping women; and when Bernard Guidonis produced his classic manual for inquisitors, on the basis of his experience as inquisitor for the whole area between Toulouse, Albi and Carcassonne from 1307 to 1324, he too had nothing to say about such matters. [19] Indeed, the inquisitors showed little enthusiasm for carrying out even the limited instructions given by the pope. In 1329 the inquisitor of Carcassonne did sentence a monk to life imprisonment for practising love-magic; but that is the only trial of an alleged magician that is known, on solid historical grounds, to have been conducted by any one of the many inquisitors of Carcassonne or of Toulouse during the fourteenth century.

In 1330 the pope in effect withdrew the authorization. He issued instructions that any sorcery trials then being conducted in France, whether by inquisitors or by bishops, should be completed as quickly as possible; that the documents should be sent to him; and that no more cases should be undertaken. [20] Thereafter such trials were carried out not by inquisitors but by commissions specially appointed by the pope. During the period 1330–50, when according to Lamothe-Langon the inquisitors of Toulouse and Carcassonne were burning witches by the hundred, they were in reality confined to their traditional role of pursuing heretics.

There is no doubt about it: there never was an inquisitorial witch-hunt at Toulouse or at Carcassonne. Not only the famous trial of 1335 but the whole saga was invented by Lamothe-Langon. We are faced with a spectacular historical hoax.

–2–

A hoax of this kind fits perfectly into the career of Lamothe-Langon. For Lamothe-Langon was not a historian at all but the author of innumerable vaguely historical novels, with a marked taste for the sinister, the mysterious and the melodramatic. He came from Toulouse: the countryside and city where he sets his drama of witches' sabbats and witch-burnings was familiar to him in every detail. Also, he specialized in fabricating spurious historical sources, which he produced in thousands upon thousands of pages. For such a man nothing would have been easier, or more diverting, than to concoct the confessions of Anne-Marie de Georgel and Catherine, wife of Pierre Delort.

The matter, and the man, call for closer attention.[21] Etienne-Léon de Lamothe (to give him his original name) was born in 1786, of a noble family: his ancestors included capitouls, his father, grandfather and great-grandfather had all been councillors of the *parlement* of Toulouse. Along with a number of similar public figures from Toulouse, his father was guillotined in Paris by the revolutionary government in 1794; which, since Mme de Lamothe was a totally ineffective person, left the eight-year-old boy to manage his life for himself. He avoided any formal schooling and educated himself in his father's library, devouring every book he could lay hands on, indiscriminately and without any kind of guidance. At the age of sixteen he began to write, and within four years he had turned out four tragedies, six comedies, three operas, a novel and sundry other works. And if these juvenilia circulated in manuscript only, by the age of twenty-two he had published four novels, including a five-volume novel on the troubadours which was translated into English, German and Italian.

Meanwhile a tumultuous love-life with a series of fashionable mistresses, first at Toulouse, then in Paris, consumed the remnants of a fortune which had never been large. Lamothe set out to find employment in the imperial administration, and he found it—first as auditor to the Conseil d'Etat, then, at the age of twenty-five, as sub-prefect of Toulouse. He carried out his duties with distinction and proved himself a good administrator. On the other hand, it would be absurd to take seriously his claim that during this period he also laid the foundations of his *Histoire de l'Inquisition* by studying manuscript sources.[22] His appointment at Toulouse lasted only two years (1811–13) and was certainly no sinecure. Moreover, he had no training in paleography; and when he quotes unpublished materials, he never supplies verbatim transcriptions—as serious historians commonly did, even at that time.

Lamothe's administrative career was closely identified with the imperial cause—during the Hundred Days he resumed service, as sub-prefect at Carcassonne—and with the final overthrow of Napoleon all prospects of official employment vanished. He tried to ingratiate himself with the royalists by writing a satirical account of his late master, entitled *Bonaparte*; but in vain. So he turned to writing as a full-time occupation. Under the names of Lamothe-Houdancourt (from 1815 to 1817) and of Lamothe-Langon (from 1817), and also under a vast number of pseudonyms, he became the most abundantly productive author in France, in an age when many authors were abundantly productive.

In the years following Napoleon's fall the public was insatiable for novels, criticism was at low ebb, publishers were concerned with quantity not quality, and the few novelists who existed were mostly poor devils whose only choice lay between non-stop production and starvation. Lamothe did at least make a great deal of money (which he spent as fast as he made it, or faster) but at the cost of becoming the supreme hack in a generation of hacks. Late in life he commented bitterly on his fate: "Despite the force of temperament and the mental energy with which I was blessed by our divine Creator, I could no longer carry on. . . . Fifty years of unremitting labour, beginning each day between three and four o'clock in the morning and continuing to two o'clock in the afternoon—labour surpassing and crushing human strength—in the end extinguished my imagination and annihilated my energy." [23] In sheer bulk his achievement was indeed prodigious— some 400 works, in prose and verse, representing some 1,500 volumes of manuscript.

The three-volume *Histoire de l'Inquisition* can be justly appreciated only against this background. Lamothe-Langon himself made high claims for the work: "For twenty years I collected valuable material . . . brought together scattered documents . . . I venture to call it a truly Benedictine work . . ." [24] In reality, his preoccupations and methods had little in common with those of the patient historians of Saint-Maur. The *Histoire* appeared after a whole series of horrific novels with titles like *Tête de mort, ou la Croix du cimetière de Saint-Aubin; les Mystères de la tour Saint-Jean, ou les Chevaliers du Temple; les Apparitions du château de Tarabel, ou le Protecteur invisible; le Monastère des frères noirs, ou l'Étendard de la mort; la Vampire ou la Vierge de Hongrie.* More-over the very year 1829, which saw the publication of the *Histoire*, also saw the publication of no less than twenty other volumes by Lamothe-Langon! For such a man the labour of historical research was clearly out of the question.

It is easy enough to divine what inspiration lay behind this particular work. In a pamphlet which he wrote to smooth the way for his history, Lamothe-Langon mentions Llorente's *Critical History of the Spanish Inquisition.* This work, by a former Spanish inquisitor, had been published in French translation in 1817–18, and by 1829 there had been three French, three German, two English and two Dutch editions. Nothing could be more natural than for Lamothe-Langon to try to imitate so successful a production. Only he failed; his history passed almost unnoticed, was never reprinted, and had no translations. Moreover when, from about 1880 onwards, French historians began serious work on the Inquisition in the south of France, they passed over Lamothe-Langon in silence, as unworthy of notice.[26] And no doubt the book would have been altogether forgotten if Joseph Hansen—himself a most honourable and devoted archivist and historian—had not, in the simplicity of his heart, reprinted the supposed reports of witch-trials it contains.

Neither Hansen himself, nor the many historians who have followed in his footsteps, would have been so easily deceived if they had examined some of the works which Lamothe-Langon produced after the *Histoire de l'Inquisition.* For from that date onwards he turned out volume after volume of spurious memoirs, attributed either to figures famous in French history or else to individuals who had been close to such figures. Four of these memoirs, each in several volumes, appeared in the very same year as the *Histoire*: *Mémoires historiques et anecdotiques du duc de Richelieu, Mémoires de madame la comtesse du Barry, Mémoires et souvenirs d'un pair de France* and above all *Mémoires d'une femme de qualité,* which achieved an international success. And thereafter, although Lamothe-Langon continued to write novels as before, this new genre became his principal and most profitable speciality: in all he produced twenty-four memoirs, totalling ninety volumes, in seventeen years.

For our present purpose the memoirs attributed to Napoleon and to Louis XVIII are particularly relevant, for they show that Lamothe-Langon did indeed possess all the skill and audacity required to fabricate and launch a historical myth. Not only are the *Mémoires de Napoléon Bonaparte* (1834) presented as the work of the emperor himself, but a projected continuation is announced in the following terms: "Here, without doubt, is the most important publication of the century. There need be no fear that anyone will confuse the great man's authentic memoirs with the multitude of memoirs and recollections that are constantly appearing. . . . These most valuable memoirs were completed on the isle of Elba. Brought back to the Tuileries, they were left in the emperor's study. . . . Later, they were placed in the hands of the same person to whom Louis XVIII had entrusted his own memoirs, about which nobody had ever raised any doubts." [27] The reference is to the spurious memoirs of Louis XVIII, which were also the work of Lamothe-Langon.

As for the *Mémoires de Louis XVIII* and the *Soirées de S.M. Louis XVIII*, it is thanks to them that one specific, notorious imposture, which would otherwise have been quickly forgotten, has continued to intrigue and deceive some people right down to our times. In the 1830s a deserter from the Prussian army, called Naundorff, appeared in France and claimed to be Louis XVII, i.e. the Dauphin who in reality had died in prison during the Revolution. The man was quickly unmasked and expelled from France. Lamothe-Langon, however, inserted into his spurious memoirs of Louis XVIII various remarks suggesting that the Dauphin had not in fact perished and might well be Naundorff. He also inserted into other spurious memoirs, attributed to other personalities, passages which seemed to corroborate this view of the matter; and so constructed a whole body of self-supporting but completely fictitious evidence which still continues, at intervals, to give rise to further outbursts of argument and to fresh crops of books. One such occasion was around 1910; at that time Dr de Santi, the Toulousain expert on Lamothe-Langon, produced a pamphlet in which he showed that the "proofs" of the pro-Naundorff faction consisted almost wholly of passages culled from books which, whatever their ostensible authors, were really all by Lamothe-Langon. Not that that put an end to the affair—a new pro-Naundorff campaign was launched in 1954! [28]

Fortified with these insights into the personality and methods of Lamothe-Langon, we may return to his most successful hoax, the imaginary witch-hunt in fourteenth-century Languedoc. Although in the preface to his history he claims to have studied manuscript sources in various archives, he makes no such claim in respect of the confessions of Anne-Marie Georgel and Catherine, wife of Pierre Delort. On the contrary, this text is described in a footnote as "extracted from the archives of the Inquisition of Toulouse, by Father Hyacinthe Sermet, metropolitan bishop of the South". Now, Antoine-Pascal-Hyacinthe Sermet really existed. [29] Born at Toulouse in 1732, he started as a

Carmelite monk and rose to be provincial of his order. He was a man of some erudition, and at one time concerned himself with the history of the Inquisition of Toulouse. Nevertheless, it is highly improbable that he ever made any extracts from the archives of the Inquisition. In the single, twelve-page article which was all that he ever published on the subject, he makes it plain that he had not discovered any unpublished sources.[30] That was in 1790, when Sermet was already fifty-eight and had reached the end of his career as a scholar. For with the coming of the Revolution he became deeply involved in politics. He was one of the clerics who accepted appointments from the revolutionary government—in 1791 he took office as the metropolitan bishop of the Haute-Garonne, in defiance of his superiors. "Le Père Sermet", as he popularly was called, became a most controversial figure, denounced by his archbishop, pouring out political pamphlets in Provençal, taking part in ecclesiastical councils sponsored by the government and even—having conferred on himself the title of "metropolitan bishop of the South"—holding a provincial council of his own at Carcassonne. He continued in this style until 1801, when the changing political climate induced him to retire on a pension; after which he spent his last few years in obscurity and died in Paris. So it is hard to see when or how Sermet could have carried out the labours which Lamothe-Lagon attributes to him. On the other hand, by the time the attribution was made he was in no position to comment, for he had been dead for twenty-one years.

But all this is beside the point. We have already demonstrated, from internal evidence, that the whole passage containing the confessions is spurious. It remains to consider what models Lamothe-Langon had before him when he concocted it.

Practically all Lamothe-Langon's voluminous manuscripts were destroyed after his death, but fortunately this particular problem can be solved without recourse to manuscript sources. In the preface to his history Lamothe-Langon mentions that he knew (how could he fail to?) the famous *Historia Inquisitionis* of the seventeenth-century Dutch Protestant Philipp van Limborch, and that he had been particularly struck by the appendix, which contains a number of sentences passed by the inquisitors of Toulouse.[31] The documents in this *Liber Sententiarium Inquisitionis Tholosanae* not only give the text of the sermons and sentences but list the various clerics who were present on each occasion; and they also mention that royal officials and capitouls were in attendance. Lamothe-Langon would have needed to look no further for the framework of his fabrication. The sermon by which Bernard Guidonis in 1322 sentenced a number of heretics to various penalties, for instance, would have provided an admirable model for the imaginary sermon which Lamothe-Langon attributes to Bernard's nephew Pierre.[32] Two other works mentioned by Lamothe-Langon will have supplied him with the names of the personages who are supposed to have been involved. An old and well-known history of Toulouse, La Faille's *Annales de la Ville de Toulouse*, gives the names of the six capitouls for 1335, in almost exactly the same order.[33] The fatal error concerning Pierre Guidonis, on the other hand, can be traced back to Percin's list of inquisitors of Toulouse, published in 1693.[34] It is typical of Lamothe-Langon that, having taken both the name and the date from Percin, and constructed a whole melodrama around them, he should add: "By an inexplicable oversight, Father Percin did not include in his list Pierre Guidonis, who was functioning as an inquisitor in 1334."[35]

To find models for the witches' confessions he will naturally have had to look to a later historical period, when the new stereotype of the witch was fully developed. An obvious source would be Pierre de Lancre's *Tableau de l'Inconstance des Mauvais Anges*, which was published in 1612. This celebrated work, which has always been easily available, reveals in great detail the beliefs of a witch-hunting magistrate at the height of the great witch-hunt, and the correspondence with Lamothe-Langon's account is exact. The initial appearance of the Devil in the form of a black man; the pact, concluded at midnight; the witch transported by a mere effort of will to a sabbat held usually on Friday nights, though in the most varied places; the Devil in the form of a gigantic black goat, presiding over the sabbat and copulating with the women participants; the promiscuous mating between the men and women present; the banquet where new-born babies are devoured, and disgusting liquids are drunk, but where no salt is ever to be seen; the cooking of poisonous herbs and of substances from exhumed corpses; the poisoning of human beings and of cattle, and the destruction of crops by means of poisonous mists—all these details are to be found in the pages of de Lancre,[36] and they also figure in the fictitious confessions of Lamothe-Langon's witches.

As for the names of the two witches, Georgel and Delort, it seems that Lamothe-Langon took them neither from the fourteenth century nor from the seventeenth but from his own times. Both are decidedly rare names in France—but both were borne by literary personages who lived in Paris at the same time as Lamothe-Langon and who worked in the same fields as he. They were the abbé Jean-François Georgel, whose six volumes of memoirs, published posthumously in 1817–18, are almost as fanciful as the memoirs that Lamothe-Langon was to produce in such abundance; and Joseph Delort, who was a contemporary of Lamothe-Langon's, and came from the same region.[37] Delort achieved precisely the kind of career that Lamothe-Langon had hoped for: he became a successful civil servant, rising to be deputy head of the section for science, literature and the arts. He also wrote historical works of a decidedly romantic kind, at the same time as Lamothe-Langon was producing his historical romances. Lamothe-Langon cannot have failed to know the works of Georgel and Delort, and everything suggests that the names of his two witches represents the private joke of a man who—as the Naundorff episode also shows—was quite a joker.

One feature of the spurious confessions remains to be accounted for: the references to the Dualist religion. No other witch, in the entire history of European witchcraft, ever seems to have maintained that God and the Devil are equal powers, locked in eternal struggle; or that the Devil is on the point of defeating God; or that this earth is the Devil's realm; or that the souls of the dead belong to the Devil and serve his purposes. These ideas were contributed by Lamothe-Langon himself. As a Toulousain, he knew something about Catharism—indeed, a major part of his history is concerned with the Inquisition's struggle against that exotic heresy. By introducing these distortions of Catharist beliefs into his portrayal of witchcraft he effected a major falsification of history.

In 1828 Karl Ernst Jarcke, writing in Berlin, launched the notion of a society of witches going back to pre-Christian times. In 1829 Etienne-Léon de Lamothe-Langon published in Paris his fabrication of an inquisitorial report attributing Dualist beliefs to a pair of fourteenth-century witches. It is hard to say which did more to bedevil research into the true origins of the great witch-hunt.

−3−

Historians might have been less willing to believe in the fourteenth-century witch-hunt in the south of France but for the fact that the same thing had apparently happened in the north of Italy. Here the authority looked absolutely unimpeachable: a legal opinion written and signed, some time around 1350, by the great Italian jurist and professor of civil law Bartolus, or Bartolo, of Sassoferrato. In his own day Bartolo's prestige was unique, and for centuries after his death his remained a name to conjure with. Certainly nobody seems to have questioned the authenticity of the legal opinion with which we are concerned. Nevertheless it is a forgery. This can be proved; and in addition the approximate date of the forgery can be established and the forger identified.

The first modern historian to draw attention to the text seems to have been Johann Joseph von Görres, who summarized it in the third volume of his *Christliche Mystik*, published in 1840.[38] Three years later another German, Wilhelm Soldan, mentioned it in his pioneering history of the witch-trials, alongside the stories which he took from Bardin and Lamothe-Langon.[39] Soon it was being used for frankly polemical purposes. In 1869 Pope Pius IX decided to make papal infallibility a dogma of the Church, and called the first Vatican council to promulgate it. In the furious controversy which this step provoked within the Church, the celebrated Bavarian historian and professor of theology Johann Joseph Ignaz von Döllinger emerged as the most formidable critic of the new dogma. In a work which attracted attention throughout western Europe, he marshalled the historical arguments against papal infallibility. Here the Bartolo text appears in a peculiarly sinister light. When dealing with the treatment of suspected witches by the Inquisition, Döllinger writes:

> At first the inquisitors . . . took legal opinions. The most famous jurist of his time, Bartolo, writing around 1350, favoured death by burning. This legal opinion, which marks the start of witch-burning, is most noteworthy. Here the evil effects of the authoritarian, crudely materialistic interpretation of the Bible, as practised by popes and their legal and theological parasites, are palpably evident. . . . The papal lawyers ruined theology and the papal theologians ruined jurisprudence. In this spirit jurists declared, as Bartolo did in this opinion, that a magic-making woman must be burned, because Christ had said that whoever left his community must be cast out, like a withered branch that one burns.[40]

Since then the text has figured in most histories of the witch-hunt. In particular, in 1900–1 Joseph Hansen printed it in full in his collection of sources and summarized it very fully in his history—which was enough to ensure its acceptance right down to the present day.[41]

In its original Latin form the opinion is presented as a reply by Bartolo to an enquiry from the bishop of Novara. Minus the references to earlier legal authorities, it can be translated as follows:

> The witch-woman concerned . . . ought to be delivered up for the ultimate penalty and burned at the stake. For she is said to have renounced Christ and her baptism; therefore she should die, in accordance with the saying of our Lord Jesus Christ in the gospel

according to John, chapter 15: "If a man abide not in me, he is cast forth as a branch, and is withered; and men gather them, and cast them into the fire, and they are burned." And the law of the gospel takes precedence over all other laws and must be followed even in disputes in the law-courts, since it is God's law.

This witch confesses that she made a cross of straw and trampled it underfoot, and that she made the cross for the purposes of trampling it underfoot. By itself this would be enough to earn her the death penalty.

Furthermore the witch confesses that she has adored the Devil, bending the knee to him. For this she should suffer the death penalty.

She confesses that she has bewitched children by touch and glance, so that they died. It is certain that they died, and their mothers voiced complaints about their deaths. For this the witch should die, as a murderess. For I have heard from holy theologians that the women who are called witches can harm, even fatally, by touch or glance, bewitching men or children or beasts, because these women have corrupt souls, which they have vowed to the demon. But this last point, as to whether witches can harm by touch or glance, and particularly whether they can kill, I leave to Holy Mother Church and to the holy theologians to decide. For the present I do not pronounce on that point, for the preceding reasons are sufficient for this witch to be delivered up for the ultimate penalty, and for her goods to be confiscated and handed over to the treasury of lord Joannes de Plotis, bishop of Novara, who is lord of the spiritualities and temporalities of the town of Orta, where the witch comes from.

As to whether, if the witch repents and returns to the Catholic faith, and is prepared publicly to abjure her error to the satisfaction of lord Joannes de Plotis, bishop of Novara, she ought to be spared temporal penalties and death in this world: there is no doubt that she ought to be spared in that case; I mean, if she returns to the faith, and gives signs of repentance, immediately after the detection of her offence. But if this happens not immediately, but after a lapse of time, I think it must be left to the judge to decide whether the signs of repentance are genuine or whether she is moved by fear of punishment; in the former case she should be spared, in the latter not. I say that this should be left to the judgement of the lord bishop Plotis and the lord inquisitor. If however it is conceded that she is a murderess, she shall not by repentance avoid death in this world; but, as I said, I leave the matter of murder to be decided by Holy Church.

(Signed) I, Bartolo of Sassoferrato.

The correspondence with the picture painted by Lamothe-Langon is striking. Just as Lamothe-Langon's inquisitor was supposed to have found witches at work in the foothills of the Pyrenees, so an Italian inquisitor was supposed to have found a witch at Orta, which is a village in the foothills of the Alps, north-west of Novara. It was natural that historians should have seen each source as a confirmation of the other. Yet in reality the similarity between the two throws no light at all on historical fact, for both sources are equally spurious.

Bartolo's legal opinions, or *consilia*, were greatly esteemed, and it is quite true that he supplied them to all sorts of eminent persons, including at least one bishop. After his death in 1357 collections of his *consilia* were made, and with the invention of printing these were published as books. The earliest edition, printed in Rome in 1473, contains only 244 *consilia*; but after years of patient research Thomas Diplovataccio was able to add a further 117, and the whole 361 are given in the Venice edition of 1521 and in all subsequent editions.[42] But one looks in vain, amongst these 361, for the *consilium* concerning the witch of Orta. That first appears in a collection or anthology of *consilia* on criminal cases by various authors, published by Giovanni Battista Ziletti (or Zileti) in Venice in 1566.[43] It figures there as one of five *consilia* attributed to Bartolo; and in the later Venice editions of Bartolo's collected works—from 1590 onwards—these five *consilia* are included, along with another *consilium* printed by Ziletti in an earlier collection, and twenty-eight not previously printed at all.[44] To examine the first dozen of the thirty-four new *consilia* is to realize that we are dealing with another ingenious hoax. The great medieval jurist has been used as a vehicle for a private joke.

There never was a bishop of Novara called Joannes de Plotis. Yet in committing this name to print, Ziletti was not misreading his manuscript source.[45] Three of the four other *consilia* which he ascribes to Bartolo in the same collection also refer to individuals with the surname of de Plotis. Even more surprisingly, out of the first eleven of the additional *consilia* which appear in Bartolo's *Omnia Opera* from 1590 onwards, no less than eight are concerned with various de Plotis—i.e. the four taken from Ziletti, plus four not previously published. And if, finally, one pursues the enquiry backwards, to the collection of *consilia* on matrimonial cases published by Ziletti in 1563, one finds yet another two opinions ascribed to Bartolo, and both of those involve members of the de Plotis family.[46] To sum up: over a period of twenty-seven years, from 1563 to 1590, Bartolo was gradually credited with more and more legal opinions concerning a family called de Plotis, of the town of

Novara—ten opinions in all, and not one of them known until two centuries after Bartolo's own time.

As portrayed in the *consilia*, the de Plotis were a very queer lot indeed, plagued by the strangest worries and dilemmas. Joannes, bishop of Novara, appears four times, and not always as a pursuer of witches. He is, for instance, disturbed to find that a notary, in drawing up a legal document, after originally referring to him as the most reverend lord Joannes de Piotis, has then altered the name to "de Plotis"; and he asks whether the man can be punished for fraud. Bartolo opines that he cannot—partly because in a Latin document it is more correct to use the Latin form, but also because that great and noble family is known to be descended from an ancient Roman, Gnaeus Plancus Plotus.[47] On another occasion the bishop is uncertain whether he ought to dissolve a marriage between a rapist and the woman he raped. Here Bartolo is less helpful, and ends by advising the bishop to refer the question to the Holy See. Yet the tone is encouraging: Bartolo is sure that his friend lord Joannes, to whom he owes so much, will himself weigh all aspects of the matter; for he well remembers the acuteness of mind which the lord Joannes displayed when, together with his brother lord Marcus Plotus, he was studying law at Bologna.[48]—All this to a bishop who never existed at all.

Other de Plotis appear in roles scarcely less exalted than the bishop's. When the emperor Charles IV wished to ask Bartolo's opinion on a delicate matter of blasphemy, he employed Marcus Aurelius de Plotis to convey the enquiry.[49] As for Count Joannes Baptista de Plotis, he was one of the emperor's councillors. When a German nobleman claimed that Germans were more honourable and noble than Italians, Joannes Baptista called him a liar; and when the emperor asked Bartolo whether this amounted to legally insulting behaviour, Bartolo replied that it would have been unworthy of an Italian, and an imperial councillor at that, to have done otherwise. But the same Count Joannes Baptista had domestic problems: he had married a girl from another noble family of Novara, only to find later that she was related to him within the forbidden degrees. In view of the fact that the count, constantly travelling on the emperor's service, had had little opportunity to look into such matters, the pope declared the marriage legitimate. Nevertheless, when the count died the question arose as to whether his children could inherit; Bartolo opined that they could.[50] Yet not all de Plotis were above reproach. Bartolo is sharp with Joannes Aloysius de Plotis, mayor of Milan, who had wrongfully imprisoned Hector de Mapamundis (meaning "Map of the World") for an offence committed by Hector's brother.[51] Moreover, in challenging Joannes Maria de Plotis to a duel, Count Sebastianus de Plotis undoubtedly offended against the ancient statutes of Novara, which Petrus de Plotis in his day had helped to draw up. It was fortunate for him that Fabianus de Plotis heard him say that he had forgotten about the challenge; for this enabled Bartolo to take a lenient view.[52]

Such is the true background of the witch of Orta: for some three centuries, until medievalists and anti-papal propagandists discovered her and found in her what they wanted to find, she was simply a minor character in a preposterous family saga. How this saga was ever accepted as the work of Bartolo is a mystery. Even apart from the absurdity of most of the incidents, the Latin style is utterly unlike his, and even the signature appended to each *consilium*—"Ego, Bartolus de Saxoferrato"—is one he never used. One can only assume that no scholar ever read these fragmented materials with enough attention to realize that they form a whole, and that that whole is a parody.

Who was the parodist? No hint is given in the *Omnia Opera* of Bartolo, nor in the work from which the faked *consilia* in the *Omnia Opera* were drawn—the collection of opinions on criminal cases first published by Ziletti in 1572. But if one inspects the two *consilia* which, though attributed to Bartolo, never reappeared in the *Omnia Opera*, one finds the answer. These are the *consilia* in Ziletti's collection of matrimonial cases, first published in 1563. In each the rubric states that, though written by Bartolo, the opinion has only now been brought to light by the illustrious doctor of both laws Joannes Baptista de Plotis.

Giovanni Battista Piotto, or de' Ploti, as he is variously called by Italian historians, was a prominent citizen of Novara in the second half of the sixteenth century.[53] A nobleman and landed proprietor, he was also a respected jurist, a pupil of the celebrated Andrea Alciati. Novara was at that time under the protection of Milan, which was itself a dependency of the Spanish crown; and Piotto acted for many years as Novara's spokesman in Milan. He was zealous in defending Novara's rights and privileges—it was thanks to him that the Spaniards desisted from demolishing the suburbs; and in due course his fellow-citizens acknowledged his services by bestowing on him the title of *padre della patria*. He was also a great producer of *consilia*—those published number more than a hundred.

These *consilia* turn a near-certainty into a certainty: nobody who studies them can doubt that Piotto was the forger of the pseudo-Bartolean *consilia* and the creator of the witch of Orta. It is not simply that the Latin style is so similar—just like the pseudo-Bartolean *consilia*, some of the *consilia* which Piotto wrote over his own name deal with the affairs of his family, and with fictitious affairs at that.[54] To appreciate the spirit in which these documents were concocted one has only to compare No. 87 in Ziletti's "matrimonial" collection, published first in 1563, with No. 15 in Piotto's collection of his own *consilia*, published in 1578.[55] The former tells how Giovanni Battista's son, Francesco Maria, made his own daughter his sole heir on condition that, when she reached marriageable age, she should marry the worthiest member of the de Plotis family. When the time came, a furious dispute arose as to whether she had not infringed the condition by marrying a jurist de Plotis when she could have had a soldier de Plotis, or even a doctor of arts and medicine. As a good jurist Giovanni Battista naturally opines that his niece has done very right. In the 1578 volume the same *consilium* reappears—but the family is now called not de Plotis but Sempronius!

Piotto seems to have written many of his *consilia* simply to exercise his skill in resolving nice points of law, or maybe to display his legal erudition; while others are obviously meant to be read as jokes—sophisticated professional jokes, comparable with the great satire on legal pedantry, the judgement of Judge Bridoye, which occupies three chapters in the *Third Book* of Rabelais. The Piotto's were a family of lawyers—Francesco Maria was one, and there were others. The existence of this captive audience is perhaps enough to account for the virtuoso displays and recondite fooleries which Giovanni Battista perpetrated in his own name. But by 1563 he had hit on a new idea: he stopped writing about his son and began, instead, to concoct *consilia* about imaginary ancestors of his, which he passed off as the work of Bartolo.

How did he manage to get them published? Above all, how did it come about that in the end they were even incorporated into new editions of Bartolo's collected works? Here the role of the jurist, editor and compiler Giovanni Battista Ziletti must have been decisive. After all, six of the forgeries were first published in his collections. And when four of the six were taken into Bartolo's *Omnia Opera* it happened in Venice, where Ziletti lived and worked: they do not figure in the Basel edition of 1589, but they do figure in the Venice edition of 1590, as they do also in the later Venice editions of 1603 and 1615. Indeed, the editors of the *Omnia Opera* explicitly acknowledge that these *consilia* had previously appeared in Ziletti's collection. But even in the forgeries which appear for the first time in the *Omnia Opera*, the influence of Ziletti can be detected in the background: a *consilium* which mentions

Marcus Aurelius de Plotis is immediately followed by a note by Ziletti, which in turn refers to a treatise by our Piotto.

There seems to have been a close understanding between the two men, and one feels that Piotto knew what he was doing when he described Ziletti as "that most learned doctor of Venice . . . zealous for public rather than private profit, bringing together many things in civil law with great labour and with a genius which is divine rather than merely human, transmitting the *consilia* of various doctors . . . to print and so to immortality . . .".[56] Certainly Piotto and Ziletti were jointly responsible for launching, in 1572, the text which has misled so many historians into believing that inquisitors were hunting witches in the diocese of Novara more than two centuries earlier.

It is true that the witch of Orta does not stand entirely alone. Around 1508 one Bernardo Rategno, who was then inquisitor for the neighbouring diocese of Como, wrote that "the sect of witches began to pullulate only within the last 150 years, as appears from the old records of trials by inquisitors, in the archives of our Inquisition at Como".[57] This seemed to confirm that inquisitorial witch-hunting in that neighbourhood could indeed be traced back to the 1350s. However, no later writer has found any trace of the documents in question, though the archives of Como have been searched by historians who had these matters in mind.[58] The earliest witch-hunts established as having taken place in that area date from a full century later—from the 1450s in the Val Leventina, from the 1480s in Como itself. As for Rategno, otherwise known as Bernard of Como, he was appointed inquisitor only after a lifetime spent as a preacher, but during the years left to him he earned himself a reputation as a ruthless hunter of witches; indeed, the passage in question comes from a tract written specially to prove that witches exist and ought to be burned.[59] No serious modern historian would have taken the statement at its face value if it had not appeared to be supported by other evidence, Italian and French. With that evidence discredited, and no other evidence forthcoming, the fourteenth-century witch-hunt at Como loses all credibility.

Nevertheless Rategno's comment is not irrelevant to the matter in hand. Though he himself died in 1516, his tract remained unknown for half a century. It was first published as an appendix to a larger work, also by Rategno, on the procedure to be adopted by inquisitors in dealing with heretics; and that was in 1566, at Milan. In the tract, witches are described as women who, in addition to killing adults and children, bow down to the Devil and—not an invariable characteristic of witches —trample on the cross. Now, Piotto lived and worked in Milan. As a lawyer who himself wrote several *consilia* about the treatment of heretics, he would hardly have overlooked an inquisitor's manual published in that very city. In the manual he would have found an assurance that 150 years earlier—i.e. in Bartolo's time—witch-hunts were taking place in the neighbourhood. Is it mere coincidence that that same year 1566 saw the publication of his pseudo-Bartolean *consilium* about the witch of Orta who killed children, bowed down to the Devil, trampled on the cross, and must pay for it by being burned alive? Instead of confirming the story of the witch of Orta, Rategno's statement may very well have inspired it.

Between them, Bardin in the fifteenth century, Rategno and Piotto in the sixteenth, and Lamothe-Langon in the nineteenth opened up what for long looked like a royal road to the origins of the great witch-hunt. It has turned out to be no such thing but, on the contrary, a false and decidedly muddy track. Once that is fully accepted it becomes possible to recognize other and better sign-posts, even when they point in unexpected directions.

8

MALEFICIUM BEFORE 1300

– I –

The stereotype of the witch as it is described at the beginning of Chapter Six, and as it existed in some parts of Europe in the fourteenth, fifteenth and sixteenth centuries, was an amalgam of four notions. A witch was imagined as (1) an individual who practised *maleficium*, i.e. who did harm by occult means; (2) an individual who was bound to the Devil as his servant; (3) an uncanny being who flew through the air at night for evil purposes, such as devouring babies, and who was associated with wild and desolate places; (4) a member of a society or sect which held periodical meetings or sabbats, where the Christian religion was systematically parodied and where the Devil was worshipped and also had sexual intercourse with his human servants.

Originally these four notions were quite distinct; and despite all the excellent work that has recently been done on the history of witchcraft beliefs and witch trials, it is still not clear how they came together. How did so complex a stereotype come into being—by what stages, in what circumstances, under whose auspices, in response to what needs and desires? The rest of this volume will be given over to trying to answer those questions.

The concept of *maleficium* provides a convenient starting-point; and as a first step we can forestall some possible confusions. Anthropologists working in present-day "primitive" societies have often found it convenient to distinguish between "sorcery" and "witchcraft". "Sorcery" commonly refers to a technique: the use of substances or objects believed to be imbued with supernatural power, usually to the accompaniment of verbal spells or gestures, with the intention of harming one's fellows. The source of "witchcraft", on the other hand, lies not in technique but in the person: the witch is full of destructive power.[1] Now in Europe this distinction was known, but it was not absolute: sorcery and witchcraft overlapped—as indeed they do in many primitive societies today. Sorcery could be practised by any ordinary person, once the technique was mastered—but it could also be practised by a witch. A witch might operate through the use of substances or objects or spells or gestures as well as by the mere deployment of his or her indwelling power. In either case the deed was called by the same Latin name. *Maleficium*, which originally meant simply an evil deed or mischief, was used in official documents from the fourth century onwards in the specific sense of "harm-doing by occult means"; and the usage persisted throughout the Middle Ages. Sorcerer and witch alike were designated by *maleficus* if male, *malefica* if female.

The world of Antiquity knew all about *maleficium*, and it would be perfectly possible to trace that part of the story back not only to ancient Rome but to Sumer; but fortunately it is unnecessary. For our purpose it is enough that *maleficium* and accusations of *maleficium* are to be found from the establishment of the first Germanic kingdoms onwards. From the sixth century to the thirteenth, laws and chronicles and epic poetry contain scattered references to the matter, most of them quite free from religious overtones. Though the evidence is not abundant, it is sufficient to show how *maleficium* had been regarded in pagan times, and how it continued to be regarded by many laymen in a Christianized Europe.

Tales of *maleficium* figure in the history of the first of the Frankish dynasties, the Merovingians. The historian of the Franks, St Gregory of Tours, tells of a case which had occurred within his own experience. When in 580 Queen Fredegond lost two of her young sons in an epidemic, she was easily persuaded that they were victims of sorcery: her hated stepson Chlodovic must have employed his mistress's mother to make *maleficia* against the boys. The woman was arrested and tortured until she confessed. Armed with this confession, Fredegond persuaded her husband, King Chilperic, to abandon Chlodovic to her vengeance; the young man was duly stabbed to death by hired assassins. Meanwhile the alleged sorceress withdrew the confession that had been wrung from her. It made no difference to Fredegond, who had the woman burned alive.

Fredegond's misfortunes continued, and so did her hunt for sorcerers. In 583 a third son caught dysentery and died. Soon afterwards the mayor of the palace, Mummulus, happened to remark that he possessed a certain herb which could quickly cure even the most hopeless cases of dysentery. The remark was reported to Fredegond, and she set to work at once. This time several women were arrested and tortured until they confessed that the mayor had employed them to kill the young prince by *maleficium*. Some of the women were burned, others were broken on the wheel; after which the torturers tackled Mummulus himself. Even after he had been repeatedly flogged and splinters had been driven under his nails, he would admit only that the women had supplied him with salves and potions, as a means of securing the good graces of the king and queen. Sent into exile, he died on the journey from the consequences of the torture.[2]

The employment of torture makes these cases atypical: Fredegond was after all both a monarch and an outstandingly ruthless politician. But in themselves the killings hardly offended against traditional norms.[3] It was an ancient custom for people who believed that *maleficium* was being used against them or against their kin to take personal retaliation. Amongst the Lombards in northern Italy and the Alamanni along the upper Rhine the private killing of suspected witches was a common practice down to the seventh century, and it was still common amongst the Saxons when they were conquered by Charlemagne towards the end of the eighth century.[4] In the archaic society of Iceland it was regarded as normal as late as the tenth century. This emerges clearly from the sagas which, though first written down between 1140 and 1220, portray society as it had existed some two centuries earlier. Thus *Eyrbyggia*, describing events around 980, tells how a widow, having brought serious illness on a young man by means of *maleficium*, was stoned to death by his kin.[5] *Laxdaela*, which covers the period 910–1026, tells how a married couple, both witches, killed a twelve-year-old boy by magical incantations; again, the victim's family caught them and stoned them to death.[6]

There was however another way of dealing with such matters. In all early Germanic law a crime was treated less as an offence against society than as an offence against an individual and his kin. But where the community or the central authority was strong enough, the injured individual or kin were not permitted simply to take retaliation on the offender; instead, the offender had to pay them a fine in compensation (*wergild*). This arrangement applied to offences of all kinds, including *maleficium*. Already the law of the Salian Franks, the *Pactus legis Salicae*, which was written down early in the sixth century but which reflects the attitudes of a still earlier period, fixes the *wergild* to be paid if someone is killed by *maleficium*, and the smaller sum to be paid if he is merely injured in his health.[7] Similar provisions are to be found in the law of the East Franks, the *Lex Ribuaria*, which was written down a century later;[8] and this way of regarding *maleficium* continued to exert an influence almost throughout the Middle Ages. Yet death, usually by burning, continued to be recognized as a proper penalty for lethal *maleficium* in certain cases—for instance when the offender was a slave or serf, or when he or she pleaded guilty, or when the *wergild* was not forthcoming.

Whatever the penalty, it was designed to provide either revenge or compensation to the supposed victim or his kin; and—save at certain times and places, where religious considerations intervened—that remained its main purpose right down to the thirteenth century. In England under Æthelstan (925–40) it was decreed that the death penalty was to be exacted where guilt was too manifest to be denied. Where the accused asserted his innocence, he must face a three-fold ordeal. If the outcome was unsatisfactory, he must spend 120 days in prison; after which his relatives might secure his release by paying a fine to the king and *wergild* to the victim's kin, and also standing surety for his future good behaviour.[9] In twelfth-century England anyone convicted of murder by *maleficium* was supposed to be handed over to the victim's kin, to be disposed of as they thought best.[10] A Swedish law of 1296 still speaks a similar language. A woman convicted of causing a man's death by *maleficium* is to be burned, unless the victim's kin decide to spare her life; in which case she is to pay them a sum in compensation, as well as fines to the royal treasury and the local community.[11]

Maleficia could be performed to produce other effects in individuals besides sickness or death. Women performed them, or got others to perform them on their behalf, for the purpose of influencing erotic feelings in men. In the ninth century, under the Carolingian dynasty, *maleficia* of this kind figured in political struggles. In 817 Charlemagne's son, the emperor Louis the Pious (Louis I of France), divided his vast dominions amongst his sons by his wife Irmengarde; but in 829, having remarried, he tried to provide a kingdom for his son by his second marriage also. His sons by his first marriage took up arms in revolt; and the story which they put about was that their father's second wife, Judith, was using *maleficium* to keep him helplessly infatuated. As a first step they demanded that all dealers in magic should be driven from the royal palace.[12] More drastic measures followed when, in 834, the eldest son, Lothair I, captured the town of Châlon-sur-Saône. There he found Gerberga, who was the sister of Count Bernard of Barcelona—the favourite of his step-mother Judith and his father's most powerful ally. Lothair had Gerberga drowned in the river "as is the custom with sorcerers". This seems to have been an act of private vengeance, comparable with Fredegond's killings; but in any case, there is little doubt that it was linked with the emperor's supposed infatuation.[13]

In due course Lothair's son, also called Lothair, became king of the district which was to be called after him, Lotharingia, or Lorraine. His reign was chiefly occupied by his efforts to divorce his wife Thietberga in order to marry his mistress Waldrada. This issue dictated his relations with his uncles, who ruled the vast kingdoms to the east and west of his own; with the Frankish bishops; and even with the pope. About 860, in the course of the interminable discussions about the projected divorce, Hincmar, archbishop of Rheims and one of the greatest scholars of the age, was asked to write an expert opinion. Amongst other things he was asked whether sorcery could make a man impotent with his wife and full of detestation for her; and whether it could provoke irresistible love between man and woman. He replied that it was generally believed that certain women could work such sorcery; he himself was convinced of it, and was even able to describe the techniques. He suspected Waldrada of practising *maleficium*: and this strengthened him in his view that the divorce should not take place.[14]

Such preoccupations were by no means confined to royal courts—country priests came across them amongst their peasant parishioners. Around the year 1000 canon law was becoming a recognized branch of scholarly study; and one of the first major compilations was the enormous *Decretum* or *Collectarium* composed by Burchard, bishop of Worms, and a few collaborators around 1008-12. The nineteenth book of the *Decretum* is called the *Corrector* or *Medicus*, because it teaches priests how to provide "corrections for bodies and medicines for souls". And one of the chapters of the *Corrector*—the fifth—is in effect a penitential: it consists of a long series of questions to be addressed by the confessor to his penitent, each question dealing with a different sin and being followed by a note of the appropriate penance.[15] This fifth chapter is known to be based on earlier penitentials, and the nature of the questions shows that it is designed for a congregation of peasants. To the historian it offers some fine insights into the popular mentality of the early Middle Ages.

Now this source shows quite clearly that many men—ordinary peasants of the tenth century or earlier—were afraid of being bewitched into impotence.[16] In particular, when a man left his mistress to marry another, he was apt to find himself impotent with his new wife. The modern psychologist knows that such things do happen, and so did the author of the *Corrector*; only he attributed them to a different cause. From his experience as a confessor he knew that deserted women sometimes practised *maleficium* against their ex-lovers; and whereas he was sceptical about the efficacy of some forms of *maleficium*, he had no doubts at all about this one. From other sources we know the technique employed: during the wedding, the outraged woman would make three knots in a lace or a string. This was intended to block the way to orgasm—and no doubt when the bridegroom knew or suspected what was afoot, it often worked.

It was when some unforeseeable, unaccountable disaster occurred that people looked to *maleficium* as an explanation. But whereas mysterious illnesses and deaths, or sudden impotence in marriage, could happen to anyone in any stratum of society, some kinds of disaster were peculiar to peasant life. There were accordingly some beliefs about *maleficium*, and also some techniques of *maleficium*, that flourished amongst the peasantry in particular. Here again the fifth chapter of the *Corrector* provides valuable insights. The confessor's questions show that peasants often practised sorcery to improve their own position at their neighbour's expense. Swineherds and cowherds would say spells over bread, or herbs, or knotted cords, which they would then deposit in a tree or at a road-fork; the object being to direct pest or injury away from their own animals and on to other people's.[17] A woman would use spells and charms to draw all the milk and honey in the neighbourhood to her own cows and bees, or else to appropriate other people's property for herself.[18] This is the reality behind Runeberg's sweeping generalizations about "magical exchange";[19] but they constitute only a small part of the world of *maleficium*. Even amongst the peasantry of the early Middle Ages, centuries before the full stereotype of the witch came into being, it was recognized that the motive for *maleficium* was often sheer malice. The *Corrector* refers to women who actually boasted that they could remove or kill chickens, young peacocks, whole litters of piglets, by a word or a glance.[20]

Other sources, older than the *Corrector*, refer to another, more dreaded form of rural *maleficium*. People claimed to be able to conjure up storms which would ruin the crops. This kind of *maleficium* too was commonly thought of as being directed against a particular individual: the eighth-century law of the Bavarians fixed the fine to be paid to anyone whose crops were damaged in this way.[21] But at times storm-making could become an organized racket. The sixth-century laws of the Visigoths deal with *tempestarii* who were touring the countryside, intimidating the peasants; people were paying them to spare their fields and blast the next man's instead. It was decreed that a storm-maker should get 200 lashes, have his head shorn and be paraded through the villages of the locality in this shameful condition.[22] Around 820 Agobard, bishop of Lyons, noted that almost everybody—nobleman and commoner, town-dweller and peasant—believed in the supernatural powers of storm-makers; but naturally it was the peasants who paid them to save their fields from magical storms.[23] Anglo-

Saxon penitentials of the eighth century treated the activities of the *tempestarii* as familiar sins that everybody knew about; and so does the *Corrector*.[24] And if in the later Middle Ages the laws took little cognizance of storm-making, it continued to be widely believed in and occasionally practised. Elena Dalok, who was arraigned before the commissary of London in 1493, freely boasted that she could make it rain at will—just as she could kill people by cursing them.[25]

From later sources we know the technique that was used to produce storms: it consisted of beating, stirring or splashing water. A pond was ideal for the purpose, but if none was available it was enough to make a small hole in the ground, fill it with water or even with one's own urine, and stir this with one's finger. There is no doubt that these things really were done—but in addition, storm-makers were often credited with the ability to fly. Later evidence on this point is abundant—even in nineteenth-century Switzerland it was still customary for peasants to deal with a storm by laying a scythe on the ground, cutting edge uppermost; the object being to wound the storm-witch and deprive her of her power.[26] But there are hints of similar beliefs already in the early Middle Ages. Again according to Bishop Agobard, peasants believed that *tempestarii* magically removed the crops from the fields and carried them away on cloud-ships, to sell in a mysterious land called Mangonia.[27]

From all this a coherent picture emerges. It is clear that many of the forms of *maleficium* that figure in the witch-trials of the fifteenth, sixteenth and seventeenth centuries had been familiar for many centuries before. Causing death or disease in human beings and animals; producing impotence in men; raising storms and destroying crops—these things belonged to the traditional world of *maleficium*, a world that existed already in the early Middle Ages and that had never ceased to exist thereafter. In medieval Europe it was generally believed that these things could be done by those possessed of the necessary occult power; while some individuals believed that they themselves possessed that power and tried to do those things.

The beliefs existed—but how large did they bulk in people's minds? If we were to judge solely by the number of recorded *maleficium* trials, we would have to conclude that they hardly bulked at all. Only a couple of cases are known. Around 970, in England, a certain widow was accused by a man called Aelsie of trying to murder him by driving nails into a puppet made in his likeness; the puppet being found in her chamber. After trial the woman was drowned at London Bridge; her son, who was also implicated, fled and was outlawed; and their estate in

Northamptonshire passed to the king, who gave it to the intended victim, Aelsie. Property had been in dispute, and the outcome of the trial settled the matter.[28] The other case, after starting with a regular trial, ended in a manner Queen Fredegond would have understood. In 1028 Count William II of Angoulême fell ill with a wasting sickness, and rumour spread that he was a victim of sorcery. Suspicion concentrated on a certain woman; and as she refused to admit anything, it was decided to hold a trial by the ordeal of single combat, the count and the suspect both being represented by champions. The count's champion was victorious; whereupon the woman was tortured and even crucified —but still, "her heart sealed by the Devil", she uttered not a word. However, three other women made confessions which resulted in the discovery of clay puppets, buried in the ground. The count, who was an unusually devout man, pardoned all four women; but as soon as he was dead, his son had them burned outside the town walls.[29]

There is little other positive evidence of *maleficium* trials before 1300. Nevertheless, it cannot be assumed that people gave little thought to these matters. We shall show later what formidable obstacles the law itself put in the way of anyone who might wish to bring a charge of *maleficium*—yet even so, one finds indications that the popular fear and anger that became so manifest at the time of the great witch-hunt were by no means absent in earlier centuries. As we have seen, in pre-Christian times it had been customary to kill suspected witches as a matter of private vengeance; but long after such practices were forbidden, witches continued to be killed. When telling how Lothair I drowned the nun Gerberga for sorcery in 834, the contemporary chronicler appends the significant comment: "as is the custom with sorcerers".[30] In 1080 Pope Gregory VII wrote to King Harold of Denmark, complaining that in Denmark storms and pestilence were being blamed on priests and women, and that the latter were being cruelly put to death; and he forbade such practices.[31] In 1128 the burghers of Ghent disembowelled a suspected witch and paraded her intestines through her village.[32]

Whether these were legal executions or lynchings, they are enough to show that *maleficium* was a matter of public concern. And in some cases popular fury can be seen unmistakably at work. In the ninth century Bishop Agobard tells how he saw four strangers—three men and a woman—seized by peasants who took them for *tempestarii*, fallen out of a cloud-ship; but for Agobard's intervention, they would have been stoned to death.[33] In 1074 the burghers of Cologne rebelled against their lord, the archbishop, and tried to kill him. The archbishop escaped from the city; but during the ensuing riots the mob found a woman who was suspected of having driven men mad by means of *maleficia*, and hurled her to death from the town walls.[34] The chronicler specifically states that this was done without any regard for the due process of law; and the same is true of a killing which took place at Freising in Bavaria in 1090. Three indigent women were rumoured to be "poisoners" and "destroyers of people and crops". They were seized by the mob and subjected to the ordeal of immersion in water; next, though the ordeal gave negative results, they were repeatedly flogged to make them confess; finally, though they did not confess, they were burned alive on the banks of the river Isar. All this was done without the collaboration or approval of the authorities—indeed it was done in an area where authority had temporarily broken down: owing to a dispute between rival candidates, the see of Freising had no bishop. The clergy clearly disapproved. The monk who tells the story speaks of the injustice of the accusations, the "devilish fury" of the mob, the "martyrdom" of the victims. Indeed, after the mob had done its work a priest and two monks actually removed the charred bodies and buried them in consecrated ground.[35] In 1279 a similar incident took place at Ruffach in Alsace, save that this time the clergy intervened in time. A nun was suspected of using a wax puppet for purposes of *maleficium*, and would have been burned by the peasants; but the local monks saved her.[36]

Doubtless there were many more such incidents: since the chroniclers were not generally much interested in the activities of the common people, one can probably assume that the recorded cases represent only the tip of the iceberg. In any case it is clear that medieval peasants and burghers could at times feel very strongly about witches. Long before, and quite independently of, the great witch-hunt, there existed a fund of popular suspicion, a readiness to perceive witchcraft at work and to identify witches. On occasion those feelings expressed themselves, illegally, in torture and killing. The day was to come when they would be able to do so legally.

–2–

The clergy had their own particular view of *maleficium*. The early Church, already, regarded all magical practices as manifestations of paganism; and paganism was identified with the worship of demons.[37] It was almost irrelevant whether the intention behind the magical practices was maleficent, harmless or beneficent—in the eyes of the Church all such practices were damnable, because they all depended on

the co-operation of those demons, the pagan gods. Like almost all their
contemporaries, the Fathers accepted without question that magic
worked, that it really could produce miracles—but these were pernicious miracles, evil devices by which the demons tricked human beings
into opposing God. That was the view of Justin Martyr early in the
second century; and it was still the view of the greatest and most
influential of all the Latin Fathers, Augustine, at the beginning of the
fifth century.

According to Augustine, by God's decree two realms have existed
from the beginning of the world, and all history has consisted in the
struggle between them. There is the City of God, which includes the
angels and all good people, and there is the City of the Devil, which
includes not only the demons but the pagan world with its cult of
demons. The Church, as the latter-day embodiment of the City of God,
is now at last victorious; but the City of the Devil still survives and is
still formidable. And one way in which the City of the Devil deploys its
power is through magic: by their command of magical resources the
demons seduce people into accepting and worshipping them as gods.
Augustine does not doubt that, with the help of demons, people can
perform *maleficia* which are otherwise beyond human capacity. If the
ungodly can abduct their neighbour's harvest; if they can harm people
by casting an evil eye on them; if they can even change them into beasts
of burden—this is because the demons have lent them supernatural
powers in return for adoration.[38] But the same applies to all forms of
magic, however harmless they may appear. The wearing of amulets,
the casting of horoscopes, even the healing of sickness by means of
spoken or written charms—all such things are to be eschewed, as pagan
and therefore diabolic aberrations.

In essentials the teaching of the Church continued to follow these
lines throughout the thousand years which comprise the history of
medieval Europe. In 314 the synod of Ancyra had decreed a five-year
penance for fortune-telling and for the curing of sickness by occult
means,[39] and in 375 the synod of Laodicaea had forbidden the wearing
of amulets on pain of excommunication.[40] Around 500 both of these
local provisions were incorporated by the monk Dionysius Exiguus in
his code of canon law, and so acquired validity throughout the area of
western Christendom. During the sixth and seventh centuries they were
reaffirmed and reinforced by various provincial synods. In 506 a Visigothic synod at Agde in Languedoc prescribed excommunication for
clerics or laymen who concerned themselves with divining the
future;[41] while Frankish synods held at Orleans and Auxerre in 511,

533, 541, 573 and 603 prescribed the same penalty for fortune-tellers. These forms of magic had of course nothing to do with *maleficia*, and the objections to them were purely religious. The synods which condemned divination and fortune-telling, the wearing of amulets and the magical treatment of the sick, were moved by precisely the same concern as the synods of Arles, Vannes, Auxerre, Narbonne, Rheims and Rouen which at intervals during the fifth, sixth and seventh centuries condemned the worship of trees and rocks and river-sources. In the eyes of the bishops it was all part of the campaign against paganism, and paganism was still equated with demonolatry.

The official attitude of the Church gradually influenced the secular authorities; and from the sixth century onwards the laws of the Germanic peoples were revised to take account of the Christian interpretation of magic. The old pagan laws had taken cognizance of magic only in the form of *maleficium*, and even then had judged it solely in terms of the harm supposedly done to life, health or property. Now, under the influence of the Church, there was a tendency to treat all magic as a criminal offence.[42] This was already the case when Visigothic law was codified, around 550. The law which decreed 200 lashes for *tempestarii* [43] decreed the same penalty for "those who invoke demons to trouble men's spirits, or who offer nocturnal sacrifices to the demons, or wickedly invoke them with impious prayers".[44] At that time the Visigothic monarchs still adhered to the Arian heresy. When, in 589, the royal house turned to the Church of Rome, the ecclesiastical and secular authorities entered into an alliance to stamp out all forms of magic. A synod at Toledo, in 693, dealt with fortune-telling. Members of the upper classes who practised it were to be heavily fined, humbler folk were to get a hundred lashes. Significantly, the same penalties were decreed for worshipping stones, trees or river-sources,[45] and judges as well as bishops were held responsible for seeing that the regulation was observed. Magic as demon-worship, demon-worship as an offence which concerned State as well as Church: the basic pattern is discernible already at that early stage.

Later a similar development took place in the vast Carolingian empire. In 787 Charlemagne, in his capitulary for the Saxons, decreed that not only maleficent sorcerers but also fortune-tellers should be handed over to the ecclesiastical authorities as slaves; while anyone offering sacrifices to the Devil—meaning Donar, Wotan and the other Germanic gods—should be put to death.[46] These measures were part of a policy for the forcible assimilation of a pagan people which had only recently been conquered and was still refractory; but even in lands where Christianity had long been established, the bishops sometimes prescribed very severe measures for stamping out magical practices. In 799 a Bavarian synod forwarded a recommendation to Charlemagne: anyone arrested on a charge of practising magic—whether storm-raising and other *maleficia*, or mere fortune-telling—was to be imprisoned and interrogated until he or she confessed. Torture could be used, though not to such a point that the prisoner died—the object must always be to induce repentance and to save a soul. Responsibility for seeing that these measures were enforced lay with the chief priest of the locality. If the secular authorities—the count and his officials—accepted bribes and let such prisoners go, the chief priest was to report them to the bishop, and the bishop was to punish them.[47]

Church and State were drawing closer together, as they had once done in the Visigothic kingdom, and with similar results: the clergy felt free to call on the secular authorities to pursue and punish those whom they regarded as Devil-worshippers. And this tendency became still more marked under Charlemagne's successors. After preliminary discussions at the synod of Paris, the bishops presented a recommendation to the Emperor Louis the Pious, at the imperial diet of 829. The cult of paganism, they complain, still survives in the activities of magicians, fortune-tellers and sorcerers. And they continue: "It is said that their *maleficia* can disturb the air, bring down hail, foretell the future, remove the fruits and milk from one person and give them to another, and perform innumerable marvels. As soon as they are found out, the guilty men and women must be subjected to discipline and punished by the prince; all the more severely because their wicked and overweening audacity does not shrink from serving the Devil."[48] No particular punishment is specified, but it would seem that death was not excluded. The very injunctions from the Pentateuch that were to resound so loudly during the great witch-hunt, five, six and seven centuries later, were already quoted by the Frankish bishops for the benefit of Charlemagne's son: "Thou shalt not suffer a witch to live."[49]—"The soul that turneth after such as have familiar spirits, and after wizards, to go a-whoring after them, I will even set my face against that soul, and will cut him off from among his people."[50]

Like his father, Louis gave legal sanction to the bishops' recommendation. And after the division of the Carolingian empire, similar situations continued to arise in both the western and the eastern halves: synods condemned in the name of God, and monarchs legislated accordingly. *Maleficium*, which had always been condemned as criminal, now evoked in addition such a deep religious horror that even secular laws were coloured by it. "The saints of God," proclaimed the Emperor Charles the Bald in 873, "have written that it is the king's duty to get rid of the impious, to exterminate the makers of *maleficia* and of poisons. We therefore expressly adjure the counts to show great diligence in seeking out and seizing, in their counties, those guilty of these crimes. . . . And not only the guilty but their associates and accomplices, male or female, shall perish, so that all knowledge of so great a crime shall vanish from our land." (51)

So already in the early Middle Ages the secular authorities did sometimes, at the urging of the ecclesiastical authorities, concern themselves with *maleficium* as a religious transgression. Nevertheless it would be quite wrong to try to link what happened in the Visigothic kingdom and the Carolingian empire with the great witch-hunt of the fifteenth, sixteenth and seventeenth centuries. The differences, both in scale and in motivation, are vast. It may be that in the earlier period some *tempestarii* and suchlike really were flogged, or tortured, or even executed, but there was certainly no widespread witch-hunt. Above all, whatever repressive measures were taken, they were taken as part of a campaign to stamp out the remnants of paganism. The notion of witchcraft as a form of heresy was utterly foreign to early medieval civilization.

And indeed it seems that after the Carolingian epoch the secular authorities were not asked to concern themselves with *maleficium* as a religious transgression for some four centuries. The Church of course continued to combat the practice of *maleficium*, as it did other magical practices; but its methods were not blood-thirsty. For one thing, certain forms of witchcraft were treated as sheer superstition. Much that had been taken seriously by Augustine was now treated with scepticism. People were discouraged from taking seriously the very types of *maleficium* that were most mysterious and uncanny. Precisely because the clergy were concerned to root out the vestiges of paganism that still survived in popular imagination, they minimized the occult power of witches—it was not permissible, for instance, to believe that witches could devour people from inside, or that they could kill people by a glance.(52) Other kinds of *maleficium* were accepted as effective by everyone, including the clergy; and here the practitioner was encouraged to confess, to do penance and to receive absolution. Thus the vernacular penitential of pseudo-Ecbert (*c.* 935) mentions that ancient and ever-popular technique, maltreating a model or puppet. If the intended victim survives, the penance is a year on bread and water, and two further years on bread and water for three days a week; if he dies, double that amount.[53] A severe penalty, certainly—but mild enough when compared with the torments which were visited upon supposed witches at the time of the great witch-hunt.

In the twelfth and thirteenth centuries the Church became more and more preoccupied with rooting out heresy, and it cannot be asserted dogmatically that during those centuries no persistent sorcerer was ever handed over by a bishop to the secular authorities, to be burned as a relapsed heretic. A passage in Walter Map suggests that such executions may not have been wholly unknown by, say, 1200.[54] On the other hand the silence of the chronicles suggests that they must have been very rare. All in all, it seems certain that there were very few trials for *maleficium*, whether as a secular or as a religious offence, between 1000 and 1300. It remains to find out why.

−3−

The greater interest in the common people which has characterized recent historiography has given rise to new interpretations of the great witch-hunt. Two British historians in particular, Mr Keith Thomas and Dr Alan Macfarlane, have concerned themselves with the question of why, in England, there were practically no witch-trials during the Middle Ages, and hundreds of such trials during the period 1560–1680; and they have sought the answer in increased tensions in village life.[55] This is not the place to consider how far their hypotheses are relevant to the great European witch-hunt as a whole; but one specific issue does call for comment. Mr Thomas has summarized it with admirable clarity in a couple of sentences in his monumental work:

"Why, if popular witch-beliefs were much the same as they had been in the Middle Ages, was it only during the sixteenth and seventeenth centuries that legal action against witchcraft attained such dimensions? To this question there are only two possible answers. Either the demand for the prosecution of witches suddenly grew, or the facilities for such prosecution had not previously existed."[56]

Thomas regards the first of these answers as by far the most plausible. The legal machinery for prosecuting the authors of *maleficia* existed in earlier centuries; if it was hardly ever used, that indicates that there was no widespread desire to prosecute witches or sorcerers. The argument sounds cogent enough. It becomes less so when one examines how, in such cases, medieval legal machinery actually worked.

Almost throughout the Middle Ages—very generally until the thirteenth century, in some parts of Europe even to the fifteenth century—the accusatory form of criminal procedure obtained. That is to say, the legal battle was fought out not between society and the accused, but between the accused and a private person who accused him. In this respect there was no difference between a civil and a criminal case; in the latter as in the former the individual complainant was responsible for finding and producing proofs such as would convince the judge.

The accusatory procedure was derived from Roman law, and it retained all those features which had characterized it under the later Empire. By and large it favoured the accused rather than the accuser. The accuser was obliged to conduct the case himself, without the assistance of prosecuting counsel. Moreover, if he failed to convince the judge he was likely to suffer as heavy a penalty as would have been visited upon the accused if he had been convicted. This was known as the talion.[57]

The intention behind the talion was simply to discourage malicious or frivolous accusations, but the effect was far more sweeping. How was the law to distinguish between a mere mistake and deliberate calumny? In practice it seldom distinguished; everyone knew that an unsuccessful complainant would almost certainly be penalized, whatever his motives. In England, under Edward I, it was decreed that an accuser who failed to make out his case should be imprisoned for a year as well as pay compensation for the imprisonment and infamy he had brought upon the accused; and this provision was altogether in keeping with a tradition which went back to Anglo-Saxon times.[58]

Everything possible was done to impress the would-be accuser with the risks involved. When notifying the judge of the proposed action, the accuser had to give a written undertaking to provide proof and, if the proof were found inadequate, to submit to the penalty of the talion as a calumniator. This inscription was an indispensable preliminary; no criminal case could proceed without it. And that was not all: once the inscription had been accepted by the judge, the accuser could not withdraw without incurring the penalty of the talion. Indeed, even while the action was in progress the accuser might, in effect, be penalized: in those cases where the accused was imprisoned pending trial, the judge commonly ordered the accuser to be imprisoned likewise, to preserve equality between the two parties.[59]

In order to condemn the accused outright, the judge required either a spontaneous confession from him or else an array of proofs which should be "clearer than the noonday light". Failing these, he would order the accused to submit to an ordeal. The ordeal, which originated not in Roman but in early Germanic law, could take various forms. The accused might be thrown into the water, bound in a certain way. If he or she floated it meant that the water, that symbol of purity, was rejecting a criminal; sinking was therefore taken as proof of innocence. Or the accused might be required to hold a red-hot iron, or plunge an arm into boiling water, for a given time. The injured limb was then bound up for a few days; if, when the bandage was removed, no scar was found, that too was proof of innocence. These ordeals were applied chiefly to members of the lower orders. Amongst the aristocracy the matter was more likely to be submitted to the test of single combat, either between the accuser and the accused or between champions representing them. All these various ordeals were regarded as appeals to God: where the human judge was uncertain, the decision was left to divine justice. But by the thirteenth century these ancient forms of ordeal were being replaced by another device, canonical purgation: the accused was required to swear before God that he was innocent, while a specified number of compurgators, or oath-helpers, swore that his oath was to be trusted.

An ordeal successfully endured, a canonical purgation successfully discharged, would bring acquittal; and in that case the accuser was required to prove that his accusation had been due to an honest mistake. If he was unable to carry out this almost impossible task, nothing could save him from the talion. The results of the system were what one would expect: nobody would become an accuser unless impelled by the most powerful motives. Only the most imperious considerations of self-interest or the most obsessive passion would induce anyone to face a long-drawn-out and highly uncertain action, which while it was in progress might involve his own imprisonment and which might end in his ruin. This was the case even when the offence in question was an ordinary felony: historians of medieval law tend to think that, so long as the accusatory procedure remained in force, only a tiny proportion of common criminals were ever brought to trial. But the inhibiting factors must have been vastly more powerful still when the offence was *maleficium*, whether real or imagined.

By its very nature *maleficium* was almost unprovable. Where puppets were produced, stuck full of pins, things might go well enough; but such cases were very exceptional. Other types of proof were far more hazardous. A misfortune—a death or an illness—was never simultaneous with the act of *maleficium* that was supposed to have caused it. Nor were there likely to be eye-witnesses to an act of *maleficium*—let alone eye-witnesses who would be prepared to testify on oath. The accused, on the other hand, had very good chances of establishing his or her innocence, whether by ordeal or by compurgation. In such circumstances, to charge anyone with *maleficium* was to take a very grave risk indeed. Sometimes the risk was taken, with disastrous results—for instance, at Strasbourg in 1451 a man who had accused a woman of *maleficium* and failed to make his case was arrested, tried for calumny and drowned in the River Ill.[60]

What was true of *maleficium* as a secular offence was even more true of *maleficium* as a religious offence. If the hazards were enough to deter a man from demanding justice even when he felt himself personally wronged, why ever should he concern himself with a matter which in no way involved his own interests? *Maleficium* as a religious offence was best left to the priest in the confessional. It was not for nothing that the clerical authors of the famous manual for witch-hunters, the *Malleus Maleficarum*, deplored the fact that even in the late fifteenth century the accusatory procedure was still in force at Coblenz. There were suspected witches in the neighbourhood, but it was simply impossible to try them under that procedure.[61]

It is not really surprising, then, that no tradition ever developed of bringing unsolicited accusations of *maleficium*; nor does the absence of such a tradition prove that during the Middle Ages the common people were not preoccupied with *maleficium*. The lynchings listed above are enough to show that *maleficium* was feared and that those who practised it, or were suspected of practising it, were hated. Indeed, they may show more than that: for lynchings are just what one would expect in a situation where fear and hatred were widespread but could find no expression through legal, institutionalized channels.

Much had to change before *maleficium* trials could become frequent, let alone before mass witch-hunts could begin. The accusatory had to be replaced by the inquisitorial procedure, while *maleficium* itself had to be seen in a new and more sinister light.

9

MAGICIAN INTO WITCH (1)

So long as the forgeries of Bardin, Lamothe-Langon and Piotto remained undetected, it seemed plausible that the great witch-hunt should have developed out of the Inquisition's struggle, during the fourteenth century, against heresy amongst the common people of southern France and northern Italy. But the demolition of the three forgeries changes everything. Traditional assumptions break down, familiar sources acquire different meanings, perspectives shift, the outlines of a new picture emerge.

It remains true that the first steps towards the great witch-hunt were taken when the inquisitorial procedure was brought to bear on new notions of *maleficium*. But these new notions of *maleficium* had nothing to do with heretical movements in southern France or northern Italy but reflected developments in quite different quarters; while the inquisitorial procedure was applied mainly not by professional inquisitors but by quite different authorities.

These bald statements call for elaboration. It is generally believed that ritual magic (or ceremonial magic, as it is sometimes called) had nothing whatsoever to do with witchcraft; and on the face of it that seems obvious. The practitioner of ritual magic operated above all by means of conjuration: he would summon one or more individual demons by name, with the object of persuading or compelling them to carry out a specific task. More often male than female, a commander of demons rather than their servant, a specialist skilled in a most elaborate technique, he was a very different figure from the witch as she was imagined at the time of the great witch-hunt. Yet if, after excluding the fabrications of Bardin, Lamothe-Langon and Piotto, one re-examines the remaining thirteenth- and fourteenth-century sources without any preconceptions, one finds that they are practically all concerned with ritual magic, and with that alone. One can also observe how, over a period of generations, ritual magic and the struggle against ritual magic helped to produce the fantastic stereotype of the witch. It turns out that the source of the new notions of *maleficium* lies there.

Although a comprehensive history of ritual magic in the Middle Ages has yet to be written, the main outlines of the story are clear.[1] Some awareness of the art had existed ever since Antiquity; [2] but in the later Middle Ages the art became far more elaborate, and it also began to evoke far more interest. A couple of contemporary comments will give a fair idea of what was involved. They come from educated men who were neither magicians nor persecutors of magicians but who, through their professional concerns, were well placed to know about such things.

Michael Scot was court astrologer and tutor to the young emperor Frederic II, and in the opening years of the fourteenth century, probably at Palermo, he wrote for him a vast work, the *Liber introductorius*, on astrology and related subjects.[3] In it he not only gives a list of the names by which demons may be invoked, he also states that, if a demon is to be imprisoned in a ring or a bottle, sacrifices have to be made first—indeed, as demons have a taste for human flesh, the magician may have to take some from a corpse, or even cut off a piece of his own.[4] A century later, also in Italy, another writer on astrology and astronomy, Cecco d'Ascoli, gives a similar indication. It was traditional to ascribe the invention of ritual magic to Zoroaster; and according to Cecco, Zoroaster discovered that "those four spirits of great virtue who stand *in cruciatis locis*, that is, in east, west, south and north, whose names are as follows: Oriens, Amaymon, Paymon and Egim, who are spirits of the major hierarchy and who have under them twenty-five legions of spirits each . . . because of their noble nature seek sacrifice from human blood and likewise from the flesh of a dead man or a cat. But this Zoroastrian art cannot be carried on without great peril, fastings, prayers and all things which are contrary to our faith." [5]

Sacrifices of blood or flesh were not the only way of soliciting the attention of demons. Around 1300 the Catalan Arnald of Villanova, who was eminent both as a writer on medicine and alchemy and as the physician and confidant of popes and kings, wrote a critique of ritual magic. He noted that some magicians tried to coerce spirits by means of artificial figures, words or "characters"; though for his part he did not accept that mere men could coerce spirits at all.[6] But already before 1250 the German monk Caesarius of Heisterbach, whose views on demons we have already considered, had hinted at a whole ritual of conjuration. In the *Dialogus miraculorum* he tells how a sceptical knight was converted to a belief in demons by a priest called Philip, who was a practitioner of ritual magic. Challenged to show what he could do, the magician took the knight to a cross-roads at noon—like midnight, a propitious time for such operations. He drew a circle on the ground with a sword, placed the knight inside it and warned him that if he allowed any of his limbs to stray across the circumference he would infallibly be seized and torn to pieces. The magician having withdrawn to perform his ritual, the knight was left to watch demonic manifestations all around him, ending with the appearance of a gigantic black demon, too hideous to look at.[7]

These scattered references effectively dispose of what would otherwise have been a formidable obstacle. It is known that the techniques of conjuring up demons were enshrined in writing as early as the thirteenth century; but very little of the extant material dates from earlier than the sixteenth or seventeenth centuries, and without confirmatory evidence we could hardly have assumed that the prescriptions we find there were known to practising magicians centuries earlier. The comments of Michael Scot, Cecco d'Ascoli, Arnald of Villanova and Caesarius of Heisterbach settle the matter: it is clear that the extant sources are closely modelled on—if indeed they are not copied from— the magical books of the Middle Ages.

At this point we are confronted by the great jungle of the pseudo-Solomonic writings. It was natural that many spurious works should be foisted on to the great king of Israel, who is glorified in the Talmud and the Koran as well as in the Bible, and whose name evokes images of superhuman wisdom and fortune even to the present day. The earliest surviving example is the *Testament of Solomon*, which seems to have originated in Palestine in the first century after Christ.[8] This is a medico-magical work and is not at all concerned with conjuring up demons; and the same could be said of most of the pseudo-Solomonic books which were written—some in Hebrew, some in Greek, some in Arabic—during the next thousand years. But from the twelfth or thirteenth century onwards pseudo-Solomonic works of quite a different kind were circulating in western Europe—true manuals on the art of conjuration, written by magicians for magicians. In the first half of the thirteenth century Guillaume d'Auvergne, bishop of Paris, in his treatise on laws warned readers against books bearing the name of Solomon and containing idolatrous images and detestable invocations.[9] Around 1267 the English philosopher Roger Bacon—at that time resident in Paris—complained that magicians were producing more and more pseudo-Solomonic works, written in grandiloquent language and containing formulae for conjuring up demons and specifications of the sacrifices to be offered them.[10] The sixteenth- and seventeenth-century sources mentioned above are variants or copies of those late medieval pseudo-Solomonic works. The most relevant to our purpose is the *Lemegeton*, otherwise known as the *Lesser Key of Solomon*, which tells us all we need to know.

Roger Bacon names, as one of the pseudo-Solomonic works circulating in the 1260s, a *Book of the offices of the spirits*, and the German abbot Trithemius still refers, in 1508, to a work called *Concerning the office of the spirits*. This work, or these works, must have had much the same character and purpose as the first part of *Lemegeton*, entitled *Goetia*.[11] A variant of *Goetia* was published by the Dutch medical doctor Johannes Weyer in 1577, under the title *Pseudomonarchia daemonum*, and was later translated into English by Reginald Scot and incorporated into the fifteenth book of his *Discoverie of Witchcraft* (1584). There we find descriptive lists of some scores of principal demons; detailing not only the forms in which each individual demon appears but also what offices he discharges and what powers he possesses. A few samples from Reginald Scot will convey something of the atmosphere:

> Purson, *alias* Curson, a great king, he commeth forth like a man with a lions face, carrieng a most cruell viper, and riding on a beare; and before him go alwaies trumpets, he knoweth things hidden, and can tell all things present, past, and to come: he bewraieth treasure, he can take a bodie either humane or aierie; he answereth truelie of all things earthlie and secret, of the divinitie and creation of the world, and bringeth forth the best familiars; and there obeie him two and twentie legions of divels, partlie of the order of vertues, & partlie of the order of thrones. . . .

> Leraie, *alias* Oray, a great marquesse, shewing himselfe in the likenesse of a galant archer, carrieng a bowe and a quiver, he is author of all battels, he dooth putrifie all such wounds as are made with arrowes by archers, *Quas optimos obijcit tribus diebus*, and he hath regiment over thirtie legions. . . .

> Glasya Labolas, *alias* Caacrinolaas, or Caassimolar, is a great president, who commeth forth like a dog, and hath wings like a griffen, he giveth the knowledge of arts, and is the captaine of all mansleiers:* he understandeth things present and to come, he gaineth the minds and love of freends and foes, he maketh a man go invisible, and hath the rule of six and thirtie legions. . . .

> Berith is a great and a terrible duke, and hath three names. Of some he is called Beall; of the Jewes Berith; of Nigromancers Bolfry: he commeth forth as a red souldier, with red clothing, and upon a horsse of that colour, and a crowne on his head. He answereth trulie of things present, past and to come. He is compelled at a certeine houre, through divine vertue, by a ring of art

* i.e. man-slayers, murderers.

magicke. He is also a lier, he turneth all mettals into gold, he adorneth a man with dignities, and confirmeth them, he speaketh with a cleare and a subtill voice, and six and twentie legions are under him. . . .

Malphas is a great president, he is seene like a crowe, but being cloathed with humane image, speaketh with a hoarse voice, he buildeth houses and high towres wonderfullie, and quicklie bringeth artificers togither, he throweth downe also the enimies edifications, he helpeth to good familiars, he receiveth sacrifices willinglie, but he deceiveth all the sacrificers, there obeie him fourtie legions. . . .

Shax, *alias* Scox, is a darke and a great marquesse, like unto a storke, with a hoarse and subtill voice: he dooth marvellouslie take awaie the sight, hearing, and understanding of anie man, at the commandement of the coniuror: he taketh awaie monie out of everie kings house. . . .

Focalor is a great duke comming forth as a man, with wings like a griphen, he killeth men, and drowneth them in the waters, and overturneth ships of warre, commanding and ruling both winds and seas. And let the coniuror note, that if he bid him hurt no man, he willinglie consenteth thereto: he hopeth after 1000. yeares to returne to the seventh throne, but he is deceived, he hath three legions. . . .

Such were the demons of ritual magic. Essentially they belong to the hosts of hell, as these were imagined by medieval Catholicism: they are fallen, evil angels. Not that astrological links are altogether lacking: some books of magic do try to relate specific demons to specific planets, and insist that a conjuration will succeed only if it is timed with due regard to planetary influences. But this is a very minor theme. By and large the demons with which a magician concerns himself are indistinguishable from the demons whose operations we considered in Chapter 4. In some cases even the names are derived from the Bible. Thus the ruler of all the demons is Baal, the sun-god of the Canaanites, who in the Old Testament is portrayed as the greatest and more fearsome of all heathen gods and the lord of all abominations; while the "mighty king" Belial is familiar from Jewish apocalyptic, where he figures as the chief power of evil, and the "terrible duke" Berith is mentioned in the Book of Judges as the god of the infidels. Other demons bear names that are quite unknown outside the ritual magic of Europe and were obviously invented *ad hoc*; but clearly they too are thought of as belonging to the same infernal hierarchy. Some of the formulae of conjuration are quite explicit on the matter: "I conjure you divels . . . I conjure you, and everie of you, ye infernall kings . . . by your hell, and by all the divels in it. . . ." [13] Moreover, the demons who are conjured up by name—the sixty-nine demons listed by Weyer and Scot, the seventy-two listed in *Goetia*—command the services of numberless lesser demons; and these are the demons whose ubiquity and incessant activity so appalled Abbot Richalmus of Schönthal. [14] Only, in the context of ritual magic these denizens of hell, instead of wreaking havoc according to their own desires, are harnessed to the magician's will.

Many of the benefits which a magician aimed to secure through his demonic contacts, whether for himself or for his employer, carried no harmful implications for other human beings. Through ritual magic one could, without effort, master the arts and sciences; one could compel the love of the mate one wanted; one could win the favour of the great and so advance one's career; one could discover the whereabouts of hidden or buried treasure; one could foresee one's future. Much the same demands exists today—and are catered for by a variety of industries, from cosmetics to sweepstakes, from personality courses to horoscopy. But if these were the commonest aims of ritual magic, they were not the only ones. Causing disease, deafness, blindness, insanity; provoking men to theft and murder; producing putrid wounds, leading to death within three days; burning the magician's own enemies— these are true *maleficia*, and all of them figure amongst the "offices of the spirits". In addition ritual magic was often sponsored by the rich and powerful, for their particular purposes: some demons specialized in producing wars and battles, sinking warships, demolishing walls, burning towns to the ground.

Whatever its objective, the act of conjuration itself followed a resolutely religious pattern—which might be of either Jewish or Christian inspiration, or a mixture of both. [15] Whether the magician was trying to scale the heights of scholarship in a flash or whether he was trying to make men kill one another, he set about it in a most pious fashion. Nowhere, in the surviving books of magic, is there a hint of Satanism. Nowhere is it suggested that the magician should ally himself with the demonic hosts, or do evil to win the favour of the Prince of Evil. Not a word is said about reversing or profaning religious rituals or observances, whether Christian or Jewish. The demons are not to be worshipped but, on the contrary, mastered and commanded; and this is to be done through the power of the God who created all spirits as well as all human beings. Throughout, the attitude is that of a devout man who can with confidence call on God for help in his undertaking. Indeed, all the books of magic stress that a magical enterprise has no prospect of success unless the magician worships God and believes absolutely in his infinite goodness.

It may seem paradoxical that anyone should hope for God's help in finding hidden treasure, let alone in burning towns to the ground; but in the context of ritual magic it is not. At the heart of ritual magic was the belief in the irresistible power of certain divine words, and above all of the Divine Name. Strings of such words and names were built into prayers. When recited aloud in appropriate circumstances, these prayers were supposed to compel the obedience of demons: at the sound of the Divine Name the demons trembled and were subdued to the magician's will. But how could any man invoke God or utter the Divine Name— at least with any hope of being heard—unless he were himself full of reverence and love for God? So it came about that even when his aims were thoroughly destructive, even when he was trying to work a *maleficium*, the magician felt himself a pious Christian or Jew.

In a sense, conjuring up a demon was one long exercise in religious devotion. Before embarking on a conjuration the magician was required to prepare himself by a period of chastity, fasting and prayer. Then the various strange instruments used in a conjuration—sword, staff, rod, lancet, hook, sickle, needle, white-handled knife, black-handled knife—had to be fumigated, asperged and consecrated. To be effective, the consecration had to include a recital of seven psalms, prayers to the angels, and a direct appeal to God. Next, as the time for the conjuration drew near, the magician washed himself in consecrated water and put on his ceremonial robes—including a hat of white leather bearing the names of God, such as El, Elohim, or else Jehovah, Adonay. Above all, the conjuration itself was carried out by invoking the power of God. Anyone interested can study the incredibly long (and tedious) formulae in Mathers's translation of the *Key of Solomon*.[16] Here a briefer example, from the *Lemegeton*, will suffice. If a demon obstinately refuses to appear after repeated invocations, the magician may proceed to the ultimate sanction—he may penalize the demon in God's name:

> Thou art still pernicious and disobedient, willing not to appear and inform me upon that which I desire to know; now therefore, in the Name and by the power and dignity of the Omnipotent and Immortal Lord God of Hosts, Jehovah Tetragrammaton,* sole Creator of Heaven, Earth and Hell, with all contained therein, the

* Tetragrammaton: the four consonants forming the Hebrew "incommunicable name" of God.

marvellous Disposer of all things visible and invisible, I do hereby curse and deprive thee of all thine office, power, and place; I bind thee in the depths of the Bottomless Pit, there to remain unto the Day of Judgment, in the lake of fire and brimstone, prepared for the rebellious spirits. . . .[17]

Stranger still, a magician could bind a spirit permanently to himself, by imprisoning it in a ring, mirror, crystal or other stone; and for this too divine assistance was indispensable. Here once more Reginald Scot may serve as a guide to the mysteries. Only after the magician had spent a day in fasting, and made his confession, and spent two further days in prayer, was he equipped to begin. A preliminary invocation of five senior demons, Sitrael, Malantha, Thamaor, Falaur and Sitrami, was carried out with a great display of Christian piety—in the name of the Father, the Son, the Holy Ghost, the Virgin Mary, all the saints, the angels and arch-angels, the patriarchs, the prophets, the apostles, the evangelists, the martyrs "and all the elect of God". The effect of such a conjuration, repeated five times, was infallible: "Then shalt thou see come out of the north part five kings, with a marvelous companie: which when they come to the circle, they will allight from their horsses, and will kneele down before thee, saieng: Maister, command us what thou wilt, and we will out of hand be obedient unto thee." The magician was now in a position to achieve his aim:

I conjure, charge, and command you, and everie of you, *Sitrael*, *Malantha*, *Thamaor*, *Falaur*, and *Sitrama*, you infernall kings, to put into this christall stone one spirit learned and expert in all arts and sciences, by the vertue of this name of God Tetragrammaton, and by the crosse of our Lord Jesu Christ, and by the bloud of the innocent lambe, which redeemed all the world, and by all their vertues & powers I charge you, ye noble kings, that the said spirit may teach, shew, and declare unto me, and to my freends, at all houres and minuts, both night and daie, the truth of all things, both bodilie and ghostlie, in this world, whatsoever I shall request or desire, declaring also to me my verie name. And this I command in your part to doo, and to obeie thereunto, as unto your owne lord and maister. That done, they will call a certeine spirit, whom they will command to enter into the centre of the circled or round christall. Then put the christall between the two circles, and thou shalt see the christall made blacke.

Then command them to command the spirit in the christall, not to depart out of the stone, till thou give him licence, & to fulfill thy will for ever. . . . And then take up thy christall, and looke therein, asking what thou wilt, and it will shew it unto thee. . . . And when the spirit is inclosed, if thou feare him, bind him with some bond . . ." [18]

"If thou feare him . . .": demons were dangerous beings, and the ritual was designed not simply to force them to serve the magician but also to protect him from them. The spiritual preparations, the preliminary mortifications and prayers, were meant to ensure that he would remain safe in body and soul. Some of the books of magic even add that unless the magician, when attempting a conjuration, is in a state of grace and has a clear conscience, he may find that instead of commanding the demon he is commanded by it. Similarly, when the magician put on his ceremonial robes, inscribed with the names of God, he was shielding himself against the destructive powers he was about to conjure up. The circle which he drew on the ground with his consecrated sword served the same purpose: it marked out a field of concentrated divine power, a barrier which no demon could cross. So long as the magician remained within the circle, he could operate in safety; but if he stepped outside it, or even allowed a single limb to stray outside, he could be seized by the demons.

It is all a far cry from the great witch-hunt. And at first glance it may seem incredible that the reality of the magician, with his abstruse technical literature, his elaborate professional techniques for mastering and binding demons, his incessant invocation of God, could have contributed anything at all to fantasies about illiterate peasant women sexually seduced by demons and enlisted in the service of Satan. Nevertheless it did contribute something, and that something can be defined.

In ritual magic demons were imagined as participating in a far more direct and individual way than had been the case with ordinary magic, such as had been practised down the centuries. Of course, the Church had always maintained that every magical operation implied the co-operation of demons; but that had been understood in a very vague and general sense. Now magicians were conjuring demons by name, summoning them to manifest themselves in visible form, giving them precise instructions; and this implied a new and closer form of collaboration between particular human beings and particular demons. Moreover, some demons were noted as being especially good providers of familiars—which pointed to a still closer, more lasting form of collaboration.

Then there was the matter of sacrifice. The magicians were not Satanists—yet some of them certainly did try to lure demons on by

offerings of flesh and blood. This had nothing to do with human sacrifice. The custom was either to cut a limb from a corpse—usually the
corpse of a criminal on the gallows—or else to slaughter an animal or
fowl. Michael Scot and Cecco d'Ascoli refer to such practices in the
thirteenth and fourteenth centuries; and some books of magic contain
detailed prescriptions for sacrificing a fowl. The magician is instructed,
for instance, to take a black virgin hen to a cross-roads at midnight and
tear it apart, while summoning up a demon; or else to kill a black cock,
tear out its eyes, tongue and heart, dry them in the sun, and reduce
them to powder, which is then offered up.[19] Admittedly, the books
containing these two prescriptions date from the seventeenth and the
nineteenth centuries respectively; but the prescriptions themselves are
certainly very ancient. All these various forms of sacrifice figure in one
or other of the fourteenth-century trials.

In these transactions a special place was reserved for the demon
Belial. The *Lemegeton* and its variants describe the situation of that
"mighty king", who in his origins was the first angel to be created after
Lucifer or Satan himself. We learn that King Solomon shut up the
seventy-two principal demons in a brass vessel and cast it into a deep
lake; but the Babylonians discovered the vessel and, supposing it to
contain a great treasure, broke it open. The spirits who were thus set
free returned to their former places, along with their attendant legions.
Only Belial took a different course: he entered into an image or idol,
whence he uttered oracles in return for sacrifices and divine honours.[20]
Such a demon figures in at least one of the fourteenth-century trials—
the posthumous trial of Pope Boniface VIII. More important, the fact
that the books of magic proclaimed, and magicians accepted, the special
status and demands of Belial was bound to appear particularly sinister
to the guardians of religious orthodoxy.

In reality, whatever sacrifices were offered, and even if they were
offered to Belial himself, God was still invoked and his omnipotence
affirmed. But that did not make the proceedings any less blasphemous,
indeed heretical, when viewed in terms of Catholic doctrine. The first
step towards the great witch-hunt was taken when the traditional
teaching of the Church was applied—not necessarily or mainly by
inquisitors—to the relatively unfamiliar phenomenon of ritual magic;
for in the process *maleficium* acquired a meaning it had not possessed in
earlier centuries.

– 2 –

In a paper on "The literature of witchcraft", delivered to the American Historical Association in 1889, George Lincoln Burr listed the theological and ecclesiastical pronouncements which in his view effectively created the stereotype of the witch. Already Thomas Aquinas, who died in 1274, "taught that there were among men other servants of the Devil, more subtle, more dangerous, than the heretics: the men and women devoted altogether to his service—the witches". By the 1320s, he continues, the Church was fully committed to the struggle against witchcraft; and this was exemplified by a bull of Pope John XXII, *Super illius specula*. Finally, the inquisitor Nicolas Eymeric produced the earliest book on witchcraft, with the object of clarifying its nature and so helping inquisitors to identify and pursue witches.[21] Burr was a serious and conscientious scholar, and his comments fitted in well with what was thought to have happened around Toulouse and Novara; so it is not surprising that this view of the matter has been accepted and perpetuated by reputable historians down to the present day. But now the events around Toulouse and Novara turn out never to have occurred, and in any case the best part of a century has passed since the lecture was delivered. It is time to re-examine the sources.

So far as Aquinas is concerned, the task is already done. More than thirty years ago another American scholar, Charles Edward Hopkin, produced an excellent thesis entitled *The share of Thomas Aquinas in the growth of the witchcraft delusion*.[22] If this had ever been published, Burr's dictum would no doubt enjoy less credence; for Hopkin found that the vast work of "the angelic doctor" has no place for anything remotely resembling witches, as witches were imagined at the time of the great witch-hunt.

Admittedly, Aquinas not only accepts that demons exist, he accepts that they can operate as *incubi* and *succubi*, i.e. that a demon can take on the form of a man or a woman, and in that form have sexual intercourse with a human being. But then, this was very generally believed, and always had been. Augustine was familiar with the idea eight centuries earlier, and both Augustine and Aquinas give, as their reason for taking it seriously, the general consensus of popular opinion. This is not the place to enquire why the belief in *incubi* and *succubi* was so widespread (a matter to be considered in a later chapter). The point is, rather, that Aquinas never connects *incubi* or *succubi* with *maleficium*. Nowhere does he even hint that, by mating with a demon, a woman can acquire magical powers, or herself become a semi-demonic being.

To discover what Aquinas thought about magic one has to look at quite different parts of his work; and what emerges then is that for him magic means almost exclusively ritual or ceremonial magic. Here and there he mentions old women who can harm people, especially children, by the evil eye; but these are brief references. Conjuration of demons is what really concerns him. He confronts this new aberration as a theologian, intent on defining its theological implications. In this task of interpretation he draws on a tradition that goes back to Augustine, and beyond Augustine to the Bible itself.

Magicians, says Aquinas, invoke demons in a supplicating manner, as though addressing superiors; yet when they come, they give them orders, as though addressing inferiors—thereby showing that they are deceived as to their own powers. Not that Aquinas doubts that the demons come—if not in the sense of becoming visible, then at least in the sense of answering questions; he even remarks that those verbal replies cannot be imaginary, since they are heard by all within earshot. But why do they come?—Aquinas insists that no demon can really be coerced by a magician; it only pretends to be coerced, for reasons of its own. The formulae and apparatus used by the magician have no power in themselves, but they are pleasing to demons as signs of reverence. In appearing to comply with a magician's command, a demon is deceiving the magician, who in reality is in a position of subjection. By this show of obedience the demon leads the magician ever deeper into sin; and that is wholly in accord with a demon's nature and desires.[23]

The particular practices which Aquinas attributes to magicians have nothing at all to do with the monstrous deeds that were later to be ascribed to witches. Indeed, in this respect he understates. He says not a word about sacrifices, whether of animals or of the flesh of corpses, and has little to say about *maleficium*. He recognizes that demons can make a man impotent with his wife, but neither that nor any other form of *maleficium* much concerns him. His interest is concentrated almost entirely on the practice of divination, i.e. foretelling the future. He insists that any attempt to foretell the future, beyond what can be foreseen by human reason or what has been revealed by God, is sinful. And the reason why it is sinful is that it involves dealing with a demon. It is one example—the commonest—of what Aquinas calls a "pact".

For Aquinas, any human being who accepts help from a demon, in the hope of accomplishing something which transcends the powers of nature, has entered into a pact with that demon. Such a pact may be either explicit or tacit. It is explicit when the human operator invokes the demon's help—and that is so whether the demon responds or not;

in other words, the act of conjuration involves an explicit pact. A tacit pact is involved when, without conjuration, a human being performs an act with a view to some effect which cannot naturally follow, and which is not to be expected, either, from the intervention of God.[24]

The notion of the pact was not new—it is to be found already in Augustine—but it took on a new significance when, in the Europe of the thirteenth and fourteenth centuries, it was applied to the magical practices then proliferating. Aquinas argues that every attempt to communicate with a demon, whether explicit or tacit, is not merely sinful but amounts to apostasy from the Christian faith. It does so because, in every such attempt, some part of the worship that ought to be rendered to God alone is diverted to one of God's creatures, and a fallen, rebellious angel at that. In all this Aquinas was speaking as a representative of contemporary orthodoxy.

In practice the ecclesiastical authorities took a far more serious view of those forms of magic which involved an "explicit pact", i.e. the deliberate invocation of particular demons, than of those which did not. In 1258 Pope Alexander IV laid down the principle that inquisitors were not to concern themselves with cases of divination as such, but only with those which "manifestly savoured of heresy".[25] This can only refer to the invocations characteristic of ritual magic. And the pronouncements of Pope John XXII in the 1320s, which Burr mistakenly supposed to be concerned with witchcraft, likewise turn out to refer to ritual magic.

In 1320 the pope, disturbed by reports that were reaching him concerning the practice of ritual magic at the papal court at Avignon itself, decided that the time had come to clarify and define the relationship between magic and heresy. After first taking written opinions from five bishops, two generals of monastic orders and three masters of theology, and then discussing the matter with them at a special consistory at Avignon, the pope wrote to the cardinal of St Sabina, who in turn wrote to the inquisitors of Toulouse and Carcassonne.[26] Henceforth the inquisitors were empowered to act against practitioners of ritual magic as heretics; and in 1326 or 1327 the pope tried to reinforce their efforts by a bull, *Super illius specula*.[27] Between them, the letter of authorization and the bull show perfectly clearly what practices were involved. On the one hand magicians were trying to win the favour of demons by adoring them, doing them homage, entering into pacts with them, giving them written documents and other pledges; on the other hand they were trying to bind demons to their service by enclosing them in specially made rings, mirrors, phials and the like, so that they

could ask them questions and extract answers, and generally compel
their assistance. The purposes for which these things were done were
themselves "most foul", but it was the involvement of demons that
made the whole undertaking heretical. The bull makes this perfectly
plain. Christians are given eight days to abandon such practices, after
which they become liable to almost all the penalties for heresy. Within
eight days, too, all books and writings on magic are to be handed over
for burning, on pain of excommunication and maybe worse penalties
as well.

The *Treatise against the invokers of demons* of Nicolas Eymeric, which
is often referred to as the earliest book on witchcraft, exists only in
manuscript; though a summary of it is included in his celebrated
Directorium Inquisitorum or *Inquisitors' Guide*.[28] Eymeric, a Spaniard,
had been functioning for some twelve years as inquisitor-general for
Aragon when he wrote it, in or just after 1369; so it can be taken as a
fair account of everything that an experienced investigator knew or
believed about the occult arts in the last part of the fourteenth century.
On inspection it turns out to be not about witchcraft but, once again,
about ritual magic.

Like Pope Alexander IV, whom he quotes, Eymeric recognizes that
some forms of divination, however deplorable, are not heretical and so
do not concern the Inquisition; such are divination by palmistry or by
drawing lots. But heresy is present in any divination that involves the
cult of demons—whether that cult take the form of *latria*, the worship
due to God alone, or of *dulia*, the adoration paid to the saints. Eymeric
knows of many ways in which *latria* and *dulia* can be expressed. When
a magician sacrifices birds or animals to a demon, or makes offerings of
his own blood, or promises the demon obedience, or kneels to it, or
sings songs in its praise, or observes chastity or mortifies the flesh out of
reverence for it, or lights candles or burns incense in its honour, or begs
something of it by means of signs and unknown names, or adjures it in
the name of a superior demon—all this is *latria*. *Dulia* includes less
familiar practices, such as praying to God through the names and merits
of demons, as though they were mediators like the saints. But Eymeric
also knows of magical ceremonies by which a demon can be invoked
without either *latria* or *dulia*; as when the magician makes a circle on the
ground, places an assistant within it, and reads spells from a book.

Eymeric's account is much fuller than anything offered by Aquinas or
by John XXII. He had certain advantages: he mentions that he had
seized and read many books of magic before burning them. His
motives are also rather different from his predecessors': as a leading

inquisitor, he is concerned to show that practitioners of ritual magic come under the jurisdiction of the Inquisition. To prove his point he cites a large number of authorities, including Aquinas and the bull *Super illius specula*—indeed, he gives the complete text of the bull, and that is the earliest copy of it we possess. His conclusion is that all ritual magic is heretical, even when neither *latria* nor *dulia* is involved; for the very act of invoking demons is heretical. Those who do these things are all heretics, and are liable to the same penalties as other heretics: if penitent, they are to be perpetually immured; if they are obdurate, or if after repenting they relapse, they are to be handed over to the secular arm for execution.

Such are the three authorities who, between them, are supposed to have created the stereotype of the witch. Obviously they did no such thing. Yet these are significant pronouncements, for they show quite clearly what, in the thirteenth and fourteenth centuries, the Church thought of practitioners of ritual magic. Other sources add nothing substantial to what these three tell us. Confronted with the spread of ritual magic in western Europe, popes, scholastics and inquisitors alike decided that it was a form of heresy and apostasy.

The magicians themselves of course saw the matter in quite a different light. Fourteenth-century manuscripts of a magic book known as the *Liber sacer*, or alternatively as the *Sworn Book of Honorius*, carry a preface which must surely have been written in response to the papal condemnations of the 1320s.[29] The pope and the cardinals, we learn, have decreed the extirpation of the magic art and the physical extermination of all magicians. The grounds for the decree are that magicians are transgressing the ordinances of the Church, invoking demons and making sacrifices to them, and moreover deceiving ignorant people by their illusions and so driving them to damnation. But, say the magicians, none of this is true; the pope and the cardinals have themselves been deceived by the Devil. In the magic art spirits are compelled to act against their will—and this is something that only the pure of heart can achieve; the wicked are therefore unable to practise the art with any success. The Devil, so far from regarding the magicians as allies, sees in them a threat to his monopoly of working wonders—which is why he has inspired legislation against them.

On the evidence of the books of magic the protest seems justified. The magicians did not regard themselves as demon-worshippers, because they knew that when they invoked a demon, they did so in the name and by the power of God. The ecclesiastical authorities were presumably also aware of this fact, but in their eyes it made no difference. Whatever the procedure, ritual magic always involved asking from demons what ought to be asked from God alone; and that was utterly damnable.

In all this *maleficium* played little part. Foretelling the future, discovering hidden treasure, tracking down a thief—these are the purposes which, in its doctrinal pronouncements, the Church commonly attributed to ritual magic. Yet other possibilities existed. As we have seen, some books of magic themselves list the many kinds of harm that demons can be induced to do. When it came to actual trials, these claims were seized upon: in trials where ritual magic figured, *maleficium* often figured too. But such trials were also heresy trials: and that is how *maleficium* acquired a new significance.

That significance seemed all the more sinister because the inquisitorial procedure, under which heresy trials were conducted, was as likely to distort the facts as to elicit them; and could also be used to fabricate deeds that were never done at all. Not that the Inquisition itself contributed much to the process. Though the Inquisition perfected the inquisitorial procedure, it never monopolized it; and very few of the heresy trials which, in the course of the fourteenth century, directly prepared the way for the great witch-hunt were conducted by professional inquisitors, whether Dominican or Franciscan. Bishops, special ecclesiastical commissioners and secular judges played a much larger part; and, as we shall see, their motives were very mixed indeed.

10

MAGICIAN INTO WITCH (2)

-I-

It seems that the first person to be formally tried for practising ritual magic was Pope Boniface VIII; and he was tried posthumously. This happened in 1310–11, in the aftermath of the pope's struggle with Philip the Fair of France, and it was the work of Philip's devoted servant, Guillaume de Nogaret.*

Boniface was the first pope to see the spiritual hegemony of the papacy openly challenged and rejected by a national monarchy.[1] The immediate source of conflict was the taxation of the clergy. England and France were at war, and Edward I and Philip IV both tried to secure contributions from their clergy towards the cost of the war. This was contrary to the canon law of the time, and Boniface was well within his rights when, in 1296, he issued a bull forbidding any imposition of taxes on the clergy without express licence by the pope. But whereas in England, thanks to the efforts of the archbishop of Canterbury, Robert de Winchelsey, the bull had some effect, Philip was able to introduce countermeasures which practically nullified it in France. And he was quick to follow up his victory: by arresting and imprisoning the bishop of Pamiers, Bernard Saisset, he openly challenged the papal claim, so laboriously established during the preceding two centuries, to control over the clergy. Boniface in turn replied with two bulls, in which he demanded the release of Saisset and reaffirmed the supremacy of the spiritual over the temporal power; but he had underestimated Philip's determination and ruthlessness.

Philip had allies in the Colonna family. That mighty Roman clan hated Boniface bitterly. They were the second oldest of the city's princely families, and had long been the most powerful. The oldest

---

* In 1301–3 Walter de Langton, bishop of Coventry and Lichfield and treasurer of England, had to face charges which included intimate dealings with the Devil; but ritual magic was implied rather than explicit. For a recent account of the episode: Alice Beardwood, "The trial of Walter Langton, Bishop of Lichfield, 1307–1312", in *Transactions of the American Philosophical Society*, New Series, vol. 54, Part 3, Philadelphia, 1964, especially pp. 7–8.

family was the Caetani, into which Boniface was born; and with his accession to the papal throne it became the most powerful as well. The Colonna saw themselves deprived of their traditional primacy, and more; for Boniface set about breaking their power—excommunicating them, confiscating their estates, even declaring a crusade against them. The Colonna responded by aligning themselves with the king of France and joining in his campaign to discredit the pope. It was the Colonna who first put about the story of Boniface's demonic contacts.

In March 1301, an assembly of bishops and great lords gathered around Philip the Fair at the Louvre, heard Nogaret denounce the pope as a heretic and demand a general council of the Church to try him; after which Nogaret left for Italy. And while Boniface prepared yet another bull, this time excommunicating the king of France, Nogaret organized a plot to seize him and drag him before a council. The Colonna were his allies, but in effect they ruined the plot. In September the pope was duly seized at his castle at Anagni; but then Sciarra Colonna went too far, insulting and harassing the old man for three days, and also provoking the inhabitants of Anagni to such a point that in the end they rose and rescued the pope. Nogaret was wounded and fled; there could no longer be any question of a general council. On the other hand Boniface was a broken man, mentally and physically; and within a month he was dead.

The consequences were to pursue Nogaret for eight of the ten years of life that remained to him. The new pope, Benedict XI, issued a bull excommunicating him and fifteen others who had taken part in the action at Agnani. The following year Benedict also died, to be succeeded by the French pope Clement V, resident at Avignon and largely dependent on the good will of the king of France. Both Philip the Fair and Nogaret had helped to secure Clement's election, and both expected favours in return. For Philip it was important that Clement should annul the bulls that Boniface had directed against him; and that he should comply, if not actively co-operate, in the suppression of the Order of the Temple. As for Nogaret, he desperately needed to be relieved of the sentence of excommunication. Between them, they hit on an ingenious device for exerting pressure on the pope: they proposed that his predecessor Boniface should be posthumously tried as a heretic, apostate and criminal.

If the trial had been carried all the way through, the outcome would have been momentous: Boniface's memory would have been sullied, his reign declared illegitimate, even his bones exhumed and burned; the king of France would have been justified and exalted; the institution of the papacy would have been further weakened. Yet it may be doubted whether either King Philip or Nogaret ever intended to push matters so far. Certainly they cannot have believed the charges against Boniface any more than they believed the charges against the Templars. This is proved by the outcome. By 1311 Pope Clement had yielded on all counts: the relevant bulls had been annulled, the Temple had been suppressed, and Nogaret had been absolved (subject to some rather hypothetical conditions). None of this would have made any difference to men who genuinely believed that the papal throne had been occupied by a heretic: they would have persisted. In the event, however, the charges against Boniface were quietly dropped. [2]

Some of the charges have a direct bearing on our theme. [3] A first hint of them was given already in June 1303. While Nogaret was away in Italy, preparing to kidnap the pope, Philip held a meeting of the Estates at the Louvre. On that occasion the king, the prelates and nobles of France, and the doctors of the University of Paris listened while one of Nogaret's assistants listed Boniface's crimes. The Colonna certainly had a hand in that speech—it even included passages lifted from a manifesto of their own. [4] And among the peculiarities attributed to the reigning pope is the following: "He has a private demon, whose counsel he takes in, and throughout, all matters. So that on one occasion he said that if all people in the world were in one region, and he in another, they would not be able to trap him, whether in law or in fact; something that would not be possible without the use of the demonic art. And this is said against him publicly." [5]

By the time of the posthumous trial the theme had undergone considerable elaboration. In 1310 Nogaret presented Pope Clement with a document which was in effect a much amplified version of the speech of 1303. [6] Here too the Colonna were involved—particularly Cardinal Peter Colonna, who is specifically mentioned as a source of information. In this document Boniface's demonic contacts bulk large. [7] He had, it seems, not one but three demons—one presented by an Italian woman; another, more powerful, presented by a Hungarian; a third, called Boniface, and the most powerful of the three, presented by Boniface of Vicenza—"Boniface given to Boniface by Boniface," the pope is supposed to have jested. In addition, he carried a "spirit" in a ring on his finger; many cardinals and clerics had observed how that ring seemed to reflect sometimes a man, sometimes an animal's head.★

★ In reality this was no doubt a ring with a talismanic stone, bearing the symbol of a planet. These symbols often comprised the image of a Greco-Roman god with animal's features. To wear a talismanic ring showing Jupiter with a lion's

The support given by these assorted demons was far more effective than the mere advisory service offered by the demon of 1303. After the election of Celestine V as pope, Benedict Caetani (as he then was) came home in a rage, filled the censers in his room, and locked himself in. As the room filled with clouds of incense his attendants, listening at the keyhole, heard him shouting, "Why have you deceived me?" and a treble voice reply: "It was impossible this time. Your papacy must come from us, you must not be a true, legitimate pope. It will come soon!" Often when great decisions were pending Boniface would shut himself into his room, forbidding anyone even to touch the door; and after an hour or so his companions would feel the earth shake and hear sounds of hissing and lowing, as of serpents and cattle, issuing from the room. They lived in fear that one day the demons he called up would strangle both him and them.

The pope expected his demons to involve themselves in his feud with the Colonna. He was often heard to exclaim furiously, "Where are the Colonna you promised to hand over to me? I gave myself to you, body and soul, for that purpose." But the demons' replies were unsatisfactory. They pointed out that whereas Boniface had the power to destroy the property of the Colonna, he was not permitted to harm their persons; so that the demons were not permitted to divulge their whereabouts. Yet in his hour of greatest need the demons did effectively oppose the Colonna: Boniface was supposed to have declared that neither God nor man, but the demons, had rescued him from the Colonna at Anagni.

Nogaret and his agents arranged for their accusations to be substantiated by witnesses. This presented no difficulties at all, for Boniface had made many enemies. A man of great abilities and energy, he had shown himself proud and arrogant, relentless towards those whom he regarded as standing in his way, abrupt and irascible even towards his adherents; a man who, with many of the qualities of a great ruler, failed to be one largely because he was less suited to gain than to forfeit loyalties. So during 1310 and 1311 a score of hostile witnesses, all selected or approved by Nogaret, offered their evidence to the pope and the papal commissioners. A first hearing took place at Groseau near Avignon in the summer of 1310; and there the witnesses, though they had some startling things to say about the late pope, made no mention of

---

face and bird's feet, for instance, was a way of winning the favour of a powerful person, increasing one's reputation and seeing one's enemies humiliated: Boniface may well have adopted it. Cf. "Picatrix". Das Ziel der Weisen von Pseudo-Magriti. Translated into German from the Arabic by Hellmut Ritter and Martin Ritter (Studies of the Warburg Institute, vol. 27), London, 1962.

demons.[8] But at a second hearing, held in Rome in the spring of 1311, three monks specifically charged Boniface with demon-worship.[9] Most of the witnesses heard in Rome had previously appeared at Groseau; but these monks were added to the list only in Rome, as though to clinch the matter.

The evidence of Brother Berardus of Soriano is particularly instructive.[10] The first episode he describes is set in the period 1277–80, i.e. at least thirty years before the trial itself. At that time the future Pope Boniface was still Benedict Caetani, a notary of Pope Nicholas III. The evidence reads as follows:

> Once when witness, along with another man called Constantius of Foligno, who was the chamberlain of the said lord Benedict (Caetani), were loitering, at a late hour, at a window of the palace where he was staying (at Viterbo), he saw how the lord Benedict went out into a garden adjoining the palace, drew a circle with a sword, placed himself in the middle of the circle, sat down, and pulled out a rooster, and also fire in an earthen jar. He saw the lord Benedict kill the cock and throw its blood on the fire. Smoke came from the mixture of blood and fire, while the lord Benedict read from a book and conjured up demons. After this conjuration witness heard a great sound, which terrified him. At length he heard a voice begging: "Give us a part." And the above-mentioned Constantius saw the lord Benedict take the cock and throw it out of the garden, saying: "Here is your part." Then the lord Benedict left the garden and passed witness and his companion without speaking to them, or to any member of his household, and went into an unoccupied room. Witness with his companion Constantius slept next to the room of the lord Benedict; and all that night he heard the lord Benedict talking, and another voice answering. Yet there was nobody else in the room.

Years later, when Benedict Caetani had become Boniface VIII, another disturbing experience befell Brother Berardus, this time in the papal palace in Rome. He found the pope at dinner with various people, including the same Constantius. There was a window in the wall of the room, covered with a piece of golden silk. After dinner the silk was removed, and the pope stood in adoration before the window for a full hour, before being carried off to his throne. Berardus stayed behind, along with Constantius; and on asking his friend what the pope had been worshipping, received the reply: "It is no painting, but the evil majesty." Thereupon Berardus went quickly up to the window and, despite Constantius's protests, opened it. Inside was an idol, and Constantius explained its significance: it contained a diabolic spirit, which the pope worshipped and regarded as his god. Everything he did was done in accordance with this spirit's teaching.

This recalls the chief demon Belial, who took refuge in an idol. But it also recalls the idol of the Templars, of which France had heard a great deal during the preceding four years. That idol too was full of demonic power—and it too was an invention of Nogaret and his men. But the similarity between the two cases does not end there. The Templars were charged with apostasy, sodomy and murder—and precisely the same charges were brought against the deceased pope. The witnesses heard by Pope Clement and his commissioners accused his predecessor of denying and mocking the central doctrines of Catholic Christianity: the triune nature of God, the divinity of Christ, the virgin birth, the real presence of Christ in the Eucharist, the end of the world and the Last Judgement. They accused him of sodomy with boys and with women. They accused him of murdering his own predecessor, Celestine V. And —to round the matter up—they accused him of favouring the Templars and accepting money from them.[11]

Only, the Templars were not accused of entering into an alliance with demons for the purpose of ruining and destroying human beings. To be accused of that, and at the same time to be portrayed as evil in every possible respect—that was a new combination, and full of sinister potentialities. Retrospectively, this trial of a dead pope can be seen as initiating a process that was to culminate, much later, in the great witch-hunt.

–2–

The persecution of Guichard, bishop of Troyes, belongs to the same period as the persecution of the Templars and the posthumous assault on Boniface VIII; and like them it was pursued by the servants of Philip the Fair, including Nogaret.[12]

Born probably around 1245, Guichard became a monk and rose in the hierarchy with quite unusual rapidity. By 1273 he was at the head of an important priory at Provins, in Champagne; and in the years following he attracted the patronage of a very powerful woman, Blanche of Artois, who was the widow of Henry III, king of Navarre and count of Champagne. His great career was made possible partly by Blanche herself and partly by her daughter Joan, who on coming of age inherited both Navarre and Champagne and also married Philip the Fair and so became, in 1285, queen of France. Promoted abbot, Guichard became the representative in Champagne both of the countess and of the queen, and so powerful that nobody could oppose his will. Finally, in 1298, the influence of the two women secured his elevation as bishop of Troyes. Over the years he had built up a fortune; as bishop he became in addition a great lord, the most dazzling prelate Troyes had ever had. He played a part at the royal court itself, being a member of the king's council. But he made enemies, both amongst the king's councillors and amongst his own clergy. Enguerrand de Marigny, who was making his career in the household of Queen Joan and was on his way to become the king's chief minister, was bound to see a dangerous rival in such an able and energetic careerist. As for the clergy of Troyes, they had ample grounds for irritation. Conciliatory so long as he was still making a career, once he had reached the episcopate Guichard showed himself as arrogant as any great secular lord; choleric, quick with insults and abuse, riding roughshod over traditional privileges. He was to pay for this when he lost the favour of his patronesses.

He began to lose it a couple of years after becoming bishop. A certain Jean de Calais, who was in charge of Blanche's revenues in Champagne, was accused of embezzling part of them and was imprisoned in Guichard's episcopal prison. The man escaped, fled to Italy and was never recaptured; and Guichard found himself accused of conniving in the escape, for money. The accusation was laid before the countess by two men: the archdeacon of Vendôme, Simon Festu, who belonged to her inner circle and was competing with Guichard for her favour; and an agent of an Italian bank called Onofrio Deghi or, in France, Noffo Dei. The countess was quickly persuaded and turned fiercely against her former favourite, who was promptly expelled from the council. In 1301 an enquiry was opened, and it turned into a downright persecution of Guichard. The sudden death of Blanche the following year brought no reprieve, for Queen Joan carried on the persecution. Although the enquiry was still in progress some of Guichard's property was seized, while Enguerrand de Marigny set about making an inventory of the remainder. And already at this stage there were hints of a tactic that was later to be used against the bishop on a massive scale: Enguerrand told Queen Joan that Guichard was employing a Jew to conjure up the demon, which would then be used to frighten her into dropping the case.[13]

So things continued until, in 1304, the fugitive Jean de Calais died in Italy, leaving letters for the king and queen, in which he proclaimed Guichard's innocence. The bishop, he declared, had had no part in his escape; it was Simon Festu who had managed the whole business, in order to destroy his rival. A reconciliation between Queen Joan and the bishop followed; Guichard paid a sum in compensation, and the enquiry was dropped. In 1306 Noffo Dei, believing himself to be dying, also withdrew his accusations against Guichard; and in June 1307, Pope Clement V formally recognized his innocence. It seemed that the bishop, who was now about sixty, could look forward to a tranquil old age. But this was not to be: the affair of Jean de Calais turned out to be a mere prelude to a far more dangerous onslaught.

This new campaign was instigated by enemies of Guichard in the household of the king's son, the young king of Navarre; though others were soon to join in. The opening moves bore a remarkable resemblance to the opening moves against the Templars. Just as, on that occasion, an obscure individual, Esquieu de Floyran, had made his way to King Philip as the bearer of horrific revelations concerning the secret activities of the order, so now another obscure individual, a hermit called Reynaud de Langres, brought horrific revelations concerning the secret behaviour of Bishop Guichard. In fourteenth-century France hermits were not necessarily pious and unworldly—many were shady characters who chose that way of life as a means of concealing their real activities. Reynaud de Langres was one such. Early in 1308 he arrived at the archiepiscopal city of Sens, where he informed first a priest, then the archbishop and finally the royal officials of the terrible things he had witnessed at the hermitage of Saint-Flavit de Villemaur, in Guichard's diocese of Troyes. Queen Joan had died suddenly in 1305, at the early age of thirty-two; and about that time, said the hermit, he had seen the bishop practising *maleficia* at night, in company with a witch of the district. More recently the bishop had approached him personally and had tried to persuade him to poison the king's brother and children. He had refused, and now went in fear of his life.

The news was at once conveyed to King Philip, and it could not have come at a more opportune time. It was the very moment when Pope Clement was making his one real attempt to save the Temple, or at least to exert some influence over its fate; and Philip was already preparing his propaganda campaign in reply. The pope was to be intimidated and defamed by every means; in particular, it was to be made plain that in defending the Templars he would be aiding and abetting heresy and so laying himself open to the charge of heresy, no less. Nothing could be more convenient for the king than to have found a bishop who could be charged not only with regicide but with having commerce with demons. He was not the man to let such a chance slip. He insisted that an enquiry be instituted—and he did so in very much the same language as he used about the Templars. The pope must act because the bishop's crimes constituted an offence not only against the king's majesty but also against the divine majesty and the Catholic faith; and if he failed to act, the king would do so, to save the honour of the Church.[14]

Clement, already harassed beyond endurance over the Templars, gave way at once. He instructed the archbishop of Sens to arrest Guichard, and in very curious terms: in addition to *maleficia* and attempted poisonings, the bull mentions that Guichard had "committed other fearful and sacrilegious crimes".[15] In this the king's hand is clearly visible; for such wording left the accusers free to produce further charges as required, without having to obtain further authority from the pope. In fact the royal officials were closely involved in the affair from the start. In flat disregard of canon law, they removed Guichard from the archbishop's custody and placed him in the royal prison at the Louvre. The first formal version of the charges was prepared by a royal official, Hengest, *bailli* of Sens, who also supplied the witnesses. And on 6 October 1308, the day before the enquiry opened, Guichard's crimes were proclaimed at an assembly held in the king's garden; it was the same device as had been employed against Boniface VIII and against the Templars.

The enquiry was carried out by a commission consisting of the archbishop of Sens and the bishops of Orleans and Auxerre. The case had grown remarkably during the six months since the hermit first told his story. Now it appeared that Guichard had boasted, repeatedly and in various places, that unless Queen Joan restored him to favour he would destroy her. To this end, like a man plunging into an abyss of evil, he summoned a woman who had the reputation of a fortune-teller and sorceress. She advised him to invoke the Devil; so he applied to a Dominican friar, Jean de Fay, who was skilled in that art. When the Devil duly appeared, Guichard did homage to him. In return, the Devil gave him the necessary instructions: to make a waxen image, to baptize it with the queen's name, to prick it with pins and, if that proved insufficient, to throw it in the fire.[16]

The charges were presented in the form of twenty-three separate items; Guichard denied each one of them, and repeated the denials under oath, standing before the Scriptures, his hand on his heart. Whereupon the commission proceeded to hear the witnesses. There were eight of them, but only three had anything interesting to say: the hermit, who repeated his original story; and Guichard's chamberlain and the fortune-teller, who had some curious details to add.

The chamberlain, called Lorin, told two contradictory stories.[17]

First he said that he had sometimes seen Guichard get up at night, but had assumed that he was off to see his mistress, in the same building. Later he remembered that he himself had, on each occasion, accompanied Guichard to the room of Jean de Fay; he had also seen the bishop and the Dominican leave the palace together, disguised as peasants and carrying a box. Less thoroughly coached than the Templars, Lorin also revealed what lay behind his evidence. After being arrested by the king's soldiers, he had been kept in chains for a fortnight. When the *bailli* Hengest first interrogated him, at Troyes, he had repeatedly denied that he had ever seen the bishop go out at night. But then Hengest had had him stripped naked and suspended, spread-eagled, in mid-air from rings in the walls; until, almost dead with pain, he had told the story required of him, and sworn to its truth.

In the case of the fortune-teller, an indigent woman of thirty-two called Margueronne de Bellevillette, the mere threat of torture was enough to extract an appropriate statement.[18] In exchange she was allowed not to incriminate herself. Nothing more was said about her having urged Guichard to make contact with the Devil—on the contrary, she now figured as an unwilling witness of the contact. Summoned to the episcopal palace, she had been unable to suggest how the bishop could regain the favour of Queen Joan. But instead of being sent packing, as might have been expected, she had been allowed to loiter. She heard Guichard deep in conversation with the Dominican, who began to read from a book of spells. After some time she saw, to her horror, a form like a black monk descend from a window high up in the wall, flying, without a ladder, until it came to rest by the bishop and the Dominican. The form had horns on its forehead, and Margueronne decided it must be the Devil. It addressed the friar: "What do you want of me, you who tire me out so?"—"The bishop here has been asking for you."—"What does he want?"—"He wants you to make his peace with the queen."—"If he wants me to make his peace with the queen, he must give me one of his limbs." Then the bishop intervened to say that he would think it over, and the Devil withdrew by the same window, as it were flying and beating its wings. That the compact was indeed made, with fatal results for the queen, was indicated by the evidence of the other witnesses.

The Devil, who had not figured at all in the hermit's original statement, was beginning to bulk large; those "other fearful and sacrilegious crimes" were beginning to take shape. But this was only the first step. The enquiry was adjourned for four months; and by the time it resumed, in February 1309, the royal officials had prepared a whole new set of accusations.[19] It is known that these were contributed in part by Guichard's old enemies, Enguerrand de Marigny, by now chief minister of Philip the Fair; Simon Festu, who had just been promoted bishop of Meaux; and Noffo Dei, who had regained his malice along with his health. But the royal officials also contributed their share. An outline of the new accusations was submitted to Nogaret; and nobody familiar with Nogaret's part in the affair of the Templars can fail to recognize his special touch in the final version.[20] Moreover, whereas only eight witnesses had appeared at the first session of the commission, for the new session the royal officials had managed to assemble a fine and varied collection. The clergy of Guichard's diocese of Troyes provided twenty-five canons, three archdeacons, two abbots, fourteen priors, as well as a multitude of ordinary priests, monks and clerks. The chamberlain Lorin had been reinforced by Guichard's cook, his porter, his barber, his mistress. Six Lombards, representing the Italian banks, were there; and so were innumerable folk, of all ranks, from Troyes and from Provins. In all, the witnesses totalled some two hundred; and though many admitted that they knew nothing against Guichard save by hearsay, between twenty and thirty were ready to confirm the gravest charges.

The tone was set by the very first item, which formed as it were an introduction to the whole: it stated that Guichard was the son of an incubus, i.e. of a demon.[21] Details were provided by no less than twenty-seven witnesses. When Guichard was being born, it was said, his mother, fearing she might die, confessed that she had been sterile for seven years, and had been able to conceive only with the help of an incubus. Because of this his father's house was called the Devil's house, or the house of the incubus; and it had been difficult to get domestics to work in it. His father knew of the matter, and as a result had never been able to stand the sight of his son. Guichard had been pursued, throughout life, by the evil fame attaching to his birth. When he was a young monk, his fellows avoided him, calling him "the incubus's son". Later, when he became prior, his wealth was interpreted as showing that he was indeed a son of the Devil. Guichard himself had often been heard to say that his home had been frequented by an incubus. So far the witnesses; as for Guichard, he admitted to knowing the story: his father's house was indeed supposed to have been plagued by an incubus, for half a year—but that was after his birth, not before. He was no demon's son.

Whatever Guichard might say, further evidence was forthcoming to confirm his demonic connections. The prior of Nesle recalled an experience he had had as a young monk of seventeen, in 1275.[22] At that time Guichard was prior of Saint-Ayoul at Provins. One evening, as he was going upstairs to his room after supper, he took off his robe and handed it to the young monk. The latter, glancing at the prior's head, saw it encircled with a fiery glow, which he recognized as consisting of demons. He threw the robe over the prior's face; but Guichard tried to reassure him, saying: "Be quiet, don't be afraid, and don't tell anyone what you've seen." The young monk told nevertheless, and now other witnesses came forward to say that they had heard of the incident.

It appeared, too, that throughout his career Guichard had kept a private demon, which he consulted at his convenience.[23] The general view was that he kept it in a glass flask; though his mistress had heard, from another woman, that he kept it in the point of his cowl. But the demon could also travel; it spied on the bishop's servants, overheard their conversation and repeated it to the bishop. Sometimes Guichard had been heard conversing with the demon; and a witness had seen him emerging from such a conversation, his hair bristling and with a sort of sweaty smoke rising from his head. At times Guichard's barber trembled so violently at the thought of the demon in the house that he was unable to shave his master.

With a demon for father, and another demon as his lifelong familiar, Guichard could convincingly be accused of multiple homicide; and so he was. It was charged that he had poisoned his predecessor at Saint-Ayoul so as to become prior in his place; that, as abbot, he had starved prisoners to death in his dungeons; that when the late queen planned to send a canon to Rome to denounce him, he had had the canon assassinated; and that he had also prepared personally, from a mixture of adders, scorpions, toads and spiders, the poison destined for the royal princes. Moreover it now appeared that the death of Queen Joan had not been the result of *maleficia* alone; a letter was produced, bearing Guichard's seal, which instructed one "Cassian the Lombard" to concoct poison to that end.

Guichard solemnly denied all these charges, while admitting some comparatively minor ones. He admitted that his household had, for a time, included two assassins, but insisted that he had not known of their guilt; he admitted accepting money in a doubtful case of heresy; he admitted trying to fabricate money, but added that, so far from profiting from the experiment, he had lost heavily. It is clear, in addition, that he openly kept a mistress; that he had dealings, and very profitable ones, with Italian bankers; that he was abrupt and violent in his behaviour towards his clergy. All in all, the bishop emerges as a man of affairs rather than of religion: energetic, able, acquisitive, none too scrupulous. On the other hand, there are no more grounds for thinking him a murderer than for crediting him with personal contacts with demons.

This was confirmed by the outcome of the enquiry.[24] It lasted a year and a half, and another fifteen months passed before, in March or April 1311, the commission submitted its report to the pope. It was the very moment when Pope Clement had finally acceded to King Philip's demand that he condemn the Temple. The king lost interest in Guichard, and allowed him to be transferred from the Louvre to Avignon; and once the pope had him in his custody, he refrained from further action. Meanwhile Noffo Dei was hanged in Paris for some unspecified crime; and before his death he affirmed the bishop's innocence, as he had done once before. In 1314—five years after the beginning of the affair— Guichard was at last set free. Though it was impossible for him to return to Troyes, the pope had no hesitation in employing his services as suffragan bishop of Constance in Germany.[25] His name had been effectively cleared: fourteenth-century chroniclers were in no doubt that the affair was a frame-up.[26] One may well wonder whether, even while it was in progress, any reasonably well informed person ever saw it in any other light.

-3-

For some twenty years, between 1318 and 1338, two popes at Avignon showed disquiet over the activities of magicians. Almost immediately on his accession, in 1317, Pope John XXII had Hughes Géraud, the aged bishop of Cahors, arrested for trying to kill him by poison and by *maleficium*.[27] Interrogated seven times by the pope in person, the bishop admitted his guilt—one cannot tell under what pressure. Although the extant accounts make no mention of demonic intervention it must surely have figured in the case, for the bishop was treated as only the most dangerous heretics were treated: he was tortured, scourged and burned at the stake, and his ashes were scattered in the Rhône. Pope John was indeed rather prone to accuse his enemies of *maleficium* reinforced by dealings with demons. In Italy the head of the Ghibelline party, Matteo Visconti, was accused by the pope's allies in Milan, the archbishop and the inquisitor, of attempting the pope's life by means of wax puppets, and also of having personal dealings with the Devil.[28] In the end nothing came of it, for the commission of cardinals appointed by the pope to try the case had to recognize that all the evidence came from a single witness, who had been bribed. But this experience did not discourage the pope. Between 1320 and 1325 he sent a whole series of missives to the bishop of Ancona and the inquisitor there, pointing out that his political opponents in that region too were heretics, idolators and worshippers of idols. It is remarkable how closely these accusations by a French pope resemble the accusations which, a few years before, had been brought against Pope Boniface VIII and against Bishop Guichard. In 1320 eight Ghibelline lords of Recanati, in the March of Ancona, were summoned to appear before an inquisitor on the grounds that they kept an idol containing a demon, who advised them in all their doings, and whom they worshipped in return.[29]

These were devices contrived by the pope for his own, political purposes. But this was not always the case. Ritual magic was a reality, and already at the beginning of his reign the pope found evidence of it at his own court.[30] In 1318 he appointed a commission consisting of the bishop of Fréjus, a prior and a provost to carry out an investigation, by inquisitorial methods. The suspects were all men, and they included eight clerics and an unspecified number of laymen. The pope claimed that news of their activities had reached him from a reliable source, and certainly all the stock features of ritual magic are there: the spells read from books, the magic circle, the consecrated mirrors and images; and also the demon who, when duly conjured up, will imperil men's salvation, or cause them to wilt away, or even kill them outright.

It is true that the pope also speaks of "a certain pestiferous society of men and angels"—but here caution is required. At first glance one might suppose that he was thinking of some secret society in which human beings consorted with demons; one might even wonder whether there was not, after all, a sect of Satanists. Only, the phrase does not mean anything of the kind. It was simply a traditional cliché, which can be traced back verbatim through Ivo of Chartres, in the twelfth century, and Hrabanus Maurus in the ninth, to Isidore of Seville in the seventh. And in the end it turns out that Isidore himself was merely adapting a passage where St Augustine, reflecting on magic, comments that the whole world outside the Christian Church was a society of wicked men and wicked angels, i.e. demons. Though ritual magic was a reality, and though books of magic themselves insisted that the magician must operate in the presence of assistants, there is no evidence whatsoever for the existence of a Devil-worshipping sect of magicians.

In 1326 another group was discovered at Agen, in south-western France.[31] A canon, another cleric and a layman were charged with invoking demons to produce storms of hail and thunder and to kill men. This too was a case of ritual magic—the canon possessed books of magic, and also had vessels full of powders and fetid liquids. His two accomplices were caught by the town guards while trying to procure more vehicles of maleficent power: they were stealing heads and limbs from corpses hanging on the town gallows. The layman was burned straightaway, while the two clerics were handed over to the ecclesiastical authorities. The pope adopted the same approach as in 1318: he appointed a cardinal to judge the case. And in the same year of 1326 he also appointed a commission of three cardinals to judge a prior and two lesser clerics, charged with using images and invoking demons for magical purposes.

As we have seen, in the 1320s the Inquisition was also empowered, and even encouraged, to proceed against practitioners of ritual magic. Yet in the event professional inquisitors seem to have dealt with very few such cases.* Only two are known in detail. In 1323 the inquisitor of Paris, acting together with the episcopal ordinary, tried two laymen, an abbot and a number of canons. It appeared that the Cistercian abbot of Sarcelles had lost some treasure and had employed a magician called Jean de Persant to recover it and to find the thief. The magician's accomplice, under torture, described his master's plan, which was curious. A cat was fed on bread soaked in water and consecrated oil, with the intention that it should be killed and its skin cut into strips to form a magic circle. Standing in the circle, the magician would invoke the demon Berith—a familiar figure in the magic books—who would then make the desired revelations. The magician was burned at the stake, along with the remains of his accomplice, who had died in prison; the ecclesiastics were unfrocked and imprisoned for life.(32)

In 1329 the inquisitor of Carcassonne sentenced a Carmelite monk called Pierre Recordi to perpetual imprisonment on bread and water, with chains on hands and feet. The man had confessed to trying to obtain possession of women by the techniques of ritual magic. He had offered wax puppets, mixed with his own saliva and with the blood of toads, to Satan. He would place the puppet under the threshold of the woman's house, and she would then have to yield or else be tormented by a demon. After the image had done its work the monk would sacrifice a butterfly to the helpful demon—who would manifest himself in

* As bishop of Pamiers 1317–26 Jacques Fournier, later Pope Benedict XII, operated as inquisitor for his diocese and tried thirty-eight cases of heresy and one case of superstitious practices. His register includes not a single case of ritual magic. Cf. J. Duvernoy, *Le registre d'Inquisition de Jacques Fournier (1318–1325)*, 2 vols., Toulouse, 1965.

a breath of air. This case at least seems to have been faked—Recordi confessed, *inter alia*, that the wax images bled when pricked; and he also said that all the images had been thrown into the river—so not one was ever produced in evidence. Moreover, he retracted the whole confession again and again, in the course of a trial which lasted several years.[33]

The Inquisition was in no sense the spearhead of the campaign against ritual magic. On the contrary, its intervention was small-scale and, one suspects, self-defeating. The very year after the sentencing of Recordi, Pope John withdrew the powers he had granted; all trials then in progress were to be completed as quickly as possible, and the documents forwarded to him. One wonders whether these second thoughts were not prompted by the Recordi case; leading Carmelites are known not to have shared the inquisitor's views, and they may have induced doubts in the pope himself. However that may be, though magicians continued to be tried under the inquisitorial procedure, it was no longer the Inquisition that tried them. When the next pope, Benedict XII, had to deal with a case of ritual magic he appointed one Guillen Lombardi to carry out the investigation. Lombardi was not a friar, as were the regular inquisitors, but a canon and later provost of a collegiate church. He was also a highly qualified lawyer; and he operated under the eye of the pope himself, for the prisoners were held in the papal prisons.[34]

It is striking how often, in the first half of the century, the accused were clerics—something which rarely happened in the great witch-hunt itself. The reason is plain: ritual magic could be practised only by those who were learned enough to study the magic books; and in that period such people were still mostly to be found amongst the clergy. Moreover clerics, being professionally concerned with demons, were more apt than laymen to fancy that they could command them. And for the same reason they were apt to be suspected, whether by laymen or by their fellow clerics, even when in reality they were innocent of any dealings with the hosts of hell. That was the state of affairs at the beginning of the fourteenth century, at the time of the trials of Pope Boniface and Bishop Guichard; it still obtained during the spate of trials under John XXII; and clerics continued to figure in the few trials known to have been held under Benedict XII and Clement VI—which brings us to mid-century.

After that date the evidence becomes very fragmentary. It is certain that ritual magic continued to be practised (it was still being practised in the seventeenth century), and also that from time to time action was taken to suppress it and to punish its adepts. On the far side of the Pyrenees the inquisitor-general of Aragon, Nicolas Eymeric, whose

writings we have already considered, certainly had some dealings with
such people: he mentions the confessions which he extracted from
them, and also the Solomonic books which he had seized and burned.
In France, on the other hand, the Inquisition seems to have been permanently handicapped by the restrictions imposed by John XXII in 1330.
In 1374 the inquisitor of France wrote to Pope Gregory XI complaining
that many people, including clerics, were invoking demons; and that
when he tried to proceed against them, his jurisdiction was contested.
The pope responded by authorizing him to prosecute and punish such
offences, but limited the authorization to two years.(35) And although
the authorization must have been renewed, only a couple more cases of
ritual magic are known to have been judged by inquisitors.

In 1380 the provost of Paris, Hugues Aubryot, was summoned before
the bishop of Paris and a Dominican inquisitor to answer a number of
charges.(36) His real offence seems to have been that he had infringed the
privileges of the Church by imprisoning clerics, including members of
the University; but the charges ranged from heretical talk to partiality
towards Jews. Moreover, though Aubryot was in his sixties, he was
accused of seducing young girls and married women by means of
magic. Although demons are not specifically mentioned, one suspects
that they were lurking somewhere in the background of this trial;
anyway Aubryot was imprisoned for life. The other case involved one
Géraud Cassendi, notary of Bogoyran near Carcassonne.(37) He was
tried by the Inquisition in 1410, on a charge of invoking demons and
seducing women and girls. A witness stated that he had seen Cassendi
take some threads of gold from an image of the Virgin and work them
into his shirt. Thus protected, he had conjured up demons by reading
from a book; whereupon many demons appeared—though they disappeared again when the witness, understandably alarmed, threw a
shoe at them. The outcome of this case is unknown.

By the late fourteenth century the secular courts in Paris were extending their powers at the expense of the ecclesiastical tribunals; and in
1390–1 two significant trials were held at the Châtelet. Here the
accused were no longer clerics or notables but women of low social
status—and nevertheless their confessions were still formulated in terms
of ritual magic.(38)

The first trial opened on 30 July 1390. A former lover of Marion la
Droiturière had jilted her and married another woman; and Marion was
accused of having employed one Margot de la Barre to make the man
impotent with his young wife. All that Margot admitted before torture
was that she knew how to perform magical cures, including cures of

impotence. The provost's court, on the other hand, was intent on unearthing weightier offences than simple, traditional magic, whether benign or maleficent. With the agreement of the *parlement* (to which the women appealed in vain), it used torture mercilessly, and ended by extracting confessions which accorded with its own preconceptions. The women confessed that they had operated by means of chaplets of herbs which the Devil, at their request, endowed with magical powers. Invoked three times in the name of the Father, the Son and the Holy Spirit, the Devil appeared physically—looking, the women said, very much as he did in the mystery plays; took the chaplets, and departed through the window, with a noise like a whirlwind. For this imaginary exercise of ritual magic, both women were burned.

The second trial, which with appeals to the *parlement* lasted some ten months, was likewise concerned with a mixture of traditional *maleficium* and ritual magic, in the context of a sexual relationship. A woman called Macete was accused of employing Jehanne de Brigue to use magic to induce one Hennequin de Ruilly to marry her. This was duly done, but Hennequin proved a brutal husband; and the two women collaborated a second time, to bring illness on the man by means of sorceries with toads and wax figures. Under torture Jehanne confessed that all this had been achieved with the help of a demon called Haussibut. Indeed, already as a child she had been taught by her godmother how to conjure up Haussibut: the method was to call on the Trinity to compel the demon to appear. It is true that when advised to offer the demon a sacrifice of flesh, in the form of her own arm, she demurred. Still, once again the case, as manipulated by the provost's court, had become a case of ritual magic; and it ended as such cases commonly did, in the burning of both the accused.

—4—

The trials we have just considered were all heresy trials, where the accused was charged, above all, with having personal dealings with a demon. In some of them *maleficium* also bulks large; and the combination of these two kinds of accusation, in the context of a trial conducted under the inquisitorial procedure, does mark a step in the direction of the great witch-hunt. Yet in itself it is only a small step. The accused in these trials were all charged as individual offenders, not as members of a sect. On the other hand, at the times and places where the witch-hunt reached its greatest intensity, witches certainly were thought of as constituting a sect—the most pernicious sect of all. The transition can be observed in two trials held in the fourteenth century. In both, the accusations are still formulated in terms of ritual magic, but the accused are thought of as an organized sect.

The earlier of the two trials was that of Lady Alice Kyteler and her associates; it was held at Kilkenny, in Ireland, in 1324–5.[39] Lady Alice was a rich woman, descended from an Anglo-Norman family which had been settled in Kilkenny for some generations. Robert le Kyteler, of Kilkenny, was engaged in trade with Flanders towards the close of the thirteenth century; and Lady Alice added to the family wealth by marrying William Utlagh, or Outlaw, a rich banker and money-lender, also of Kilkenny. Later she married three more husbands: Adam le Blund, of Callan; Richard de Valle; and Sir John le Poer.[40] She and her son by her first marriage, William Outlaw, attracted much hatred. Like his father, William Outlaw was a banker and money-lender; and there are documents to show that many of the local nobles were heavily in debt to him. The reputation of mother and son is mirrored in a tale preserved in the *Annals of Ireland*. Lady Alice was believed to be in the habit of raking filth from the streets towards her son's door, muttering under her breath:

> "Unto the house of William my sonne
> Hie all the wealth of Kilkennie town." [41]

But the fiercest hatred came from the sons and daughters whom Lady Alice's husbands had had by earlier marriages. These stepsons and step-daughters of hers complained bitterly that, by her sorceries, she had killed some of their fathers and had so infatuated others that they had given all their wealth to her and her son William, to the perpetual impoverishment of the rightful heirs. They added that even her present husband was reduced to such a state by powders, pills and sorceries that he was wasting away, deprived of his nails, without hair on his body. Indeed it was said that Sir John le Poer, being warned by his wife's maid, forcibly opened her boxes and found there a sackful of horrible things, which he transmitted to the local bishop. They had not far to go, for Kilkenny was the episcopal city of the diocese of Ossory.

The bishop, Richard de Ledrede, went quickly into action: early in 1324 he held a formal enquiry, with which he was able to associate a number of knights and nobles. The witnesses included the dispossessed heirs of the four husbands, who "urged the bishop with public clamour, demanding remedy and aid"; but the charges went far beyond *maleficium* and multiple homicide. Alice Kyteler and William Outlaw were presented as sorcerers who were also involved in sundry heresies, in fact as heading an organized heretical group. Ten men and women were accused along with them; to judge by their names, all belonged to the ruling Anglo-Norman stratum, and one at least, a cleric in minor orders called Robert of Bristol, is known to have come from a family with large estates.

In the supposed practices of this group, *maleficium* and demon-worship were interwoven. The *maleficia* were manifold. The group was accused of concocting powders, pills and ointments from herbs, the intestines of cocks, horrible worms, nails from corpses, the swaddling-clothes of babies who had died unbaptized; and of making candles from human fat. These substances were boiled in the skull of a decapitated robber, and were employed, to the accompaniment of incantations, to bring sickness or death to faithful Christians, or else to excite love or hatred. Moreover, it was said that at their nocturnal meetings these people did what only the clergy were entitled to do: fulminated excommunications against individuals, cursing each part of the body from the sole of the foot to the crown of the head. In particular the women anathematized their own husbands.[42]

All these things were done in a truly heretical spirit. It was said that, to ensure the success of their sorceries, the members of the group became apostates from Christianity—though on a curiously temporary and provisional basis. According as their aims were more or less ambitious, they denied the faith of Christ and of the Church either for a month or for a whole year; during which time they would not attend mass or take the Eucharist, nor go to church, nor believe anything that the Church believed. By magical means they sought the counsel of demons, and they also sacrificed animals to demons; Lady Alice had three times offered up the blood and limbs of cocks to her private demon, just as Pope Boniface was supposed to have done.[43]

There is nothing manifestly impossible in all this, but the charges include a further item, and one which must give us pause. It concerns that private demon of Lady Alice's, who appeared sometimes in the guise of a cat, sometimes in the guise of a shaggy black dog, sometimes in the guise of a Negro. Lady Alice received him as her incubus and allowed him to copulate with her. In return, he gave her wealth—all her considerable possessions had been acquired with his help. Moreover, the demon was known to other members of the group. He even gave them his name, which was the Son of Art, or Robin, son of Art; and he also explained that he belonged to the poorer demons in hell.[44]

Now, in the contemporary account of the proceedings against Lady Alice—which is the sole source for these matters—all the charges are listed together, as though they were interdependent; so if one charge is manifestly false, the rest must also be suspect. Moreover the charges are listed twice over—and the second time they appear in the context of a confession extracted under torture. An associate of Lady Alice called Petronilla of Meath was flogged six times, on the bishop's orders; after which she produced "publicly, in the presence of the assembled clergy and people", all the above particulars—both those relating to concoctions and *maleficia* and cursings and those relating to Robin, son of Art.[45] Indeed, Petronilla admitted that she herself had acted as go-between (*mediatrix*) for Lady Alice and her demon lover; and she provided details. With her own eyes, in full daylight, she had seen Robin materialize in the form of three Negroes bearing iron rods in their hands, and in this strange guise have intercourse with the lady. She had even dried the place after their departure, using the bed-cover.[46] Unless one is prepared to accept all this, there are no grounds for believing any of the charges against Lady Alice.

All the charges, in fact, are designed to serve one and the same purpose: to show that Lady Alice had no right to her wealth, that it had been wrested from its rightful owners by truly diabolic means, that it was tainted at the source. *Maleficia* had been practised, poisons had been concocted, anathemas had been pronounced, men had been murdered, to secure this wealth. Worse still, all this had been done with the help of a demon who had not only received, as his fee, worship and animal sacrifice—like Pope Boniface's demon—but also had mated with Lady Alice.

Armed with this information, Bishop de Ledrede wrote to the lord chancellor, Roger Outlaw, prior of Kilmainham, demanding that the accused parties be immediately imprisoned. But Roger Outlaw, who was Lady Alice's brother-in-law and William Outlaw's uncle, declined to act; so the bishop had to proceed as best he could, without the help of the secular arm. He cited Lady Alice to appear before him on a certain day; but when the day came it was found that she had fled the town. Next the bishop cited William Outlaw, on charges of heresy and of aiding and protecting heretics; but nothing came of that either, for the seneschal of Kilkenny intervened.

The seneschal was a powerful nobleman called Sir Arnold le Poer, a distant relative of Lady Alice's fourth husband, Sir John le Poer. Whether out of friendship, or out of self-interest, or simply because he thought the whole business nonsense, he sided with William Outlaw. Together with Outlaw he went to see the bishop and asked him most earnestly to withdraw the indictment; and when this failed, loaded him with reproaches and threats. Next day he went further; he sent a band of armed men to arrest the bishop and lodge him in Kilkenny jail, where he kept him until the day for which William Outlaw had been cited had passed. And when, on his release, the bishop again cited Outlaw to appear before him, and appealed to the seneschal for help, he met with a sharp rebuff. [47]

Ledrede excommunicated Lady Alice; whereupon the lady indicted the bishop for defamation of character, and her allies, Sir Arnold le Poer at their head, had him cited to appear before the parliament in Dublin. But the bishop had never been lacking in self-confidence, and now he defended his conduct and argued his case with such vigour that the assembly was won over. At last he was able to proceed with the arrest of Lady Alice's associates. They were thrown into prison at Kilkenny; and soon Ledrede had the gratification of reciting the charges against them in the presence of the king's justiciar, the lord chancellor, the treasurer, and the king's council, all assembled for the purpose in his own episcopal city. All the accused were found guilty and were sentenced to various punishments. Some, including Petronilla of Meath, were burned alive; others were whipped through the streets of Kilkenny; others were banished and declared excommunicate; others were sentenced to the penance of wearing crosses sewn on their garments. [48] William Outlaw, after a period in prison, was permitted to recant, to do penance, and to be reconciled with the Church—though he did have to use some of his great wealth in providing a leaden roof for the bishop's cathedral. As for Lady Alice, who was cast as the chief culprit, she escaped burning only because her powerful kinsfolk got her out of Ireland and into England. [49]

The whole affair makes sense only if it is seen as one episode in a struggle between, on the one side, Lady Alice's kinsfolk and allies and, on the other side, her stepsons and stepdaughters. Financial considerations seem to have played a part on both sides. It is known that the lord chancellor, Roger Outlaw, was heavily in debt to the bishop; while Lady Alice's accusers must certainly have found allies amongst the various nobles who were in debt to her or to her son. Ever since the early middle ages, the rich and powerful had been prone to use *maleficium* and accusations of *maleficium* as weapons in the struggle for wealth and power. This was one more instance—but with a difference: the demonic bulks far larger here than it had done in earlier centuries. For this Bishop Ledrede must surely be held responsible. So far as we can tell, Robin, son of Art, did not figure in the accusations brought against Lady Alice by her husbands' heirs; but he bulks large in Petronilla's confession, which was extracted by the bishop's men. And everything

we know of Ledrede's previous and subsequent career shows him to
have been preoccupied with notions of heresy and demon-worship in a
way which was far more familiar in France than in England, let alone
in Ireland.(50)

A Franciscan of English origin, Ledrede had in fact visited France and
the papal court at a time when the trials of the Templars and Pope
Boniface and Bishop Guichard were still fresh in everyone's memory.
He was appointed to the see of Ossory by Pope John XII and consecrated at Avignon in 1317; and already in 1320—four years before the
Kyteler affair—he held a synod of his chapter and clergy, where he
made legislation against such persons in the diocese as might be tainted
with unorthodoxy. Later, after the affair was over, he ruthlessly pursued
Lady Alice's ally, the seneschal of Kilkenny Arnold le Poer, as a
heretic; never resting until he had him excommunicated and imprisoned in Dublin castle, where after some years the man died—
unabsolved, and accordingly deprived of the last rites and even of
burial. Later still, Ledrede himself was summoned before the court of
the archbishop of Dublin, as well as before secular tribunals, for various
crimes, including the instigation of murder. He took refuge at Avignon,
where he was able to persuade the pope, Benedict XII, that Ireland was
full of demon-worshipping heretics, whom he alone opposed.

He was absent from Ireland—in effect exiled—for nine years; and
when he was allowed to return and resume his functions, he found that
his superior, the archbishop of Dublin, was keeping an inconveniently
close watch on the diocese of Ossory. This started a new dispute; once
more Ledrede turned to the reigning pope, this time Clement VI, and
managed to convince him that the archbishop was protecting heretics.
This was in 1347, almost a quarter of a century after the Kyteler affair.
Whether or not there was any connection between the two episodes,
the bishop certainly showed the same mentality in both. For him, as for
King Philip the Fair, it was automatic to denounce an opponent as a
heretic or a protector of heretics; perhaps even to regard him as such.

Once such a man was persuaded that Lady Alice was guilty of *maleficium* he was practically bound, given his background, to assume that she
must also be an out-and-out heretic. Indeed, all his actions were based
on that conviction. When he first wrote to the lord chancellor, demanding the arrest of the lady and her associates, he referred to them as
heretics; and he appended a copy of the recently published papal
decretal *De haereticis*. When he had the king's officers assembled at
Kilkenny, he regaled them by reading the same decretal aloud, ex-
pounding it in the vernacular, and adding an excursus of his own on the

penalties appropriate to heretics and their protectors.[51] But he went further. The notion of the incubus or copulating demon, which had already been used against Bishop Guichard of Troyes through his mother, had a more obvious application when the accused was herself a woman. The bishop of Ossory applied it. For the first time in European history (so far as is known), a woman was accused of having acquired the power of sorcery through having sexual intercourse with a demon —and not a young woman either, but one who must have been well over sixty.* In the proceedings against Lady Alice Kyteler, as conducted by Richard de Ledrede, a new image of the witch begins to emerge.

Yet the Kyteler case is not a typical witch-hunt, of the kind that was to become so common at the time of the great witch-hunt. That much has often been noted, but it has not proved easy to explain, or even to define, its peculiarities. It becomes perfectly easy when it is realized that the frame of reference was still provided by ritual magic. Then everything makes sense. Petronilla of Meath referred to her mistress as the most practised mistress of the art in the realm, indeed in the whole world: such a description fits one of those magicians who were lords of demons rather than one of the later witches, who were their abject servants. Lighted candles were used in the ceremonies: the Solomonic books have much to say about that. Animals were torn limb from limb at country cross-roads, as sacrifices: this was a stock feature of ritual magic. One of Petronilla's achievements was, by incantations, to make some women take on the appearance of horned goats: such tricks belong exclusively to the world of ritual magic. Above all, Lady Alice's demon, though he has certain features in common with the demon-seducers of the later witch-trials, is only fully understandable when viewed in terms of Solomonic lore. He claims to be one of the lesser demons of hell, and iron bars form part of his equipment—and in the *Key of Solomon* spirits of the lowest order were described as being "like soldiers, armed with spears". Even his name, which has caused so much puzzlement, ceases to be a riddle. In calling him Robin, Petronilla of Meath was no doubt uttering the name of the first local wood-spirit that occurred to her—as countless other women, under torture, were to do in later centuries. But in adding a patronymic she was surely— probably at Ledrede's instigation—indicating a connection with ritual magic. In ritual magic the magician was often called the Master of the Art, the animal whose skin provided the parchment for the magic

* It seems that her son William was already adult in 1302, i.e. twenty-two years before the trial; see T. Wright, *Narratives of sorcery and witchcraft*, vol. I, London, 1851, p. 26.

formulae was called the Victim of the Art. What, then, could be more fitting than that this early demonic familiar should be called *filius Artis* —meaning not that he was the son of another demon, called Art (in any case a theological impossibility) but that he was a son of the magic art?

The second trial in which a sect of witches figures was held three quarters of a century later, some time between 1397 and 1406; and still the frame of reference was supplied by ritual magic. This was a Swiss trial, held at Boltigen in the Simmerthal—a region which had recently been conquered by the city of Bern; and it was conducted by a secular judge, Peter of Greyerz (Gruyères), who represented the authority of Bern.*

The chief accused was one Stedelen. Under torture, this man confessed to a variety of *maleficia*. He had afflicted a whole farmstead with sterility, causing the farmer's wife no less than seven miscarriages and making all the cattle infertile; this had been done by burying a lizard under the threshold. He also knew how to produce hail-storms and devastate the crops; how to make children fall into the water and drown before their parents' eyes; how to kill people with thunderbolts; how to harm his neighbours in their belongings and their bodies—in fact, how to perform all the traditional forms of *maleficium*. In answer to the judge's questions, accompanied by repeated torture, he explained how storms were made. It appeared that a group of *malifici* and *maleficae* came together in a field and begged the prince of all demons to send them one of his demonic subjects, whom they designated by name. A black cock was sacrificed at a cross-roads, its flesh being thrown high in the air, where the lesser demon snatched it up. After which the demon would make hail-storms and cast thunderbolts—though not, Stedelen added, always at the places suggested.

In the confession which Peter of Greyerz extracted from Stedelen the world of *maleficium* and the world of ritual magic come together more clearly even than in the Kyteler affair. And in other confessions extracted by the same judge—and by the same methods—the whole is fused with that stereotype of the heretical sect which had been developed over the preceding three centuries. Here we learn that the "sect" of *malefici* around Bern were accustomed not only to kill babies by magical

* Peter of Greyerz told the story of the trial to the Dominican Johannes Nider, who included it in his book *Formicarius*, which he wrote in 1435–7; the relevant passages are reprinted in Hansen, *Quellen*, pp. 90–9. Nider himself was not, as has sometimes been suggested, in any way involved in the trial. He was not an inquisitor, and the trial had in any case taken place many years before he heard of it. Peter of Greyerz ceased to hold office in the Simmerthal in 1406.

means but to use the infant corpses for concocting potions which, in turn, possessed magical power. A candidate for membership of the sect was taken by the masters into a church on a Sunday morning, before the blessing of the holy water. There he was required to renounce Christ and Christianity and to do homage to a demon, known as "the little master", who manifested himself in human form. Next he drank from the potion—whereupon the "images of the art" were revealed to him. It is the age-old fantasy, adapted to include ritual magic.

For there is no doubt that it was as much a fantasy in this as in all earlier cases. Not only were all the confessions obtained by torture—Peter of Greyerz also maintained that in order to evade capture, the leaders of the sect could emit evil smells which incapacitated their captors, and could even turn themselves into mice. He also believed that when he himself fell downstairs one night in the dark, it was because invisible witches had pushed him.

These two trials, at Kilkenny in Ireland and at Boltigen in Switzerland, bring us to the threshold of the great witch-hunt. Neither was a simple reflection of age-old, popular beliefs about *maleficium*. In both, the essential elements were supplied not by an illiterate peasantry but by the upper, educated strata of society. Both the awareness, however distorted, of ritual magic, and the fantasy of a sect of demon-worshipping heretics, had originated amongst the literate. And so, of course, had the inquisitorial procedure, with the use of torture.

On the other hand, neither Bishop de Ledrede nor Peter of Greyerz was a professional inquisitor. Both men were clearly fanatics, driven by their own inner demons, rather than officials coolly following the routine of a great bureaucratic machine. Dominated by demonological obsessions, they used the inquisitorial procedure to justify and confirm those obsessions. Between them, they produced a true prelude to the great witch-hunt.

Yet before the great witch-hunt could begin, the idea of witchcraft had to undergo a further transformation: intellectuals had to persuade themselves that witches could fly. So long as witches were supposed to proceed to their meetings on foot, those meetings could not plausibly be represented as either very frequent or very large. It was a different matter when men in positions of authority began to maintain that witches proceeded by magical means, invisibly, through the air. Here too the first steps were taken in the fourteenth century.

11

THE NIGHT-WITCH
IN POPULAR IMAGINATION

–I–

The ancient Romans already knew of a creature which flew about at night, screeching, and lived on the flesh and blood of human beings. Their literature in the first two centuries after Christ abounds in references to it. They called it a *strix*, from a Greek word meaning "to screech"; usually they thought of it as an owl, and granted it feathers and even eggs, but they were also clear that it was no mere bird. Pliny the Elder admitted that he could not fit the *strix* into any recognized species of bird; and he added that according to popular belief it offered its breasts to babies to suck.[1] Its purpose in so doing was sinister: Serenus Sammonicus, who wrote about medical science, considered that its milk was poison.[2].

Ovid has worse things to say about *striges*. In the *Fasti* he describes them as ravenous birds, with hooked beaks and grasping talons, grey feathers, and eyes that stare fixedly out of big heads. These owl-like creatures may, he says, be natural birds, or they may be old women magically transformed into birds—but in any case they fly about at night in search of babies unprotected by their nurses. When they find one they drag it from its cradle and tear out and eat its entrails, until their own stomachs are distended with swallowed blood. The poet also describes devices for holding these birds at bay. You must touch the lintels and threshold with a sprig of arbutus and place a wand of white-thorn at the window. Above all you must offer the *strix*, as a substitute for the baby's entrails, the entrails of a young pig, saying: "Birds of night, spare this child's vitals! A young victim dies instead of this little baby. Take, I beg you, another heart instead of that heart, other vitals instead of those vitals! We offer you this life instead of a better life."[3]

These visitations were not confined to babies. Petronius tells of a dead boy whose entrails were devoured by a *strix* which then substituted a straw doll for the human body; a slave who tried to drive the creature off with his sword became black and blue all over, as though he had been scourged, and died after a couple of days. And the author comments that adults who suddenly lose their strength, and particularly men who lose their potency, commonly think they are being eaten by a *strix*.[4] Both Petronius and Ovid refer to a special food—a mixture of ham and bean-soup—which was taken to counteract the effects of being inwardly devoured.

From all this it is plain that *striges* were indeed thought of not as ordinary birds but as beings into which certain women could transform themselves. There is a relevant comment in Ovid's description, in the *Amores*, of the procuress and witch Dipsas. She is an old hag, who specializes in destroying the chastity of the young, but she also possesses vast magical powers. Dipsas not only understands the occult use of herbs, she can conjure up the dead, cleave the solid ground, make a river flow back to its source. Moreover, says Ovid, "if I may be believed, I have seen the stars drip blood, and blood darken the moon. I believe that then (Dipsas), transformed, was flying through the darkness of the night, her hag's carcase clad in feathers. This I suspect, and such is the report." [5]

Apuleius, in *The Golden Ass*, throws more light on the matter with his portrait of that Thessalian lady, Pamphile. Like Dipsas, Pamphile is a super-witch, who by sorcery can subdue the elements, trouble the planets and even disturb the gods; and she too is accustomed to change herself into a bird on certain nights. She does this by means of a magic concoction of laurel and dill dissolved in water, which she drinks and with which she rubs herself from head to foot; whereupon feathers spring out of her skin, her nose turns into a beak and her nails into claws, she begins to hoot like an owl and at last flies off in quest of a lover. Moreover if a young man is so imprudent as to repulse Pamphile, she destroys him. For Pamphile, we are told, is continually on fire with lust; every handsome young man attracts her; and if anyone is rash enough to reject her, she will either change him into a beast or kill him outright.[6]

In other words, the *strix* is a witch who is a woman by day but at night flies through the air on amorous, murderous or cannibalistic errands. Thus the grammarian Festus, in his work on the meanings of words, defines the late Latin word *strigae* as "the name given to women who practise sorcery, and who are also called flying women".[7]

Most of these writers knew perfectly well that there were no such things as *striges* or *strigae*; they were simply using the idea to ornament their fiction.* And certainly the law took no cognizance of these mysterious creatures. It did recognize maleficent sorcery, and people

* Horace openly mocks the belief, in *Ars poetica*, lines 338–40.

were frequently tried and sentenced as sorcerers. But nobody was taken into custody for being a *strix*.

Yet the literary references are clearly to a belief which was taken seriously in some quarters, and it may well be that amongst the common people belief in *striges* was real and widespread. Certainly this was the case amongst the Germanic peoples before they came under first Roman and then Christian influence. The notion of a witch as an uncanny, cannibalistic woman had developed amongst them too—it seems, independently of outside influence. And the earliest body of Germanic law, the *Lex Salica*, which was written in the sixth century but which reflects the beliefs and attitudes of a still earlier age, treats the *stria* or *striga* as a reality, and her cannibalism as something that really occurred. It hints at assemblies of witches with cauldrons; it fixes the fine to be paid "if a *stria* shall devour a man and it shall be proved against her"; and it also fixes the fine in the event that "anyone shall call a free woman a *stria* and shall not be able to prove it".[8]

Later laws, more permeated by Christian influence, no longer recognize the *stria* herself as a reality, but they show quite clearly that belief in the *stria* was still widespread. The laws of the Alamanni, which date from the first half of the seventh century, decree a fine for a woman who calls another a *stria*.[9] The last of the Germanic codes, the laws of the Lombards, which was promulgated by King Rothar at Pavia in 643, also warns against this kind of slander.[10] Indeed it goes further: "Let nobody presume to kill a foreign serving-maid or female slave as a *striga*, for it is not possible, nor ought it to be at all believed by Christian minds that a woman can eat a living man up from within." [11] The belief that was being attacked here reappears in Charlemagne's capitulary for the Saxons, in 789: "If anyone, deceived by the Devil, shall believe, as is customary amongst pagans, that any man or woman is a *striga*, and eats men, and shall on that account burn that person to death or eat his or her flesh, or give it to others to eat, he shall be executed".[12] From this it emerges that at the end of the eighth century the still largely pagan Saxons not only believed in cannibalistic *strigae*, but were themselves accustomed to eat them—doubtless as a way of neutralising their supernatural destructive power once and for all.

Nor is the evidence wholly confined to the laws. So little German literature has survived from the early Middle Ages that it would be unrealistic to expect vernacular texts to set alongside Ovid and Apuleius. Nevertheless there is one revealing passage in the translation which the Swiss monk Notker Labeo (*c.* 952–1022) made of that curious fifth-century encyclopaedia, Martianus Capella's *De nuptiis Mercurii et*

Philologiae. Commenting on the fact that certain savage tribes were supposed to practise cannibalism, Notker remarks that "here at home", witches are said to do the same.[13]

The notion of cannibalistic witches, then, was familiar to many of the Germanic peoples in the early Middle Ages. Moreover the linguistic evidence suggests that, like their Roman precursors, these creatures were imagined as flying at night. The Latin of the early medieval laws is, admittedly, fairly debased—and nevertheless the clerics who wrote it must certainly have known that *striga* was derived from *strix*, and that a *strix* was something that flew about, screeching, in the dark. If they had not wished to convey this idea they could very well have used the term *malefica*, which also meant "witch" but had no bird-like associations.

In any case, by the beginning of the eleventh century there is firm evidence that in parts of Germany the image of the cannibalistic woman often, if not invariably, included the ability to fly about at night. It is to be found in the fifth chapter of Burchard's *Corrector*, which has already afforded us such valuable insights into the *maleficium* beliefs of the early Middle Ages. One of the questions proposed in this penitential reads as follows:

> Have you believed what many women, turning back to Satan, believe and affirm to be true; as that you believe that in the silence of the quiet night, when you have settled down in bed, and your husband lies in your bosom, you are able, while still in your body, to go out through the closed doors and travel through the spaces of the world, together with others who are similarly deceived; and that without visible weapons, you kill people who have been baptized and redeemed by Christ's blood, and together cook and devour their flesh; and that where the heart was, you put straw or wood or something of the sort; and that after eating these people, you bring them alive again and grant them a brief spell of life? If you have believed this, you shall do penance on bread and water for fifty days, and likewise in each of the seven years following.[14]

This passage has several points of interest. It expounds the fantasy of the cannibalistic night-witch in much greater detail than any earlier Germanic source. It confirms the hint which the *Lex Salica* had dropped some five centuries earlier, that night-witches were imagined to move and act collectively, and to cook their victims before eating them. Above all it supplies strong evidence that in Germany the figure of the cannibalistic night-witch belonged to the world of traditional folkbeliefs.

Two and a half centuries later this was still the case. In the mid-thirteenth century a poet from the Tirol mocked these same popular

beliefs about cannibalistic night-witches. Jokingly, he says that he has
gone from university to university, in many countries; nowhere has he
heard any scholar lecture on these uncanny beings. Indeed, he adds, it
would be a wondrous thing to see a woman riding on a calf or a broomstick or a poker, over mountains and villages. For himself, he could
never believe it, whoever might say it, unless he saw it with his own
eyes. It is also all lying nonsense that a woman can cut out a man's
heart and put straw in its place.[15] The Englishman Gervase of Tilbury,
who around 1211 wrote a book of table-talk for the delectation of the
Emperor Otto IV, was also familiar with the idea that certain men and
women fly by night through vast distances, enter homes, dissolve
human bones, suck human blood, and move infants from place to
place. It is true that he gives St Augustine as his authority; nevertheless,
he is clearly reflecting a contemporary belief, for he also says that
physicians attribute such ideas to nightmares.[16] And anyway there is
nothing in Augustine that could have served as a source.

Because the night-witch was known to the Romans also, it has often
been assumed that the Germanic peoples must have taken the idea from
them; or more precisely, that wherever the night-witch appears in a
medieval text, it is due to the influence of Latin literature.[17] Yet the
balance of evidence is heavily against this view. The earliest written
Germanic law, the Lex Salica, treats the night-witch as a reality—and
no Roman law ever did that. And later laws, which deny the reality of
the night-witch, are clearly directed not against the sophisticated
fancies of literati raised on Ovid, but against beliefs which were so deep
and widespread amongst the common people that they were liable to
express themselves in insults and violence. Down to the thirteenth
century, it was the educated elite who, in the name of Christian
doctrine, rejected the night-witch; while the common people continued
to believe in her. And one can go a little further. Burchard's penitential
shows that some women assimilated the belief so completely that they
imagined themselves to be night-witches. It condemns such women—
not for doing harm to others but for indulging in a pagan superstition.
What they were really doing was living out, in their dreams, a collective fantasy or folk-belief that was traditional amongst the Germanic
peoples.

–2–

There was another popular belief, of a very different kind, concerning
women who travelled at night in a supernatural manner. Around 906
Regino, formerly abbot of Prüm, was asked by the archbishop of

Trier to write a guide to ecclesiastical discipline for the use of bishops when carrying out visitations of their dioceses. He included in his book a canon which probably originated in a lost capitulary of the ninth century and which later received the title *Canon Episcopi* from its opening phrase, "Episcopi episcoporumque ministri".[18] * The key passage reads as follows:

> . . . there are wicked women who, turning back to Satan and seduced by the illusions and phantoms of the demons, believe and openly avow that in the hours of the night they ride on certain animals, together with Diana, the goddess of the pagans, with a numberless multitude of women; and in the silence of the dead of night cross many great lands; and obey (Diana's) orders as though she were their mistress, and on particular nights are summoned to her service. Would that they alone perished in their perfidy, without dragging so many others with them into the ruin of infidelity! For a numberless multitude of people, deceived by this false view, believe these things to be true and, turning away from the true faith and returning to the errors of the pagans, think that there exists some divine power other than the one God.

And the canon reminds priests of their duty: they must, from the pulpit, warn their congregations that this is all illusion, inspired not by the spirit of God but by that of Satan. For Satan knows how to deceive foolish women by showing them, while they sleep, all kind of things and of people. But who has not, in dreams, gone out of himself, so that he believed he was seeing things which he never saw when awake? And who would be so foolish as to think that things that happened only in the mind have also happened in the flesh? Everyone must be made to realise that to believe such things is a sign that one has lost the true faith, and that one belongs not to God, but to the Devil.

So far the *Canon Episcopi*. A century after Regino of Prüm, Burchard of Worms included the gist of it in his *Decretum*;[19] whence it was

---

* The preceding canon in Regino's book is taken from the fourth-century synod of Ancyra, and this has often led to the Canon Episcopi being ascribed to the same council. This is however mistaken. It is also mistaken to think that the text of the canon was known to Augustine; the treatise *De spiritu et anima*, where it is to be found, though frequently attributed to Augustine is in reality an eleventh-century work. There is no foundation, either, for the idea that a Roman synod of the year 367 dealt with the belief in nocturnal meetings under Diana's leadership. The source is a life of Pope Damasus I (see C. Baronius, *Annales Ecclesiastici* vol. V, Lucca, 1739, pp. 535, 572 (ad an. 382 (para 20) and ad an. 384 (para 19)); but it gives no detail of the supposed synod. The text in Regino of Prüm is the earliest of the extant sources on this matter.

taken over by the later canonists Ivo of Chartres and Gratian, and so passed into the enduring corpus of canon law. It bulks large in most modern histories of European witchcraft; yet if one studies it carefully, it has no obvious bearing on witchcraft at all. The women it criticizes do not imagine themselves as night-witches, addicted to murderous and cannibalistic enterprises, but as devotees of a supernatural queen who leads and commands them on their nocturnal flights.

This supernatural queen deserves closer attention. Like Regino, Burchard calls her "Diana, goddess of the pagans", but he adds the phrase "or Herodias"; and in another paragraph of the *Corrector* he refers to her as "Holda".[20] Between them, these names lead straight to one particular body of folk-belief.

The Roman goddess Diana continued to enjoy a certain cult in the early Middle Ages. A life of St Caesarius, who was bishop of Arles early in the sixth century, mentions "a demon whom the simple people call Diana". Gregory of Tours describes how, in the same century, a Christian hermit in the neighbourhood of Trier destroyed a statue of Diana which, though no doubt of Roman origin, was worshipped by the native peasantry.[21] Further east, in what is now Franconia, the cult was still vigorous late in the seventh century; the British missionary bishop St Kilian was martyred when he tried to convert the east Franks from their worship of Diana.[22] Goddess of the moon and lover of the night, Diana was also, in one of her aspects, identified with Hecate, goddess of magic. And it was characteristic of Hecate that she rode at night, followed by a train of women, or rather of souls disguised as women—restless souls of the prematurely dead, of those who had died by violence, of those who had never been buried.

With Diana, Burchard equates Herodias, the wife of Herod the tetrarch and the instigator of the murder of John the Baptist. Legends clustered around this figure. Already in the tenth century we hear of her from Ratherius, who was a Frank by origin but who became bishop of Verona. He complains that many people, to the perdition of their souls, were claiming Herodias as a queen, even as a goddess, and were affirming that a third part of the world was subject to her; as though, he remarks, that were the reward for killing the prophet.[23] In the twelfth century a Latin poem on Reynard the Fox, called *Reinardus*, provides further details. It describes how Herod's daughter, here also called Herodias instead of Salome, falls in love with the Baptist, who repulses her. When his head is brought to her on a platter she still tries to cover it with tears and kisses, but it shrinks away. Its lips begin to blow violently, until Herodias is blown into outer space, where she must hover for evermore, a sorrowful queen. Yet she has some consolations. She has her cult, and a third part of mankind serves her. And from midnight until cockcrow she can sit on oaktrees and hazel-bushes, resting from her eternal travelling through the empty air.[24]

But it is the queen's other name, Holda, that shows most clearly how her followers regarded her.[25] When Burchard gives this as an alternative to Diana and Herodias, he is evoking a figure who was to remain prominent in German folklore right down to the nineteenth century—and nowhere more so than in Hesse, where Burchard was born. Holda (Hulda, Holle, Hulle, Frau Holl, etc.) is a supernatural, motherly being who normally lives in the upper air, and circles the earth. She is particularly active in the depths of winter; snowflakes are the feathers that fall when she makes her bed. She travels in the twelve days between Christmas and Epiphany, and this brings fruitfulness to the land during the coming year—from which one may conclude that originally she was a pagan goddess associated with the winter solstice and the rebirth of the year. She can sometimes be terrifying—she can lead the "furious army" which rides through the sky on the storm, she can also turn into an ugly old hag with great teeth and a long nose, the terror of children. Yet in the main she becomes terrifying only when angered—and what angers her is above all slackness about the house or the farm.

For Holda is not always in the sky; she visits the earth, and then she functions as patroness of husbandry. The plough is sacred to her, she assists the crops. She is particularly interested in the women's work of spinning and weaving; and if she punishes laziness she rewards diligence, often by pushing gifts through the window. She is also concerned with childbirth—babies come from her secret places, her tree, her pond. Fruitfulness and productivity of every kind are her special pre-occupations.

When Holda goes on her nocturnal journeys she is accompanied by a train of followers. These are the souls of the dead, including the souls of children and of babies who have died unbaptized (but here one must remember that often the soul itself is imagined as a child). And this makes sense of the passages in the *Canon Episcopi* and in Burchard's *Corrector*; the women who imagined themselves to fly at night, in the train of Diana or Herodias or Holda, were sending their souls to join, temporarily, the wandering souls of the dead—and on errands which were not murderous and destructive but, on the contrary, beneficent and sustaining.

Such beliefs, or fantasies, were by no means confined to Germany. Guillaume d'Auvergne, bishop of Paris, who died in 1249, has similar tales to tell from France. He has heard of spirits who on certain nights take on the likeness of girls and women in shining robes, and in that guise frequent woods and groves. They even appear in stables, bearing wax candles, and plait the horses' manes. Above all these "ladies of the night" visit private homes, under the leadership of their mistress Lady Abundia (from *abundantia*), who is also called Satia (from *satietas*, meaning the same). If they find food and drink ready for them, they partake of them, but without diminishing the quantity of either; and they reward the hospitable household with an abundance of material goods. If on the other hand they find that all food and drink have been locked away, they leave the place in contempt. Inspired by this belief, foolish old women, and some equally foolish men, open up their pantries and uncover their barrels on the nights when they expect a visitation. The bishop, of course, knows just what to think of such practices. Demons trick old women into dreaming these things; and it is a grievous sin to think that abundance of material goods can come from any other source than God.[26]

A generation later Lady Abundia appears in that vast encyclopaedia in verse, Jean de Meun's *Roman de la Rose*, which was to become the most popular vernacular work in the whole of medieval literature. Many people, we are told, foolishly imagine that at night they become witches, wandering with Lady Habonde. They also say that the third child in a family always has the capacity to do this (just as one third of mankind serves Herodias). Three times a week they journey, entering every house through the chinks and holes, ignoring locks and bolts. Their souls, leaving their bodies behind, travel with "the good ladies" through houses and through strange places. Jean de Meun himself has no use for such imaginings, which—like Guillaume d'Auvergne—he regards as a speciality of foolish old women. In his view dreams are the explanation of all these journeys.[27]

Belief in the mysterious ladies and their nocturnal visitations was sufficiently widespread to inspire practical jokes, or at least stories of practical jokes. A Latin treatise compiled in France in the first quarter of the fourteenth century tells how some ruffians tricked a rich and credulous peasant.* Dressed as ladies, they forced the door of his house one night and went dancing through the rooms. Singing "Take one, give back a hundred", they took away all his most valuable belongings. Meanwhile the peasant looked on as though bemused, and when his wife tried to stop the looting, told her: "Shut up and close your eyes!

* A practical joke recounted by Boccaccio has a very similar basis (*Decameron*, ninth story of the eighth day).

We'll be rich, for these are the good beings and they will increase our belongings a hundredfold." [28] Another anecdote concerns an old woman's attempt to extract a reward from the parish priest. She describes how she and the "ladies of the night" entered his home, though it was locked up, and found him naked on his bed. If she had not had the presence of mind to throw a cover over him, the ladies would have punished this disrespectful behaviour by beating him to death. Unimpressed, the priest beat her about the shoulders with a cross, to teach her not to believe in dreams.

The "ladies of the night" were known in Italy too. The thirteenth-century archbishop Jacobus de Voragine mentions them in his collection of legendary lives of the saints, which under the title of *Golden Legend* became one of the most popular and widely translated religious works of the Middle Ages. He tells how the fourth-century bishop, St Germanus, after dining at the house of some friends, was astonished to see the table re-laid. When he asked for whom the meal was meant, the answer was: "For the good women who enter at night." He sat up and watched—and suddenly he seemed to see "a multitude of demons in the form of men and women". His hosts, summoned from their beds, recognized the visitors as their neighbours; but the bishop, unconvinced, tried exorcism, and with excellent results. The visitors admitted to being devils who had disguised themselves as particular friends of the family. As demons go, these were harmless enough—they intended nothing worse than a practical joke, and yielded to exorcism quite happily. Nevertheless the moral is clear: if you believe in "the good women", demons will enter your house. [29]

Although Jacobus de Voragine does not mention the supernatural queen, she was just as familiar in Italy as in France and Germany. The fourteenth-century Dominican Jacopo Passavanti in his guide to asceticism shows how the fantasy described in the *Canon Episcopi* had persisted through five centuries, undergoing some elaboration yet still recognizably the same: "It happens that demons taking on the likeness of men and women who are alive, and of horses and beasts of burden, go by night in company through certain regions, where they are seen by the people, who mistake them for those persons whose likenesses they bear; and in some countries this is called the *tregenda*. And the demons do this to spread error, and to cause scandal, and to discredit those whose likenesses they take on, by showing that they do dishonourable things in the tregenda. There are some people, especially women, who say that they go at night in company with such a tregenda, and name many men and women in their company; and they say that the mistresses of the throng, who lead the others, are Herodias, who had St John the Baptist killed, and the ancient Diana, goddess of the Greeks".[30]

Even today, many Sicilian peasants believe in mysterious beings whom they usually call "ladies from outside", but also sometimes "ladies of the night", "ladies of the home", "mistresses of the home", "beautiful ladies" or simply "the ladies". According to the few who have ever seen them, these are tall and beautiful damsels with long, shining hair. They never appear by day, but on certain nights, especially Thursdays, they roam abroad under the leadership of a chief "lady". When they find a well-ordered house they will enter through cracks in the door or through the keyhole. Families who treat them well and offer them food and drink, music and dancing, can expect every kind of blessing in return. On the other hand any sign of disrespect or any resistance to their commands will bring poverty and sickness on the house—though even then they are quick to forgive, if they find themselves properly treated at their next visit. Though they are feared, as supernatural and uncanny beings, they are not confused with witches. Whereas witches are human beings, and essentially evil, the "ladies from outside" are spirits, and essentially good. In fact they are guardians, not destroyers.[31]

From all this there emerges a coherent picture of a traditional folkbelief. Its origins seem to lie in a pre-Christian, pagan world-view. It is certainly very ancient; and despite certain variations of detail, it has remained constant in its main features over a period of at least a thousand years and over a great part of western Europe. It is concerned with beneficent, protective spirits, who are thought of above all as female, and who are sometimes associated with the souls of the dead. In the past, it has been taken seriously in peasant communities: people tidied up their houses and left food and drink to win the favour of these spirits. Moreover some people—notably old women—used to dream or fantasy that they could attach themselves to these spirits and take part in their nocturnal journeyings. And here this age-old folkbelief can be brought into relation with equally ancient beliefs about witches. In both cases, we find that women are believed—and sometimes even believe themselves—to travel at night in a supernatural manner, endowed with supernatural powers by supernatural patrons. One belief is indeed the opposite of the other; with the cannibalistic witch, symbol of destruction, disorder and death, one can contrast the woman who joins the radiant "ladies" on their benign missions for the encouragement of hospitality and good housekeeping.

Inevitably, the official attitude of the Church to the "ladies of the night" was very different from that of the half-pagan peasantry. Just as, down to the thirteenth century, the Church denied the existence of night-witches, so it denied that these more welcome visitors were what they seemed to be. Belief in either kind of nocturnal voyager was condemned as pagan superstition. From the *Canon Episcopi* in the ninth century to Guillaume d'Auvergne in the thirteenth, there is unanimity amongst the orthodox: the "ladies of the night" belong to the world of dreams. The demons are indeed involved, but only in so far as they try, by means of these dreams, to seduce the dreamers from the true faith. To take such dreams for reality, above all to believe that one has oneself taken part in a nocturnal journey—this is to turn away from Christianity, it is to fall into the errors of the pagans and the snares of the Devil. Even so, it is not a horrific sin; and the penance imposed is much lighter than the penance for praying or lighting candles at a former pagan shrine.

But in the thirteenth century the attitude begins to change. Already Jacobus de Voragine takes a different view of the matter, and this is still truer of Jacopo Passavanti in the fourteenth century. The traditional picture of the nocturnal visitors changes; no longer tall, beautiful ladies, they have all the appearance of known individuals of both sexes, in fact they look just like one's neighbours. And the traditional interpretation also changes. These are no mere apparitions in a dream, they are demons visiting this earth in the guise of human beings; and they can also be seen and heard by human beings who are fully awake and in full possession of their senses. Something that hitherto has happened only in the minds of silly old women has taken on an objective, material existence. The implication is clear: a human being who takes part in such a gathering is no longer merely relapsing into pagan superstition, but is actually consorting with demons. The old fantasy of the supernatural queen and her train is beginning to blend with the new fantasy of the witches' Sabbat.

At the same time the Church becomes much more severe in its dealings with women who thought themselves followers of Diana. Between 1384 and 1390 two women were actually tried before the tribunal of the Inquisition in Milan—not for imagining that they followed Diana, but for following her.[32] Both gave substantially the same evidence. Twice a week for many years they had been going to the "society" or "game" around "Signora Oriente", or Diana, or Herodias, and paying homage to that supernatural queen. The "society" included dead as well as living persons (as we have seen, Diana's followers always had included the souls of the dead). It also included animals—one of every kind except the donkey and the wolf. The animals were eaten by the company, but later the queen would resuscitate them. The company would also visit the houses of the rich; and wherever they found a house in good order and ready for them, the queen would bless it. For the rest, it was the queen's custom to instruct her followers about the use of herbs to cure sickness, and about the divining of theft and sorcery.

All this belongs to the body of traditional, pagan beliefs about "white" magic. But one of the women also confessed to sexual intercourse with a devil called Lucifelus—a feature so out of keeping with the rest that one suspects it was suggested by the inquisitor. Moreover, in the end both women were handed over to the secular arm and executed. It is a far cry, indeed, from the *Canon Episcopi*.

Folk-beliefs about the "ladies of the night" would never, by themselves, have given rise to the great witch-hunt of the fifteenth, sixteenth and seventeenth centuries; but they did provide materials which could be exploited by the witch-hunters. The "ladies of the night" were, after all, imagined as a highly organized body, under a supernatural leader—and this meant that, in the eyes of the orthodox, the women who dreamed that they joined this throng were dreaming of submitting themselves to the absolute rule of a demon. Cannibalistic night-witches, on the other hand, had not traditionally been imagined in this way. Though there are hints—in the *Pactus legis Salicae* and again in Burchard's *Corrector*—that they operate collectively, the early medieval sources never suggest that they associate with demons, let alone that they are organized under demonic leadership. Night-witches and "ladies of the night" alike belonged to the world of popular imagination, particularly peasant imagination; and there they were kept quite separate from one another. But to the educated, looking at these fantasies from outside and from above, the distinction was not necessarily so absolute. John of Salisbury, an Englishman who spent much of his time in France, has this much to say in his *Policraticus*, which he wrote between 1156 and 1159:[33]

> ... they assert that a certain woman who shines by night,* or Herodias, or the mistress of the night, summons gatherings and assemblies, which attend various banquets. The figure receives all

---

* "nocticulam", probably a slip for "noctilucam", which was used by Classical authors as an epithet for the moon and therefore Diana; cf. Varro, *De lingua latina*, IV, 10; and Horace, *Carmina*, iv, 6, line 38.

kinds of homage from her servants, some of whom are handed over for punishment, while others are singled out for praise, according to their deserts. Furthermore, they say that infants are exposed to the *lamiae*;* some of them being dismembered and gluttonously devoured, while the mistress takes pity on others and has them put back in their cradles.

Here the two ideas—of the "ladies of the night" and of night-witches who steal and devour babies—are ingeniously combined: both are commanded by the moon-goddess or by Herodias, and the image of the nocturnal banquet merges into that of the cannibalistic orgy. Of course John of Salisbury and the educated elite of his time regarded both ideas as mere delusions. "Who is so blind," asks John, "as not to recognise this as the wicked work of deceiving devils? It is clear that these things are put about from silly women and from simple men of weak faith." And he goes on to show how this "plague" can be cured: one must refuse to take these lies and follies seriously and, when one meets them, expose their demonic origin.

But a time was to come when the attitude of the educated elite would be very different from this. In the fourteenth and fifteenth centuries some of the literate began to take over both fantasies from the "silly women and simple men", and blended them into a single fantasy about organized masses of witches flying by night, intent on cannibalistic orgies, and guided by demons. And that did indeed contribute to the outbreak of the great European witch-hunt.

−3−

It is clear that already in the Middle Ages some women believed themselves to wander about at night on cannibalistic errands, while others believed themselves to wander about, on more benign errands, under the leadership of a supernatural queen. Later, after the great witch-hunt had begun, some women genuinely believed that they attended the sabbat and took part in its demonic orgies: not all the confessions, even at that time, are to be attributed to torture or the fear of torture. In an age such as ours, with its interest in psychedelic experiments, one is bound to ask whether these delusions could have been the result of drugs.

Writing in 1435–7, the German Johann Nider tells the story of a peasant woman who imagined herself to fly at night with Diana.[34] When a visiting Dominican tried to disabuse her, she offered to show him how she did it. One night, in the presence of the Dominican and

* A Classical equivalent for *strigae*.

another witness, she placed herself in a basket, rubbed herself with an ointment, and fell into such a stupor that not even falling to the floor could wake her. When finally she awoke she assured the observers that she had been with Diana, and could hardly be persuaded that she had never left the spot at all. At the same date the Spaniard Alfonso Tostato also tells of such women, and adds that while in their stupor they are insensible to blows and even to fire.[35] A century later the Italian Bartolommeo Spina knew of women who anointed themselves and, in a deep stupor, imagined themselves to fly through the air with their mistress and a host of dancers.[36] And by 1569 the Dutch physician Johannes Weyer was even able to supply recipes of solutions and ointments that were supposed to be favoured by witches.[37]

How seriously should all this be taken? The fact that some of the recipes include real narcotics, such as belladonna, has roused curiosity. Some bold spirits, notably in Germany, recently tried them out on themselves—and promptly experienced very much what the witches are supposed to have experienced.[38] Yet there are grounds for doubt. Not one of those tales about women anointing themselves even pretends to come from an eyewitness—even Nider, who goes into most detail, merely repeats what his teacher had once told him about an unnamed Dominican. Moreover the earliest recipes, from the fifteenth century, consist not of narcotics but of such disagreeable but non-toxic substances as the flesh of snakes, lizards, toads, spiders and (of course) children; and the ointments are less commonly applied to the witch's body than to the chairs and broomsticks on which she rides.[39] All in all, there is hardly more reason to take these stories seriously than to believe that the witch Pamphile, in Apuleius, was really able, with the help of a concoction of laurel and dill, to grow an owl's feathers, beak and claws and fly off hooting.[40] The true explanation lies in quite a different direction—not in pharmacology but in anthropology; for the night-witch is known in many non-European societies today.

The anthropological literature on witchcraft is vast and continues to grow at a prodigious rate, but to clarify this particular problem one need only turn to J. R. Crawford's *Witchcraft and sorcery in Rhodesia*.[41] Mr Crawford's book, which is based on judicial records of witchcraft and sorcery allegations between 1956 and 1962, shows very clearly what the Shona peoples of Rhodesia believe about night-witches. They believe that certain women strip themselves naked and fly through the air at night, usually on a hyena, ant-bear, owl or crocodile. The purpose of the flight is cannibalism or, rather, necrophagy—something which the Shona regard with even greater horror, if possible, than does our own society. The witch is supposed to exhume newly buried corpses and eat the flesh—but also to kill people, especially children, in order to devour them.(42) That is the general belief amongst the Shona, and it has many counterparts in other areas of Africa, and, indeed, in Asia and Central and Southern America also. The point, however, is that some Shona women apply it to themselves. The following comes from a confession of a woman called Muhlava:

'I know a native woman by the name of Chirunga, she is a witch. We go about at night bewitching people. We have gone out five times. The accused came to my hut one day and said she wanted to be friendly with me. Later she came again and we went to the fields and there I made certain incisions on the accused on the hips. I applied some magic to these cuts, some white medicine. This is the same stuff that Tsatsawani had given me some years previously. The accused was at this time quite a young girl, she was not married and was still living with her parents. I explained to Dawu, the accused, that this meant she was now a witch. I explained that we should go about at night bewitching people. Once I went out with Chirunga and the accused to see my husband. They both came to my hut, that is the accused and Chirunga. They came riding hyenas at night. We all went to my husband's hut. They came with me in order to bewitch my husband Chidava. This was also to teach the accused. I cannot explain the reason for this, it only comes to us in a dream. We poured some *maheo* or sweet beer into Chidava's mouth, there was bewitching medicine in it. We then sprinkled some more medicine on his body. We then left and went to bed. The accused and Chirunga then took their hyenas and rode away into the night. Three days later my husband died. A little later my two friends, the accused and Chirunga, came at night on hyenas and we all went to the place where the body was buried. We exumed the body of my husband, we skinned the body, we cut a piece of meat and took it to my hut. We reinterred the body in the grave. At the hut we cooked the meat and ate it, it was good. We departed then. Some time later we three went to visit Meke, the brother of Chidava. We all rode hyenas. Near the kraal we talked amongst ourselves and decided to kill Meke. We went into the village and we found him sleeping. We each of us laid hands on him. The next morning Meke was ill. The kraal head then came to us and said that we should not bewitch the man Meke so we relented and Meke lived. After this the accused married and went to live in Maranda's area. Quite recently myself and the mother of the accused were attending a beer drink. A report was made to us by Maswirira. Two days later I went to visit the accused in chief Maranda's area. I went at night on a hyena's back. I stood outside the hut where the accused was sleeping. The infant was in the accused's arms. We pulled the baby and later I rode off on my hyena. . . . We wanted to bewitch the child—I cannot tell the reason because it only came to us as if we were dreaming. We fought over the child. We wanted to bewitch the child so it would die. We wanted to eat it. The child was never dropped during the struggle. I then returned to my kraal. . . .'[43]

Muhlava's confession was largely corroborated by that of her friend Chirunga Tsatsawani. To appreciate both at their full value it is necessary to add Crawford's comment:

Any suggestion that the alleged witches were forced to confess is, I think, belied by the very nature of the confessions themselves. Forced confessions are generally grudgingly made and retracted as soon as the threat is removed. The confessions in [this case] were not of this nature and were first made in front of a definitely sceptical European policeman and then repeated or admitted in front of a European magistrate and later a European judge. As far as one can tell there is no reason to suppose that the police brought any pressure to bear on these people. There would, in any event, be no reason to bring pressure to bear on such talkative persons. Again, there seem to be no reasons one can suggest why the community in which these people were living should demand confessions of the sort which were made, for—even if a confession were demanded—a mere confession of witchcraft lacking in circumstantial detail would suffice.

While, no doubt, no normal, well-adjusted person would give the evidence these alleged witches gave, there is no reason to suppose that any of them was insane. Certainly they were considered sane enough to give evidence or to stand trial and, in any event, it is hardly possible that a group of women in one village should be similarly attacked by identical forms of the same mental disorder.[44]

This, surely, is the heart of the matter: these confessions correspond precisely with the ideas about night-witches which are general amongst the Shona. The deeds were all purely imaginary—the cannibalism as much as the hyena-ride: Chidava's body was exhumed by the police and subjected to a post-mortem, and no trace of any interference was found. On the other hand, there is nothing to suggest that the imaginings were produced by drugs. The collective fantasy has simply taken possession of the minds of certain women, to the extent that they believe themselves to be night-witches: "I cannot explain the reason for this, it only comes to us in a dream. . . . I cannot tell the reason because it only comes to us as if we were dreaming."

Set against this background the discoveries of the Italian scholar Dr Carlo Ginzburg, which he has described in his fascinating book *I Benandanti*, take on a fresh significance.[45] By archival research Ginzburg unearthed the existence, in the late sixteenth century, of a curious group of anti-witches at Friuli, near Udine in north-eastern Italy. These peasants saw themselves as entrusted with the task of going out, during the Ember days, to fight witches who were trying to destroy the fertility of the crops and also to kill children. Their steeds could be goats or cats as well as horses, their weapons consisted of sticks of fennel; the outcome of the battle decided whether the coming year would be one of plenty or of famine. Because of this, Ginzburg decided that he had stumbled upon a survival of an age-old fertility cult; and other writers have adopted and developed the idea.[46] Yet there is nothing whatsoever in Ginzburg's material to justify such a conclusion.

The experiences of the Benandanti—the rides, the battles with the witches, the rescuing of the crops and the children—were all trance experiences. The Benandanti—as they themselves repeatedly stated— underwent these experiences in a state of catalepsy: throughout the relevant period they lay motionless in bed, in a stupor. It was, they said, their spirits that went out to do battle; indeed, if a spirit failed to return promptly, the body died.[47] Moreover, the summons to enlist in the Benandanti came to a person in his sleep; it was brought by an angel—described as golden, like the angels on altars—and the same angel stood by the banner of the Benandanti during the battle.[48]

The Benandanti believed absolutely that their experiences were real, and that they were collective; but they never for a moment suggested that they were bodily—the witches too were said to fight only in spirit. As with the Shona women, "it only came to them as if they were dreaming". Indeed, to be a Benandante at all it was necessary to have been born with a caul, which was regarded as a bridge by which the soul could pass from the everyday world into the world of spirits.

What Ginzburg found in his sixteenth-century archives was in fact a local variant of what, for centuries before, had been the stock experience of the followers of Diana, Herodias or Holda. It has nothing to do with the "old religion" of fertility postulated by Margaret Murray and her followers. What it illustrates is—once more—the fact that not only the waking thoughts but the trance experiences of individuals can be deeply conditioned by the generally accepted beliefs of the society in which they live.

This is merely to re-state, in modern terms, what was taken for granted by educated people almost to the close of the Middle Ages. As we have seen, until the late fourteenth century the educated in general, and the higher clergy in particular, were quite clear that these nocturnal journeyings of women, whether for benign or for maleficent purposes, were purely imaginary happenings. But in the sixteenth and still more in the seventeenth centuries, this was no longer the case. And that is what made the great witch-hunt possible: witch-hunting reached massive proportions only where and when the authorities themselves accepted the reality of the nocturnal journeyings. For without such journeyings, no witches' sabbats.

It remains to ask what started such a great change of outlook

12

THE MAKING OF THE GREAT
WITCH-HUNT

–1–

The importance of the most famous of the witch-hunters' manuals, the *Malleus Maleficarum*, published in 1486, has been exaggerated. The most intensive period of witch-hunting, when great holocausts took place in one region of Europe after another, began only towards the close of the following century. On the other hand, the stereotype of the witch was already fully developed half a century before the *Malleus* appeared— and more fully and more horrifically than in the *Malleus* itself. The *Malleus* has little to say about the witches' sabbat or about nocturnal flying, but both figure prominently in records of trials from the 1420s and 1430s onwards.

These trials were a by-product of the persecution of the Waldensians —which meant that they occurred most frequently in those areas where pockets of Waldensians either survived or were believed to survive. As we have seen, by the fifteenth century these were, in the main, mountainous areas; for whole colonies of Waldensians had taken refuge in the French and Swiss Alps. This circumstance is responsible for the notion, first propounded by Joseph Hansen, but still flourishing, that the fantasy of the night-witch was fostered by the peculiar conditions of mountain life.[1] In reality, this fantasy was extremely widespread in the Middle Ages, and in no way peculiar to mountain populations—as is obvious from the preceding chapter. And when the fantasy penetrated into the thinking of judges, ecclesiastical and secular, the results were as quickly apparent in the populous plains as in the remote Alpine valleys. A new kind of trial came into being; and the earliest examples ranged from the Alps to the area around Lyons, to Normandy, to Artois.

In all these trials the inquisitorial procedure was employed, though not necessarily by the Inquisition: inquisitors, bishops and secular judges were all involved, sometimes separately, sometimes in col- laboration. The earliest trial seems in fact to have been mainly a secular affair. In 1428 the peasant communes of the Swiss canton of Valais— admittedly, under the guidance of their suzerain, the bishop of Sion—

decided that anyone accused of witchcraft by more than two persons should be arrested; tortured if no confession was forthcoming; and burned on the strength of the confession so obtained. According to Hans Fründ, chronicler of Lucerne, writing some ten years later, a regular witch-hunt began in that same year of 1428, in the two valleys south of the Rhône known as the Val d'Anniviers and the Val d'Hérens.[2] In the confessions extracted from some of the accused there appears, for the first time, the image of the flying, Devil-worshipping witch that was to inspire the great witch-hunt.

Torture was employed, and so ruthlessly that many who refused to make false confessions died under it. But not all possessed such extraordinary strength of character; and the picture that emerged from their utterances was both lurid and complex. In part, it reflects the traditional misconceptions about ritual or ceremonial magic. For many years, it appeared, great numbers of men and women had been formally renouncing God, the saints and the Church and had been pledging themselves to the Devil; paying him an annual tribute of a sheep or a lamb, or else promising him one of their own limbs, to be collected after death. Such things recall the trials of Pope Boniface, Bishop Guichard, and Alice Kyteler. On the other hand, the powers which the Devil bestowed in return belong largely to the age-old world of peasant *maleficia*: power to make people or animals sicken or die, power to render men impotent and women sterile, power to drain cows of their milk and to devastate cornfields.

Yet other features of the picture clearly have a quite different source, in fantasies concerning night-witches. For the Devil, who usually appeared in the form of a black animal, provided his followers with a salve to apply to chairs, on which they would fly from one village to another; he would also, on occasion, transport them himself from mountain-top to mountain-top. Like Diana's troop, these followers of the Devil's would invade people's cellars and drink the best wine; but they were also *striges*, who killed, cooked and ate children, both their own and other people's. This was done at a nocturnal meeting, where the Devil would also make an appearance, to preach a sermon warning his followers not to go to church or to make confession to any priest. The result of this earliest formulation of the witches' sabbat was the burning of a number of men and women—which the chronicler puts now at 100, now at 200, and which must surely have been large.

On the French side of the Alps the trials were mostly initiated by the Inquisition—which in that area was staffed by Franciscans instead of by Dominicans.[3] For a century, Waldensian families had been solidly implanted in the four valleys of the Briançonnais known as Freys-sinière, Argentière, Valpute and Valcluson. Now the whole population of those remote areas came to be suspect—and suspect not simply of heresy but of the new-style witchcraft.

As in Valais, the stereotype still owes something to the tradition of ritual or ceremonial magic. Before the Devil or a subordinate demon will appear, he has to be invoked—he does not present himself of his own accord and force his attentions on the future witch, as he does in the later witch-trials. Moreover the witch is as likely to be a man as a woman. Thomas Bègue, who was executed in 1436, confessed to conjuring up a demon by calling, three times, on "Mermet diable"; whereupon Mermet appeared, first in the guise of a black cat, then as an old Negro dressed in black, with horns on his feet. Jeannette, widow of Hugues Brunier, admitted having invoked a demon named Brunet, who materialized as a black dog and then, again, as a Negro dressed in black; also, she sacrificed a black cock to him each May-day. Other demons, when invoked under names like Guillemet or Griffart, would appear in the form of black cats, or black crows, before turning into Negroes. It is all still very close to the world of Alice Kyteler and her Negro Robin, "son of the art".

But the notion of apostasy, and collective apostasy at that, now looms much larger. There is no question here of a temporary renunciation of God and the Church. Once conjured up, the demon demands conver-sion: Christ is to be renounced for ever, by some symbolic gesture such as trampling or spitting on the cross; homage must be paid to himself or to his master, the Devil; quite often he insists that one or more of the convert's children shall be sacrificed. As in the case of Alice Kyteler, the Devil or his demon has sexual intercourse with his followers, varying his sex to suit theirs—but he may go further: the Devil's mark, the stigma on the flesh, which was to bulk so large in the great witch-hunt, already figures in some of these trials.

Above all, the fantasy of the witches' sabbat, or "synagogue" as it was usually called, is described for the first time in all its grotesque detail. The Devil or the subordinate demon provides male and female witches with the means to go to the sabbat, however distant it may be. Some receive a little black horse, others a red mare, others a fantastic beast like a greyhound; but most are given a stick and some ointment to grease it with—and so equipped, they fly like the wind. At the sabbat, demons and witches together banquet under the supervision of the Devil himself, who may appear either in the guise of a black cat or as his infernal self, crowned, clad in black, with shining eyes. The witches worship him on their knees. They also report on the acts of *maleficium* which they have performed since the last sabbat; the Devil praises or blames them accordingly and issues instructions for future *maleficia*. The body of a newly killed child—often a child of one of the witches— is cooked, to make the magical powders required for these purposes; after which demons and witches dance together, while the Devil plays the drum or the bagpipes. Finally each witch has intercourse with his or her particular demon—until, at cock-crow, the assembly breaks up and the witches return home on their magical steeds.[4]

There is no reason at all to think that most of the men and women who confessed to these strange performances really were Waldensians. It seems, rather, that ecclesiastical and secular authorities alike, while pursuing Waldensians, repeatedly came across people—chiefly women —who believed things about themselves which fitted in perfectly with the tales about heretical sects that had been circulating for centuries. The notion of cannibalistic infanticide provided the common factor. It was widely believed that babies or small children were commonly devoured at the nocturnal meetings of heretics. It was likewise widely believed that certain women killed and devoured babies or small children, also at night; and some women even believed this of them-selves. It was the extraordinary congruence between the two sets of beliefs that led those concerned with pursuing heretics to see, in the stories which they extracted from deluded women, a confirmation of the traditional stories about heretics who practised cannibalistic infanticide.

They not only saw a confirmation—they were also led to embark on an elaboration. For the supposedly cannibalistic women were also supposed to go about their fearsome business by flying. Now the notion of a flying sect of heretics had great advantages: it made it possible to account for assemblies which were frequent, and often vast, and which nevertheless nobody ever saw. Already in 1239, at Châlons-sur-Marne, the inquisitor Robert le Bougre—a French counterpart to Conrad of Marburg—had tortured one of his female victims into confessing that she flew through the air to serve at the heretics' banquets at Milan, hundreds of miles away.[5] The notion did not catch on at that time, but it did so a couple of centuries later. And here fantasies about night-witches and also fantasies about those other night-flyers, the "ladies of the night" who followed Diana or Herodias or "Signora Oriente", were of decisive importance.

In the course of the fifteenth century inquisitors and lay magistrates began to combine these various fantasies with the stereotype of a Devil-worshipping, orgiastic, infanticidal sect. A few untypical inquisitors, from Conrad of Marburg to Alberto Cattaneo, had supplied what seemed to be confirmation of that stereotype; they had been able to do so thanks to the inquisitorial procedure, and in particular to the use of torture. Bishop Ledrede of Kilkenny and the Swiss judge Peter of Greyerz had integrated *maleficium* into the picture, along with features borrowed from ritual magic; again torture played its part. Now the nocturnal flight was added. In earlier centuries that fantasy had been rejected by the educated, but it was a different matter now. Precisely because the notion of nocturnal travels for purposes of cannibalism not only fitted in with the existing stereotype but made it much more credible, it appealed strongly to those concerned with tracking down and trying heretics. Tales which a few of the accused provided spontaneously had to be confirmed by the rest—and again, torture was used to ensure this. In the end it became a commonplace, accepted by the greater part of society, that there were heretics who, in addition to perpetrating the horrors traditionally attributed to heretics, flew at night to their assemblies. In popular parlance all these activities were identified with Waldensians—in French it was even called *Vauderie*. In reality, a new crime had been invented—one which, in later times, lawyers were to give a technical name, *crimen magiae*.

The pursuit of Waldensians, though most intensive in mountainous regions, was by no means confined to them; and nor were witch-trials. In 1438 Pierre Vallin of La Tour du Pin was tried for witchcraft, and he was a vassal of the lord of Tournon: the whole area, which lies to the south and south-east of Lyons, is a mere 200 metres above sea level. The trial is of interest for two reasons: it shows how closely secular and ecclesiastical authorities collaborated in pursuing the newly invented crime, and also why the new-style witch-trials tended to turn into mass trials. The trial took place in two stages: in the first, Pierre Vallin was prosecuted and sentenced by officers of the archbishop of Vienne and of the Inquisition; in the second, by the fiscal of the lord of Tournon.[6] Already at the first of the two trials the accused confessed that he had given himself to a demon called Belzebut, body and soul, no less than sixty-three years before; and regularly rode on a stick to the "synagogue", or sabbat, where children were eaten. At the second trial the secular authorities were interested in extracting from the unfortunate man the names of accomplices, i.e. of fellow-witches who had also ridden on sticks to the sabbat. Pierre Vallin had already been tortured and had already, in effect, been sentenced to death; now he was tortured again to obtain this information. In the end he supplied some ten names. It is noteworthy that they were mostly names of men, and that the interrogators pressed him to name priests and clerics and nobles and rich men in particular. The time had not yet come when attendance at the sabbat would be practically confined to women, and to peasant women at that.

In 1453 and 1459 two sensational trials took place in northern France. In the first, at Evreux in Normandy, the accused was Guillaume Adeline, who was a noted doctor of theology and had formerly been a Professer at Paris; the judges consisted of an inquisitor and a representative of the bishop of Evreux.[7] It was alleged that a written compact with Satan had been found on Adeline's person, binding him to preach sermons against the reality of the sabbat; with the result that judges had been discouraged from prosecuting frequenters of the sabbat, and the number of those frequenting it had increased accordingly. Adeline eventually confessed not only that he had indeed entered into such a compact with Satan, but that he himself had been in the habit of flying on a broomstick to the sabbat. He found there a demon called Monseigneur, who sometimes changed himself into a he-goat; where-upon Adeline would do him homage by kissing him under the tail. Those attending the sabbat were also required to renounce formally every aspect of the Christian faith. Perhaps because of his eminence, perhaps because he enjoyed the support of the University of Caen, Adeline was sentenced not to death but to perpetual imprisonment in a dungeon, on a diet of bread and water. After four years of this regime he was found dead in his cell, in an attitude of prayer.

The company to which Adeline is supposed to have belonged is referred to as the sect of Waldensians—but by that time the term was very generally used as a synonym for "witches". Attendance at the sabbat or (as it is called here) the "synagogue" of "Waldensians" or witches is what mattered; *maleficia* are barely hinted at. The same applies to the most celebrated of fifteenth-century witchcraft-trials, the Vauderie of Arras. That affair also shows most vividly how a trial of a single individual, when conducted under the inquisitorial procedure by authorities who were convinced of the reality of the nocturnal flight and the sabbat, could launch a mass trial.[8] In 1459 a hermit at Langres, before being burned as a witch, was forced by torture to name all whom he had seen at the sabbat. They included a young prostitute of Douai and an elderly painter and poet of Arras, hitherto noted for his poems in honour of the Virgin Mary. The matter was at once taken up by the inquisitor of Arras; but the leading part was soon taken over by two other Dominicans—Jean, titular bishop of Beirut, who was acting as suffragan for the absent bishop of Arras, and Jacques du Boys, who was both a doctor of laws and dean of the general chapter of the Dominican Order. Both the accused named further participants at the sabbat, who in turn were arrested and tortured until they implicated many more. At the insistence of du Boys and of the bishop of Beirut, burnings began. These two insisted that anyone opposing the burnings must himself be a witch, and that anyone who dared to assist the prisoners should be burned also. In their view, Christendom was full of witches—many bishops and cardinals and, indeed, a full third of nominal Christians were secret witches. Before the burnings the inquisitor preached a sermon and read a description of the sabbat. Asked if the description was true, all the prisoners assented; but when the inquisitor went on to abandon them to the secular arm for burning, they shrieked out that they had been cruelly deceived. They had been promised that, if they would confess, a short pilgrimage would be their only penance; they would be burned only if they persisted in denial. As the flames rose around them they continued to cry that they had never been to the *Vauderie*, that the confessions had been extracted by torture and by false promises.

Arrests continued, and they began to involve some of the richest citizens of Arras. Terror reigned in the city, for nobody could be sure that his turn might not come next. The economy of Arras was also adversely affected; a great manufacturing city, it suffered as its merchants lost their credit. In the end the evidence of the trials was laid before the duke of Burgundy at Brussels, who in turn took counsel of a great assembly of clerks, including the doctors of Louvain. The reality of the sabbat was debated, but no conclusion was reached. The duke thereupon took a severely practical decision: he sent his herald to be present at all examinations. The arrests stopped at once, although the lists of accused were by no means exhausted. Four trials were still pending, and the inconsistency of the sentences reflects the confusion which by this time was prevailing in the minds of the judges; for one trial resulted in a burning, another in what was in effect a life sentence, and two simply in fines—enormous fines, admittedly, paid partly to the Inquisition and partly to the various secular officials. In vain the bishop of Beirut and Jacques du Boys urged the inquisitors to continue the persecution—the inquisitors refused. Moreover they showed by their behaviour that they themselves no longer believed in the sabbat-stories. One woman, after repeated torture, had confessed to attending the sabbat and had duly been sentenced to be burned along with the whole of the first batch; but her heretic's mitre had not been ready, her execution had been postponed, and now, with the change of policy, she was merely banished from the diocese and ordered to make a short pilgrimage.

This was not the end of the matter. One of those arrested was the Chevalier Payen de Beaufort, an old man and head of one of the richest families in the province of Artois. He at once appealed to the *parlement* of Paris; and though his appeal was disregarded and suppressed, he had sons who were able to pursue the matter. By this time the persecution was in any case practically at an end; and it proved possible to remove de Beaufort and other prisoners from Arras to the Conciergerie in Paris. It was the beginning of a legal investigation in which, for the first time, both sides could be given a hearing. The prime mover in the whole affair, Jacques du Boys, promptly went mad, and died within the year. As for the investigation itself, it was pursued with all the procrastination for which the *parlement* was celebrated, and lasted some thirty years. In 1491, when almost all those concerned were dead, a decree was read with great pomp at the very spot in Arras where the sentences had been pronounced. The accused and condemned were formally rehabilitated, while those of their persecutors who were still alive were fined; part of the sum to be spent on founding a mass for the souls of the victims, and erecting a cross on the spot where they had been burned. Anyone who believes in the reality of the sabbat—whether persuaded by Montague Summers or by Margaret Murray—would do well to consider the verdict passed by the *parlement* of Paris and publicly proclaimed, and acclaimed, at Arras.

– 2 –

In these fifteenth-century trials the role of the demonic associate undergoes a radical change. In the trials of the preceding century the demon had been more or less subservient to the human being who conjured him up. Boniface, Guichard, even Kyteler were all imagined as commanding the services of their demons, even if they had to offer sacrifices to induce them to appear at all. This is no longer the case with Vallin or Adeline. Vallin has given himself body and soul to his demon; he has served him obediently for 63 years; he calls him master; he kneels before him, kissing his left hand as a sign of homage; he pays him an annual fee in cash; he has even given him his own baby daughter to kill. Adeline does homage to his goat-demon by kissing him under the tail, and he signs a written compact with Satan. In the trials in the French Alps we meet with other new features, which were to become quite normal in the great witch-hunt of the sixteenth and seventeenth centuries: men and women confess both to having sexual intercourse with demons at the sabbat, and to having intercourse in private with their special demons. And here too the demons are beginning to emerge as dominant partners; sometimes the witch, male or female, is even marked with the Devil's mark.

In short, a drastic inversion of roles has begun: the demon is changing from servant into master. This is how he figures in the witch-trials of the sixteenth and seventeenth centuries—and when the witch is a woman, he figures as her sexual master as well. Primarily this change reflected an ever-growing obsession with Satan and the demonic hosts, an ever-growing sense of their deadly fascination and overwhelming power. But it is also true that the notion of demon as master was already enshrined in certain specific, well-established traditions; and that will certainly have facilitated the change.

For instance, the idea that a human being could enter into an agreement with Satan or a subordinate demon was far from new. It figures already in a story concerning that leader of the Greek Church in the fourth century, Basil the Great, bishop of Caesarea. A slave asks a sorcerer for help in securing the love of a senator's daughter. The sorcerer arranges for the Devil to appear at night at the tomb of a pagan, where the slave renounces his baptism, denies Christ and pledges himself to the Devil in writing. The Devil carries out his part of the bargain—but then Basil intervenes. Thanks to his prayers the written pledge is miraculously taken from the Devil and delivered to him. He tears it up in front of the assembled people, and so frees the slave from the Devil's clutches.[9]

This story became widely known, also in Europe; but another, similar tale from Asia Minor had even greater resonance. It was first told by a patriarch of the Greek Church, Eutychius, who claimed to have been an eye-witness of these strange events. In the sixth century, in the reign of the Byzantine emperor Justinian the Great, there lived in Cilicia a man called Theophilus. He was the steward of the church of Ada, and was generally thought worthy of a bishopric; but thanks to slander put about by his enemies, he was dismissed from office. In despair he turned for help to a Jewish sorcerer, who arranged for him to meet the Devil in person. Theophilus signed a document renouncing Christ and the saints and pledging himself to the Devil, who thereupon secured his reappointment. But then came years of bitter remorse and harsh penance; until the Virgin was moved to intercede with God, and the dangerous document was miraculously wrested from the Devil.[10] Translated out of Greek into Latin in the eighth century, rendered into

Latin verse in the tenth century, the story of Theophilus provided the
plot for many plays, in many languages, during the later Middle Ages.
From the thirteenth century onwards it was one of the most familiar
and best loved tales.[11]

There are other indications that in the later Middle Ages people
became increasingly fascinated by such fantasies. Around 1180 the
Englishman Walter Map tells how a certain Eudo was persuaded to
accept the Devil as his master, in return for riches.[12] And naturally
Caesarius of Heisterbach, around 1220, is able to offer his novice an
instructive case. He knows of two magicians who deceived the populace
of Besançon with their miracles—until the day when a cleric conjured
up the Devil and discovered the source of their power. They had signed
a pact with the Devil, and each carried a copy under his armpit,
beneath the skin. The bishop promptly had the precious documents cut
out, after which the magicians could without difficulty be burned
alive.[13] These were mere fictions, but they were not necessarily
regarded as such; and it is not surprising that when witch-hunting
began in earnest, the notion of the diabolic pact should have found a
practical application.

The notion that demons could mate with human beings was not new,
either. Though the Bible supplied only one solitary example of such
miscegenation, and that a dubious one,[14] the literature and mythology
of Rome seemed to supply plenty. Augustine regarded it as sheer
impudence to deny that fauns have intercourse with women, considering the many testimonies to that effect.[15] The implication was clear;
for as the seventh-century encyclopaedist Isidore of Seville pointed out,
the hairy creatures which pursued women, and which were known to
the Romans as fauns and to the Gauls as Dusii, were really demons.[16]
But after all, many of the gods of Greece and Rome were notorious
pursuers of women; and as we have seen, all Christian theologians,
whether in the early or the medieval Church, were agreed that these
gods were demons too.

Some medieval legends carry the idea much further, and tell how
offspring could be born of the union of a demon with a woman. Ever
since the first century Christians had been familiar with the idea that,
in the days immediately preceding the Second Coming, a supernatural
magician and monarch called Antichrist would rule the world from
Jerusalem. In the tenth century a French monk, collating current
notions about Antichrist, noted that his mother was expected to be a
Jewish prostitute who, at the moment of conceiving, would receive
Satan into her womb in the form of a spirit.[17] Indeed, it was the mis-

carrying of a similar plan that resulted in the birth of Merlin, the Welsh enchanter in Arthurian romance. Exasperated by the Incarnation, Satan chose a special family, exterminated all its members save one daughter, and then sent a demon to beget Antichrist with her. Fortunately the woman's confessor had the presence of mind to baptize the child at birth, with the result that he became not the malignant magician Antichrist but the benign magician Merlin. It was also commonly believed that certain whole peoples, such as the Huns, were born of demons mating with women.

All this belongs to the world of legend; but the copulating male demon, or incubus as he was called, gradually began to invade the lives of real women. There is a hint of this as early as the ninth century, in the writings of Hincmar, archbishop of Rheims (the same who concerned himself with *maleficium* as a cause of impotence).[18] Hincmar tells how a demon sometimes deceives a woman by taking on the appearance of the man she loves; he also knows of a nun who was grievously tormented by an incubus, until a priest exorcized it.[19] But it is only from the twelfth century onwards that incubi figure at all prominently in the chronicles. Writing around 1120, Guibert de Nogent tells how at a time when his father had been made impotent by *maleficium*, his mother was visited one night by an incubus; fortunately a "good spirit" arrived just in time to avert the worst.[20] Guibert adds that he knows many tales of incubi, but forbears to tell them lest he alarm his readers.

Around 1150 St Bernard had to deal with a more serious case.[21] Arriving at Nantes, he found a woman who was much vexed by an incubus. The demon would come to her at night and take its pleasure of her, always without waking her husband. For six years she concealed her shame, but in the end fear of God's judgement drove her to confess to a priest. Unfortunately none of the penances or remedies prescribed —neither prayer nor pilgrimages—proved effective; the demon returned every night and was becoming more and more lascivious. So when Bernard appeared the woman threw herself at his feet and implored his aid. The man of God spoke gently to her, promised her the help of heaven and told her to return next day. That night the incubus visited her again, adding blasphemies and threats to his usual misconduct. But Bernard devised a remedy: he gave her his staff to take to bed with her. This kept the demon at bay, but he stood outside the room, uttering fearsome threats and promising to resume his debauchery as soon as Bernard had gone. This called for more vigorous counter-measures. The following Sunday Bernard summoned the whole population to church. While the congregation held lighted candles, the saint mounted the pulpit and told the whole lamentable story; after which he solemnly anathematized the demon and forbade it, in Christ's name, ever to molest any woman in future. That worked; as the candles were extinguished, the demon's power was destroyed. The woman made confession and received the Eucharist; after which she never saw her incubus again.

A century later, Caesarius of Heisterbach has several tales about incubi. There was, for instance, the sad case of the priest Arnold, lately of Bonn.[22] Though a priest, Arnold had a daughter so beautiful that she was constantly importuned by men, and especially by the canons of the cathedral. One day a demon came to her in the form of a man, and by sweet talk seduced her. They made love often and with great satisfaction; but in the end the girl repented and confessed to her father, who promptly sent her away across the Rhine. Thereupon the demon appeared to Arnold, shouting, "You wretched priest, why have you taken my wife from me? You have done it to your hurt." And he dealt him such a blow on the chest that the unfortunate man vomited blood, and died within three days. Caesarius tells also of a woman at Breisach on the Rhine who, feeling death approaching, confessed to a priest that she had been making love with a demon. It had given her such pleasure that she had resisted confessing for seven years; and now her soul passed from her before she could finish her confession and receive absolution.[23]

It is clear that these are all regarded as serious cases. When a woman yields to an incubus, she imperils her eternal salvation. Compared with this, the transgression of a man with a succubus, i.e. a demon in female form, is slight indeed. Here too Caesarius has an instructive example to offer. John, a theologian of Prüm in the Rhineland, tried to persuade a woman to come to him one night. She did not in fact come, but a demon came in her place, in her likeness and with her voice. In the morning his visitor informed the cleric that he had been in bed not with a woman but with a demon. But John merely uttered a strange word (which Caesarius, out of modesty, cannot repeat) and laughed at the demon, quite unperturbed by his strange adventure.[24] People never did regard succubi with the same horrified fascination that they brought to incubi.

If one compares the various stories about incubi which were current in the Middle Ages, a coherent pattern emerges. In each case the raw material of the story is provided by the woman herself; it is she who, of her own initiative, reveals that she has been having intercourse with an incubus. In some cases it seems that the lover who is imagined as an incubus is really a man—and it may well be that simple women were sometimes fooled in this way. In other cases the lover is clearly imaginary, a product of erotic dreams or reveries, or maybe of hallucinations. But the reason why such commonplace phenomena as erotic imaginings or extra-marital affairs were interpreted in such a sinister sense lies, of course, in the existence of a corpus of demonological lore. Without demons, no incubi.

It was a two-way process. If in the first place priests taught women to look out for incubi, by the thirteenth century theologians were reflecting on the experiences that women were reporting. Guillaume d'Auvergne, bishop of Paris, treats of the matter at some length, and in exactly the same spirit as he brings to the tales of Lady Abundia and the "ladies of the night." [25] He is quite clear that demons cannot really have intercourse with women, because they have no true bodies and therefore no genitals; so it must be that women simply dream or imagine these things. On the other hand the bishop insists that, even if such dreams and imaginings sometimes have natural causes, they are usually the work of demons. Guillaume was more sceptical than most. Thomas Aquinas, for instance, was convinced not only that demons can mate but that they can procreate, and by a most ingenious method: as a succubus a demon receives seed which, transforming itself into an incubus, it then transmits to a woman. [26]

Neither the tales about pacts with the Devil nor the fantasies about incubi were originally connected with witchcraft—but when the new stereotype of the witch began to take shape, when the witch began to be imagined less as the master than as the instrument of the demonic powers, they were there to help the process along. Ancient legends, nocturnal experiences of neurotic or sexually frustrated women—all alike were transformed into further proofs that there existed a sect in which human beings operated under the direct promptings of demons, to whom they were helplessly enslaved.

To the creation of this imaginary sect, written works contributed little. Very few of the relevant writings antedate the Arras Vauderie, let alone the earliest trials in the Dauphiné and in Switzerland. The most celebrated, Nider's *Formicarius* (1435–87), adds practically nothing to the age-old notion which simply equated witchcraft with *maleficium*; and, as we have seen, it explicitly denies the reality of the nocturnal flight. [27] The French poem by Martin Le Franc, *Le champion des dames* (1440), shows that the notions of the sabbat and the nocturnal flight were familiar at that date, but not that the author himself took them seriously.[28] The *Errores Gazariorum* (*c.* 1450)—"Gazarii" by that time meaning Waldensians—would appear to be the work of an inquisitor living in Savoy or by the Lake of Geneva.[29] It is based on the evidence already extracted during the trials, and treats that evidence as reliable; but—even apart from the fact that they exist only in a single manuscript—these few pages cannot possibly have fostered the trials themselves. We are left with the *Flagellum haereticorum fascinariorum* (*The scourge of the heretic-witches*) by Nicolaus Jacquier.[30] The author was inquisitor for northern France in the 1450s and was familiar with the proceedings against Guillaume Adeline; and his aim was, quite specifically, to demonstrate the reality of the nocturnal flight, as against the authority of the *Canon Episcopi*, which had represented the orthodox view ever since the tenth century. This is indeed a polemical and propagandist work; but it was written only one year before the Arras Vauderie—by which time innumerable smaller trials had already been held.

It is true that in the sixteenth and seventeenth centuries a vast, international body of literature would be produced, arguing for and against the reality of the sabbat, the nocturnal flight, the association of human beings and demons. But that is another matter. The origin of the new stereotype of the witch lay elsewhere—not in literature but in the evidence extracted during the trials themselves. The grain of truth in the evidence lay in the fact that some people really believed themselves to fly at night, and that some women believed themselves to copulate at night with incubi. The rest came from the imagination of certain inquisitors, bishops and magistrates, who used and abused the inquisitorial procedure to obtain all the confirmation they needed.

The trials we have considered cannot be explained in terms of the tensions of village life, nor do they centre on accusations of *maleficium*. Adeline was no peasant but an eminent ecclesiastic, and he was supposed to have attended the sabbat in the hope that the Devil would protect him from a knight who wanted to harm him. In the Arras affair the accused are mostly townsfolk, some of them very rich; and *maleficium* is barely mentioned. In both trials the very act of attending the sabbat, and the apostasy that that implies, provide the centre of the accusation. On the other hand recent scholarship—particularly recent British scholarship—has shown that interpersonal hatreds and resentments amongst the peasantry did indeed, in the sixteenth and seventeenth centuries, express themselves in formal accusations of *maleficium*, which in turn provided the starting-point for many witch-trials.

That aspect of the matter has also to be considered.

-3-

It was no novelty for peasants to suspect certain of their neighbours of harming them by occult means. As we have seen in an earlier chapter, peasant fear of *maleficium* had sometimes expressed itself in violence and killing even when official sanction was altogether lacking. From the fifteenth century onwards, first in one region and then in another, that sanction became available: peasant fears could now find expression in formal accusations. As the authorities became more concerned with new concepts of witchcraft, so they became more willing to lend an ear to popular complaints about *maleficium*. The problem is to disentangle what was in the minds of the peasants from what was in the minds of the authorities; for in most regions where witches were tried at all, they were tried by judges who were convinced in advance that any witch must belong to a Satanic conspiracy against Christendom.

Fortunately the impasse is not total. The Swiss Confederation in the fifteenth and sixteenth centuries, and England in the sixteenth and seventeenth centuries, possessed legal systems which permitted the common people to bring charges of *maleficium* before the courts. Many of the depositions have been preserved in their original form, uncontaminated by any demonological interpretations which may have preoccupied the judges. There exists, for instance, a collection of depositions made in the Canton of Lucerne between the mid-fifteenth and the mid-sixteenth century, consisting of accusations brought by some 130 villagers against thirty-two witches;[31] not one of these depositions so much as mentions the Devil, but every deposition without exception mentions *maleficia*. These documents do indeed convey something of the atmosphere in which, at village level, such suspicions and accusations flourished.

It is worthwhile to examine a typical deposition in detail. In the year 1502 men from the villages of Schötz, Ettisweil and Albersweil complained to the village mayor of the Willisau district concerning the *maleficia* of Dichtlin (i.e. Benedicta), wife of Hans in der Gasse, and her daughter Anna.[32] It is clear that the women had already been arrested once on charges of sorcery, and had been released. Now their neighbours were returning to the offensive; and this, translated from the Swiss-German dialect of the early sixteenth century, is what they had to say:

> First, Cunrat Kurman says that six or eight years ago he had a chill, and Anna came and brought him some stewed apple; it was well spiced with good things, so he liked it very much and ate

heartily, for it was very good, as it seemed to him. And when she brought it she told his wife that nobody but he was to eat of it, neither his wife nor the child; and she would be back. And when he had eaten the stewed apple he fell on the floor and was unconscious for two hours. Then they laid him on a bed, where he lay for another two hours, knowing nothing, bereft of reason, quite deaf and senseless, and was no longer like a Christian person. He is sure that this came from what he had eaten.

Jost Meyger says that ten or twelve years ago his late mother was working as a midwife, and so was Dichtlin. Women called his mother in more than they did Dichtlin; and in time his mother went down with a long illness, and when she came to die, she swore, as she hoped to be saved, that it was Dichtlin's doing. And Jost also swears upon his life that his mother had her illness from Dichtlin.

Item: Kuni Hinter der Kilchen says that eight or nine years ago he had four young pigs. They went into Dichtlin's garden, and his wife chased them out again. Dichtlin said: "What are you doing?" His wife answered: "I've chased the pigs out of your garden, so they shan't spoil your vines, I did it for the best." And Dichtlin said: "The Devil reward you! You've done it so that you can keep to the nest for 13 days". Soon afterwards she was brought to childbed; then she remembered those words and decided that was the nest. But when she got up from childbed she was lame, and she still is lame. And Kuni and his wife swear on their lives that the lameness came from Dichtlin.

A little while ago Kuni went out to mow. He came to the River Luthern and found Anna standing and looking into a pool in the stream. He said: "What are you doing?" She replied: "I'm fishing". Later he saw her standing in the pool in the Luthern, splashing the water between her legs with both hands. And before he got home, there was a heavy downpour.

Item: Jost Brun says that Anna came and caught crayfish in the stream, and she was in a black mood. They met at the white bridge, and a storm came up; and as they were looking at the storm, Anna said the storm might do harm in some places, but not here. She said also: "The storm came up behind Freibach and is going towards Hutweil." That gave him nasty doubts about her.

Ulli Meyer says, she had an ox, it was sprightly and ran up and down in the lane in front of the women's house. Next day it was dead. That they had killed it he did not say, nor did he know it.

Schinnouwer says he went down to cut a joist and found Anna fishing in the Luthern and as he was coming home, a big storm blew up. But he did not say she had made it, for he did not know that.

Ulli of Aesch says, the women went fishing four times, and each time, just as they were coming home, a great storm came up. Also, a beggar told him he had seen the two women sitting in the stream; and as he passed by they called him back, saying: "Be a good fellow, give us our shifts" (they were hanging on a bush). He did so, and saw clearly that they were holding something or other between their legs; though he did not know what it was. That same night there was a great hailstorm.

Next Ulli Hüsly told how once his wife had called a midwife in, and not Dichtlin, and God gave her a child. Then Dichtlin threatened his wife, wagging her finger and saying "What will you bet, you will be the worse off?" And a storm came and a thunderbolt fell on his house and burned up everything he possessed. And he says he will swear on his life that this came from Dichtlin.

Ulli Ruttiman says: When the two women were recently released* they went home. Herr Peter Wechter and he also went there. And they all met, and the women said many things in anger. Among other things Anna said, "We won't forget the way the rogues treated us, and we won't forget how the piper tied us up on the cart." And they made many threats and said: "We'll go away." And the daughter said: "If anything happens after this, it will happen to me just as much as to my mother, I'll be blamed for everything."

Jörg Tanner says that when he was Hentz Cläwi's servant Dichtlin's husband, Hans in der Gassen, walked up with him from Altishofen. Hans in der Gassen said to Jörg: "You and your master have put a fir-tree in the cavity. It could easily happen that that will bring him more harm than profit." Two or three days later Hentz Cläwi, a healthy, sprightly fellow, fell ill and soon he was dead. But Jörg did not know that Hans in der Gassen did it, or who did it.

And then Ulli Schärer, Ulli Mor and Hans Wellenberg said unanimously that the two women went fishing a fourth time. As they came home it thundered all the way and they hardly escaped the storm.

The picture that emerges from this document is clear enough. A dozen witnesses voice accusations or suspicions against a family—in effect against a mother and her daughter, though with some suggestion that the father too may be implicated. All the accusations and suspicions are concerned with *maleficia*—eight of them with making storms by

* i.e. from imprisonment.

means of homeopathic or imitative magic (splashing the water in the river), two with causing the death of a human being, two with causing mysterious illness (a spell of unconsciousness, a permanent crippling) one with causing the death of an ox, one with destroying property by thunderbolt. The elder woman is a midwife; and where a motivation for the *maleficia* is mentioned, it is her jealousy of rivals in her profession.

The picture can be completed from other depositions in the Canton of Lucerne. In 1454, in the town of Lucerne itself, Dorothea, the wife of Burgi Hindremstein, was accused by several witnesses.[33] When her child was knocked over by another child, Dorothea brought illness upon the latter. When her daughter became involved in a quarrel with another woman, Dorothea cursed the woman so that she was covered in sores. When a creditor of her husband's demanded payment of an overdue debt, Dorothea killed his cow by sorcery. When Dorothea herself quarrelled with a woman, she made her enemy's cow give blood instead of milk, until she was mollified with a gift of flour. The case was aggravated by the fact that Dorothea's mother had been burned as a witch and that she herself had had to flee from the Canton of Uri. Weighing the evidence, the council of Lucerne decided that such a woman was better dead than alive, and accordingly sentenced her to be burned.

Very similar is the case of the woman known as "the Oberhauserin", accused by a number of her neighbours in Kriens in 1500.[34] When a neighbour stole this woman's cherries, she bewitched his milk; and when by means of counter-magic he made her ill, she did the same to him. In the end he had to win her favour, whereupon she cured him. On another occasion the Oberhauserin enticed a maid away from her employers; in the resulting quarrel, she used sorcery to bring further misfortunes upon the household—sickness in the cattle. A man who had a small difference with her was thrown by his horse, fell sick and finally died—protesting that he was being killed by sorcery. Two brothers refused her the loan of a hoe: they were deluged with hail. Rightly or wrongly, people accused the Oberhauserin of boasting of her powers; at least she seems to have reacted to the accusations by threatening those who made them. And here, too, as in the case of Dichtlin, not only the woman but her daughter and her husband were regarded with fear; she was expected to perform *maleficia* on their behalf as well as on her own. When, after talking with her husband, a man lost two head of cattle, he at once assumed that he must, unwittingly, have caused offence by his remarks.

Harmful storms, sickness in man and beast—these were the commonest accusations; but it was not unknown for a villager suffering from impotence to attribute it to *maleficium*. In 1531 one Sebastian, of the village of Rüti in the Willisau, felt himself persecuted by a woman called Stürmlin, because he had married the girl whom Stürmlin had chosen for her own son.[35] His account of the woman, her actions and her power, is full of real dread. He was impotent with his wife, and had no doubt that this was Stürmlin's doing. He told how Stürmlin would often come, unannounced, into his room, and depart without saying a word, leaving him and his wife terrified. Once in church Stürmlin shot him such a glance that his hair stood on end; and later that day, when he set out to visit her, he developed such a pain in the neck that he could hardly speak. When he took a bath with his wife, in the hope that this might cure their trouble, Stürmlin appeared and said that the bath might prove too strong for one or other of them; whereupon his wife was seized with violent cramps. Sometimes the man would forbid Stürmlin the house, and then the results were disastrous; all the cattle died, while the horses over-ate till they were unfit for work. Yet at other times the couple would ask the woman to help them. Stürmlin seems in fact to have been a "wise woman", specializing in magical cures, and by no means an irreconcilable enemy of the young people. When Sebastian reproached her with his misfortunes, she merely asked him not to slander her, as it might make it harder for her to help him with her prayers. She gave the couple all kinds of magical devices— a notched stick to help with prayer, a special candle to light on Maundy Thursday. Nevertheless it is clear that Sebastian and his wife worked themselves into such a state of hysteria that the mere thought of Stürmlin was enough to produce all kinds of disorders.

Such are the accusations voiced by peasants in the Canton of Lucerne. Alongside them one may set an English case, of purely popular inspiration, in which the authorities did nothing at all beyond recording the accusations.[36] In 1601–2 a justice of the peace in Devonshire, Sir Thomas Ridgeway (later Earl of Londonderry), took evidence from twelve witnesses concerning *maleficia* which were supposed to have been perpetrated in the village of Hardness, near Dartmouth. The accused were a fisherman, Michael Trevisard, his wife Alice and his son Peter; and the accusers were ordinary villagers, who appealed to the magistrates for protection. Ridgeway had the deposition written down, no doubt for use at the assizes; though it is not known whether the accused persons were ever brought to trial. The "examination" (i.e.

deposition) of one of the witnesses, Alice Butler, of Hardness, is typical: [37]

1. This examinate* saith that she, sitting at a door or bench in Hardness aforesaid about Christide last was twelvemonth with one Michael Trevysard of Hardness aforesaid, used these words: "I would my child were able to run as well as any of these children that run here in the street!" Then said Trevysard, "It shall never run!" "No? That's hard!" says this examinate again. "No, it shall never run," answered Trevysard, "till thou hast another," repeating the same words a dozen several times at the least with great vehemency. Whereupon this examinate, being much troubled in mind, especially upon a fear conceived by her before through the general bad report that went of him, departed from him. And the very same week the same child sickened, and consumed away, being well one day and ill another, for the space of seventeen weeks or thereabout, and then died.

2. This examinate further saith, that Peter Trevysard, son of the said Michael Trevisard, came to this examinate's house to borrow a hatchet, which Alice Beere, servant to this examinate, denied, to whom the said Michael answered, "Shall I not have it? I will do thee a good turn ere twelvemonth be at an end." And shortly the said Alice Beere sickened, continuing one day well and another day ill, for the space of eleven weeks, and then died. In which case both the husband of this examinate and a child of theirs fell sick, and so continued seventeen or eighteen weeks, and then died.

Equally relevant is the charge brought by Joan Baddaford against Alice Trevisard. In the course of some petty squabble Alice had told Joan's husband, John Baddaford, to "go to Pursever Wood and gather up his wits"—doubtless a way of calling him dim-witted. Unfortunately, said Joan, "within three weeks after the said John Baddaford made a voyage to Rochelle, in the Hope of Dittsham, and returned home again out of his wits, and so continued by the space of two years, tearing and renting his clothes, in such sort as four or five men were hardly able to bind him and keep him in order". [38] Moreover, Joan complained, Alice Trevisard had threatened that within seven years she should lose all her property; and this too had come to pass. And these events were only the culmination of a long history of disputes. Already three years earlier Joan had demanded a penny from Alice Trevisard for washing some clothes; Alice paid, but with the comment that the

* i.e. informant.

penny should do Joan "little good". And sure enough, when Joan spent the penny on drink "she had no power to drink thereof, but the same night fell sick, and continued so by the space of seven weeks following". The explanation must have seemed obvious: it has always been regarded as dangerous to receive anything, whether as a gift or as payment, from a witch.

So it came about that Joan Baddaford went, with several of her neighbours, to Sir Thomas Ridgeway's home to lay a complaint against Alice Trevisard. On the way back they happened to meet Alice herself and began to rail at her. Probably they threatened her with burning, for although witches were not in fact burned in England, the common people were not always aware of this. At any rate, Alice said to Joan, "Thou and thine may be burned before long be!" A few days later her child, sitting on the hearth, was burned on the neck (or so it seemed to her) even though the fire was not kindled; and within three weeks it wasted away and died.

Another complainant was William Tompson, a sailor, who had had a nocturnal dispute with Alice in the streets of Dartmouth. In the end he struck her with a musket-rod; whereupon she uttered the threat, "Thou shalt be better thou hadst never met with me!" William Tompson had scarcely returned to sea when his ship caught fire and foundered; he himself was picked up by a Portuguese vessel and carried to Spain, where he was imprisoned for a year. When at last he returned to Dartmouth Alice Trevisard, meeting his wife, expressed her vexation and added, "He shall be there again within this twelve months." And so it came to pass. William was captured by the Spaniards and kept in prison, this time for twenty-five months.

Christian Webbar, a widow, let a tenement in Hardness to Michael Trevisard, who failed to pay the rent. When Christian demanded the arrears, Alice Trevisard cursed her, "It shall be worse for you." Alice threw water on Christian's stairs; but a neighbour saw her and warned Christian to avoid those stairs. Alice herself carelessly used the stairs and at once fell under the influence of her own sorcery: "within one hour after, the said Alice . . . fell grievously sick, and part of the hands, fingers, and toes of the said Alice rotted and consumed away, as yet appears by her"; while Christian too fell sick.

There were many others at Hardness who had grievances against the Trevisards. George Davye had a quarrel with Michael Trevisard; within a week his child leapt from his mother's arms into the fire and was badly burned. When Trevisard heard of this he boasted that he could heal the child if he wished, but he would never do anything to

help John Davye or his family. And the following week Davye himself, who was away at sea, was badly hurt in an accident. Henry
Oldreve was another who suffered after a dispute with Trevisard: he
lost twenty fat wethers in one week and then himself fell sick and died.
William Cozen also quarrelled with Trevisard, and within a quarter of
a year his daughter-in-law was crippled: "her neck shrunk down
between her two shoulders, and her chin touched her breast, and so
remaineth still in a very strange manner".

As for Susan Tooker (or Turke), she had complaints to bring
against all three Trevisards, father, mother and son. Some years before
Alice Trevisard had threatened: "I will not leave thee worth a gray
groat!"; and sure enough, Susan's husband, on his very next voyage,
lost ship and goods, and in a calm sea. Young Peter, being refused a
drink by Susan, replied "that it had been better to have delivered him
drink". Next day Susan sickened, and she remained sick for seven
weeks. And Susan had a tale to tell of Michael Trevisard as well. When
Mr Martin, as mayor of Hardness, set up a fold or pound, Michael
Trevisard mocked him, saying that wind and weather would tear it up.
Mr Martin had done his best to counter the threat, moving the pound
to places quite sheltered from the weather; "yet sithence it hath been
plucked up very strangely, for it riseth up altogether, being timber of
an exceeding great weight and bigness". There was also the case of
Joan Laishe, who had once refused Alice Trevisard a half-pennyworth
of ale. "That shall be a hard half-pennyworth," cried Alice, "I shall not
leave you worth a groat!" Two days later one of Joan's ale-casks fell to
the ground and burst and all the ale was lost.

Like the Lucerne material, this story of the Trevisard family of
Hardness, Devon, shows just how suspicions and accusations of
maleficium arose amongst the common people when they were left to
themselves, without interference from the secular or ecclesiastical
authorities or from professional witch-hunters. And the picture that
emerges is confirmed by the researches of Dr Alan Macfarlane on some
hundreds of witchcraft prosecutions in Essex at the same period.[39]
Macfarlane found that the accusations arose not necessarily as a result
of a direct quarrel between two persons, but when a number of village
families fell out with the same person or the same family. For each
"witch" there were, on an average, four people who believed themselves to be the witch's victims. But the number of those involved was
far greater, for it included the families and friends of the "victims".
Often the whole population of a village would get caught up in the
tension and gossip; the formal accusation would then express the

consensus at which the village community had arrived after a lengthy exchange of complaints and rumours.

Accusations were made between people who knew each other intimately. Almost always, the "witch" belonged to the same village as the "victims"; often he or she was a neighbour, someone with whom the "victims" had been closely involved, socially or economically. Indeed Macfarlane argues that an accusation of witchcraft was often in effect (though not of course consciously) a device for severing a close relationship which had become a burden. The refusal to give food or money, or to lend some household implement, would then symbolise the breaking of the bond between two neighbours. The person who made such a refusal would feel uneasy and expect retaliation; and any misfortune which befell him would be interpreted in the light of his expectation. Moreover to be able to bring a charge of witchcraft against the person he had himself treated shabbily would relieve him of his sense of guilt: " . . . it was the victim who had made an open breach in neighbourly conduct, rather than the witch. It was the victim who had reason to feel guilty and anxious at having turned away a neighbour, while the suspect might become hated as the agent causing such a feeling." [40] This is certainly a pattern one soon comes to recognize in studying these cases; but there are other patterns also. In the Lucerne material, the "witch" Dichtlin, who was a midwife, was felt to be jealous of another more successful midwife. In the Devonshire material, Michael Trevisard provoked a crisis by refusing to pay his rent. There are many possible causes for friction between neighbours in a village; and any one of them could give rise to accusations of *maleficia* in certain circumstances.

These circumstances can be defined. On the one hand, a certain kind of misfortune had to occur; on the other hand, there had to be somebody about who could plausibly be regarded as a witch. The misfortune could vary greatly in form. A strange, unfamiliar illness, or an unforeseeable accident, might strike a man, a woman, a child, a house, and ox, a litter of piglets, a brood of chicks. A cow might fail to yield as much milk, bees might fail to produce as much honey, a field might fail to bear as much crops as expected. A storm might bring devastation. But the decisive fact was always that particular individuals felt singled out for affliction. Collective disasters, such as famines and plagues, were another matter: it does not seem that peasants, left to themselves, attributed such things to witches—that happened only when and where the new, demonological conception of the witch had taken over. Even when peasants wondered about a storm, they thought of the harm done to particular fields or particular buildings. At village level, the starting point for *maleficium* accusations was normally the unexpected misfortunes of particular individuals.

But who was selected for the role of witch? The most striking fact is the preponderance of women. Admittedly, male witches did exist. The touring storm-raisers of the early Middle Ages, who so effectively terrorized the peasants, seem to have been mostly men. But in later centuries *maleficium* at village level was almost a female monopoly.

The Lucerne material, for example, lists thirty-one women accused, and only one man—and that one was a foreigner (presumably an Italian) who could make himself understood only through an interpreter; moreover, he claimed that his *maleficia* were really performed by a woman companion. As for the Essex cases examined by Dr Macfarlane, out of 291 witches tried at the assizes between 1560 and 1680, only twenty-three were men, and eleven of these were connected with a woman. With the Trevisards of Devon, the whole family was suspect; yet there too the woman Alice seems to have been the most feared—even where the original quarrel was with one of the men, the resulting *maleficia* were sometimes attributed to Alice.

Until the great European witch-hunt literally bedevilled everything and everybody, the witch was almost by definition a woman. In fact, on the basis of the vast mass of data available, one can be rather more precise. Witches, in the sense of practitioners of *maleficia*, were usually thought of as married women or widows (rather than spinsters) between the ages of fifty and seventy. At that time one was old at fifty—and the older these women were, the greater their power was supposed to be. Some of those executed were over eighty.

Of course, not all elderly married women or widows were accused of performing *maleficia*; and the evidence points to certain types as particularly liable to attract suspicion. For instance, witchcraft—in the sense of the ability and will to work *maleficia*—was widely believed to run in families. In particular, the daughter of a woman who had been executed as a witch often found herself in a dangerous position. We have seen how, in deciding to burn Dorothea, wife of Burgi Hindremstein, the town councillors of Lucerne were influenced by the fact that, years before, her mother had been burned.[41] In fact the daughter had been harried by her mother's fate all her life. She had escaped being burned along with her mother only by fleeing from her native Canton of Uri, and suspicion followed her everywhere. However friendly Dorothea's behaviour, it was construed in the most unfavourable manner possible; she could do nothing right. Once at a carnival feast, she was able to produce a dish of millet for ten persons at short notice—and in due course this hospitable gesture was adduced as proof of her witchcraft!

With other women, it was some personal peculiarity that singled them out for suspicion. Many of those accused of *maleficia* were solitary, eccentric, or bad-tempered; amongst the traits most often mentioned is a sharp tongue, quick to scold and threaten. Often they were frightening to look at—ugly, with red eyes or a squint, or pock-marked skin; or somehow deformed; or else simply bent and bowed with age. Such women were felt to be uncanny—like the strange apparition that was seen in the Canton of Schwyz in 1506. According to a contemporary chronicler, that too was in the form of an old woman, dressed in dirty old clothes and outlandish headgear—but in addition it had great long teeth and cloven feet. Many, we are told, died of terror at the very sight of it; and plague swept through the land.[42] The kind of imagination that could create such a being was also capable of transforming old women, weighed down by their infirmities, into embodiments of malevolent power.

Finally there were the midwives and the practitioners of folk medicine. Infant mortality was very high—and who had better opportunities than midwives for killing babies? No doubt they often did kill them, through ignorance or ineptitude. But that was not the explanation that came to people's minds; and it is striking how often the village midwife figures as the accused in a witchcraft trial.

As for the practitioners of folk medicine, they were obvious suspects.[43] In an age when scientific medicine had hardly begun, and when professionally qualified doctors were in any case seldom available to the peasantry, the countryside produced its own medicine men or medicine women. These people were not necessarily charlatans; many of them used herbal remedies, and also techniques of suggestion, that had real therapeutic value. But some also used the techniques of magic, such as spells; moreover, their art often included divining whether a sickness was due to *maleficium*, and if so, applying counter-magic. Not surprisingly, such "white witches", male and female alike, were apt to be perceived as simply witches. After all, if a person endowed with supernatural powers failed to cure a sickness or prevent a death, might that person not actually have caused the affliction? To disappointed patients and their relatives it must have seemed obvious enough.*

* The Lucerne material includes a case of a "wise woman" who, having failed to cure a man of impotence, was held to have caused it (p. 210 of the Hoffmann-Krayer material cited in the Notes).

Many "witches", under torture, confessed to using herbs, roots, leaves and powders to harm man or beast; and although that proves nothing as to their guilt, it does suggest that they were at home in folk medicine.

Such were the women whom their neighbours most easily came to think of as witches—but how did the women think of themselves? Did they feel themselves to possess some supernatural power for evil? Or were they outraged at the accusation? The answer is that both situations could occur.

The Lucerne material includes, in addition to the depositions of the accusers, some statements by the accused. Thus is 1549 Barbara Knopf of Mur was accused by several neighbours of bewitching and killing cattle, and of crippling and blinding human beings. Arrested and taken to prison, she denied every accusation and added—in the words of the magistrate—that "she had done nothing, only she had a nasty tongue and was an odd person; she had threatened people a bit, but had done nothing wicked. She desired to be confronted with those who said such things about her and she would answer them. . . .[44] That is how a woman arrested on a charge of *maleficium* usually reacted, when no torture was used. These answers have the ring of truth. There is in fact no reason to suppose that most women accused as witches regarded themselves as such.

But some did. As we have seen, *maleficia* really were practised; some women really did try to harm or kill people or animals, or to destroy crops or property, by occult means. These things had been done since time immemorial and they were still being done during the great witch-hunt—indeed, in some remote and backward regions they are still being done today. And it is not difficult to think of one category of women who must always have been particularly tempted by such practices. "Wise women" or "white witches", who felt able to perform cures by supernatural means, must also have felt able to inflict harm by supernatural means; and some of them certainly did attempt the latter as well as the former. In the Lucerne material, the "wise woman" Stürmlin may or may not have intended to inflict impotence on the young man who had jilted her daughter and married another.[45] But less ambiguous cases have also been recorded. In a trial in Fortrose in Black Isle, north of Inverness, in 1699, a woman boasted of her power to harm as well as to heal; thereby accusing herself, it seems, quite voluntarily. The evidence reads as follows:

> Margaret Bezok alias Kyle spouse of David Stewart in Bal-
> maduthy declared she threatened John Sinclair using a phrase that
> she would quicklie overturn his cart and within a week thereafter

his wife fell ill, and that she was brought to see the seek wife and touched and handled her and heard that thereafter she convalesced.

John Sinclair in Miuren declared that she said Margaret did threaten ut supra and that thereafter his wife distracted within less than a week and continued in that distemper till the said Margaret was brought to see her, and that she handled and felt his wife who thereafter grew better but continues something weak still and that it is eight weeks since the first threatening.[46]

This little tale completes nicely our picture of the traditional, age-old world of *maleficium* and *maleficium* beliefs as it existed amongst the peasantry of western Europe.

−4−

There existed, then, two completely different notions of what witches were.

For the peasantry, until its outlook was transformed by new doctrines percolating from above, witches were above all people who harmed their neighbours by occult means; and they were almost always women. When the authors of the *Malleus Maleficarum* produced quasi-theological reasons to explain why witches were generally female, they were simply trying to rationalize something which peasants already took for granted.[47]

Why was it taken for granted? The answer has sometimes been sought in the circumstances of village life in the early modern period. It has been argued that, as the traditional sense of communal responsibility declined, elderly women who were unable to provide for themselves came to be felt as a burden which the village was no longer willing to shoulder;[48] or else that spinsters and widows increased so greatly in number that they came to be felt as an alien element in a society where the patriarchal family still constituted the norm.[49] Such factors may well have provided an additional impetus for witch-hunting in the sixteenth and seventeenth centuries, but they certainly do not fully account for the notion that the witch is, typically, a woman. At least in Europe, the image of the witch as a woman, and especially as an elderly woman, is age-old, indeed archetypal.

For centuries before the great witch-hunt the popular imagination, in many parts of Europe, had been familiar with women who could bring down misfortune by a glance or a curse. It was popular imagination that saw the witch as an old woman who was the enemy of new life, who killed the young, caused impotence in men and sterility in women, blasted the crops. And it was also popular imagination that granted the witch a chthonic quality. The *Malleus* again reflects a popular, not a theological belief when it recommends that a witch who is to be taken into custody should first be lifted clear of the earth, to deprive her of her power.[50]

The other notion of the witch came not from the peasantry but from bishops and inquisitors and—to an ever-increasing degree—from secular magistrates and lawyers. Admittedly, rural magistrates were often themselves of peasant origin; but they were literate, which meant that a view of witchcraft which was enshrined above all in written texts was current amongst them, and in this view a witch was above all a member of a secret, conspiratorial body organized and headed by Satan. Such a witch could just as well be a man as a woman, and just as well young as old; and if, in the end, most of those condemned and executed as witches were still elderly women, that was the result of popular expectations and demands. As we have seen, the earliest witch-trials were quite free from such one-sidedness; and still at the height of the great witch-hunt, in the sixteenth and seventeenth centuries, many men, young women and even children were executed.

The complaint against these people was not primarily or necessarily that they harmed their neighbours by occult means but that they attended the sabbat. Collective worship of the Devil in corporeal, usually animal form; sexual orgies which were not only totally promiscuous but involved mating with demons; communal feasting on the flesh of babies—these constituted the essence of witchcraft as it was imagined and formulated by educated specialists during the fifteenth, sixteenth and seventeenth centuries. Practices which in earlier centuries had been vaguely ascribed to certain heretical groups, notably the Waldensians, now constituted an independent offence, which in time came to be called the *crimen magiae*. Admittedly, *maleficium* was not excluded—at the end of the sabbat the Devil commonly required his followers to report on the harm they had recently brought about, and instructed them on the harm they were expected to do during the coming weeks or months. Nevertheless, in this version of witchcraft, *maleficium* was of secondary importance. Here a witch was not simply a malicious, dangerous person but an embodiment of evil; above all, an embodiment of apostasy.

Left to themselves, peasants would never have created mass witch-hunts—these occurred only where and when the authorities had become convinced of the reality of the sabbat and of nocturnal flights to the sabbat. And this conviction depended on, and in turn was sustained by, the inquisitorial type of procedure, including the use of torture. When suspected witches could be compelled, by torture, to name those whom they had seen at the sabbat, all things became possible: the mayor and town councillors and their wives were just as likely to be accused as were peasant women.

The great witch-hunt itself lies outside the scope of this book, but a few brief comments are called for. It reached its height only in the late sixteenth century, and it was practically over by 1680—with the trials at Salem, Massachusetts, in 1692 as a belated epilogue. It was an exclusively western phenomenon—eastern Europe, the world of Orthodox Christianity, was untouched by it. Within western Europe, no distinction can be drawn between Roman Catholic and Protestant countries—both were equally involved. On the other hand, not all areas of western Europe were equally involved. Spain, Italy, Poland, the Low Countries, Sweden experienced mass witch-hunts, but only in limited areas and for limited periods. England saw little of mass witch-hunts, though some hundreds of women were executed (by hanging, not burning) for doing harm by occult means. In Scotland, France, the German states, the Swiss Confederation, mass witch-hunts were carried out with great intensity and ferocity. Yet even there, the centres of activity constantly shifted: an area which had never burned a single witch would suddenly begin to burn witches by the dozen; another, which had been burning witches for years, would suddenly stop; in some areas little or no witch-hunting took place. Everything depended on the attitude of the authorities—the prince, or the town council, or the magistrates. The authorities in turn could be influenced to take up witch-hunting by the writings of such codifiers as Bodin or Del Rio, or by the example of neighbouring states. They could also be influenced to abandon it by writings of such men as Weyer or Spee, or by some particular paradox arising from the trials—not least the risk that they themselves would be accused of attending the sabbat.

Many attempts have been made to estimate the total number of individuals burned as witches in Europe during the fifteenth, sixteenth and seventeenth centuries, but it is a fruitless enterprise: the records are too defective. Some of the best-known estimates, which put the figure at some hundreds of thousands, are fantastic exaggerations. On the other hand those who would argue, from the statistics for English witch-trials, that there never was a great European witch-hunt at all are also in error. For certain areas of the European mainland reasonably complete records do exist, and some of these have been studied in detail. They show beyond all possible doubt that the great witch-hunt is no myth.

Dr Guido Bader, in a thesis published in 1945, gives statistics for executions in the Swiss cantons between 1400 and 1700.[51] He found that, in the Confederation as a whole, 8,888 persons were tried and 5,417 are known to have been executed—though he adds that the real number of executions was probably far higher. The number of trials and executions varied enormously from canton to canton. In the single canton of Vaud 3,371 persons were tried between 1591 and 1680—and all, without exception, were executed; for the half-century from 1611 to 1660 alone, the figure is 2,500.[52]

Dr H. C. Erik Midelfort has made a detailed study of south-west Germany.[53] He calculates that in a period of a little more than a century, from 1561 to 1670, at least 3,229 persons were executed in that area.[54] The figures for particular places are even more startling. In the little town of Wiesensteig, sixty-three women were burned in a single year, 1562.[55] In the small, secluded territory of Obermarchtal, with a population of some 700 poor peasants, in the three years 1586-8 forty-three women and eleven men were burned, i.e. nearly 7 per cent of the population.[56] Such massive killings occurred only when supposed witches were forced by torture to denounce others whom they had seen at the sabbat. Midelfort gives an example: "When Ursula Bayer denounced eight other persons, we know that four of them were executed with her on 16 June 1586, and two later; only two escaped trial and torture."[57] In June 1631 the small town of Oppenau, in Württemberg, with a population of 650, was drawn into the witch-hunt that had been proceeding in the neighbouring territories for a couple of years. In less than nine months fifty persons had been executed in eight mass burnings, and 170 further denunciations were awaiting consideration by the court—at which point the judges began to have doubts about the correctness of their proceedings.[58] It would be easy, but pointless, to multiply the examples; those given are enough to show how untypical the English case was. The decisive factors are not in doubt: really massive witch-hunts occurred only where the concept of witchcraft included the sabbat and where judicial procedure included torture—and in England, save in rare instances, neither circumstance applied.

The great witch-hunt is only now beginning to be studied on a European scale, but already this much is certain: it was not, in the main, a cynical operation. Financial greed and conscious sadism, though by no means lacking in all cases, did not supply the main driving force: that was supplied by religious zeal. Even torture appeared, to most of those who employed it, not only legitimate but divinely required. The witch was regarded as being not only allied to the Devil but in the grip of a demon, and the purpose of torture was to break that grip. Each trial was a battle between the forces of God and the forces of the Devil —and the battle was fought, *inter alia*, for the witch's own soul: a witch who confessed and perished in the flames had at least a chance of purging his or her guilt and achieving salvation. On the other hand, it was held that God would give an innocent person strength to withstand any amount of torture. And it is true that the few—about one in ten, at the height of the witch-hunt—who could hold out were usually set free. In this sense torture became the successor to, and substitute for, trial by ordeal.[59]

The great witch-hunt can in fact be taken as a supreme example of a massive killing of innocent people by a bureaucracy acting in accordance with beliefs which, unknown or rejected in earlier centuries, had come to be taken for granted, as self-evident truths. It illustrates vividly both the power of the human imagination to build up a stereotype and its reluctance to question the validity of a stereotype once it is generally accepted.

Much work remains to be done before the dynamics of the great witch-hunt can be fully understood. Meanwhile it is at least possible to suggest one fruitful line of enquiry. When operating separately the two different notions about witches inspired two very different kinds of witch-trial; but they could also be combined, and this is what commonly happened at the height of the great witch-hunt. A certain collusion, no doubt unconscious, occurred between the peasantry on the one hand and the authorities—and notably the magistrates—on the other. An old woman is arrested for witchcraft. At once, neighbours come forward to accuse her of harming their children or their cattle— whereupon the magistrates compel her to admit not only to those acts of *maleficium* but also to having entered into a pact with a demon, having copulated with him for years and having formally renounced Christianity. They also compel her to speak of the sabbat and to name those whom she saw there.[60] Behind the accusations from below and the interrogations from above lie divergent preoccupations and aims. Just how they interlocked deserves detailed examination. It might well provide the key to what still remains one of the most mysterious episodes in European history.*

* I was delighted to hear, just as this book was being completed, that Dr Christina Larner, of Glasgow, had been awarded a grant by the Social Science Research Council to organize and carry out, in Scotland, a research project which should throw much light on this central problem.

NOTE ON THE ILLUSTRATIONS

Plate 1 reproduces a miniature in a manuscript, dated about 1460, of a Latin tract or sermon by Johannis Tinctoris, *Contra sectam Valdensium.* Tinctoris was a former professor of theology and rector of Cologne University. In 1460 he was living in retirement, as a canon at Tournai; and the "Waldensians" whom he attacked were the victims of the witch-hunt in 1460 at Arras. The miniature shows how the witches' sabbat was imagined at the time when the fantasy was just taking shape. The witches fly to the sabbat on monstrous beasts, they worship the Devil in the form of a goat, but they clearly belong to the upper strata of society and include as many men as women.

Plate 2 reproduces an illustration in the second edition of Pierre de Lancre's *Tableau de l'inconstance des mauvais anges,* Paris, 1613. De Lancre was a distinguished magistrate of Bordeaux who in 1609, at the behest of King Henry IV, carried out a major witch-hunt in the Basque country. The illustration shows how the sabbat was imagined at the height of the great witch-hunt. Lancre explains the details: Satan in the likeness of a goat, preaching from a golden pulpit; a witch presenting a child she has abducted; witches and demons feasting, chiefly on human flesh, including that of unbaptized children; obscene dances of witches and demons, with musicians providing the accompaniment. He also points out the witches on the extreme right are poor folk and are not admitted to the banquets, while those on the left are lords and ladies and are responsible for the high ceremonies of the sabbat—a further proof that where witch-hunting was at its most intense, it was by no means directed solely against poor old women. The witches in the foreground are preparing *maleficia*, while the flying witches are supposed to be raising storms at sea.

The first two illustrations are both the work of people who believed in the reality of the happenings they portrayed. This was no longer the case with Goya. In an unpublished introduction to the series of Caprichos he described his aim: to conjure up "forms and movements which have

1. "Waldensians" adoring the Devil in the form of a he-goat. From a manuscript of a French translation of a Latin tract or sermon by Johannis Tinctoris, *Contra sectam Valdensium*. Copyright Bibliothèque royale Albert Ier, Brussels (MS 11209, folio 3 recto). Date about 1460.

2. The witches' sabbat as imagined at the height of the great witch-hunt.

From Pierre de Lancre's *Tableau de l'inconstance des mauvais anges*, second edition, Paris, 1613.

3. Goya: Capricho No. 71, with the caption: "Si amanece, nos vamos" ("When day dawns, we have to go").

4. Goya: Painting of witches, often known as El aquelarre (The witches' sabbat), in the Museo de la Fundación Lázaro Galdiano, Madrid.

5. Goya, Painting of witches, often known as El hechizo (The bewitching), in the Museo de la Fundación Lázaro Galdiano, Madrid.

6. Goya: Capricho No. 45, with the caption: "Much hay que chupar" ("There's plenty to nibble at").

7. Goya: Saturn devouring one of his sons, in the Prado, Madrid.

8. Rubens: Saturn devouring one of his sons, in the Prado, Madrid. Reproduced from the Mansell Collection, London.

hitherto existed only in our imagination". The paintings and engravings reproduced in Plates 3, 4, 5 and 6—all of which belong to the period 1795–9—are satirical in intention. As Edith Helman has shown in her book *Trasmundo de Goya* (Madrid, 1963), they were inspired by an eye-witness account of a famous witch-burning held at Logroño in 1610; and they mock the witches' confessions that were read out on that occasion. Goya knew perfectly well that there were no such things as witches' sabbats. Nevertheless, thanks to his extraordinary powers of imagination and intuition, he was able to re-create the phantasmagoria with all the compulsive vividness which it possessed for earlier generations.

Plate 3, which reproduces a Capricho entitled "Si amanece, nos vamos" ("When day dawns, we have to go"), shows a senior witch instructing junior colleagues. It has been suggested that the sack is meant to be imagined as full of dead infants; and the presence of the two children in the background seems to point in the same direction. Certainly Plates 4, 5 and 6 show what a large place the killing and devouring of infants occupied in the traditional notion of witchcraft. The Capricho reproduced in Plate 6 actually bears the caption "Mucho hay que chupar" ("There's plenty to nibble at"). Together with Goya's famous painting of Saturn devouring one of his sons (Plate 7), and the painting by Rubens which probably inspired it (Plate 8), they provide inconographical support for the argument of the Postscript that follows.

POSTSCRIPT:
PSYCHO-HISTORICAL SPECULATIONS

In recent years various attempts have been made, above all in the United States, to adopt a psycho-analytical approach to the material of history; but these attempts have been largely confined to interpreting the behaviour and personalities of dead individuals. There is another possibility. I believe, and have believed for the last thirty years, that in so far as the insights of psycho-analysis can be brought to bear on history at all, collective fantasies or (in the widest sense of the term) social myths constitute the most fruitful field for their application.[1] In this admittedly speculative postscript I propose to apply them, with all due tentativeness, to the collective fantasy with which we are concerned.

For what we have been examining is above all a fantasy at work in history (and incidentally, in the writing of history). It is fantasy, and nothing else, that provides the continuity in this story. Gatherings where babies or small children are ceremonially stabbed or squeezed to death, their blood drunk, their flesh devoured—or else incinerated for consumption later—belong to the world of fantasy. Orgies where one mates with one's neighbour in the dark, without troubling to establish whether that neighbour is male or female, a stranger or, on the contrary, one's own father or mother, son or daughter, belong to the world of fantasy. And so does the Devil or subordinate demon who, in the guise of a monstrous tom-cat or goat-man, presides over and participates in some of these performances. Human collectivities, large and small, certainly are capable of grotesque and monstrous deeds—no century has proved it more abundantly than our own. Nevertheless, there is no good reason to think that these particular things ever happened: we have examined case after case, and have found hardly any where the accusation did not include manifestly impossible features.

The fantasy was not of equal importance, nor did it fulfil the same functions, at all stages in the long and complex story. Against the Christians of Lyons in the second century, and again against the Knights Templars in the fourteenth, it was cynically and consciously exploited to legitimate an exterminatory policy which had already been decided on. When amateur inquisitors of fanatical disposition—men such as Conrad of Marburg, Alberto Cattaneo, John of Capestrano —wove it into the charges against the Waldensians or the Fraticelli, the effect was to intensify the persecution of a group that was already marked out for persecution. The great witch-hunt, on the other hand, never would have occurred at all but for the fantasy of a child-eating, orgiastic, Devil-worshipping sect. Admittedly, at that point other beliefs clustered around the central fantasy—beliefs about *maleficium*, about ritual magic, about witches who flew by night, about pacts, about incubi. But the witch-hunt reached massive dimensions only where the minds of the authorities were obsessed by the central fantasy itself. In the great witch-hunt that fantasy became, as it were, an autonomous force. The law was re-shaped to take account of it: in the form of the witches' sabbat it became the core of a new offence, the *crimen magiae*. And on the charge of committing that imaginary offence, many thousands of human beings were burned alive.

This book has told, in detail, the story of how the fantasy operated over a lengthy period of European history. It has tried to describe the complex process of social interaction by which, with the passage of time, the fantasy became standardized and sanctified, a matter of consensus. But it is also natural to ask just where the fascination of such a fantasy lay. Clearly it represents a total inversion of social norms: the acts attributed to these real or imaginary out-groups were acts which were totally forbidden, which indeed were regarded with horror, as the quintessence of everything that human beings ought not to do. But perhaps we can be rather more specific than that.

The title "Europe's Inner Demons" is intentionally ambiguous. It suggests, of course, that the groups which were demonized did not consist of inhabitants of distant countries but lived—or, in the case of the witches, were imagined as living—in the heart of Europe itself. But it is also meant to convey that for many Europeans these groups came to embody part of their innermost selves—their obsessive fears, and also their unacknowledged, terrifying desires. The nature of these endopsychic demons is indicated by the specific accusations brought against the demonized groups. Certain accusations have recurred again and again in the course of our story. Their meaning may become clearer when they are viewed in a broader context.

The theme of cannibalistic infanticide, for instance, is not confined to these accusations—it is met with also in the myth and folklore of Europe.[2] It was known already in ancient Greece. Thus the Titan Cronus (whom the Romans identified with the god Saturn), being warned that he would be deposed by one of his own children, tried to swallow them all. But his wife Rhea saved the youngest, Zeus, who in due course forced his father to disgorge the other children and finally, after a mighty struggle, overthrew him. One of Zeus's sons, Tantalus, cooked his son Pelops as a meal for the gods—but the gods, displeased, brought Pelops back to life and cast Tantalus into the lower world for punishment. The Germanic folk-tales collected by the Brothers Grimm include a number of variations on the same theme. In the original version of Snow White the wicked queen eats what she believes to be the lungs and liver of the small girl whose death she has ordered— though in reality the lungs and liver are those of a young boar. Snow White, of course, survives, and at her wedding watches the wicked queen dance in red-hot slippers until she is grilled alive. In the story of Hansel and Gretel the two children, sent from home, wander through the forest until they are captured by a repulsive hag who kills and eats children. Hansel is fattened for the purpose, but when the day comes Gretel pushes the hag into her own oven and leaves her to burn to ashes.[3] In a Magyar variant three girls, driven from home, come to the castle of a cannibal giant and giantess. When they are about to be roasted and eaten, the youngest girl pushes the giant into the oven; after which his wife is knocked on the head and the girls take possession of the castle.

Now all these tales are inspired by the same preoccupation. Cronus and Tantalus are fathers intent on destroying their offspring. The wicked queen, the hag, the giant and giantess too are adults who try to destroy children, but in the end are destroyed by them. The common theme is generational conflict, between those who at present hold power and those who are destined to inherit it. And the means by which the adults try to retain power is, precisely, cannibalistic infanticide.

This surely throws a new light on our problem. We have already seen that cannibalistic infanticide belongs both to the traditional stereotype of the heretical sect and to the traditional stereotype of the witch, and that for that very reason it was relatively easy, given the appropriate circumstances, to combine the two notions. We can probe deeper now. It seems plain that both stereotypes draw on one and the same archaic fantasy. Psycho-analysts would maintain that the unconscious roots of this fantasy lie in infancy or early childhood. Psycho-analysts of the Kleinian school would argue, more specifically, that infants in the first two years of life experience cannibalistic impulses which they project on to their parents; and that the source of the fantasy lies there. Other psycho-analysts would advance different interpretations. It has been argued that many parents really do harbour unconscious cannibalistic impulses towards their children, and that the children are subliminally aware of the fact.[4] It has also been argued that children themselves can harbour unconscious cannibalistic impulses towards a younger sibling—the baby brother or sister whom they see as an interloper or potential rival; and that in later life this intolerable, repressed desire, projected, can breed monstrous fantasies.[5] Psycho-analysis, though a most fruitful aid in interpreting the world of fantasy, is anything but an exact science; and such matters are best left to professionals to debate. I shall limit myself to a more general hypothesis, which I regard as eminently plausible. It is, that the theme of cannibalistic infanticide, which has bulked so large in this book, owes part of its appeal to wishes and anxieties experienced in infancy or early childhood, but deeply repressed and, in their original form, wholly unconscious.*

It is, fortunately, a simpler matter to interpret the theme of the erotic orgy. No great psychological sophistication is required to see that the monotonous, rigidly stereotyped tales of totally, indiscriminately promiscuous orgies do not refer to real happenings but reflect repressed desires or, if one prefers, feared temptations. And if, in pre-Freudian times, the inclusion of incest between mother and son, father and daughter, might have seemed to militate against such an interpretation, it will hardly do so now. When a real or imaginary outgroup is accused of holding orgies of this kind, it is certainly the recipient of unconscious projections.

The theme was known already to the pagan populations in the Roman Empire, but in the Christian Europe of the Middle Ages and the early modern period it took on a new meaning. In the "synagogue of Satan" and its successor the "witches' sabbat", the orgy is combined with a sacrilegious parody of divine service, eroticism goes hand in hand with apostasy. What in Antiquity had been imagined as a merely human debauch now came to be imagined as a ritual inversion of

* Witches and medieval heretics are not the only cases where this theme has been woven into the stereotype of an outgroup. In my books *The Pursuit of the Millennium* and *Warrant for Genocide* I have argued that it has often been woven into the stereotype of the Jew. As late as 1913 a Russian Jew, Mendel Beiliss, was tried for killing a Christian boy so that the blood could be used in the unleavened bread which is ritually eaten at Passover. Within the present generation it was widely believed even amongst educated Chinese that European children stole Chinese children and shut them in a room to be devoured by rats—a barely disguised version of the same belief.

Christianity, carried out under the supervision, and with the participation, of Satan or of a subordinate demon.

It is easy to see why the notion of unbridled sexuality could so easily be combined with that of a cult in which Christianity was systematically repudiated and burlesqued. Christianity, whether medieval or post-medieval, Catholic or Protestant, has generally tended to exalt spiritual values at the expense of the animal side of human nature. The imaginary cult of a Devil who materializes as a tom-cat or a goat-man, and in that guise is kissed by or mates with his followers, male or female, would seem to be a clear example of "the return of the repressed"—the repressed in this case being human animality, distorted and made monstrous by the very fact of repression.

What is involved is not anti-clericalism—that was open, avowed and very widespread throughout the later Middle Ages. Nor is it intellectual agnosticism—that first appeared in the seventeenth century, and then only in very restricted circles. It is, rather, *unconscious* resentment against Christianity as too strict a religion, against Christ as too stern a taskmaster. Psychologically it is altogether plausible that such an unconscious hatred would find an outlet in an obsession with the overwhelming power of Christ's great antagonist, Satan, and especially in fantasies of erotic debauches with him. It is not at all surprising that the tension between conscious beliefs and ideals on the one hand, and unconscious desires and resentments on the other, should lead some frustrated or neurotic women to imagine that they had given themselves, body and soul, to the Devil or to a subordinate demon. Nor is it surprising that these same tensions, operating in a whole stratum of society, should end by conjuring up an imaginary outgroup as a symbol of apostasy and of licentiousness—which is practically what witches became in many parts of Europe. In that case the tens of thousands of victims who perished would not be primarily victims of village tensions but victims of an unconscious revolt against a religion which, consciously, was still accepted without question.

It may well be that the entire story told in this book is ultimately understandable only in such terms as these. As far back as the records go, people had always been apt to imagine troublesome or eccentric old women as being linked in a mysterious and dangerous way with the earth and with the forces of nature, and as themselves uncanny, full of destructive power. But from the twelfth century onwards a new element appears—at first amongst monks, then amongst other literate elements in the population: the need to create a scapegoat for an unacknowledged hostility to Christianity. Perhaps the great witch-hunt became possible when the two resentments—the one avowed and widespread, the other unavowed and socially far more restricted—fused in a blind, terror-stricken hatred of a sect or society of witches that in reality did not exist at all.

The hypothesis at least deserves consideration. It might lead on to further insights. It might even prove possible to find out why the notion of erotic orgies around a monstrously erotic Devil became increasingly fascinating in the later Middle Ages, and reached its height only in the early modern period; and why it bulked so much larger in northern and central than in southern Europe.

That task lies outside the scope of this study, which is already vast enough. What began as an enquiry into the origins of the great witch-hunt has led in some unexpected directions and has produced some unexpected results. On the one hand various widely accepted notions have turned out to be baseless, while on the other hand various factors which have generally been overlooked have turned out to be of decisive importance. The story itself, I think, is now tolerably clear. But again and again I have felt that the fears and hatreds which I was studying had origins and meanings which were unknown to those who were moved by them to torture and to kill. The purpose of these "Psycho-historical speculations" is to suggest what those origins and meanings may have been.

BIBLIOGRAPHICAL NOTES

ABBREVIATIONS

Bouquet. *Recueil des Historiens des Gaules et de la France (Rerum Gallicarum et Francicarum scriptores)*, ed. M. Bouquet *et al.*, Paris, 1738–1876.

Hansen, *Quellen*. J. Hansen, *Quellen und Untersuchungen zur Geschichte des Hexenwahns und der Hexenverfolgung im Mittelalter*, Bonn, 1901.

Hansen, *Zauberwahn*. J. Hansen, *Zauberwahn, Inquisition und Hexenprozess im Mittelalter und die Entstehung der grossen Hexenverfolgung*, Munich and Leipzig, 1900.

MGSS. *Monumenta Germaniae historica, Scriptores*, ed. G. H. Pertz *et al.*, Hanover and Berlin, 1826 ff.

MGH, Leges. *Monumenta Germaniae historica, Leges*, Hanover and Leipzig, 1835 ff.

Pat. graec., Pat lat. Patrologiae cursus completus, Series graeca, Series latina, ed. J. P. Migne, Paris, 1857–66.

In the case of well-known works by ancient or medieval writers, particular editions are specified only where this is required for ease of reference.

CHAPTER ONE: PRELUDE IN ANTIQUITY

– I –

1 Minucius Felix, *Octavius*, cap. ix and x; cf. cap. xxvii, xxx, xxxi, where the Christian rebuts these accusations.

2 Tertullian, *Apologeticum*, cap. xvi.

3 *Ibid.*, cap. viii.

4 Pliny the Younger, *Epistola x*, 96–7.

5 Tatian, *Oratio ad Graecos*, xxv, 3.

6 Justin, *Apologia II*, 12.

7 Justin, *Dialogus cum Tryphone Judaeo*, cap. x, 1.

8 Athenagoras, *Legatio pro Christianis*, iii, 34–5.

9 For these accusations against Christians: J. P. Waltzing, "Le crime rituel reproché aux chrétiens du 2ᵉ siècle", in Académie Royale de Belgique, *Bulletin de la Classe des Lettres . . .*, series 5, vol. 10, Brussels, 1924, pp. 205–39; F. J. Dölger, *Antike und Christentum*, vol. 4, Münster i.W., 1924, pp. 187–228: "Sacramentum infanticidii".

10 On this persecution, see Eusebius, *Historia Ecclesiastica*, ed. Kirsopp Lake, lib. V; cap. i, 1. For a penetrating recent account: W. H. C. Frend, *Martyrdom and Persecution in the Early Church*, Oxford, 1965, chapter 1.

11 Eusebius, *Historia Ecclesiastica*, lib. V, cap. i.

12 Frend, *op. cit.*, p. 5; J. Vogt, "Zur Religiosität der Christenverfolger im römischen Reich", in *Sitzungsberichte der Heidelberger Akademie der Wissenschaften, Philosophisch-historische Klasse*, Jahrgang 1962, pp. 7–30.

13 Frend, *op. cit.*, pp. 7, 10.

14 Eusebius, *loc. cit.*, para 52.

15 *Ibid.*, para 26.

–2–

16 On this fantasy: A. Jacoby, "Der angebliche Eselskult der Juden und Christen", in *Archiv für Religionswissenschaft*, vol. 25, Leipzig and Berlin, 1927, pp. 265–82; and E. Bickermann, "Ritualmord und Eselskult", in *Monatschrift für Geschichte und Wissenschaft des Judentums*, Dresden, 71 Jahrgang, 1927, pp. 171–87, 255–64.

17 Apion's stories are preserved in the answer of the Jew Josephus: *Contra Apionem*, cap. ii, 9.

18 Epiphanius, *Panarion*, xxvi, 12.

19 Sallust, *Catilina*, xx.

20 Dio Cassius, *Romaika (History of Rome)*, lib. XXXVII, 30.

21 *Ibid.*, lib. LXXI, 4.

22 Plutarch's *Lives: Poplicola*, iv.

23 Polyaenus, *Strategica*, VI, 7, 2.

24 Josephus, *Contra Apionem*, 91–6.

25 I Corinthians 11 : 23–5.

26 Concil. Trident., Sessio xiii, Canon 2.

27 Tertullian, *De Corona*, cap. iii (*Pat. lat.* vol. 2, col. 80; and cf. *ibid.*, Note (j)).

28 Tertullian, *Liber II ad uxorem*, cap. iv and v (*Pat. lat.*, vol. 1, cols. 1294–7).

29 John 6:53.

30 Justin, *Apologia I*, 26.

31 Irenaeus, *Adversus Haereses*, lib. I, cap. xxv, 3, 4; cf. lib. I, cap. xxcii, 2.

32 Clement of Alexandria, *Stromateis*, lib. III, cap. ii; cf. lib. III, cap. iv.

33 On the *Agape*: H. Lietzmann, *Mass and the Lord's Supper*, trans. D. H. G. Reeve, Lieden, 1954, etc.; B. Reicke, *Diakonie, Festfreude und Zelos in Verbindung mit der altchristlichen Agapenfeier*, Uppsala and Wiesbaden, 1951. (Uppsala Universitets Årsskrit, 1951, No. 5.)

34 Ethiopic translation of the *Church Order* of Hippolytus, summarized in Lietzmann, *op. cit.*, p. 163

35 Livy, *Ab urbe condita*, lib. XXXIX, cap. viii–xix. For a recent account: Frend, *op. cit.*, pp. 109–12.

36 Livy, *loc. cit.*, cap. viii, 5–7; cap. xiii, 11–12 (trans. E. T. Sage).

37 *Ibid.*, cap. xvi, 3–7 (trans. E. T. Sage).

38 For the following see Frend, *op. cit.*, *passim.*; cf. G. E. M. de Ste Croix, "Why were the Christians persecuted?", in *Past and Present*, London, No. 26 (November 1963), pp. 6–38 (esp. pp. 24–31); and J. Vogt, "Zur Religiosität der Christenverfolger in römischen Reich", in *Sitzungsberichte der Heidelberger Akademie der Wissenschaften, Philosophisch-historische Klasse*, Jahrgang 1962, pp. 7–20.

39 Tertullian, *Apologeticum*, cap. xl, 1–2.

CHAPTER TWO: THE DEMONIZATION OF MEDIEVAL HERETICS (1)

–1–

1 Philastrius, *Diversarum hereseon*, xlix, 3.

2 Epiphanius, *Panarion*, xlviii, 4.

3 Augustine, *De haeresibus*, xxvi.

4 Theodoret, *Haereticarum fabularum compendium*, iii, 2.

5 e.g. Jerome, *Epistola xli*, 4.

6 Augustine, *De moribus Ecclesiae Catholicae et de moribus Manichaeorum*, lib. II, cap. vii.

7 Text, in Latin translation, in F. C. Conybeare, *The Key of Truth, a manual of the Paulician Church in Armenia*, Oxford, 1899, pp. 152–4.

8 Michael Psellos, *Peri energeias daimonon*, cap. v (*Pat. graec.*, vol. 122, cols. 831–3). Cf. K. Svoboda, *La démonologie de Michel Psellos*, Brno, 1927 (esp. pp. 47–8).

9 Adhémar de Chabannes, *Historia Francorum*, lib. III, cap. 59 (MGSS vol. IV, p. 143).

10 Paul, monk of Saint-Père of Chartres, *Liber Aganonis*, in *Cartulaire de l'abbaye de Saint-Père de Chartres*, ed. M. Guérard, vol. I, Paris, 1840, p. 112. Modern scholars, relying on the eighteenth-century edition of the *Liber Aganonis* in Bouquet, vol. X, have commonly regarded the document containing the first real sabbat-story as contemporary with the events at Orleans, i.e. as dating from around 1022. But this is a mistake; see Guérard's introduction, p. cclxxvi, Note 2.

11 Walter Map, *De nugis curialium*, Distinctio I, cap. xxx (Camden Society, vol. 50, London, 1850, p. 61).

12 Alain de Lille, *De fide catholica contra haereticos sui temporis*, lib. I, cap. lxiii (*Pat. lat.* vol. 210, col. 366). Map may well have heard the story from Alain de Lille, for both men were at the Lateran Council in Rome in 1179. The derivation of "Cathar" from *cattus* was widely accepted; for an example see I. von Döllinger, *Beiträge zur Sektengeschichte*, vol. II, Munich, 1890, p. 293.

13 Gulielmus Alvernus, *Tractatus de legibus*, cap. xxvi, in *Opera Omnia*, Orléans 1674, vol. I, p. 83.

–2–

14 On Conrad of Marburg and his activities: *Gesta Treverorum, Continuatio IV*, in MGSS vol. XXIV, pp. 400–2; *Chronica Albrici Monachi Trium Fontium*, in

MGSS vol. XXIII, pp. 931–2; *Annales Wormatienses*, in MGSS vol. XVII, p.s 39. For a good modern account: P. Braun, "Der Beichtvater der heiligen Elisabeth und deutsche Inquisitor Konrad von Marburg", in *Beiträge zur hessischen Kirchengeschichte* (ed. Diehl and Koehler), Neue Folge, Ergänzungsband IV, Darmstadt, 1911, pp. 248–300, 331–63. Some valuable corrections to Braun are supplied by L. Förg, *Die Ketzerverfolgung in Deutschland unter Gregor IX. Ihre Herkunft, ihre Bedeutung und ihre rechtlichen Grundlagen*, Berlin, 1932. B. Kaltner, *Konrad von Marburg und die Inquisition in Deutschland*, Prague, 1882, though dated, is also worth consulting. On Conrad's probable aristocratic descent, and connection with the Premonstratensians, see K. H. May, "Zur Geschichte Konrads von Marburg", in *Hessisches Jahrbuch für Landesgeschichte*, vol. I, Marburg, 1951.

15 *Annales Wormatienses, loc. cit.*

16 *Chronica Albrici*, p. 931.

17 Cf. H. Finke, *Konzilienstudien zur Geschichte des 13 Jahrhunderts*, Münster, 1891, pp. 30 seq.

18 *Gesta Treverorum, Contin. IV*, p. 402.

19 MGH, *Epistolae Saeculi XIII e regestis Pontificum Romanorum*, vol. I, No. 560, pp. 453–5.

20 *Annales Erphordenses Fratrum Praedicatorum*, in *Scriptores Rerum Germanicarum: Monumenta Erphesfurtensia*, ed. O. Holder-Egger, Hanover, 1899, p. 86.

21 Text in *Chronica Albrici*, pp. 931–2.

22 Cf. Förg, *op. cit.*, pp. 79, 91.

23 *Chronica Albrici*, p. 931.

CHAPTER THREE: THE DEMONIZATION OF MEDIEVAL HERETICS (2)

–1–

1 Text in *Chronica Albrici*, p. 931.

2 For bibliography see G. Gonnet and A. Hugon, *Bibliografia Valdese*, Torre Pellice, 1953 (*Bollettino della Società di Studi Valdesi*, No. 93) and G. Gonnet, *Sulle fonti del Valdismo medioevale*, in *Protestantesimo*, vol. XII, Rome, 1957, pp. 17–32. The beginnings of the movement are described in C. Thouzellier, *Catharisme et Valdéisme en Languedoc à la fin du xii⁰ siècle*, Paris, 1966, and K.-V. Selge, *Die ersten Waldenser*, 2 vols., Berlin, 1967. As a general survey the fourth edition of E. Comba, *Storia dei Valdesi*, Torre Pellice and Turin, 1950, remains valuable. A fine collection of texts on this as on other movements, in English translation, is contained in: W. L. Wakefield and A. P. Evans, *Heresies of the high middle ages*, New York and London, 1969.

3 Matthew 19:21.

4 *Tractatus de haeresi Pauperum de Lugduno*, printed without author's name in E. Martène and U. Durand, *Thesaurus anecdotorum*, vol. V, Paris, 1727. The relevant passages are at cols. 1779–80, 1782.

5 Cf. K. Schrödl, *Passavia sacra*, Passau, 1879, pp. 242–3; and H. Haupt, "Waldensertum und Inquisition im südöstlichen Deutschland bis zur Mitte des

14ten Jahrhunderts", in *Deutsche Zeitschrift für Geschichtswissenschaft*, vol. I, Freiburg in Breisgau, 1890, pp. 306 seq. and 322–8; E. Tomek, *Kirchengeschichte Oesterreichs*, Innsbruck, Vienna, Munich, 1935, p. 215; P. P. Bernard, "Heresy in fourteenth century Austria", in *Medievalia et Humanistica*, vol. X, Boulder, Colorado, 1956, pp. 50 seq.

6 *Anonymi auctoris brevis narratio* . . ., in H. Pez, *Scriptores rerum Austriacarum*, vol. II, cols. 533–6. An expanded version is in *Annales Matseenses*, in MGSS vol. IX, pp. 825–6.

7 *Annales Matseenses, loc. cit ·*

8 Cf. B. Dudík, *Iter Romanum*, vol. II, Vienna, 1855, pp. 136–41, which includes the text of the bull.

9 John of Winterthur, *Chronica*, in MGSS, new series, vol. III, pp. 144–5.

10 *Gesta archiepiscoporum Magdeburgensium*, in MGSS vol. XIV, p. 434.

11 John of Winterthur, *op. cit.*, p. 151.

12 Cf. H. Haupt, "Husitische Propaganda in Deutschland", in *Historisches Taschenbuch*, 6th series, 7th year, Leipzig, 1888, p. 237; D. Kurze, "Zur Ketzergeschichte der Mark Brandenburg und Pommerns vornehmlich im 14 Jahrhundert: Luziferianer, Putzkeller und Waldenser", in *Jahrbuch für die Geschichte Mittel- und Ostdeutschlands*, vol. 16–17, Berlin, 1968, pp. 50–94.

13 John of Winterthur, *op. cit.*, p. 145.

14 Nicolas Eymeric, *Directorium Inquisitorum*, Rome, 1578, p. 206.

15 For the transcript of the interrogation see *Processus contra Valdenses, Pauperes de Lugduno* . . ., ed. G. Amati, in *Archivo storico italiano*, vol. I, 2, pp. 16–52, and vol. II, 1, pp. 3–61 (both Florence, 1865). For the relevant passages of Antonio Galosna's confession see vol. II, pp. 3, 9, 12–31. See also C. Cantù, *Gli Eretici d'Italia*, vol. I, Turin, 1865, pp. 83–6; G. Boffito, "Eretici in Piemonte al tempo del gran scisma (1378–1417)", in *Studi e Documenti di Storia e Diritto*, 18th year, Rome, 1896, pp. 381–431 (esp. pp. 387, 407–8); and G. Gonnet, "Casi di sincretismo ereticale in Piemonte nei secoli XIV e XV", in *Bollettino della Società di Studi Valdesi (Bulletin de la société d'histoire vaudoise)*, vol. CVIII, Torre Pellice, 1960.

16 Cf. Amati's introduction to the *Processus*, pp. 14–15. For the sentence see *Instrumentum Sententiae late per Dominum Inquisitorem contra duos Valdenses*, ed. G. M. di San Giovanni, in *Miscellanea di Storia Italiana*, vol. XV, Turin, 1876, pp. 75–84. For the trial of 1451: G. Weitzecker, "Processo di un valdese nell'Anno 1451", in *La Rivista Cristiana*, vol. IX, Florence, Turin, Rome, 1881, pp. 363–7.

17 On this episode see J. Chevalier, *Mémoire historique sur les hérésies en Dauphiné*, Valence, 1890, and J. Marx, *L'Inquisition en Dauphiné*, Paris, 1914.

18 J. Marx, *op. cit.*, p. 170.

19 *Ibid.*, pp. 26–7.

20 Gabriel Martin, *Inscription en faux* . . . *contre le livre intitulé: De la puissance du pape* . . . *par le sieur Marc Vulson*, Grenoble, 1640, pp. 219–31. The archival sources on which Martin claims to base his account are lost; but the account is confirmed by other archival sources studied by Marx (see Marx, *op. cit.*, p. 26, n. 1).

21 Cf. Amati, *op. cit.*, vol. I, 2, p. 40.

22 Franciscus Marcus, *Decisiones aureae*, Lyons, 1584, vol. II, p. 362.

23 A transcript of the interrogation is in the Morland collection of Waldensian manuscripts in Cambridge University Library: Dd. III. 26 (c) H 6. It is printed in Peter Allix, *Ancient Churches of Piedmont*, London, 1690, pp. 307–17.

24 Marx, *op. cit.*, p. 26, n. 6.

−2−

25 For the record of the interrogations and confessions see *Processus contra hereticos de opinione dampnata existentes, coram dominis deputatis ad instantiam domini Antonii de Eugubio procuratoris fiscalis factus*, in F. Ehrle, "Die Spiritualen, ihr Verhältnis zum Franziskanerorden und zu den Fraticellen", *Archiv für Literatur- und Kirchengeschichte des Mittelalters*, vol. IV, Freiburg in Breisgau, 1888, pp. 110–38. The same document is also in A. Dressel, *Vier Documente aus römischen Archiven*, 2nd edn., Berlin, 1872, pp. 3–48. Ehrle's edition is the more accurate; and the references below are all to this edition. However, Dressel, at pp. 18–25, gives the text of a letter from the commissioners to the pope, summarizing the results of the interrogations, which is not to be found in Ehrle.

26 e.g. Ehrle, *op. cit.*, pp. 135–8, and R. Guarnieri, *Il Movimento del libero spirito*, Rome, 1965, p. 480.

27 On the Fraticelli see D. L. Douie, *The nature and the effect of the heresy of the Fraticelli*, Manchester, 1932, and the briefer accounts in M. Reeves, *The influence of prophecy in the later middle ages*, Oxford, 1969, pp. 212–28; and G. Leff, *Heresy in the later middle ages*, Manchester and New York, 1967, vol. I, pp. 230–55. The particular group of Fraticelli considered here figures only in Douie, pp. 243–6.

28 Text in *Processus*, pp. 112–16.

29 *Ibid.*, p. 117.

30 *Ibid.*, p. 127.

31 *Ibid.*, p. 118.

32 *Ibid.*, p. 121

33 *Ibid.*, p. 126.

34 *Ibid.*, p. 126.

35 *Ibid.*, pp. 120, 129.

36 *Ibid.*, p. 130.

37 *Ibid.*, p. 131.

38 *Ibid.*, p. 127.

39 See above, p. 18.

40 Guibert de Nogent, *Histoire de sa vie, (1053–1124)*. ed. G. Bourgin, Paris, 1907, lib. III, cap. xvii, pp. 212–13.

41 L. Banchi, *Le Prediche volgari di San Bernardino da Siena*, vol. II, Siena, 1884, p. 356.

42 On John of Capestrano see J. Hofer, *Johannes Kapistran. Ein Leben im Kampf um die Reform der Kirche*, revised edn., 2 vols, Rome and Heidelberg, 1964–5.

43 *Ibid.*, vol. I, pp. 339–42.

44 Wadding, *Annales Minorum*, 2nd edn., vol. XII, Rome, 1735, p. 25. Wadding takes this information from the Chronicle of Antoninus, archbishop of Florence.

45 Cf. Nicolas de Fara, *Vita S. Johannis a Capistrano*, in *Acta Sanctorum*, 10 October, p. 448, para. 25; Christophorus a Varisio (Varese), *Vita S. Johannis a Capistrano, ibid.*, p. 500, para. 37.

46 See above, p. 45.

47 Blondus Flavius, *De Roma Triumphante libri X*, Basel, 1531. The volume includes *Italia Illustrata*, although this is a separate work. The relevant passage is at pp. 337–8. *Italia Illustrata* was compiled in 1453.

48 *Ibid.*

49 Cf. the variant readings of the above passage as given in B. Nogara, *Scritti inediti e rari di Biondo Flavio*, Rome, 1927, p. 223.

50 Codex 18626, 67 recto, in Staatsbibliothek, Munich.

51 See above, p. 47.

52 Joannis Genesius de Sepúlveda, *De vita et rebus gestis Aegidii Albornotii Carrilli*, in *Opera Omnia*, vol. IV, Madrid, 1780, pp. 57–8.

–3–

53 Some serious modern historians think that libertine consequences were drawn; but the weightiest piece of evidence adduced—the confessions of two captured Catharist leaders as summarized by Geoffroy de Vigeois (*Chronicon*, in M. Bouquet, *Recueil des historiens des Gaules et de la France*, vol. XII, p. 449) and by Geoffroy d'Auxerre (ed. J. Leclercq, in *Studia Anselmiana*, Fasc. 31, Rome, 1953, p. 196)—seems to me very dubious evidence indeed. Nothing in the panoply of sources displayed by e.g. G. Koch, *Frauenfrage und Ketzertum im Mittelalter*, Berlin, 1962, pp. 113–21, proves that the Cathars practised promiscuity, let alone that they held orgies.

54 See, for instance, the mid-thirteenth century *Summa contra hereticos*, by the Milanese Franciscan Jacobo de Capellis, published by C. Molinier in his "Rapport . . . sur une mission exécutée en Italie", in *Archives des Missions scientifiques et littéraires*, 3rd series, vol. XIV, Paris, 1888, pp. 133–336. The relevant passage is at pp. 289–90.

55 See above, p. 9.

56 Cf. F. Baethgen, "Franziskanische Studien", reprinted in his *Mediaevalia: Aufsätze, Nachrufe, Besprechungen*, Stuttgart, 1960, pp. 331–41.

57 An exception was the late Rev. Montague Summers; see *A History of witchcraft and demonology*, London and New York, 1926, p. 25.

58 Cf. C. H. Lea, *The Inquisition of the middle ages*, vol. II, p. 358.

59 See above, p. 30.

60 Some of these sources are mentioned in the first section of this chapter. Others are: *Gesta Treverorum, Continuatio IV*, in MGSS vol. XXIV, p. 401; and the second part of the document entitled *Manichaei cujusdam confessio*, in I. von Döllinger, *Beiträge zur Sektengeschichte*, vol. II, Munich, 1890, pp. 370–3.

61 See N. G. Garsoïan, *The Paulician heresy. A study of the origin and development of*

Paulicianism in Armenia and the eastern provinces of the Byzantine Empire, The Hague and Paris, 1967 (esp. pp. 232–3).

62 See above, p. 18.

63 See J. B. Russell, *Dissent and reform in the early middle ages*, Berkeley and Los Angeles, 1965, pp. 205–15; and works listed below, n. 67. The date at which Bogomile influence reached the West has been much debated; but even those who believe that it did so in the eleventh century admit that at that time it must have been confined to ethics and ritual; cf. C. Thouzellier, "Tradition et résurgence dans l'hérésie médiévale", in *Hérésies et sociétés dans l'Europe pre-industrielle, 11ᵉ–18ᵉ siècles*, ed. J. Le Goff, Paris and The Hague, 1968, pp. 105–16. Western heresy knows nothing of Dualist metaphysics before the mid-thirteenth century.

64 See above, p. 22.

65 Radulphus Ardens, *Homilia XIX in Dominica VIII post Trinitatem*, in *Pat. lat.*, vol. 155, col. 2011.

66 Geoffroy de Vigeois, *loc. cit.*

67 Standard works on the Dualist religion, of relatively recent date, are: D. Obolensky, *The Bogomils*, Cambridge, 1948; H. Söderberg, *La religion des Cathares*, Uppsala, 1949; A. Borst, *Die Katharer*, Stuttgart, 1953. For a comprehensive bibliography: H. Grundmann, *Bibliographie zur Ketzergeschichte des Mittelalters*, 1900–66 (Sussidi Eruditi No. 20), Rome, 1967, pp. 23–41.

68 See below, p. 177.

CHAPTER FOUR: CHANGING VIEWS OF THE DEVIL AND HIS POWERS

– I –

1 G. Roskoff, *Geschichte des Teufels*, Leipzig, 1869, though inevitably dated, is still the fullest general history of ideas about Satan and the demonic hosts. The same ground is covered more briefly by E. Langton, *Satan, a portrait*, London, 1945, and H. A. Kelly, *Towards the death of Satan*, London, 1968. For the development of Christian and Jewish ideas down to the New Testament see also E. Langton, *Essentials of demonology*, London, 1949.

2 Amos 3:6.

3 Isaiah 45:7.

4 See H. V. Kluger, *Satan in the Old Testament*, trans. H. Nagel, Northwestern University Press, Evanston, U.S.A., 1967.

5 For texts see R. H. Charles, *The Apocrypha and Pseudepigrapha of the Old Testament*, 2 vols., Oxford, 1913. For a good survey see H. H. Rowley, *The relevance of Apocalyptic*, 2nd edn., London, 1947. How far the growth of Jewish demonology was due to Iranian influence, and how much Satan owes to the Zoroastrian spirit of destruction Ahriman, has been much debated and remains uncertain. For recent contributions see J. Duchesne-Guillemin, *Ormazd et Ahriman*, Paris, 1953, and R. C. Zaehner, *The dawn and twilight of Zoroastrianism*, London, 1961.

6 *I Enoch* 10:1–11 (Charles, *op. cit.*, vol. II, pp. 193–4).

7 *I Enoch* 15:11 (*ibid.*, p. 198).

8 *I Enoch* 19:1 (*ibid.*, p. 200).

9 *Jubilees* 11:4 seq. (*ibid.*, p. 29).

10 *Testament of Levy* 19:1 (*ibid.*, p. 315).

11 G. Vermes, *The Dead Sea Scrolls in English*, London, 1962, p. 124.

12 *Ibid.*, pp. 140–1.

–2–

13 For recent accounts see G. B. Caird, *Principalities and Powers: a study in Pauline theology*, Oxford, 1956, and H. A. Kelly, *op. cit.*

14 John 8:44.

15 II Corinthians 4:4.

16 Acts 26:18.

17 I Corinthians 10:20. The Greek text of the New Testament uses "diabolos" for Satan only. For a lesser evil spirit the word is "daimon" which, though the Revised Version renders it as "devil", ought to be translated as "demon".

18 John 12:31.

19 John 16:11.

20 Hebrews 2:14.

21 I Peter 5:8.

22 Revelation 20:10.

–3–

23 *I Enoch* 69:4–6 (Charles, *op. cit.*, vol. II, p. 233).

24 Latin *Vita*, 9, 1 (*ibid.*, p. 136); *Apocalypsis Mosis*, 16–20 (*ibid.*, pp. 145–6).

25 Ephesians 6:12; cf. Ephesians 2:2.

26 Augustine, *Enarratio in Psalmum cxlviii*, 9 (*Pat. lat.*, vol. 37, col. 1943).

27 Augustine, *De divinatione daemonum*, cap. iii, 7 (*Pat. lat.*, vol. 40, cols. 584–5).

28 Ephesians 6:12.

29 Irenaeus, *Adversus haereses*, lib. V, cap. xxiv.

30 Tertullian, *Apologeticum*, cap. xxii.

31 Origen, *Contra Celsum*, lib. VIII, 31–2.

32 Justin, *Apologia I*, 55 seq.

33 Justin, *Apologia I*, 5, 12 and 14; Origen, *Exhortatio ad martyrium*, 18 and 32 (*Pat. graec.*, vol. 11, cols. 585–8, 603).

34 Cyprian, *Liber de unitate Ecclesiae*, 15 (*Pat. lat.*, vol. 4, col. 527).

35 Jerome, *Liber contra Vigilantium*, 9 (*Pat. lat.*, vol. 23, cols. 363–4).

36 Tertullian, *Apologeticum*, cap. xxiii; Cyprian, *Ad Demetrianum*, 15 (*Pat. lat.*, vol. 4, cols. 574–5).

37 Sulpicius Severus, *Dialogus III*, cap. vi.

38 *Shepherd of Hermas*, Mandates VII and XII.

39 Irenaeus, *Adversus haereses*, lib. II, cap. xxxii.

40 Tertullian, *Apologeticum*, cap. xxiii.

41 Origen, *Homilia in librum Jesu Nave*, XV (*Pat. graec.*, vol. 12, cols. 897 seq.).

-4-

42 Theodoret, *Historia Ecclesiastica*, lib. V, cap. xxi.

43 Gregory the Great, *Dialogi*, lib. III, cap. vii.

44 *Acta Sanctorum*, 5 August, para. 9.

45 Caesarius of Heisterbach, *Dialogus miraculorum*, Book III, chapter 26. A convenient edition of the *Dialogus* in Latin is that by J. Strange, 2 vols., Cologne, 1851. There is an English translation by H. von Scott and C. C. Swinton Bland, 2 vols., London, 1929. On the demonological aspects of the work see Ph. Schmidt, *Der Teufels- und Dämonenglaube in den Erzählungen des Caesarius von Heisterbach*, Basel, 1926.

46 *Ibid.*, Book V, chapter 2.

47 *Ibid.*, Book III, chapters 6, 7.

48 *Ibid.*, Book V, chapter 5.

49 *Ibid.*, Book V, chapter 7.

50 *Ibid.*, Book V, chapter 44.

51 *Ibid.*, Book V, chapter 42.

52 *Ibid.*, Book V, chapter 18.

53 *Ibid.*, Book V, chapter 17.

54 *Ibid.*, Book V, chapter 9.

55 *Ibid.*, Book V, chapter 28.

56 *Ibid.*, Book V, chapter 30.

57 *Ibid.*, Book V, chapter 31.

58 *Ibid.*, Book V, chapter 24.

59 *Ibid.*, Book V, chapter 26.

60 *Ibid.*, Book XII, chapter 4.

61 Richalmus, *Liber Revelationum de insidiis et versutiis daemonum adversus homines*, in B. Pez, *Thesaurus anecdotorum novissimus*, vol. I, part 2, Augsburg, 1721, cols. 374 seq.

62 Richalmus, *op. cit.*, cap. lxxiii, col. 440.

63 *Ibid.*, cap. xliv, col. 440.

64 *Ibid.*, cap. lxx, col. 438.

65 *Ibid.*, cap. iii, col. 385.

66 *Ibid.*, cap. iv, col. 387.

67 *Ibid.*, cap. xli, col. 421.

68 *Ibid.*, cap. xii, col. 398.

69 *Ibid.*, caps. xvii, xxii, xxviii, xxx, cols. 403–4, 410–11, 414–16, 417–18.

70 *Ibid.*, cap. i, col. 380.

71 *Ibid.*, cap. i, col. 382.

72 *Ibid.*, cap. xxxvi, col. 420.

73 *Ibid.*, cap. vi, col. 391.

74 *Ibid.*, cap. iii, col. 384.

75 *Ibid.*, cap. iv, col. 385.

76 *Ibid.*, cap. i, col. 377.

77 *Ibid.*, cap. xc, col. 448.

78 *Ibid.*, cap. xii, col. 396.

79 *Ibid.*, cap. cxxiii, col. 464; cf. cap. xxi, cols. 408-10.

80 *Ibid.*, cap. liv, col. 428.

81 *Ibid.*, caps. iii, iv, cols. 384-90.

82 *Ibid.*, cap. iii, col. 385.

83 *Ibid.*, cap. xlvi, col. 423.

84 *Ibid.*, cap. iv, col. 390.

85 *Ibid.*, cap. xxx, col. 418.

CHAPTER FIVE: THE CRUSHING OF THE KNIGHTS TEMPLARS

-I-

1 The literature on the Knights Templars is so vast that a bibliographical survey itself fills two volumes. For books and articles published down to 1926 see M. Dessubré, *Bibliographie de l'Ordre des Templiers*, Paris, 1928; and for later publications H. Neu, *Bibliographie des Templer-Ordens, 1927-1965*. Neu's bibliography also contains many references to much earlier works; and owing to its system of classification is easier to use than Dessubré. Two competent general histories in English are: G. A. Campbell, *The Knights Templars*, London, 1937; and E. Simon, *The Piebald Standard. A biography of the Knights Templars*, London, 1959. Unfortunately neither of these works gives any reference to sources. On the destruction of the order the standard works are still H. Finke, *Papsttum und Untergang des Templerordens*, 2 vols., Münster i. W., 1907; and the two works by G. Lizerance: *Clément V et Philippe le Bel*, Paris, 1910, and *Jacques de Molay*, Paris, 1913. A great collection of original sources concerning the destruction is in Michelet's *Procès des Templiers*, 2 vols., Paris, 1841, 1851; and a useful selection, including some not known to Michelet, in G. Lizerand, *L'Affaire des Templiers*, Paris, 1923. Further important documents are in Finke, vol. II. For a French translation of a selection of Michelet's documents see R. Oursel, *Le procès des Templiers*, Paris, 1955. Oursel's own conclusions, however, do not all stand up to detailed examination.

2 Raymond Lull, *Liber de fine*. The work is printed as an appendix to A. Gottron, *Ramon Lulls Kreuzzugsideen*, Berlin and Leipzig, 1912, pp. 65-93. See also J. N. Hillgarth, *Ramon Lull and Lullism in fourteenth-century France*, Oxford, 1971 (esp. pp. 66, 72-3).

3 The surviving fragments are combined in an Aragonese document dating from early in 1308. For the text see Finke, *op. cit.*, vol. II, p. 118. Cf. letter from Christian Spinola to James II of Aragon, *ibid.*, p. 51; also Finke's comments in vol. I, pp. 121-2.

4 Pierre Dubois, *De recuperatione Terre Sancte*, ed. C. V. Langlois, Paris, 1891, especially pp. 98-9, 131-40. The tract was written between 1305 and 1307. On Dubois, see E. Zeck, *Der Publizist Pierre Dubois*, Berlin, 1911; especially, for his relationship to Lull, pp. 147 seq.

5 For Jacques de Molay's reply: Lizerand, *L'Affaire des Templiers*, pp. 2-14.

–2–

6 For Esquiu de Floyran see document in Finke, *op. cit.*, vol. II, pp. 83–5; and Almaricus Augerii, *Vita Clementis V*, in E. Baluze, *Vitae paparum Avenionensium*, ed. G. Mollat, Paris, 1914, vol. I, pp. 93–4. Like Esquiu, Almaric came from Béziers; but he wrote half a century later. The version of the story in Villani, *Istorie fiorentine*, is demonstrably inaccurate. See also Finke, *op. cit.*, vol. I, pp. 111–14; and C. V. Langlois, review of Finke in *Journal des Savants* for 1908, pp. 423–5.

7 Text in Lizerand, *op. cit.*, pp. 16–28.

8 For a bibliography of the debate concerning the guilt or innocence of the order, see Neu, *op. cit.*, pp. 41–50. Since the publication of Neu there has appeared G. Legman, *The guilt of the Templars*, New York, 1966. It need not be taken seriously.

9 Text in Lizerand, *op. cit.*, pp. 206–12.

10 For examples and references see Michelet, *op. cit.*, vol. II, pp. 292, 294, 295, 297; and cf. text in Finke, *op. cit.*, vol. II, p. 363.

11 Text in Finke, *op. cit.*, vol. II, pp. 342–64.

12 *Chronique de Saint-Denis*, in Bouquet, vol. XX, p. 686.

13 Cf. text in Finke, *op. cit.*, vol. II, pp. 351, 353, 361.

14 *Ibid.*, pp. 342, 344, 345, 348.

15 Cf. Finke, *op. cit.*, vol. I, pp. 147–50.

16 This emerges already from the order for the arrest of the Templars; see text in Lizerand, *op. cit.*, p. 26.

17 Cf. Michelet, *Procès des Templiers*, vol. I, p. 75.

18 For the text of these early confessions see Michelet, *op. cit.*, vol. II, pp. 277 seq.

19 For the confession of Hugues de Pairaud: Lizerand, *op. cit.*, p. 43.

20 Cf. texts in Finke, *op. cit.*, vol. II, pp. 342–64.

21 Texts in Finke, *op. cit.*, vol. II, pp. 309–12.

22 *Ibid.*, pp. 307–9.

23 Cf. Finke, *op. cit.*, vol. I, p. 181 with footnote (1).

24 Text in Rymer, *Foedera*, edn. of 1745, vol. I, para. 4, pp. 99–100.

25 For the Latin text of the summons: Lizerand, *op. cit.*, pp. 102–6.

26 For the Latin text of the oration: *ibid.*, pp. 110–24.

27 Cf. the oration in Lizerand, *op. cit.*, pp. 124–36.

28 Cf. Michelet, *op. cit.*, vol. I, p. 36.

29 Text in Lizerand, *op. cit.*, pp. 176–88.

30 Deposition of Aimery de Villiers-le-Duc, in Lizerand, *op. cit.*, pp. 188–92.

31 Text in G. Villani, *Istorie fiorentine*, lib. VIII, cap. 92.

CHAPTER SIX: THE NON-EXISTENT SOCIETY OF WITCHES

–2–

1 K. E. Jarcke, "Ein Hexenprozess", in *Annalen der deutschen und ausländischen Criminal-Rechts-Pflege,* vol. I, Berlin, 1828 (esp. p. 450).

2 F. J. Mone, "Ueber das Hexenwesen", in *Anzeiger für Kunde der teutschen Vorzeit,* Jahrgang 8, Karlsruhe, 1839 (esp. pp. 271–5, 444–53).

3 Cf. J. M. Roberts, *The mythology of the secret societies,* London, 1972.

4 J. Michelet, *La Sorcière,* chap. xi (p. 128 in the edition by P. Viallaneix, Paris, 1966).

5 *Ibid.,* chaps. xi, xii (pp. 127, 138 in Viallaneix).

6 Cf. G. Mongrédien, *Madame de Montespan et l'affaire des poisons,* Paris, 1953.

7 See below, p. 232.

8 P. Viallaneix, preface to *La Sorcière,* pp. 17–18.

9 E. Le Roy Ladurie, *Les paysans de Languedoc,* Paris, 1966, pp. 407–14.

10 Margaret Murray first expounded her views a few years earlier, in two articles in *Folk-Lore,* vols. XXVIII (1917) and XXXI (1920).

11 E. Rose, *A razor for a goat,* Toronto, 1962, pp. 14–15.

12 Cf. Florence Hershman, *Witchcraft U.S.A.,* New York, 1971, pp. 149–56.

13 A. Runeberg, *Witches, demons and fertility magic,* Helsingfors, 1947, pp. 230–1.

14 R. Burns Begg, "Notice of Trials for Witchcraft at Crook of Devon, Kinross-shire, in 1662", in *Proceedings of the Society of Antiquaries of Scotland,* vol. XXII, Edinburgh, 1888, pp. 212 seq., 223.

15 M. Murray, *The Witch-cult in western Europe,* Oxford, 1962, pp. 139, 99.

16 T. Potts, *Discovery of Witches in the County of Lancashire reprinted from the original edition of 1613,* Manchester, 1845.

17 Murray, *op. cit.,* p. 140.

18 J. Glanvill, *Sadducismus Triumphatus,* London, 1689, pp. 353–4.

19 Murray, *op. cit.,* p. 141.

20 *Ibid.,* p. 98.

21 (G. R. Kinloch, ed.), *Reliquiae Antiquae Scoticae, illustrative of civil and ecclesiastical affairs,* Edinburgh, 1848, pp. 121–3.

22 Murray, *op. cit.,* pp. 141–2.

23 R. Pitcairn, *Criminal Trials . . .,* Edinburgh, 1833, vol. III, Appendix, p. 613.

24 *Ibid.,* p. 604; cf. pp. 609–11.

25 *Ibid.,* p. 607.

26 Murray, *op. cit.,* pp. 100, 144.

27 A. Horneck (trans.), *An Account of what happened in the Kingdom of Sweden in the years 1669, 1670 . . .,* London, 1688, p. 584. This translation of a German pamphlet forms an appendix to Glanvill's *Sadducismus Triumphatus.*

28 Cf. J. B. Russell, *Witchcraft in the middle ages,* Cornell University Press, 1972, pp. 41–2.

29 A. Runeberg, *Witches, demons and fertility magic*, p. 230.

30 *Ibid.*, p. 86.

31 E. Rose, *A razor for a goat*, Toronto, 1962, pp. 141–2.

32 *Ibid.*, p. 143.

33 *Ibid.*, pp. 167–8.

34 *Ibid.*, pp. 197–9.

35 Murray, *op. cit.*, pp. 50–9.

36 W. R. Halliday, in *Folk-Lore*, vol. XXXIII (1922), p. 228, note.

37 Cf., in Pitcairn, *Criminal Trials*, vol. I, part 3, *Newes from Scotland. Declaring the damnable life of Doctor Fian a notable Sorcerer* . . . [1591], p. 216, and especially, in the indictment against Agnes Sampson, pp. 235, 239.

38 M. Summers, *The history of witchcraft and demonology*, London, 1926, p. xi.

39 *Ibid.*, p. 4.

40 *Ibid.*, pp. xi, 5–8.

41 J. B. Russell, *Witchcraft in the middle ages*, Cornell University Press, 1972, p. 3.

42 *Ibid.*, p. 3, and cf. p. 22.

43 *Ibid.*, p. 26, and cf. p. 266.

44 *Ibid.*, pp. 87–93, 160–3, 176–80, 197, 223.

45 *Ibid.*, p. 100.

46 *Ibid.*, pp. 283, 285.

47 *Ibid.*, pp. 52, 58, 59; and cf. p. 268

48 *Ibid.*, p. 41.

49 *Ibid.*, p. 43.

50 *Ibid.*, p. 132.

CHAPTER SEVEN: THREE FORGERIES AND ANOTHER WRONG TRACK

–I–

1 W. G. Soldan, *Geschichte der Hexenprocesse*, Stuttgart and Tübingen, 1843, pp. 180, 186–7, 189.

2 J. Hansen, *Zauberwahn, Inquisition und Hexenprozess im Mittelalter und die Entstehung der grossen Hexenverfolgung*, Munich and Leipzig, 1900, pp. 309, 315–17, 326, 335, 337.

3 Hansen, *op. cit.*, pp. 309–10. The other references to Angela de la Barthe are at pp. 188, 234.

4 E.-L. de Lamothe-Langon, *Histoire de l'Inquisition en France*, vol. II, Paris, 1829, pp. 614–15.

5 T. Bouges, *Histoire ecclésiastique et civile de la ville et diocèse de Carcassonne*, Paris, 1741, pp. 200–1.

6 D. de Vic and J. Vaissete, *Histoire générale de Languedoc*, vol. IV, Paris, 1742, Avertissement, p. v. The text of the "chronicle of Bardin" is in the Preuves, at cols. 2–47. For Molinier's comments see the new edition, vol. X, Toulouse, 1885, Notes, cols. 424–36.

7 He gives the source himself: J. J. Percin, *Monumenta conventus Tolosani Ordinis FF. Praedicatorum*, Toulouse, 1693, p. 109.

8 Cf. Vic and Vaissete, *op. cit.*, Preuves, col. 5. Percin's history makes no mention of the trial of Angela de la Barthe in its section on the inquisitors of Toulouse.

9 Cf. Vic and Vaissete, *op. cit.*, col. 18.

10 *Ibid.*, cols. 17–18.

11 *Biographie toulousaine*, vol. I, Paris, 1823, pp. 400–1.

12 Hansen, *Zauberwahn*, pp. 315–30.

13 Hansen, *Quellen und Untersuchungen zur Geschichte des Hexenwahns und der Hexenverfolgung im Mittelalter*, Bonn, 1901, pp. 450–3.

14 Lamothe-Langon, *op. cit.*, vol. III, pp. 235–40.

15 That Pierre Guidonis was inquisitor at Toulouse in 1344 is stated in J. Quétif and J. Echard, *Scriptores Ordinis Praedicatorum*, vol. I, Paris, 1719, p. 625, on the strength of a single phrase in a single manuscript. M. J. C. Douais repeated it in *Les frères prêcheurs en Gascogne au xiii* et au xiv* siècle*, Auch, 1885, p. 453; but he omitted the name from the list of inquisitors (which includes those only rarely mentioned in documents) in his later work, *Documents pour servir à l'histoire de l'Inquisition dans le Languedoc*, Paris, 1900, pp. cxxx–cxxxiv.

16 For the list of capitouls: G. La Faille, *Annales de la Ville de Toulouse*, vol. I, p. 73, Toulouse, 1687; A. L. C. A. Du Mège, *Histoire des Institutions . . . de Toulouse*, vol. II, Toulouse, 1844, p. 45. Cf. E. Roschach, "Les listes municipales de Toulouse du xii* au xviii* siècle", in *Mémoires de l'Académie des Sciences . . . de Toulouse*, 8th series, vol. VII (1885), pp. 1–22.

17 Lamothe-Langon, *op. cit.*, vol. III, p. 226.

18 For the letter of John XXII to the inquisitors: Hansen, *Quellen*, pp. 4–5. For the background of the papal intervention: Anneliese Maier, "Eine Verfügung Johannes XXII. Über die Zuständigkeit des Inquisition für Zaubereiprozesse", in *Archivum Fratrum Praedicatorum*, vol. XXII, Rome, 1952, pp. 226–46.

19 Bernard Gui, *Manuel de l'Inquisiteur*, ed. G. Mollat, 2 vols., Paris, 1926–7. What magic meant to an inquisitor at that time is shown at pp. 20–4 of vol. II. The sentences of Guidonis himself, as given in the *Liber Sententiarum Inquisitionis Tholosanae* in Philip Limborch's *Historia Inquisitionis*, Amsterdam, 1692, pp. 394 seq., includes not a single case of magic or sorcery.

20 Text in Hansen, *Quellen*, pp. 6–7.

–2–

21 On Lamothe-Langon see R. Switzer, *Etienne-Léon de Lamothe-Langon et le roman populaire français de 1800 à 1830*, Toulouse, 1962; L. de Santi, "Episodes de l'histoire de Toulouse sous le premier Empire", in *Mémoires de l'Académie des Sciences et des Belles-Lettres de Toulouse*, 10th series, vol. XII, Toulouse, 1912, pp. 87–100.

22 Lamothe-Langon, *Histoire de l'Inquisition en France*, vol. I, Preface, pp. xxxiv–xxxv.

23 Quoted by de Santi, *op. cit.*, p. 88.

24 Lamothe-Langon, *Alliance de la censure et de l'Inquisition*, Paris, 1827, pp. 8, 10;

and cf. Lamothe-Langon, *Le Chancelier et le censeurs*, vol. I, Paris, 1828, p. vii.

25 *Ibid.*

26 e.g. Ch. Molinier, *L'Inquisition dans le Midi de la France au xiii⁰ et au xiv⁰ siècle*, Paris, 1880; L. Tanon, *Histoire des tribunaux de l'Inquisition en France*, Paris, 1893.

27 Lamothe-Langon, *La dame du comptoir*, Paris, 1844, p. 4 of the cover.

28 Cf. Switzer, *op. cit.*, p. 65.

29 On Sermet see the article in Michaud's *Biographie universelle*.

30 Le Père Sermet, "Recherches historiques sur l'Inquisition de Toulouse", in *Mémoires de l'Académie royale des sciences, inscriptions et belles-lettres de Toulouse*, vol. IV (1790), p. 46. The documents mentioned by Sermet as having been discovered by the Abbé Magi were published in the same volume; they refer to the year 1245 only.

31 Lamothe-Langon, *Histoire de l'Inquisition*, vol. I, Introduction, p. xxxvi.

32 Philippus a Limborch, *Historia Inquisitionis*, Amsterdam, 1692. *The Liber Sententiarum* is at pp. 334 seq. For the attendance at the sermon of Bernard Guidonis see p. 334.

33 G. La Faille, *Annales de la Ville de Toulouse*, Toulouse, vol. I, 1687, p. 73.

34 J. J. Percin, *op. cit.*, p. 110. Cf. p. 102, where the name of Pierre Guidonis is associated with a supposed letter from King Philip VI, dated 1334. The letter derives, through La Faille, from Bardin, and is almost certainly spurious. Percin was in any case the first to connect it, quite arbitrarily, with the name of Pierre Guidonis.

35 Lamothe-Langon, *op. cit.*, vol. III, p. 231. Percin also supplies Lamothe-Langon with other information about the names and dates of inquisitors, much of it wrong.

36 Pierre de Lancre, *Tableaux de l'Inconstance des Mauvais Anges*, Paris, 1612, especially pp. 66–75, 89–90, 128–31, 140, 145, 175, 195–8, 216–17.

37 On Georgel see the article in Michaud, *Biographie universelle*. The name is so uncommon that no other Georgel appears in Michaud. His book is entitled *Mémoires pour servir à l'histoire des événemens de la fin du dix-huitième siècle, depuis 1760 jusqu'en 1806–1810*. On Delort see the article in Rabbe and Bois-jolin, *Biographie universelle et portative des contemporains*, vol. II, Paris, 1834. The name is so uncommon that no Delort appears in Michaud's *Biographie universelle*. Unlike Lamothe-Langon, Joseph Delort was clearly a trained historian with some competence in paleography. Cf. his *Essai critique sur l'histoire de Charles VII . . .*, Paris, 1824, p. 2, and the "pièces justificatives" at pp. 173 seq.

–3–

38 J. J. von Görres, *Die christliche Mystik*, vol. III, Regensburg, 1840, pp. 54–5.

39 W. G. Soldan, *Geschichte der Hexenprozesse*, Stuttgart and Tübingen, 1843, p. 189.

40 Janus (pseudonym of Döllinger), *Der Papst*, Munich, 1869, pp. 275–6; Döllinger, *Das Papstthum*, Munich, 1892, p. 126 (revised edition of the above).

41 J. Hansen, *Quellen*, pp. 64–6; *Zauberwahn*, pp. 334–7.

42 Cf. J. L. J. Van de Kamp, *Bartolus de Saxoferrato 1313–1357*, Amsterdam, 1936 (in Dutch), pp. 35 seq.

43 Ioannes Baptista Zilettus, *Consilia seu responsa ad causas criminales*, vol. I, Venice, 1566. Further editions of the collection were published at Venice in 1572 and at Frankfort on Main in 1578. I have used the Venice edition of 1572.

44 The thirty-four additional *consilia* figure in vol. X of the *Omnia Opera* in the Venice editions of 1590, 1602 and 1615.

45 Hansen, *Quellen*, p. 56, n. 1, suggested that Ioannes de Plotis must be a misreading of Ioannes Visconti, who was bishop of Novara from 1331 to 1342.

46 For *consilia* dealing with the de Plotis family: in Ziletti, *Consilia ad causas criminales* (1572), *consilia* v, vi, vii and viii; in Bartolo, *Omnia Opera*, vol. X, Venice, 1602, pp. 183 seq., additional *consilia* i, ii, iii, iv, vii, viii, ix, xi; in Ziletti, *Consilia matrimonialia*, Venice, 1563, *consilia* lxxxviii and lxxxix.

47 Bartolo, *Omnia Opera*, p. 185, additional *consilium* iv.

48 Ziletti, *Consilia matrimonialia*, pp. 350–2, *consilium* lxxxix.

49 Bartolo, *Omnia Opera*, p. 187, *consilium* vii.

50 *Ibid.*, p. 183, *consilium* i.

51 *Ibid.*, p. 184, *consilium* iv.

52 *Ibid.*, p. 189, *consilium* viii.

53 On Giovanni Battista Piotto see C. Morbio, *Storia della Città e Diocesi di Novara*, Milan, 1841, p. 229, and A. Rusconi *et al.*, *Monografie Novaresi*, Novara, 1877, pp. 51–2.

54 Examples are in an earlier collection by Ziletti, *Criminalia consilia atque responsa*, vol. I, Venice, 1559, pp. 289–312, *consilia* cviii and cix. See also the following Note.

55 Ziletti, *Consilia matrimonialia*, pp. 292–6, *consilium* lxxxvii; Ioannes Baptista Plotus, *Consilia sive responsa*, Novara, 1578, pp. 78–81, *consilium* xv.

56 In Ziletti, *Consilia . . . ad causas criminales* (1572), p. 158.

57 Bernard of Como, *Tractatus de strigiis*, Milan, 1566 (as appendix to the author's *Lucerna Inquisitorum*). The tract is reprinted, from a later edition, in Hansen's *Quellen*, pp. 279–84. Hansen's dating of around 1508 is altogether plausible, and other suggestions that have been made—for instance, the 1480s—do not fit with what is known of Bernard's life.

58 Cf. C. Cantù, *Storia della Città e Diocesi di Como*, 3rd rev. edn., vol. I, Como, 1899, pp. 477–85.

59 For an outline of Rategno's biography see Hansen, *Quellen*, pp. 279–80. For his reputation as a witch-hunter see the Latin verses by Benedetto Giovio, of Como, quoted by Cantù, *op. cit.*, p. 485. They were written before 1529.

CHAPTER EIGHT: *MALEFICIUM* BEFORE 1300

–1–

1 Cf. E. E. Evans-Pritchard, *Witchcraft, oracles and magic among the Azande*, Oxford, 1937, pp. 21, 387. It is now recognized that the distinction is not as absolute in all African societies as amongst the Azande.

2 Gregory of Tours, *Historia Francorum*, lib. V, cap. xxxix, xl; lib. VI, cap. xxxv.

3 For the early Middle Ages see Elisabeth Blum, *Das staatliche und kirchliche Recht des Frankenreichs in seiner Stellung zum Dämon- Zauber- und Hexenwesen*, Paderborn, 1936; and cf. H. Brunner, *Deutsche Rechtsgeschichte*, vol. I, pp. 678–81, Leipzig, 1887. Edith Kiessling, *Zauberei in den germanischen Volksrechten*, Jena, 1941, is influenced by Nazi ideology and is also unreliable in its handling of facts.

4 *Pactus Alamannorum*, Fragmentum II, para. 33, in MGH Leges, sectio I, vol. V, part I, p. 23; *Edictus Rothari*, 376, in *Leges Langobardorum*, ed. F. Beyerle, Witzenhausen, 1962, p. 91; *Capitulatio de partibus Saxoniae*, para. 6, in MGH Leges, sectio II, vol. I, pp. 68–9.

5 *Eyrbbygia* (*The story of the Ere-dwellers*), trans. William Morris and Eírikr Magnússon, London, 1892, chapters 15–20 (esp. p. 48).

6 *The Laxdale Saga*, trans. Muriel Press, London, 1964, chapter 37, pp. 119–21.

7 *Pactus legis Salicae*, tit. xix, 1 (ed. K. A. Eckhardt, vol. II, 1, Göttingen, 1955, p. 180).

8 *Lex Ribuaria*, cap. lxxxiii (ed. K. A. Eckhardt, 2nd edn., Hanover, 1966, p. 77).

9 Text in F. Liebermann, *Die Gesetze der Angelsachsen*, vol. I, Halle a. S., 1903, pp. 152–5.

10 *Leges Regis Henrici Primi*, cap. 71, in B. Thorpe, *Ancient Laws and Institutes of England*, 1840, p. 251.

11 *Uplandslag*, cap. xix, in *Schwedische Rechte*, trans. C. von Schwerin, Weimar, 1935, p. 142 (*Germanenrechte*, vol. VII).

12 Paschasius Radbertus, *Vita Walae*, in MGSS vol. II, pp. 553 seq.

13 Nithard, *Historiae*, lib. I, cap. v in MGSS vol. II, p. 653; cf. *Vita Hludowici*, *ibid.*, p. 639, and Thegan, *Vita Hludowici*, *ibid.*, p. 601.

14 Hincmar, *De divortio Lotharii et Theutbergae*, in Pat. lat., vol. 125, cols. 716–18. Cf. H. Schrörs, *Hinkmar, Erzbishof von Reims*, Freiburg in Bresgau, 1884, pp. 175–205.

15 Text in H. J. Schmitz, *Die Bussbücher und die Bussdisziplin der Kirche*, vol. I, Mainz, 1883, pp. 409–52. On the sources and composition see P. Fournier, "Etudes critiques sur le Decret de Burchard de Worms", in *Nouvelle Revue historique de droit français et étranger*, vol. 34 (1910). Chapter 5 of the *Corrector* is considered at pp. 217–21.

16 Schmitz, *op. cit.*, p. 446 (para. 169).

17 *Ibid.*, p. 425 (para. 68).

18 *Ibid.*, pp. 423–4 (para. 63) and p. 446 (para. 168).

19 See above, p. 116.

20 Schmitz, *op. cit.*, p. 425 (para. 69).

21 *Lex Baiuworum*, lib. XIII, cap. viii (MGH Leges, sectio I, vol. V, pp. 410–11).

22 *Lex Wisigothorum*, lib. VI, tit. 2, 4 (MGH Leges, sectio I, vol. I, p. 259).

23 Agobard, *Liber contra . . . vulgi opinionem de grandine et tonitruis*, cap. i (Pat. lat., vol. 104, cols. 147 seq.).

24 For references to the Anglo-Saxon penitentials see G. L. Kittredge, *Witchcraft in Old and New England*, Cambridge, Mass., 1929, p. 152.

25 *Ibid.*, pp. 129, 155.

26 A. Lütolf, *Sagen, Bräuche, Legenden aus den fünf Orten*, Lucerne, 1862, p. 220.

27 Agobard, *op. cit.*, col. 148.

28 B. Thorpe, *Diplomatarium Anglicum aevi Saxonici*, London, 1865, pp. 229-30. See also J. Crawford, "Evidences for witchcraft in Anglo-Saxon England", in *Medium Aevum*, Oxford, vol. XXXII (1963), pp. 112-13.

29 Adhémar de Chabannes, *Historia Francorum*, lib. III, cap. 66 (MGSS vol. IV, p. 146).

30 See above, Note 13.

31 *Monumenta Gregoriana*, ed. P. Jaffé, in *Bibliotheca rerum Germanicarum*, vol. II, Berlin, 1865, p. 413.

32 Galbert of Bruges, *Passio Karoli Comitis*, cap. 112 (MGSS vol. XII, p. 614).

33 Agobard, *op. cit.*, col. 148.

34 Lambert of Hersfeld, *Annales*, ad an. 1074 (23 April), in *Opera*, ed. O. Holder-Egger, Hanover and Leipzig, 1894, p. 190. For reasons for accepting Lambert's account see A. Eigenbrodt, *Lampert von Hersfeld und die neuere Quellenforschung*, Cassel, pp. 71-2.

35 *Annales S. Stephani Frisingensis*, in MGSS vol. XIII, p. 52.

36 *Annales Colmarienses Maiores* ad an. 1279, in MGSS vol. XVII, p. 206.

–2–

37 See above, pp. 64, 66-7.

38 Augustine, *De doctrina christiana*, lib. II, cap. 20 (*Pat. lat.*, vol. 34, cols. 46-47); *Quaestiones 83*, quaestio lxxix (*Pat. lat.*, vol. 40, cols. 90-3).

39 Synod of Ancyra, canon 24, in Mansi, *Sacrorum Conciliorum nova et amplissima collectio*, vol. II, Florence, 1759, p. 522.

40 Synod of Laodicaea, canon 36, in Mansi, *op. cit.*, vol. II, p. 570.

41 Synod of Agde, canon 42, in Mansi, *op. cit.*, vol. VIII, col. 333.

42 For developments in the early middle ages see Elizabeth Blum, *Das staatliche und kirchliche Recht des Frankenreiches in seiner Stellung zum Dämonen-, Zauber- und Hexenwesen*, Paderborn, 1936.

43 See above, p. 152.

44 *Lex Wisigothorum* lib. VI, tit. 2, 4 (MGH Leges, sectio I, vol. I, p. 259).

45 Synod of Toledo, 693, canon 2, in Mansi, *op. cit.*, vol. XII, col. 70.

46 *Capitulatio de partibus Saxoniae*, paras. 21, 23, 9 (MGH Leges, sectio II, vol. I, p. 69).

47 *Statuta Rhispacensia* (MGH Leges, sectio II, vol. I, p. 228).

48 MGH Leges, sectio II, vol. II, pp. 44-5.

49 Exodus 22:18.

50 Leviticus 20:6.

51 Bouquet, vol. VII, p. 686.

52 Burchard's *Corrector*, in Schmitz, *Die Bussbücher* . . ., p. 425 (para. 69).

53 *Poenitentiale Ecgberti*, iv, 7, in B. Thorpe, *Ancient Laws and Institutes of England*, 1840, p. 379.

54 Walter Map, *De nugis curialium*, Distinctio IV, cap. 6 (Camden Society, vol. 50, London, 1850, p. 164).

– 3 –

55 K. V. Thomas, *Religion and the decline of magic*, London, 1971; A. Macfarlane, *Witchcraft in Tudor and Stuart England*, London, 1970.

56 Thomas, *op. cit.*, p. 460.

57 On the accusatory procedure and the talion see P. Fournier, *Les officialités au moyen âge*, Paris, 1880, pp. 233 seq.; L. Tanon, *Histoire des tribunaux de l'Inquisition en France*, Paris, 1893, pp. 253–63; F. Pollock and F. W. Maitland, *The history of the English law before the time of Edward I*, 2nd edn., vol. II, Cambridge, 1952, p. 539.

58 Cf. Pollock and Maitland, *loc. cit.*

59 Cf. Fournier, *op. cit.*, p. 244. That this provision could apply also in cases of *maleficium* is evident from the Swedish *Uplandslag*, cap. xix; cf. Note 11 to section 1 above.

60 R. Reuss, *La justice criminelle à Strasbourg*, pp. 265–6, Strasbourg, 1885.

61 *Malleus Maleficarum*, Part I, question ii, cap. 1.

CHAPTER NINE: MAGICIAN INTO WITCH (1)

– 1 –

1 Valuable indications and materials will be found in A. E. Waite, *The Book of Black Magic and of Pacts*, privately printed (Edinburgh and London), 1898; L. Thorndike, *A History of magic and experimental science*, New York and London, vols. I and II, 1923, and vol. III, 1934; and E. M. Butler, *Ritual Magic*, Cambridge, 1949. D. P. Walker, *Spiritual and demonic magic from Ficino to Campanella*, London, 1958, and W. Shumaker, *The occult sciences in the Renaissance*, University of California Press, 1972, are concerned with the magic of a later period.

2 For discussions of conjuration in the third century: Thorndike, *op. cit.*, vol. I, New York and London, 1923, pp. 308–13, 436–52. For the persistence of the idea, if not the practice, in early medieval Europe: *ibid.*, pp. 629–31.

3 On Michael Scot: Thorndike, *op. cit.*, vol. II, chapter 51; and J. W. Brown, *An enquiry into the life and legend of Michael Scot*, Edinburgh, 1897.

4 *Liber Introductorius*, Bodleian MS 266, fols. 172 and 22 verso.

5 Cecco's commentary: Joannes de Sacro Bosco, *Sphera, cum commentis*, cap. III, Venice, 1518, fol. 21.

6 Cf. Thorndike, *op. cit.*, vol. II, pp. 848–50.

7 Caesarius of Heisterbach, *Dialogus miraculorum*, vol. I, lib. v, cap. 1.

8 Cf. C. C. McCown, *The Testament of Solomon*, Leipzig, 1922.

9 Guilielmus Alvernus, *Tractatus de legibus*, cap. 27, in *Opera Omnia*, Orléans, 1674, vol. I, p. 89.

10 *Epistola Fratris Rogeri Baconis de secretis operibus Artis et Naturae, et de nullitate Magiae*, in J. S. Brewer (ed.), *Opera . . . inedita*, vol. I, London, 1859, pp. 523–32 (vol. XV of *Rerum Britannicarum medii aevi scriptores*).

11 Two seventeenth-century English manuscripts of *Lemegeton* are in the British Museum: Sloane 2731 and Sloane 3648.

12 Reginald Scot, *The Discoverie of Witchcraft*, first edn., 1584, pp. 378–89.

13 *Ibid.*, p. 412.

14 See above, pp. 71–73.

15 Cf. Waite, *The Book of Black Magic and of Pacts*, pp. 111 seq. On the possible Jewish origin of the *Clavicula*: H. Gollancz, *Clavicula Salomonis. A Hebrew manuscript newly discovered . . .*, London, 1903.

16 S. M. L. Mathers, *The Key of Solomon the King*, London, 1889.

17 Quoted in Waite, *op. cit.*, p. 200.

18 Reginald Scot, *The Discoverie of Witchcraft*, Book 15, cap. 12, pp. 413–14.

19 Waite, *op. cit.*, pp. 106–7, 230, summarizing from the nineteenth-century *Dragon rouge* and the seventeenth-century *Grimoire of Honorius*. The passage from the *Dragon Rouge* exists also in an Italian version: *La Clavicola del Re Salomone* (with additions), Florence, 1880, pp. 114–16.

20 Reginald Scot, *op. cit.*, p. 383.

–2–

21 G. L. Burr, "The literature of witchcraft", in *Selected Writings* (ed. L. O. Gibbons), Cornell University Press, 1943, pp. 166–89. Originally printed in the *Papers* of the American Historical Association, vol. IV (1890), pp. 237–66.

22 C. E. Hopkin, *The share of Thomas Aquinas . . .*, dissertation, University of Pennsylvania, Philadelphia, 1940.

23 Thomas Aquinas, *Contra Gentiles*, lib. III, cap. cvi (*Opera*, vol. XVII, Venice, 1782, pp. 314–15); *Quaestiones disputatae de Potentia*, quaestio vi, art. x (*ibid.*, vol. XIV, 1781, pp. 189–92).

24 Thomas Aquinas, *Commentum in quatuor libros Sententiarum Magistri Petri Lombardi*, lib. II, Distinctio VII, quaestio iii, art. ii (*ibid.*, vol. IX, 1777, p. 97).

25 Text in Hansen, *Quellen*, p. 17.

26 Text in Hansen, *Quellen*, pp. 4–5. For the background of the papal intervention: Anneliese Maier, "Eine Verfügung Johannes XIII. Über die Zuständigkeit der Inquisition fur Zaubereiprozesse", in *Archivum Fratrum Praedicatorum*, vol. XXII (1952), pp. 226–46.

27 Text in Hansen, *Quellen*, pp. 5–6.

28 There is a manuscript of Eymeric's *Tractatus contra daemonum invocatores* in Paris: Bibliothèque Nationale, Manuscrit latin No. 1464, fol. 100–61. On the date of composition of the *Tractatus* see J. Quétif and J. Echard, *Scriptores Ordinis Praedicatorum*, vol. I, Paris, 1719, p. 710. The relevant passages in the *Directorium* are lib. II, quaestio xlii, "De sortilegis et divinatoribus", and especially quaestio xliii, "De invocantibus daemones" (pp. 234–9 in the Rome edition of 1578).

29 Thorndike, *A history of magic . . .*, vol. II, p. 284.

CHAPTER TEN: MAGICIAN INTO WITCH (2)

–1–

1 On Boniface see T. S. R. Boase, *Boniface VIII*, London, 1933; and on the relations between the papacy and the French monarchy: G. Digard, *Philippe le Bel et le Saint-Siège*, 2 vols., Paris, 1936; H. Finke, *Aus den Tagen Bonifaz VIII*, Münster i. W., 1902.

2 Cf. G. Lizerand, *Clément V et Philippe le Bel*, Paris, 1910, p. 217. For a general account of this posthumous trial see A. Corvi, *Il processo di Bonifacio VIII*, Rome, 1948.

3 For the text of the accusations see P. Dupuy, *Histoire du Differend d'entre le Pape Boniface VIII et Philippe le Bel Roy de France*, rev. edn., Paris, 1655, pp. 101–6, 324–46, 350–62.

4 Cf. Digard, *op. cit.*, vol. II, pp. 165–7.

5 Dupuy, *op. cit.*, p. 103.

6 *Ibid.*, pp. 324–46.

7 *Ibid.*, pp. 331–3; and cf. pp. 355–6.

8 *Ibid.*, pp. 543–75.

9 *Ibid.*, pp. 526 seq., witnesses I, XIV, XVI.

10 *Ibid.*, pp. 537–8.

11 *Ibid.*, pp. 526–75. For a summary of the evidence, *ibid.*, pp. 523–6. For an analysis of the evidence see Finke, *op. cit.*, pp. 227–68.

–2–

12 On this case see A. Rigault, *Le procès de Guichard, évêque de Troyes*, Paris, 1896; and for a good summary, G. Paris, "Un procès criminel sous Philippe le Bel", in *La Revue du Palais*, vol. II, Paris, 1898, pp. 241–61.

13 Cf. Rigault, *op. cit.*, p. 200.

14 For the text, translated into French from an unpublished document: Rigault, *op. cit.*, p. 57.

15 *Ibid.*, p. 58.

16 Rigault, *op. cit.*, Pièces justificatives, No. XIII, especially pp. 271–2.

17 Rigault, *op. cit.*, pp. 92–3.

18 *Ibid.*, pp. 74–5.

19 *Ibid.*, pp. 125 seq.

20 *Ibid.*, pp. 102, 115, 238 seq.

21 *Ibid.*, pp. 125–7; and cf. pp. 116–19.

22 *Ibid.*, pp. 128–9.

23 *Ibid.*, pp. 197–9.

24 *Ibid.*, pp. 213 seq.

25 K. Eubel, "Vom Zaubereiwesen anfangs des 14 Jahrhunderts", in *Historisches Jahrbuch*, vol. 18, 1897, pp. 608–36.

26 Cf. G. Paris, *op. cit.*, pp. 253–4, and the extract from *Renard le contrefait* (finished by 1322, at Troyes), *ibid.*, pp. 258–60.

–3–

27 Cf. Abbé E. Albe, *Autour de Jean XXII, Hugues Géraud . . .*, Cahors-Toulouse, 1904.

28 C. Raynaldus, *Annales ecclesiastici*, Lucca, 1738, etc. Cf. K. Eubel, "Vom Zaubereiwesen anfangs des 14 Jahrhunderts", in *Historisches Jahrbuch, 18,* Bonn, 1897, pp. 72 seq., 608 seq.

29 F. Bock, "I processi di Giovanni XXII contro i Ghibellini delle Marche", in *Bolletino dell'Instituto storico italiano per il medio evo,* No. 57, Rome, 1941, pp. 19–43 (esp. p. 36).

30 Text in Hansen, *Quellen,* pp. 2–4.

31 J.-M. Vidal, *Bullaire de l'inquisition française au XIVᵉ siècle . . .*, Paris, 1913, document 72, pp. 118–19.

32 Cf. H. C. Lea, *History of the Inquisition of the middle ages,* London, 1888, vol. III, p. 455.

33 *Ibid.,* pp. 455, 657.

34 Text in Hansen, *Quellen,* pp. 10–11; cf. *ibid.,* p. 8.

35 Text in Hansen, *Quellen,* pp. 15–16.

36 L. Tanon, *Histoire des tribunaux de l'Inquisition en France,* Paris, 1893, p. 121.

37 Text in Hansen, *Quellen,* pp. 454–5.

38 The trial proceedings are published in full in H. Duplès-Agier, *Registre criminel du Châtelet,* 2 vols., Paris, 1861 and 1864; vol. I, pp. 327–62; vol. II, pp. 280–343.

–4–

39 The basic source for the Kyteler affair is T. Wright, *Narrative of the proceedings against Dame Alice Kyteler for sorcery,* London, 1843 (Camden Society); this is a contemporary source. The *Annals of Ireland* (in *Chartularies of St Mary's Abbey, Dublin,* ed. J. T. Gilbert, vol. II, London, 1884 (Rolls Series), pp. 362–4) are a less reliable source, as they cannot have been composed before 1370 and may even date from the end of the fifteenth century. Holinshed's account in his *Chronicle of Ireland,* London, 1587, p. 69, is based on the *Annals.*

40 *Proceedings,* Additional Note, pp. 59–60.

41 *Annals of Ireland,* p. 362. This detail sounds like a piece of genuine folklore, deriving from the period itself.

42 *Proceedings,* p. 2.

43 *Ibid.,* p. 1.

44 *Ibid.,* p. 2.

45 *Ibid.,* p. 31.

46 *Ibid.,* p. 32.

47 *Ibid.,* p. 14.

48 *Ibid.,* p. 40.

49 *Ibid.,* pp. 36–7.

50 On Ledrede see the article in the *Dictionary of National Biography.*

51 *Proceedings,* pp. 22–3, 27.

CHAPTER ELEVEN: THE NIGHT-WITCH IN POPULAR IMAGINATION

-1-

1 Pliny, *Historia naturalis*, VIII, 22.

2 Q. Serenus Sammonicus, *De Medicina*, lix, 1044-7, ed. Keuchen, Amsterdam, 1662, p. 34.

3 Ovid, *Fasti*, VI, lines 131-68.

4 Petronius, *Satyricon*, cap. 134.

5 Ovid, *Amores*, I, beginning of Eighth Elegy.

6 Lucius Apuleius, *The Golden Ass*, chapter 16.

7 Sextus Pompeius Festus, *De verborum significatione Fragmentum* (*Pat. lat.* vol. 95, col. 1668).

8 *Pactus legis Salicae*, tit. lxiv, 1-3 (ed. K. A. Eckhardt, vol. II, 1, Göttingen, 1955, pp. 349-51). The passage which refers to the witch's cannibalism as real is to be found in a relatively late version, dating from 567-96; cf. Eckhardt, *op. cit.*, vol. I, 1954, pp. 216-18.

9 *Pactus Alamannorum*, Fragmentum II, para. 31, in MGH Leges, sectio I, vol. V, part 1, p. 23.

10 *Edictus Rothari*, 197, 198 (in *Leges Langobardorum*, ed. F. Beyerle, Witzenhausen, 1962, p. 53).

11 *Ibid.*, 376 (ed. Beyerle, p. 91).

12 *Capitulatio de partibus Saxoniae*, para. 6, in MGH Leges, sectio II, vol. I, pp. 68-9. H. Jankuhn ("Spuren von Anthropophagie in der Capitulatio de partibus Saxoniae", in *Nachrichten der Akademie der Wissenschaften in Göttingen. I. Philosophisch-historische Klasse*, Göttingen, 1968) argues that the capitulary proves the existence of witchcraft practices which included cannibalism. I am not persuaded.

13 P. Piper (ed.), *Notkers und seiner Schule Schriften*, vol. I, 1883, p. 787. The text is in Old High German.

14 Text in H. J. Schmitz, *Die Bussbücher und die Bussdisziplin der Kirche*, vol. I, Mainz, 1883, p. 446 (para. 170 of chapter 5 of the *Corrector*).

15 Text in Hansen, *Quellen*, pp. 638-9.

16 Gervase of Tilbury, *Otia Imperialia*, lib. iii, cap. 86

17 e.g. in the classic German work known as Soldan-Heppe-Bauer: *Geschichte der Hexenprozesse*, vol. I, Munich, 1911, pp. 86-9.

-2-

18 Text in Regino of Prüm, *Libri de synodalibus causis et disciplinis ecclesiasticis*, ed. F. G. A. Wasserschleben, Leipzig, 1840, p. 354.

19 Twice, in fact: in Book 19 (the *Corrector*), chapter 5, para. 90, and also in Book 10, chapter 1, para. 3. On the variants of the canon, in Regino and in Burchard: J. B. Russell, *Witchcraft in the middle ages*, pp. 75-80, 291-3.

20 *Corrector*, chapter 5, para. 70.

21 Gregory of Tours, *Historia Francorum*, VII, 15.

22 *Acta Sanctorum*, 8 July, p. 616.

23 Ratherius, *Praeloquiorum libri*, I, 10, in *Pat. lat.*, vol. 136, col. 157.

24 *Reinardus Vulpes*, ed. F. J. Mone, Stuttgart and Tübingen, 1832, lib. I, lines 1143–64.

25 On folklore traditions concerning Holda see "Perchta", in Baechtold-Stäubli, *Handwörterbuch des deutschen Aberglaubens*, vol. 6, Berlin and Leipzig, 1934–5, pp. 1478 seq. (Perchta is the South German equivalent to the central German Holda); also J. Grimm, *Deutsche Mythologie*, 4th edn., Berlin, 1875, pp. 220–40; V. Waschnitius, "Perht, Holda und verwandte Gestalten", in *Sitzungs-berichte der kaiserlichen Akademie der Wissenschaften in Wien. Philosophisch-Historische Klasse*, vol. 174, Vienna, 1913, pp. 4–179; and W. Liungman, *Traditionswanderungen Euphrat-Rhein*, vol. II, Helsinki, 1938, especially pp. 656 seq.

26 Guilielmus Alvernus, *De universo creaturarum*, Part III, xii, 2, cap. 22, in *Opera Omnia*, Orléans, 1674, vol. I, pp. 1036, 1066.

27 *Roman de la Rose*, ed. E. Langlois, vol. IV, Paris, 1922, lines 18424 seq.

28 The work is the *Speculum Morale*, which appears as the fourth part in all printed editions of the *Speculum Majus* of Vincent of Beauvais (*c.* 1190–1264), but which is now known to be by a later hand. The relevant passage is at Book III, part iii, Distinctio xxvii.

29 Jacobus de Voragine, *Legenda aurea*, cap. 102.

30 Jacopo Passavanti, *Lo specchio della vera penitenza*, ed. F. L. Polidori, Florence, 1856, pp. 318–20.

31 On latter-day Sicilian beliefs see G. Pitrè, *Usi e costumi credenze e pregiudizi del popolo siciliano*, vol. IV, Florence, 1952, pp. 163 seq.; and cf. G. Bonomo, *Caccia alle streghe*, Palermo, 1959, pp. 65–7. Pitrè's book was originally published in 1889.

32 See Bonomo, *op. cit.*, pp. 15–17, 59–60.

33 John of Salisbury, *Policraticus, sive De nugis curialium et vestigiis philosphorum*, lib. II, cap. 17 (ed. C. C. I. Webb, Oxford, 1909, vol. I, pp. 100–1).

–3–

34 Johann Nider, *Formicarius*, lib. II, cap. iv. Text in Hansen, *Quellen*, pp. 89–90.

35 For the text from Alfonso Tostato, written in 1436: Hansen, *Quellen*, p. 109, n. 1.

36 Bartolommeo Spina, *Quaestio de strigibus*, cap. 30–1 (first published 1523).

37 Johann Weyer, *De Praestigiis Daemonum*, Basel, 1563, pp. 219–20; cf. Giambattista Porta, *Magia Naturalis*, lib. VIII, cap. ii (edition in twenty books, first published Naples, 1589).

38 S. Ferckel, " 'Hexensalbe' und ihre Wirkung", in *Kosmos*, vol. 50, Stuttgart, 1954, pp. 414 seq.; E. Richter, "Der nacherlebte Hexensabbat. W. E. Peuckerts Selbstversuch", in *Forschungsfragen unserer Zeit*, vol. 7, Zeren, 1960, pp. 97–100; H. Marzell, *Zauberpflanzen, Hexentränke: Brauchtum und Aberglaube*, Stuttgart, 1963, pp. 47 seq.

39 e.g. in the chronicle of Mathias Widman of Kemnat, *c.* 1475, in Hansen, *Quellen*, p. 233. Cf. Johann Hartlieb, *Buch aller verbotenen Kunst*, ed. D. Ulm,

Halle a. S., 1914, cap. 32, p. 20.

40 See above, p. 207.

41 J. R. Crawford, *Witchcraft and sorcery in Rhodesia*, London, 1967.

42 *Ibid.*, pp. 112-13, 116.

43 *Ibid.*, pp. 47-8.

44 *Ibid.*, p. 60.

45 C. Ginzburg, *I Benandanti*, Turin, 1966.

46 *Ibid.*, p. 9; cf. J. B. Russell, *Witchcraft in the middle ages*, pp. 41-2.

47 Ginzburg, *op. cit.*, pp. 9-11, 20-4; and cf. pp. 43, 60-1, 67.

48 *Ibid.*, pp. 12-13.

CHAPTER TWELVE: THE MAKING OF THE GREAT WITCH-HUNT

–1–

1 Hansen, *Zauberwahn*, pp. 400-1.

2 Report by the Lucerne Chronicler Hans Fründ, first published in Hansen, *Quellen*, pp. 533-7.

3 Cf. J. Marx, *L'Inquisition en Dauphiné*, Paris, 1914 (esp. pp. 32-42); see above, pp. 38 seq.

4 Text in J. Chevalier, *Mémoire historique sur les hérésies en Dauphiné avant le 16ᵉ siècle*, Valence, 1890, pp. 131 seq.

5 *Chronica Albrici Monachi Trium Fontium*, in MGSS vol. XXIII, p. 945.

6 Record of the entire proceedings in Hansen, *Quellen*, pp. 459-66.

7 Record of the proceedings in Hansen, *Quellen*, pp. 438-72. Cf. Jacques Du Clercq, *Mémoires*, Book III, chapter 11 (ed. C. B. Petitot, Paris, 1826, pp. 60-93); and Nicolas Jacquier, *Flagellum haereticorum fascinariorum*, p. 27 (written 1458, printed Frankfort, 1581).

8 The basic sources for the study of the Arras Vauderie are Jacques du Clercq, *op. cit.*, Book V, and a tract against the sect called the *Recollectio*, printed in Hansen, *Quellen*, pp. 149-83. Amongst the many modern accounts, that by H. C. Lea, *A history of the Inquisition of the middle ages*, vol. III, London, 1888, pp. 519-30, remains unsurpassed.

–2–

9 For the Greek text: L. Radermacher, "Griechische Quellen zur Faustsage", in *Sitzungsberichte der Wiener Akademie der Wissenschaften*, vol. 206 (4), Vienna, 1927, pp. 122-48. For a ninth-century Latin translation: Hincmar, *De divortio Lotharii et Theutbergae*, Interrogatio XV (*Pat. lat.* vol. 125, cols. 721-6).

10 For the Greek text: Radermacher, *op. cit.*, pp. 164-218. For a ninth-century Latin translation see *Acta Sanctorum*, 4 February, pp. 489-92.

11 Cf. K. Plenzat, *Die Theophiluslegende in den Dichtungen des Mittelalters*, Berlin, 1926 (*Germanische Studien*, vol. 43). For surveys of these and similar legends: P. M. Palmer and R. P. More, *The sources of the Faust tradition*, New York,

1936; L. Kretzenbacher, *Teufelsbündner und Faustgestalten im Abendlande*, Klagenfurt, 1968.

12 Walter Map, *De Nugis Curialium*, Distinctio IV, cap. vi (Camden Society, vol. 50, London, 1850, p. 155).

13 Caesarius of Heisterbach, *Dialogus miraculorum*, Book V, chapter 28.

14 See above, p. 62.

15 Augustine, *De civitate Dei*, lib. XV, cap. 23.

16 Isidore of Seville, *Originum sive etymologiatum libri XX*, lib. VIII, cap. 11 (*Pat. lat.* vol. 82, col. 326).

17 Adso of Montier-en-Der, *Epistola ad Gerbergam reginam de ortu et tempore Antichristi*, in E. Sackur, *Sibyllinische Texte und Forschungen: Pseudomethodius, Adso und die tiburtinische Sibylle*, Halle, 1898, pp. 106–7.

18 See above, p. 151.

19 Hincmar, *De divortio Lotharii et Theutbergae*, Interrogatio XV (*Pat. lat.* vol. 125, col. 725).

20 Guibert de Nogent, *Histoire de sa vie (1053–1124)*, ed. G. Bourgin, Paris, 1907, lib. I, cap. xiii, pp. 43–4.

21 Arnaud (or Ernaud), abbot of Bonneval, *Liber Secundus* of *Sancti Bernardi Vita Prima*, cap. vi (*Pat. lat.* vol. 185, cols. 287–8).

22 Caesarius of Heisterbach, *Dialogus miraculorum*, Book III, chapter 8.

23 *Ibid.*, Book III, chapter 9.

24 *Ibid.*, Book III, chapter 10.

25 Guilielmus Alvernus, *De universo creaturarum*, Part III, cap. xxx, in *Opera omnia*, Orleans, 1674, vol. I, pp. 1070–3. See above, pp. 213–14.

26 Thomas Aquinas, *Summa Theologica*, Part I, quaestio li, art iii (*Opera*, Venice, 1787, vol. XX, pp. 243–4); *Commentum in quatuor libros Sententiarum Magistri Petri Lombardi*, lib. II, Distinctio VIII, quaestio i, art. iv, solutio ii (*ibid.*, 1777, vol. X, p. 105).

27 Text in Hansen, *Quellen*, pp. 88–9; and see above, pp. 219-20.

28 *Ibid.*, pp. 99–104.

29 *Ibid.*, pp. 118–22.

30 *Ibid.*, pp. 133–45.

– 3 –

31 E. Hoffmann-Krayer, "Luzerner Akten zum Hexen- und Zauberwesen", *in Schweizerisches Archiv für Volkskunde*, vol. III, Zurich, 1899, pp. 22–40, 82–122, 189–224, 291–325.

32 *Ibid.*, pp. 117–21.

33 *Ibid.*, pp. 33–8.

34 *Ibid.*, pp. 103–17.

35 *Ibid.*, pp. 198–204. For similar cases, see *ibid.*, pp. 95–7, 193–7, 210–11.

36 G. L. Kittredge, *Witchcraft in Old and New England*, Cambridge, Mass., 1929, pp. 6–20.

37 *Ibid.*, p. 8. The original depositions are at Harvard.

38 *Ibid.*, p. 10.

39 A. Macfarlane, *Witchcraft in Tudor and Stuart England*, London, 1970. See also C. L'Estrange Ewen, *Witch hunting and witch trials*, London and New York, 1929, and *Witchcraft and demonianism*, London, 1933.

40 Macfarlane, *op. cit.*, p. 174.

41 See above, p. 242.

42 Diebold Schilling, *Luzerner Bilderchronik*, ed. R. Durrer and P. Hilber, Geneva, 1932, p. 143, with picture at Tafel 280.

43 Cf. E. Delcambre, *Le concept de la sorcellerie dans le duché de Lorraine au XVIᵉ et XVIIᵉ siècle*, Nancy, 1948, Fascicule 3, pp. 205 seq.; J. Schacher, *Das Hexenwesen im Kanton Luzern*, Luzern, 1947, pp. 98 seq.

44 Hoffmann-Krayer, *op. cit.*, p. 317.

45 See above, p. 243.

46 Quoted, from a manuscript in the Library of the University of Glasgow, by Dr Christina Larner in her thesis *Scottish demonology in the sixteenth and seventeenth centuries and its theological background*, Appendix II, pp. 272–5. The thesis was submitted at the University of Edinburgh in 1961 under Dr Larner's maiden name, Christina Ross.

–4–

47 *Malleus Maleficarum*, part I, question vi.

48 A. Macfarlane, *op. cit.*, pp. 161, 205–6; K. V. Thomas, *Religion and the decline of magic*, London, 1971, pp. 560–7.

49 H. C. E. Midelfort, *Witch hunting in Southwestern Germany*, Stanford University Press, 1972, pp. 184–5.

50 *Malleus Maleficarum*, part III, question viii.

51 G. Bader, *Die Hexenprozesse in der Schweiz*, Affoltern a. A., 1945.

52 *Ibid.*, pp. 219, 217.

53 Midelfort, *op. cit.*

54 *Ibid.* p. 32

55 *Ibid.*, p. 89.

56 *Ibid.*, pp. 96–8.

57 *Ibid.*, p. 97.

58 *Ibid.*, p. 137.

59 The point is well documented in E. Delcambre, "Les procès de sorcellerie en Lorraine. Psychologie des juges", in *Tijdschrift voor rechtsgeschiedenis*, vol. XXI, Groningen, Brussels, The Hague, 1953, pp. 389–420; see also the same author's "La psychologie des inculpés lorrains de sorcellerie", in *Revue historique de droit français et étranger*, series 4, vol. XXXII, Paris, 1954, pp. 383–404, 508–26.

60 For a particularly clear example, studied in detail, see P. Villette, "La sorcellerie à Douai", in *Mélanges de Science religieuse*, vol. 18, Lille, 1961, pp. 123–73.

POSTSCRIPT: PSYCHO-HISTORICAL SPECULATIONS

1 Apart from my own writings, this approach has found most favour in France; e.g. A. Besançon, *Le Tsarévitch immolé*, Paris, 1967; L. Poliakov, *Le Mythe aryen*, Paris, 1971.

2 Cf. J. A. Macculloch, *The childhood of fiction: a study of folk tales and primitive thought*, London, 1905, pp. 278 seq.

3 In *Kinder- und Hausmärchen gesammelt durch die Brüder Grimm* (first published 1837) Hansel and Gretel is No. 15, Snow White No. 53.

4 Cf. W. Lederer, "Historical consequences of father-son hostility", in *The Psychoanalytic Review*, vol. 54, No. 2, New York, 1967, pp. 52–80; W. Lederer, *The fear of women*, New York and London, 1968, pp. 61–6; G. Devereux, "The cannibalistic impulses of parents", in *The Psychoanalytic Forum*, vol. I, No. 1, Beverley Hills, California, 1966, pp. 114–24.

5 Cf. F. Fornari, "Fantasmes d'agression", in *Études polémologiques*, No. 10, Paris, October 1973.

INDEX

Abundia (Habonde), supernatural queen, 214, 237

Accusatory procedure, 22–3, 24, 160–3

Adeline, Guillaume, alleged witch, 230, 232, 238

Adhémar de Chabannes, chronicler, 21

Aelsie, in *maleficium* case, 153–4

Æthelstan, Anglo-Saxon king, 150

Agape, early Christian feast, 10, 11, 17

Agobard, bishop of Lyons, 152

Alciati, Andrea, lawyer, 143

Alain de Lille, theologian, 22

Alexander III, pope, 78

Alexander IV, pope, 176, 177

Animal-god, worship of, as accusation, xi; against early Christians, 2; against Jews, 5–6 *See also* Devil-worship; Demons: in animal form

Antichrist, 19, 129, 235

Angelo of Poli, member of Fraticelli, 46–7

Antiochus Epiphanes, Seleucid monarch, 5, 7–8

Antonio of Sacco, member of Fraticelli, 47–8

Apion, Greek writer, 5, 7–8

Apollodorus of Cassandreia, tyrant, 6–7

Apostasy,
temptation to, 97, 261–2; witch as symbol of, 102, 252; invocation as, in Aquinas, 176; in Kyteler case, 199; in Simmerthal case, 205; in early witch-trials, 226 *See also* Sacrilege

Apuleius, 207, 208, 220

Arnald of Villanova, on ritual magic, 165

Athenagoras, Christian apologist, 3

Attalus, Christian martyr, 4

Aubryot, Hugues, provost of Paris, 196

Augustine, St,
on Montanists, 16; on Manichees, 17; on fallen angels, 66; on magic, 156, 159, 175, 176, 193; on incubi and succubi, 175, 234; not concerned with night-witches, 210; or with flying women, 211 *n*.

Augustus, emperor, 13

Bacchanalia, 11–12

Bacon, Roger, 167

Bader, Guido, 254

Baile, Jean, archbishop of Embrun, 39, 42

Bardin, Guillaume, chronicler, 127–8, 139, 164

barilotto, 46–8, 52–3; defined, 50, 52

Barre, Margot de la, sorceress, 196

Barthe, Angela de la, fictitious witch, 127–8

Bartolo of Sassoferrato, lawyer, 138, 139, 140–1, 143, 144; *consilium* falsely ascribed to, 139–40; other spurious *consilia*, 141–3

Basil the Great, St, 233

Beaufort, Payen, notable of Arras, 232

Bègue, Thomas, alleged witch, 227

Beiliss, Mendel, 259 *n*.

Belial, Beliar, demon, 62, 168, 173, 185

Benandanti, 223–4

Benedict XI, pope, 181

Benedict XII, pope (Jacques Fournier), 39, 194 *n*., 195, 202

Beniols, Hugues de, inquisitor, 127

Berardus of Soriano, monk, 184–5

Bernard, St, 75, 235–6

Bernard of Bergamo, "priest" of Fraticelli, 45, 46, 51

About the Author

Norman Cohn holds the Aston-Wolfson Chair at the University of Sussex, England, and has taught at various universities in England, Scotland, and Ireland. His other books include THE PURSUIT OF THE MILLENNIUM: Revolutionary Millenarians and Mystical Anarchists of the Middle Ages, and WARRANT FOR GENOCIDE: the Myth of the Jewish World-Conspiracy and the Protocols of the Elders of Zion.

The MERIDIAN Quality Paperback Collection

☐ **THE ARYAN MYTH: A History of Racist and Nationalist Ideas in Europe by Léon Poliakov.** A leading historian of anti-semitism traces the origins and progress of the Aryan myth in the Western world, exploring the development of legends and myths which were transformed into pseudo-scientific "theories," and which led, eventually, to the most terrible mass movement history has to date recorded.
(#F478—$4.95)*

☐ **NO BIGGER THAN NECESSARY: An Alternative to Socialism, Capitalism and Anarchism by Andrew M. Greeley.** A challenging proposal for a system far better suited to human problems and purposes, founded on natural groupings, such as the family and the neighborhood, and designed to respond to the wants and needs of those it is supposed to serve.
(#F471—$3.95)

☐ **THE TRANSFORMATION OF SOUTHERN POLITICS: Social Change and Political Consequence Since 1945 by Jack Bass and Walter DeVries.** Replete with graphs, maps, and other statistical information, this definitive work provides a total profile of the South—what it has been, what it has become and where it may be going.
(#F470—$5.95)

☐ **SIN, SICKNESS, AND SANITY: A History of Sexual Attitudes by Vern Bullough, Ph.D., and Bonnie Bullough, Ph.D.** This fascinating work is a comprehensive summary of our knowledge of past sexual attitudes as well as an appraisal of the causes and direction of the sexual revolution today.
(#F562—$6.95)

☐ **THE TERRORISM READER: A Historical Anthology edited by Walter Laqueur.** This unique anthology brings together the most notable proponents, critics, and analysts of terrorism from ancient times to today.
(#F480—$5.95)

* Not available in Canada
In Canada, please add $1.00 to the price of each book.

Buy them at your local bookstore or use this convenient coupon for ordering.

THE NEW AMERICAN LIBRARY, INC.
P.O. Box 999, Bergenfield, New Jersey 07621

Please send me the MERIDIAN BOOKS I have checked above. I am enclosing $_____(please add $1.50 to this order to cover postage and handling). Send check or money order—no cash or C.O.D.'s. Prices and numbers are subject to change without notice.

Name_____

Address_____

City_____State_____Zip Code_____

Allow 4-6 weeks for delivery.
This offer is subject to withdrawal without notice.